SECURING FREEDOM
IN THE GLOBAL COMMONS

SECURING FREEDOM
IN THE GLOBAL COMMONS

Edited by Scott Jasper

STANFORD SECURITY STUDIES
An Imprint of Stanford University Press
Stanford, California

Stanford University Press
Stanford, California

Special discounts for bulk quantities of Stanford Security Studies are available to corporations, professional associations, and other organizations. For details and discount information, contact the special sales department of Stanford University Press. Tel: (650) 736-1782, Fax: (650) 736-1784

Printed in the United States of America on acid-free, archival-quality paper

Library of Congress Cataloging-in-Publication Data
Securing freedom in the global commons / edited by Scott Jasper.
    p. cm.
 Includes bibliographical references and index.
 ISBN 978-0-8047-7010-1 (cloth : alk. paper)--ISBN 978-0-8047-7011-8 (pbk. : alk. paper)
 1. National security. 2. Security, International. 3. Global commons. 4. National security--United States. I. Jasper, Scott.
 UA10.5.S3725 2010
 355'.0335--dc22   009042486

Typeset by Bruce Lundquist in 10/14 Minion

Contents

List of Illustrations

Figures

Photographs

Tables

Foreword

Patrick M. Cronin

SECURING FREEDOM IN THE GLOBAL COMMONS may be the signal security challenge of the twenty-first century. Our world is intricately connected across the sea, air, space, and cyber domains. But who protects them? No one country controls access to the commons, but every country increasingly depends on open access to them. Indeed, the economic welfare of man and woman in this century, almost regardless of where they live, is tethered to the commons. Yet complex trends and new threats across the global commons, unthinkable even a decade ago, confront us with draconian consequences, exacerbated by economies and societies rising on the insecure foundation of networks and globalization. The exigencies of global counterinsurgency and counter-terror campaigns have impelled creative defense thinkers to grope for alternative solutions. Cold War arsenals have atrophied to the point that the need for their redesign and refurbishment is not only conceivable, but blatantly obvious. We are living in a world in which state power is simultaneously multiplying and shrinking. It is multiplying because of the emergence of new global and regional powers and the resurgence of old ones; it is shrinking because of the rise of non-state actors, transnational movements, and even super-empowered individuals. Thus, a volume that plumbs the depth and width and height of the global commons is an essential foundation on which to rethink and perhaps recalibrate concepts of how to maintain security in our time.

This book is written by distinguished academics and expert practitioners who have studied or worked extensively in topics related to the global commons. Although delivered primarily from a U.S. viewpoint, the perspectives garnered from their research and personal experience are meant to inform a wider international audience, by presenting frameworks for consideration by U.S. allies and partners. The book's implications are explicitly international, because it raises the issues of affordability and feasibility in the context of common responsibility and common action in defense of security in the global commons. Moreover, this is not just an American affirmation. International allies such as the North Atlantic Treaty Organization, Japan, and Australia, to name but a few, also have highlighted the necessity for action in the global commons. A key challenge will be to organize collective thinking and integrate responses to enable coherent and practicable solutions.

Against this backdrop, Scott Jasper asks us to confront the new realities of the global commons of outer space, international waters and airspace, and cyberspace. *Securing Freedom in the Global Commons* provides the basis for considering what these commons are; how they are interrelated; and how their preservation and protection from criminal or adversary exploitation are indispensable elements of national and international security. The volume provides a forum in which its contributors explicitly describe the various military-operational implications for securing strategic access and retaining freedom of action in the global commons. It also raises valuable definitional issues about the commons themselves, namely that their extension into and connectivity with one another and "non-common" national territories has yet to be parsed fully.

Advantage and vulnerability are the obverse and reverse themes of the world presented by *Securing Freedom in the Global Commons*: It is a world compacted and leveled, and dramatically more efficient; made increasingly vulnerable by the mixed blessings of networks and globalization; marked by widely uneven leaps ahead in living standards and the flow of goods, services, and information. The irony of fractionalization looms large in this world, diminished by exploitation of the global commons but enabling a veritable kaleidoscope of interests and conflicts, and the proliferation of both interests and states too small or weak to support themselves. This is a world characterized by chaos and instability; the uneven distribution of resources and misery; and endemic conflict. But opportunities also abound. In short, it will increasingly be a world in which the global commons will exacerbate as well as mitigate institutional and national vulnerabilities.

This world and its current conflicts seem to have polarized our institutions:

Should we be preparing for small, long wars, or for something more substantial? Among others, Andrew Bacevich framed the basic terms of this debate in *The Atlantic* magazine. Using the U.S. Army as an example, but speaking to the broader national military debate, he laid out the ostensible divide between "Crusaders" and "Conservatives." Crusaders believe that "(f)or the foreseeable future, political conditions abroad rather than specific military threats will pose the greatest danger to the United States . . . winning battles becomes less urgent than pacifying populations and establishing effective governance." Bacevich contrasts this perspective with the concern of the Conservatives that "an infatuation with stability operations will lead the Army to reinvent itself as 'a constabulary,' adept perhaps at nation-building but shorn of adequate capacity for conventional war-fighting," that, for instance, "the Army's field-artillery branch—which plays a limited role in stability operations, but is crucial when there is serious fighting to be done—may soon be all but incapable of providing accurate and timely fire support."[1]

It is, however, unnecessary and counter-productive to choose between present and future alternative threats. The comprehensive review offered by *Securing Freedom in the Global Commons* lays out why the present and future each is important, and the attendant necessity of having to hold in our minds two ideas at the same time. Reviewing this putative conundrum from the perspective of the global commons, this volume clarifies that these challenges are elements of a greater whole confronting our strategies and resources.

Securing Freedom in the Global Commons is more than just an intellectual exercise by defense academics and military operators. It has intrinsic, practical relevance to current policy debates of elemental concern to the U.S. Department of Defense and American allies worldwide, but not by simply choosing between competing ideas. Its in-depth discussion of threats, opportunities, and challenges in the global commons paces the debate in planning and budgets: How do we confront the war our allies and we are fighting now, while at the same time hedging against threats to the global commons, construed in planning regimes as the rise of non-state, transnational strategic competitors; the specter of a proliferated world (weapons of mass destruction or effect); and the rise of authoritarian capitalist states. In our present world, we see a rising—and rising and rising—China; a resurgent and assertive Russia; an increasingly militarized Iran; an isolated but potentially unstable nuclear North Korea; and a panoply of non-state actors, from pirates to hackers, who find it increasingly feasible to hold states at risk.

The contributions of this volume notwithstanding, the debate in the United States oscillates around these on-offer planning cases. The U.S. National Defense Strategy of June 2008 laid out a hedging strategy against China, Russia, Iran, and North Korea. Despite his insistence on "fighting the wars we have," and his determination to terminate or truncate several high-profile defense programs—including the F-22 stealth fighter—Secretary of Defense Robert Gates made the case for a balance between current operations and future threats in the journal *Foreign Affairs*,[2] and in a series of American War College addresses in the spring of 2009.[3] Frank Hoffman of the Foreign Policy Research Institute points out that Secretary Gates "has directly challenged his strategists and the military chiefs, declaring that the defining principle of the new National Defense Strategy is 'balance' and announcing that throwing money at the Department of Defense's problems was no longer acceptable."[4] These same complexities receive broad treatment in *America's Security Role in a Changing World*. As I wrote in that volume, the problem transcends any one instrument of policy: "Worldwide trends suggest that the United States will increasingly have to approach complex challenges and surprises through wider and more effective partnerships and more integrated strategies."[5] Hybrid solutions are required.

Hybridity may not be an easy concept to grasp, but it is transforming the character of conflict. In one manifestation of his notable body of work on hybrid warfare, Hoffman explored the relevant idea of the breadth of overlapping challenges facing the United States and allies, rather than the choices between them:

> [F]uture contingencies will more likely present unique combinational or hybrid threats that are specifically designed to target U.S. vulnerabilities. Instead of separate challengers with fundamentally different approaches (conventional, irregular or terrorist), we can expect to face competitors who will employ all forms of war and tactics, perhaps simultaneously. Criminal activity may also be considered part of this problem as well, as it further destabilizes local government or abets the insurgent or irregular warrior by providing resources, or by undermining the host state and its legitimacy.[6]

In the U.S. Naval Institute *Proceedings*, Under Secretary of Defense for Policy Michèle Flournoy proclaimed that the rise of China implies that the United States cannot depend on uncontested access to the maritime, air, space, and cyberspace commons.[7] While *Securing Freedom in the Global Commons* is not about China per se—it is explicit in its treatment of the entire range of threats—China represents the single most acute threat to security in the global commons. This is so because, convinced it has a free hand,

> China is challenging access to the global commons through a broad, consciously directed array of military developments. China's military has moved beyond its focus on Taiwan and now possesses antisatellite weapons, advanced land attack ballistic missiles, new classes of submarines and surface ships and the emerging ballistic missile capability to hit ships at sea at least 1,000 miles from China's coasts.
>
> These developments are designed to re-order the balance of power in China's favor by diminishing American strategic mobility and free access to Pacific waters, Pacific airspace, and the "high terrain" of space and cyberspace. A good example of this is China's development of land-mobile antiship ballistic missiles. This antiaccess capability is unprecedented anywhere in the world and has numerous implications for the U.S. Navy, probably best summarized as losing air and sea dominance—and perhaps control—in the Asian-Pacific region. This puts at risk American influence, regional security and alliance interdependence.[8]

The broader inference clearly is that the United States should have serious talks with its allies about gaps in strategic defenses, and about common interests in defending the global system.

Andrew Krepinevich, writing in *Foreign Affairs*, contributed to the debate by highlighting the fragility of security in the global commons; the transitory nature of traditional power; and the necessity of new alternatives for strategy, doctrine, capabilities, and operations.

> The United States can either adapt to contemporary developments—or ignore them at its peril. There is, first of all, a compelling need to develop new ways of creating military advantage in the face of contemporary geopolitical and technological trends. That means taking a hard look at military spending and planning and investing in certain areas of potential advantage while divesting from other assets. And Washington must keep in mind that efforts to field new capabilities and put in place new ways of operating typically take time, often a decade or more, to come to fruition.[9]

Under the skillful stewardship of Michèle Flournoy, policy officials inside the Office of the Secretary of Defense began in 2009 to think about the salience of securing freedom in the global commons as a planning exercise for a fundamentally new articulation of national security strategy.

The organization and specifics of *Securing Freedom in the Global Commons* argue persuasively for a balanced strategy that combines partnered capacities against today's disruptions with the need to hedge against future threats. It is in the global commons that much of this activity will take place, where offenses and defenses will square off. And it is in the global commons where the international system will be defended or deconstructed.

From this perspective, even though the world is in a financial crisis, and underinvested in today's campaigns, we have to invest in protecting the global commons.[10] In fact, this is what the U.S. Department of Defense is doing: continuing with the basic building blocks of missile defense; proceeding with advanced aerospace systems (if not additional F-22s); and establishing the new U.S. Cyber Command. In this construct, for instance, the Defense Department is funding systems relevant to operations in the global commons, such as Terminal High Altitude Area Defense (THAAD) and SM-3 missiles; the Littoral Combat Ship and Joint High Speed Vessel; and fifth-generation tactical fighter capability—the F-35—in quantity at sustainable cost.

> This is a reform budget, reflecting lessons learned in Iraq and Afghanistan yet also addressing the range of other potential threats around the world, now and in the future. . . . Some will say I am too focused on the wars we are in and not enough on future threats. The allocation of dollars in this budget definitely belies that claim.[11]

In making its arguments, this volume lays out the thematic basis for rational decisions for current and ongoing investments in any budgetary environment, despite financial constraints and whatever campaigns might be underway; funding defense of the global commons is more than a hedge; as the Navy's Maritime Strategy makes clear, it is the glue that holds the entire global enterprise together.

The authors of *Securing Freedom in the Global Commons* represent the best and brightest at a diverse array of commands and institutions. The heart of the volume they have produced is a systematic review of each of the four commons, the military operational implications of each, and their functional salience for decision makers. The authors review the character of each of the commons, explore connections and dependencies, examine operational vulnerabilities, and offer strategic alternatives for policy development and acquisition planning.

The global commons are the arena in which political, economic, and military competitions are going to play out against the backdrop of demographics, culture, commerce, and geography. *Securing Freedom in the Global Commons* has been written at the beginning of a long wave of strategic planning. It clarifies the centrality of the commons as a practical operational construct, and provides the basis for responding to challenges. In describing the terrain of both stability and uncertainty in the security environment, this volume will be of enduring value and immense interest not only for a broad international audience of strategic thinkers, academics, policy officials, military commanders, and parliamentarians, but for students of security studies and the general public as well.

Acknowledgments

MY AFFILIATION WITH THE GLOBAL COMMONS stems from nearly 4000 flight hours in the venerable P-3C Orion aircraft surveying the vast oceans and littorals of the globe. I was inspired to construct this volume by the stark recognition of real threats to the maritime commons, as seen in the diesel submarines and missile boats that I tracked in the Arabian Gulf. The development of capabilities for preserving access to the other commons of air, space, and cyberspace would allow platforms like the P-3C Orion to defeat these and other threats posed by adversary asymmetric strategies. During assignment to the U.S. Fifth Fleet in Bahrain, I witnessed the remarkable vision displayed by Rear Admiral John Ryan, U.S. Navy, as he introduced the P-3C Anti-Surface Warfare Improvement Program, which incorporates long-range electro-optic cameras and infrared-red maverick missiles; the kinds of innovative capabilities espoused in this volume. His example of leadership and foresight galvanized my pursuit of this project. I am thankful to Richard Hoffman, Director of the Center for Civil-Military Relations, for his unstinting support as this analysis developed and has been brought to completion.

I would like to thank each of my authors for taking the time to share their perspectives and expertise, garnered over years of study and practice. In particular I am grateful for the guidance of Professors Dan Moran of the Naval Postgraduate School and Gregory Cox of the Center for Naval Analysis, who helped frame the book's academic focus. Also, I would like to recognize Paul Giarra's sage advice, Scott Moreland's extensive literature research, and Elizabeth Skinner's insightful comments and precise copy editing, all of which significantly improved the project. My sincere appreciation also goes to Geoffrey Burn and his staff at Stanford University Press for their professional direction and exacting production.

Most importantly, I would like to thank my dear wife and best friend, Annie, and our wonderful boys, Christopher, Kevin, and Brian, for their patience and understanding as I pursue my academic quest to contribute to international security.

Scott Jasper

List of Acronyms

ADIZ—Air defense identification zones

AIS—Automatic information system

ASAT—Anti-satellite weapon

BMD—Ballistic missile defense

C4ISR—Command, control, communications, computers, intelligence, surveillance, and reconnaissance

CENTRIXS—Combined Enterprise Regional Information Exchange Systems

CMDA—Comprehensive maritime domain awareness

COA—Course of action

DoD—Department of Defense

DPRK—Democratic People's Republic of Korea (North Korea)

DSS—Decision support system

EEZ—Exclusive economic zone

EMP—Electromagnetic pulse

ESA—European Space Agency

EU—European Union

FIR—Flight information region

GBI—Ground-based interceptor

GPA CONOPS—Global Persistent Attack Concept of Operations

GPS—Global Positioning System

GS CONOPS—Global Strike Concept of Operations

IADS—Integrated Air Defense System

ICAO—International Convention on Civil Aviation

ICBM—Inter-continental ballistic missile

IMB—International Maritime Bureau

ISR—Intelligence, surveillance, and reconnaissance

ITU—International Telecommunication Union

IW—Information warfare

JNTC—Joint National Training Capability

JTEN—Joint Training and Experimentation Network

JTIMS—Joint Training Information Management System

JTS—Joint Training System

LEO—Low earth orbit

LOS—(UN Convention on the) Law of the Sea

LRIT—Long-range identification and tracking

MAD—Mutual assured destruction

MDA JIC—Maritime Domain Awareness Joint Integrating Concept

METL—Mission essential task list

MFP—Multiple Futures Project

MSSIS—Maritime Safety and Security Information System

NATO—North Atlantic Treaty Organization

NM—Nautical miles

NSPD—National Security Presidential Directive

OAS—Organization of American States

OCA—Offensive counter-air (operations)

OECD—Organization for Economic Cooperation and Development

OODA—Observe, Orient, Decide, Act

ReCAAP—Regional Agreement on Combating Piracy and Armed Robbery

RMAC—Regional Maritime Awareness Capability

RV—Requisite variety

SAM—Surface-to-air missile

SATCOM—Satellite communications

SCADA—Supervisory Control and Data Acquisition

SCUBA—Self-contained underwater breathing apparatus

SOLAS—(International Convention for the) Safety of Life at Sea

SSA—Space situational awareness

SSBN—Ballistic missile-capable submarine

THAAD—Terminal High Altitude Area Defense

UAV—Unmanned aerial vehicle

UJTL—Universal Joint Task List

UN—United Nations

UNCLOS—United Nations Convention on Law of the Sea

UNCOPUOS—UN Committee on Peaceful Uses of Outer Space

UNDPKO—United Nations Department of Peacekeeping Operations

USSR—Union of Soviet Socialist Republics

WMD/E—Weapons of mass destruction/effect

SECURING FREEDOM
IN THE GLOBAL COMMONS

1 Disruptions in the Commons

Scott Jasper and Paul Giarra

Defining the Commons

> "Transnational terrorism, the proliferation of weapons of mass destruction, piracy, climate change and energy security, cyber attacks, to name just a few—the threats to our collective security in a globalized world—that do not stop at national borders and cannot be successfully addressed by any nation alone."
>
> *General John Craddock, U.S. Army, Supreme Allied Commander, Europe*[1]

The North Atlantic Treaty Organization (NATO) clearly recognizes its essential role in confronting and defeating these and other threats and challenges. For NATO and its partners around the world, national security and prosperity depend on the safekeeping of a global system comprising mutually interdependent networks of commerce, communication, and governance. The essence of globalization, fueled by vertiginous technological innovation, has created new realities of connectivity and continuity on which the supercharged global system depends. These developments confront military planners with profound challenges. The globalized system can tend toward instability and dysfunction, especially when vulnerable social structures are threatened by hostile actors. The military opportunities of globalization—networking, speed, and connectivity—are a two-edged sword: defense planners will have to consider new configurations of infrastructure and operational vulnerability, diminished deterrence, the potential for elemental or systemic disruption, and the implications of preemption and decapitating attacks.

1

The global commons—outer space, international waters and airspace, and cyberspace[2]—constitute the underlying infrastructure of the global system. In old English law, the term "commons" referred to a tract of ground shared by residents of a village, belonging to no one, and held for the good of all.[3] Extrapolating from this construct, global commons have been characterized as natural, or man-made, "assets outside national jurisdiction."[4] Global commons are similar to but less wide-ranging than the elucidation of the term "military domains." A case in point would be the maritime domain, described as "the world's oceans, seas, bays, estuaries, islands, coastal areas, littorals, and the airspace above them,"[5] which encompasses far more than just "international waters." That said, the global commons can extend to domains that may be either within or outside of national jurisdiction, so long as the international community has a lawful right to the asset, such as international straits or innocent passage in a territorial sea. Although some might consider the commons to include ungoverned spaces like Antarctica,[6] for the purpose of analytical consistency regarding defense objectives related to the global commons, the U.S. Secretary of Defense's definition cited above is used throughout the volume.

The maritime and air commons are relatively traditional constructs, albeit with new circumstances and implications. The space and cyberspace commons add new, crucial, and yet somewhat imprecise conceptual and operational dimensions. The U.S. military's definition of cyberspace was revised in May 2008 to be "a global domain within the information environment consisting of the interdependent network of information technology infrastructures, including the Internet, telecommunications networks, computer systems, and embedded processors and controllers."[7] While this interpretation was meant explicitly to describe cyberspace, the absence of previous references to the use of the electromagnetic spectrum initially led to confusion over the role of electronic warfare.

In and through these traditional or emerging global commons, nation-states and non-state actors conduct global enterprise, for good or ill. In essence, the global commons as a set combines in numerous ways into physical and virtual utilities that serve as conduits for the free flow of trade, finance, information, people, and technology in the world's economic system. Likewise, the global commons entail much of the operating space of the international security environment, enabling the physical and virtual movement and operations of allied forces as well as those of transnational, regional, and emergent peer competitors.

As nodal and systemic conduits, most of the commons "are areas that belong to no one state and that provide access to much of the globe."[8] Conversely, the pathways of the commons, like a global vascular system, can also accelerate the vulnerability of critical economic and national infrastructures; the transfer of advanced weapons and military technology; the spread of ideas and ideologies; the movement and communications of criminals and terrorists; and the diversion of dangerous materials. Securing freedom of access to, transit through, and use of the global commons is fundamental to safeguarding the globalized systems.

Integrating the Commons

> "We are [also] witnessing new forms of conflict. Cyber attacks against a country's electronic infrastructure have now happened, against Estonia—and they can be crippling. Piracy, long believed to have been eradicated, is back as a major international concern—and in more than just one essential maritime route on which our trade and oil and gas supplies depend."
>
> *Jaap de Hoop Scheffer, NATO Secretary General*[9]

It is misleading to conceptualize or deal with the interests of stakeholders in the global commons independently, that is, to differentiate between the military, civil, or commercial spheres, or to segregate military service roles. This is because the domains of the commons are inherently interwoven—military maritime, space, aerospace, and cyberspace operations overlap with civilian and commercial activities—and because the networks that enable operations or activities in the various overlapping sectors are themselves threaded together. For instance, 80 percent of U.S. Department of Defense satellite communications for operations in Iraq and Afghanistan is managed by private-sector companies such as Globalstar, Inmarsat, and Iridium.[10] Military dependence on commercial satellite services will continue until the launch of more secure, higher-capacity connectivity solutions in the 2010 to 2016 timeframe, such as the Wideband Global Satellite and the Advanced Extremely High Frequency system.[11]

The importance of the global commons underlies the power of networks in a military, civil, and commercial context, and new manifestations of networked and interdependent security. Enterprise integration, however, brings with it new levels of vulnerability. First, connectivity enables access. Civil and commercial networks are accessible by design, and thereby vulnerable at very low cost. Likewise, military systems and networks are integrated among services, and with parallel and supporting civilian or commercial applications and networks, at unprecedented levels of connectivity. This greatly enables elemental access to networks, and thereby enhances both the usefulness and the vulnerability of the systems and applications that depend on networks. To protect cyberspace advantages, for example, the infrastructure the U.S. military uses to both launch and defend against cyber attacks runs through the public internet system, which leaves the U.S. military open to attack by adversaries through the same public channels.[12]

Second, systemic integration among and between the military, civil, and commercial sectors enhances the potential for mass disruption and even collapse of critical infrastructures or functions, potentially with effects on the scale of even the most extreme kinetic or weapons-of mass-destruction attacks. To illustrate, the cyberspace linkages in Supervisory Control and Data Acquisition (SCADA) systems, which regulate the operations of most critical infrastructure industries (such as utility companies that manage the electrical power grid), make attractive cyber targets.[13] Cyber attacks on these and other civil or commercial functions that result in energy disruption, financial sector collapse, water system failure, or air traffic disruption would produce cascading impacts on the support infrastructure for military operations.

This dynamic between integration, capability, and vulnerability presents fundamentally different challenges for international defense planners. Securing freedom in the global commons requires protection against attacks from and through these physical and virtual domains, while preserving and enhancing the capability to operate in the global commons for strategic and operational advantage. Strategic trends and drivers in the global system will both define challenges and dictate appropriate solutions that will have to fit the new realities. For example, the current world population growth rate of 60 million people per year will strain economic systems and require global energy production to rise by 1.3 percent per year. By the 2030s, oil requirements could go from 86 to 118 million barrels per day. If energy output falls short of demand, the implications for international tension and future conflict are ominous.[14]

Defense planners will have to refer to the history and nature of national policies and international regimes that influence or govern activities in the commons. National domestic concerns can affect international regime formation. Regimes are explicit or implicit principles, norms, rules, and decision-making procedures around which actor expectations converge in a given issue-area.[15] By entering, or not, into international agreements, nations accept, or reject, constraints on their absolute freedom of action. Treaties may impose unequal

demands on nations, due to the need for signatories to accept a common denominator for policy objectives.[16] For instance, the 2006 U.S. National Space
Policy states that "the United States will oppose the development of new legal
regimes or other restrictions that seek to prohibit or limit U.S. access to or use of
space."[17] Accordingly, the United States does not vote for United Nations General Assembly resolutions intended to prevent an arms race in outer space.[18]

Legal regimes can limit vulnerability and guide appropriate responses, but
sometimes only in theory. A case in point: the ubiquitous nature of cyberspace is problematic when it comes to determining attack attribution and
prosecution rights, as was seen in Estonia in April 2007. Amid a furious row
with Russia over the removal of a Soviet-era war monument from the center
of the Estonian capital, swarms of computers from more than fifty countries
conducted an anonymous cyber riot that swamped the websites of Estonian
ministries, banks, newspapers, and broadcasters with bogus requests for information.[19] International laws and legal codes were not prepared to rule on this
cyber aggression, which might have merited designation as an act of war even
despite the absence of armed force by a clearly identified enemy.

Protecting the Commons

> "The President must prioritize the safety and reliability of high traffic
> energy shipping routes, such as the Straits of Hormuz. Maintaining
> open and reliable lanes of commerce protects the U.S. and the global
> economy from potentially devastating supply disruption and resulting
> price volatility."
>
> General James L. Jones, U.S. Marine Corps (Retired),
> President and Chief Executive Officer, Institute for 21st Century Energy[20]

The protection of the global commons is intrinsic to safeguarding national
territory and economic interests. Protecting the commons as the locus of the
global system is part of the ongoing competition for control that traditionally has been an aspect of rivalry among peers. National leaders and defense
planners must contend with the reality that globalization has reduced the barriers to entry for competitors. This reduction has devalued the traditional
competitive advantage of dominant global powers, and changed the terms of
competition, which in turn has enabled the rise, virtually unprecedented in its
speed, of a range of transnational, regional, and emergent peer competitors

who are presenting elemental and systemic challenges to international order and legal regimes.

In the case of cyberspace, the skills and tools used in intrusions by criminals are also ideal for state-sponsored computer network attacks. "Robot" networks, or "botnets," made up of computers that are infected with malicious code, can disrupt internet traffic, harvest information, or distribute spam, viruses, or other "malware."[21] Remarkably, some 15 percent of online computers may be botnet-infected machines, unknowingly controlled through the internet by a malign master.[22] Botnets, like the Storm Worm botnet that spread infectious malware through millions of e-card links, typically facilitate criminal activity[23] but also have political utility. As many as one million botnets were used in the distributed denial-of-service attacks on the Estonian websites. Some observers charge that the Russian government rented botnets from transnational cybercriminals to orchestrate the onslaught for political reasons.[24]

Elemental and systemic challenges are constantly changing, as seen in the cyber-threat landscape, where the majority of malicious activity has become Web-based. Attackers are targeting or altering vulnerable sites (like the social networking sites MySpace and Facebook) that are likely to be trusted by end-users, to gain confidential information during code execution or file download.[25] Underground economy servers, like the Dark Market forum,[26] then sell end-user bank account credentials, credit card information, and identities. While denial-of-service and confidential data loss mostly disturb civil or commercial functions,[27] of even greater concern to the military are designer attacks that are engineered for deep penetration into specific computer systems to steal defense secrets[28] or manipulate data, like the spoofing of global positioning system (GPS) coordinates in precision-guided munitions so a bomb hits the wrong place.[29]

The irony of the commons is that their powerful role in enhancing economic growth and prosperity, the exchange of information, and the flow of goods and services in a globalized world is the very basis of increased insecurity. This is partly familiar, and partly unprecedented. Traditional challenges that emanate from the global commons persist: state actors could aspire to interrupt or deny strategic maneuver in key regions, and challenge assured access to strategic resources, such as in the Strait of Hormuz, where roughly a quarter of the world's oil must pass on tankers.[30] Hostile state actors could deliver mass-effect attacks from the maritime, air, or space commons in an integrated littoral campaign. They could also use cyberspace to mount disruptive attacks on critical, yet vulnerable, infrastructure networks. Depriving allied populations of electricity, communications, and financial services might not be enough to provide the margin of victory in a conflict, but it could damage the political will to win.[31]

Just as state competitors do, non-traditional threats likewise add to defense challenges. Maritime terrorists and other non-state actors, such as modern-day pirates, can disrupt the flow of energy resources and manufactured goods along global lines of communications or at points of entry to critical national infrastructure. Criminal organizations that thrive on the smuggling of weapons, narcotics, and humans also use the commons at low cost for tremendous disruptive effect, sometimes adapting in creative ways to avoid capture. Drug cartels have expanded the ways they transport drugs, using submarines built of fiberglass, wood, and steel, technically known as self-propelled semi-submersibles, to move ten to fifteen tons of cocaine at a time.[32] The custom-built submarines do not fully submerge but are so low to the water, rising less than two feet, that they avoid radar detection, and are usually camouflaged with paint to avoid aerial surveillance.[33]

The powerfully disruptive effect that pirates have on freedom of navigation for commercial shipping in the maritime common is another case in point. The International Maritime Bureau defines piracy as the act of boarding any vessel with intent to commit theft or any other crime, and with an intent or capacity to use force in furtherance of that act. While over 230 actual or attempted attacks occurred worldwide annually from 2004 through 2008, incidents off Somalia and the Gulf of Aden—a key choke point passed each year by over 20,000 vessels, which must reduce speed to ensure safe passage and thus heighten their exposure to interception—surged 200 percent to 111 in 2008.[34] All types of vessels are being targeted, attacked, and hijacked by armed Somali pirates, including crude-oil supertankers and chemical tankers,[35] large luxury cruise ships,[36] and freighters ferrying military cargo.[37] Despite the presence of international warships patrolling maritime corridors, eliminating pirate mother ships[38] and apprehending suspected pirates,[39] the brazen pirates, hailing from a violent failed state that has little to offer its population, are undaunted from seeking luxury lifestyles funded by million-dollar cash ransoms.[40]

While piracy is predicated on financial gain, maritime terrorism, like its land-based form, is motivated by political goals beyond the immediate act at sea, aiming primarily to gain publicity and inflict damage. A number of planned maritime terrorist plots, most directly connected to al Qaeda and its affiliates, have been preempted before execution, including suicide strikes against Western shipping interests, the use of small boats to ram supertankers transiting straits, and attacks on heavily-laden cruise liners.[41] These incidents galvanize fears in the West that militants connected with the international jihadist network are moving to extend operations beyond land-based theaters. One scenario commonly posed by analysts is an attack designed to shut down a port or block a sea-lane in order to disrupt the mechanics of the global maritime trade complex of integrated supply chains. While long-term disruption to the global economy is unlikely, significant localized financial damage would resonate with the underlying operational and ideological rationale of al Qaeda and the wider global jihad.[42]

These myriad vulnerabilities are all the more challenging in doctrinal and operational terms because they cross domains in the global commons. For example, in the commercial sector, air and maritime trade are linked along air lanes or sea routes to airfield or port nodes by networked cyber-information and space-navigation systems. Likewise, in military operations, commanders combine myriad cyber-system applications and space-based assets to conduct network-enabled operations. Cyber systems and space utilities depend on a constellation of satellites that are inherently vulnerable: they are visible to all and follow an established and predictable route, making them easy targets.[43] Cross-domain attacks are especially dangerous because some hostile actors may seek not merely to disrupt the global system, but to destroy it.

Exploiting the Commons

> "What all these potential adversaries—from terrorist cells to rogue nations to rising powers—have in common is that they have learned that it is unwise to confront the United States directly on conventional military terms."
>
> *Robert M. Gates, U.S. Secretary of Defense*[44]

The global commons embraces the world's economic system as well as the global security environment. Resourceful adversaries will leverage accessible technologies and unconventional methods to deny freedom in the commons for defense, governmental, and commercial entities. The global commons enables asymmetric approaches[45] in which adversaries exploit access to the commons in order to circumvent traditional advantages, negate core strengths, and exploit the vulnerabilities of competitors. Sample scenarios include a drug trafficker who obtains GPS coordinates on a satellite phone to make a rendezvous at sea, or a finance technician moving money via laptop to support terrorist operations, while sipping coffee in an internet café.[46] Another scenario has insurgents using aerial imagery displayed by the Google Earth internet tool (at fifteen-meter resolution) to pinpoint mortar attacks on vulnerable areas inside military bases,[47] or even worse, using half-meter resolution imagery collected by the WorldView-1 next-generation satellite constellation.[48]

Adversary asymmetric methods range from computer network intrusion tools to offensive counter-space weapons. Effects can devastate not just military operations, but also civil and commercial systems. A case in point is the dual-use global positioning system, designed to provide military and civilian users with continuous, worldwide positioning, navigation, and timing services. In addition to use by the military in weapon and command systems such as Joint Direct Attack Munitions and Blue Force Tracking, three-dimensional GPS location signals are used by millions of civilians in everything from cars, boats, and airplanes to cell phones. Precise GPS timing signals are used to synchronize banking computers, electrical power grids, and communications systems, and to time-stamp business transactions.[49] Disruption of the military GPS utility would cascade through a key mainstay of civilian transportation and economic activity.

Asymmetric strategies are devised to strike at crucial vulnerabilities, often by applying layered capabilities in coordinated operations. Competitors could combine offensive computer network operations and electronic warfare with kinetic first strikes to disrupt battlefield network information systems that support power projection and warfighting capabilities.[50] To destroy unified command and control capabilities through a computer network attack, methods available to adversaries include hacker or virus attacks, information pollution or harassment, and surveillance or reconnaissance techniques.[51]

Competitors could negate allied space-based force enhancement functions—intelligence, surveillance, and reconnaissance; missile warning; environmental monitoring; satellite communications; and space-based positioning, navigation, and timing—that increase military effectiveness.[52] Such actions can involve the electronic jamming of communication links; physical or cybernetic attacks on satellite ground stations; the use of ground-based lasers to dazzle or blind satellites' optical- or thermal-imaging sensors; and attacks in space by metal pellet clouds, microsatellite mines, or high-altitude nuclear detonations.[53] China demonstrated a hit-to-kill anti-satellite (ASAT) capability in January 2007, when it destroyed an aging Chinese weather satellite with a kinetic kill vehicle.[54] Attacks in space generate destructive debris as well as indiscriminate long-term impacts on space security.

An increasing number of state actors have the ability to use ballistic missiles, some capable of carrying weapons of mass destruction, to destroy civilian population centers or military build-up areas. In less than four decades, the number of nations possessing these weapons has gone from nine to twenty-four; more than twenty nations possess or seek to acquire nuclear, biological, or chemical weapon payloads.[55] The testing of two-stage ballistic missiles (such as the Sajil),[56] coupled with progressive nuclear activities,[57] demonstrates the dangerous ambitions of Iran and North Korea and the need for defense against attack.[58] Internationally criticized launches of Iranian Safir-2[59] and North Korean Unha-2[60] missiles for placing satellites into orbit indicate the steadfast commitment of these states to expand their intercontinental ballistic missile capabilities. Additionally, state competitors might see the building of ballistic missile submarines (China's Jin SSBN with Julang-2 missiles) as insurance against allied ballistic missile defenses.[61]

Existing fourth-generation fighter aircraft (e.g., Russia's Sukhoi Su-27 Flanker and MiG-29 Fulcrum) have the ability to deny the local air superiority essential for allied strike options against high-value targets. More alarming yet, fifth-generation fighter aircraft (Sukhoi T-50 PAK-FA), with passive electronically scanning array radar, are already in prototype assembly.[62] Peer or near-peer adversaries could also deploy advanced air defense systems,[63] such as land-based long-range and high-altitude surface-to-air missile (SAM) systems (SA-20 Gargoyle or SA-21 Growler), or high-speed man-portable SAMs (SA-18 Grouse);[64] or destroyers designed for anti-air warfare (like the Luzhou DDG equipped with SA-N-20 SAMs controlled by the TOMBSTONE phased-array radar).[65]

An adversary's niche capabilities at sea could threaten maritime access to regions or straits of strategic importance. Sophisticated mines, quiet diesel-electric submarines (Kilo, Song, or Qaaem),[66] ships with rocket-powered super-cavitating torpedoes (Hoot),[67] and swarming formations of naval speedboats[68] might deny the sea control necessary for power projection. The interdiction of vital shipping passages could be achieved by an "impenetrable line" of defense fortified with midget submarines (Yono)[69] and fast attack craft (Combattante II or Tir) equipped with radar-guided anti-ship cruise missiles (Noor).[70] A multi-faceted area-denial strategy might include coastal defenses based on long-range anti-ship cruise missiles (YJ-62C),[71] anti-ship ballistic missiles (1500 km-plus range DF-21 MRBM variant) with maneuvering reentry vehicles and terminal guidance,[72] modern destroyers (Sovremenny DDG with SS-N-22 Sunburn missiles),[73] helicopters (Harbin Z-9) with anti-ship missiles (TL-10),[74] and ski-ramp design aircraft carriers with fixed-wing (Su-33) fighters.[75]

Operating in the Commons

> "Our maritime, air, and ground forces must have the capability and capacity to prevail in a warfighting environment in which potential adversaries are rapidly closing the technological gap. Ensuring the survivability of our networks, both military and those commercial networks that support military operations, is becoming increasingly critical in a battlespace sure to place additional emphasis on the domains of space and cyberspace."
>
> *Admiral Timothy J. Keating, USN, Commander, U.S. Pacific Command*[76]

It is essential that allies have the ability to counter technologically sophisticated adversaries in the commons, to secure freedom from attack as well as preserve the freedom to attack. In geostrategic terms, the commons provide the profound advantage of what amount to external lines of communication. This high-ground advantage is a crucial precursor to resolving conflict and crisis decisively and favorably, especially in distant, austere, or inaccessible environments. Capabilities that ensure the ability to operate effectively in the commons are fundamental to any definition of operational and strategic success. In military terms, this equates to advantages in global mobility, precision engagement, information operations, and space capabilities.

The integration and synchronization of space capabilities is contributing greatly to successful operations in Iraq and Afghanistan. To illustrate, a raid by a special forces team might be supported by commercial satellite imagery and a weather mosaic of the area, GPS location signal accuracy predictions for handheld receivers and air-delivered precision-guided munitions, and improvised-explosive-device detection along travel routes. The team's location during the raid's execution could be pinpointed by blue-force tracker devices that process GPS signals. Satellite communications could be used to fly a Predator unmanned aerial vehicle overhead and stream full-motion video to the command center. Rockets or bombs guided by GPS signals could destroy the target of the raid.[77]

Proven capabilities like space-based support provide integrated offensive and defensive options, which in turn allow a broader range of strategic choices for the military operations underway today and those that can be expected tomorrow. Promising capabilities for cyberspace attack could offer a decisive military advantage that ensures operational freedom of action at the place and time of a commander's choosing, while denying the same to the adversary. The effects of emerging cyberspace attack technologies include sensor disruption, data manipulation, interference with decision support, command and control disruption, and the degradation of weapon systems.[78]

Military-Operational Implications

"The imbalance between our readiness for future global missions and the wars we are fighting today limits our capacity to respond to future contingencies, and offers potential adversaries, both state and non-state, incentives to act."

Admiral M. G. Mullen, USN,
Chairman of the US Joint Chiefs of Staff Guidance[79]

Recent international incidents demand preparation for wider disruptions to freedom in the global commons. The series of cyber attacks that spread through Georgian commercial and government websites as Russian troops entered South Ossetia in 2008 may have heralded the coming of a new feature of modern warfare.[80] Although the concerted distributed denial-of-service attacks only temporarily shut down web servers (Georgia relocated strategic IP-based cyber capabilities to other defensive points in the United States, Poland, and Estonia),[81] and thus had little impact on the outcome of the conflict, they presage a wider trend of great concern.

A capabilities-based approach to defense planning considers how adversaries may challenge us, more than who they might be or where we might face them. This approach identifies the capabilities required to defeat adversaries who wage warfare in the commons. Freedom of action calls for innovative and interdependent capabilities, which include the ability to conduct or ensure:

- *Maritime Security*
  Pervasive and persistent sensor networks
  Diverse tactical and national sensor modes (RADAR/IR/EO/SIGINT/Acoustics)

Sensor data analysis and integration

Combat identification and threat assessment[82]

Maritime law enforcement or interdiction operations

- *Cyberspace Control*

  Attack deterrence, mitigation, survivability, and attribution

  Vulnerability detection and response

  Data, electronic system, and infrastructure protection

  Electronic systems, network, and infrastructure attack

- *Space Assurance*

  Satellite redundancy, encryption, hardening, and maneuverability

  Space situational awareness (hazard identification, intent ascertainment, and action attribution)

  Operationally responsive space (demand surge and rapid reconstitution)

  Code of conduct for common understanding of acceptable behavior[83]

- *Ballistic Missile Defense*

  Sea-, land-, and space-based warning, surveillance, and tracking

  High-volume short-, medium- and long-range missile interception

  Defeat of complex ballistic missile countermeasures

- *Air Superiority*

  Surface-based enemy air defense detection, degradation, or destruction

  Airborne warning and control for offensive and defensive counter-air measures

  First look, first shot, and first kill of airborne threat by airborne assets[84]

- *Sea Control*

  Operations and fighting at greater ranges than today against advanced multidimensional maritime recon-strike networks

  Defeat of increasingly sophisticated undersea combat networks

  Sea-based command of combat units that enable expeditionary maneuver[85]

  Escort or protection of merchant shipping and military sealift vessels[86]

To achieve synchronized operations in the global commons that effectively counter transnational, regional, and emergent peer competitors, these capabilities must be linked to the range of likely threats, and integrated in terms of both theory and practice. To properly and promptly apply these capabilities, leaders must be intellectually prepared to understand and act in complex, real-time situations. The development of perceptive, reflective, and collaborative leadership skills empowered by visual decision-enabling tools and practiced in realistic joint-training events, is essential for achieving operational success.

Way Ahead

> "It will continue to fall to the United States and its partner nations to protect and sustain the peaceful global system of interdependent networks of trade, finance, information, law and governance. Maintaining freedom of action and access around the globe is as much a requirement for the functioning of this system as it is for the conduct of military operations."
>
> *Admiral M. G. Mullen, USN, Capstone Concept for Joint Operations*[87]

The U.S. Capstone Concept, which visualizes how joint forces will operate in response to a wide variety of security challenges, recognizes that maintaining sufficient control of the global commons will remain an imperative of future joint force design. The three key strategic challenges to national security that the United States and its allies face are the:

- rise of non-state, transnational strategic competitors;
- specter of a proliferated world (weapons of mass destruction or effect);
- rise of authoritarian capitalist states.[88]

The members of the alliance need to win against violent extremist movements that use the very instruments of globalization to threaten free and open societies. They must dissuade hostile, nuclear-armed states that seek to exploit the instability caused by regional conflict. They need to hedge against the growing military modernization of ascendant state competitors who actively seek to counter allied advances in some or all domains of warfare. The ability to respond across the range of these challenges depends on demonstrated military capabilities that can promote security, deter conflict, and win wars.[89]

The failure to field this broad set of necessary capabilities risks the loss of traditional military preeminence in the global commons. The proliferation of sophisticated weaponry and weapons of mass destruction with advanced delivery systems arms and empowers transnational, regional, and emergent peer competitors to challenge allied freedom of action. In times of conflict, allied forces operating in or moving through the global commons must be prepared to endure persistent attack. Adversaries will strike at vulnerabilities through asymmetric methods, often at long range with precise kinetic and non-kinetic weapons. Critical infrastructure networks (energy, banking, telecommunications, water, etc.) cannot be assumed to be off-limits, even though the consequential impact on the global economic system could have cascading effects on the competitor itself by devastating commercial trade or financial markets.

In this uncertain security environment characterized by asymmetric threats, a suitable national military objective is to "prevent conflict and surprise attacks through actions that deter aggression and coercion while retaining the capability to act promptly in defending the nation."[90] The need to deter a wide array of potential adversaries that threaten the peaceful global system is daunting, given the differences in what they value, what ends they pursue, the means at their disposal, and the ways they operate. The central idea in deterrence is to decisively influence the adversary's decision-making calculus in order to prevent hostile actions. Decisive influence is achieved by credibly threatening to deny benefits from or impose unacceptable costs on a course of action, while simultaneously encouraging restraint. Allied forces must tailor their means of response to convince adversaries that pursuing adverse courses of action in the global commons will result in worse outcomes than will other alternatives.[91] Should deterrence fail, allies must be prepared to apply overwhelming military force.

This volume provides a forum in which its contributors explicitly describe the various military-operational implications for securing strategic access and retaining freedom of action in the global commons, the conduits of the world economy. Drawing upon significant experience and practical knowledge, the authors provide innovative structures and best practices that apply in a multinational context. In a collaborative manner, each contributor examines national-level approaches and initiatives that are designed to minimize vulnerabilities and preserve advantages, while recognizing that global security can best be achieved through international cooperation and fundamental agreements. This compilation provides an intellectual framework for making the kinds of programmatic decisions and institutional changes that are crucial to ensuring stability and prosperity in the global commons.

PART I
DETERMINANTS OF SECURITY

2 Strategic Trends and Drivers

Jeffrey Becker

Models for Forecast

The global commons will be shaped in the future, as they have been in the past, by forces other than raw military power, including the less tangible factors of national will, individual perception, and leadership decisions concerning the nature of cooperation or conflict within the commons. The purpose of this chapter is to render a relatively clear image of factors loose in the international system that will influence these "ungoverned" spaces over the next decades. Because any changes in the geopolitical and military landscape will influence the global commons, strategic planners and operational military commanders will be enjoined to consider what influential factors will evolve, and how they will shape the global commons.

Attempts to characterize the future are, of course, fraught with difficulty. Among the array of forces, ideas, and actors present and active in the world, some are important to a clear understanding of what may be coming, while others that seem critical at present may appear less so with the benefit of hindsight. George Friedman describes the difficulty of forecasting the future in this way:

> [T]hings that appear to be so permanent and dominant at any given moment in history can change with stunning rapidity. Eras come and go . . . conventional political analysis suffers from a profound failure of imagination. It imagines passing clouds to be permanent and is blind to powerful, long-term shifts taking place in full view of the world.[1]

In 1890, natural philosopher William James described how, without organizing principles, concepts, and an ability to discriminate between the enduring and the ephemeral, the world around us appears to be one of disconnected, causeless happenstance and chaos.[2] Our ability to reason and to build concepts and mental models of the world allows us to impose a sense of order and explain and make sense of what we perceive. Given these warnings, how is one to select the most consequential factors from among the near-infinite set of the possible, and distinguish the causal from the ephemeral?[3] This chapter will provide two conceptual tools, the notions of trends and drivers, to aid in this process of organization.

The exploration of trends and drivers allows us to explain how international politics, conflict, and war will be conducted through the media of the global commons. A trend is the direction and speed of change in some important feature of the international environment that will allow us to imagine possible characteristics of the future. Drivers are the end result of the confluence of two or more trends. They describe how troubling knots of trends combine and thus form a wider context for discussion of the global commons. Drivers can provide perspective on the shape of actors and events in the commons over the next two decades. The trends and drivers examined in this chapter should be seen as a field guide to be used as the reader weighs and considers the more specific topic areas presented later in this volume.

Trends in the International Environment

An important set of six trends in the international environment will shape the global commons over the next several decades: demographics, natural resource scarcity (such as energy and water), future key terrain, identity networks, global finance (including dollars, debt, and defense), and science, technology, and engineering. Each of the six trends has been selected because of its power to define the conditions, circumstances, and influences that affect strategic decisions and the use of military forces in relation to the global commons. It is important, as one is considering these trends, to keep in mind that the ultimate causes of competition, conflict, and war among peoples, cultures, states, and civilizations originate from three enduring motivations based in human nature: 1) *fear*, which springs from the uncertainty and unpredictability of the intentions of others; 2) *honor*, which is derived from essential differences over ideas about the nature of justice and order in human relations; and 3) *interest*, which relates to the desire to secure and enjoy the material foundations for human well-being.[4]

Demographics

Demographics describe the characteristics of all or part of a human population, such as size, growth rate, distribution, birth and death rates, racial mix, and so on. Countries with larger populations have more geopolitical "weight" than smaller ones for the simple fact that there are more people with which to build an army, to work factories and farms, and to tax for revenue. In some cases, however, larger populations may undermine the potential power and capabilities of a poor nation if it cannot properly care for them. Resources that might be directed toward technical research, the military, or infrastructure projects might instead be directed toward simply feeding, caring for, and housing large poor, sick, or aging populations.

At a global level, the rate of population growth rose from about 1.5 percent per year in 1950–51 to a peak of over 2 percent in the early 1960s, due to significant reductions in the rate of early mortality; people were living longer than they had in the past. Growth rates thereafter declined as couples in the advanced industrialized countries deferred childbearing till later in life and effective contraceptive methods became widely available. Although the world population continues to grow, the rate of growth is beginning to slow. The 6.7 billion people on Earth produce 131 million children a year, an annual rate of population growth of some 1.14 percent.[5] At this rate, the world population in 2030 will be roughly 8.3 billion.[6]

Although "when it comes to forecasting the future, the birthrate is the nearest thing to hard numbers,"[7] perhaps the biggest surprise of the last decade is that the most alarming predictions of human population growth have not come to pass (see Figure 2.1). In places such as Europe, Japan, Russia, and China, population growth has actually gone into reverse, with possibly drastic declines in population looming. Indeed, in Japan alone over 2,000 schools closed over the past decade, as the number of elementary and junior high students fell from 13.42 million in 1994 to 10.86 million in 2005; another 300 per year are expected to close over the next decade.[8]

In Western Europe also, population growth is well below replacement levels, a trend that will severely test Europe's welfare states in the near future. Today, one hundred workers support twenty retirees, but by 2050 that ratio will change to fifty retirees per hundred workers as pensioners come to make up nearly 40 percent of the total population (in contrast to today's 20 percent).[9] At

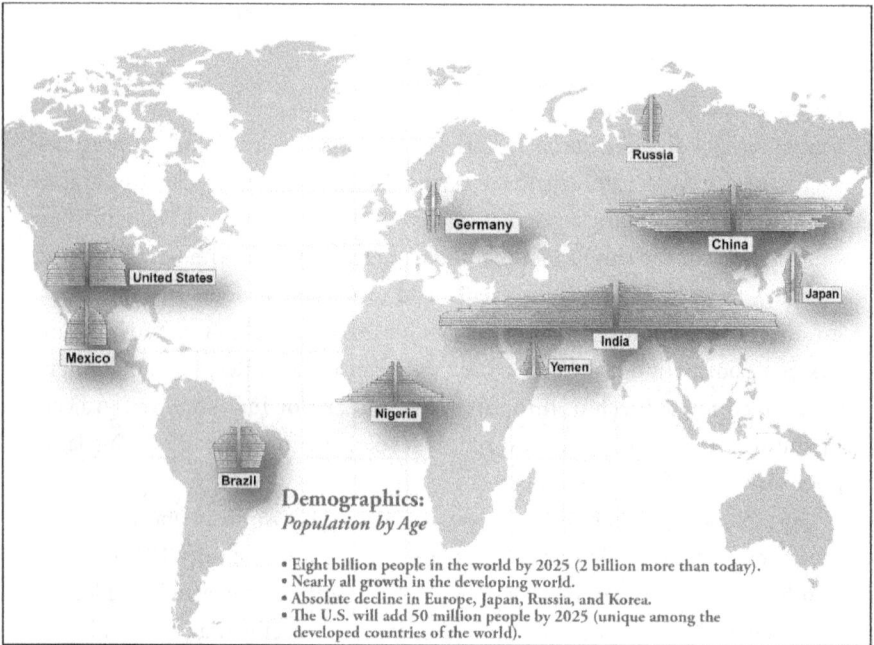

FIGURE 2.1 World Population Pyramids. A population pyramid is a demographer's tool used to track the size and age composition of a country or group. Each bar represents an age group in four-year increments (youngest at the bottom) with males on the left and females on the right. The pyramids above show projected populations of selected countries in the 2030 time frame and the width of each pyramid is to scale.

SOURCE: U.S. Census Bureau: "The Joint Operating Environment, Challenges and Implications for the Future Joint Force," United States Joint Forces Command, Norfolk, Virginia, December 2008.

the dawn of the twentieth century, no country had a median age greater than thirty; now only in Africa and the Middle East does this remain true. "Today, eight of the 16 nations of Western Europe have a median age of 40 or higher. By 2050, 6 will have a median age of 50 or higher. So will Japan, the East Asian Tigers, and 17 of the 24 nations in Eastern Europe and the Russian sphere."[10]

Energy

Energy resources are central to the functioning of the modern world economy. Until quite recently in human history, the world was powered by human or animal muscles for most agricultural and industrial purposes. In 2006, the world consumed 472 quadrillion BTUs of marketed energy per year, and by 2030, total world consumption is projected to increase by 44 percent to 678 quadrillion BTUs per year.[11] The current demand for energy is satisfied by burning oil, coal, and natural gas, by hydroelectric, wind, and solar power (collectively known as "renewable" energy), and by harnessing nuclear power to generate electricity. In addition to the production of electricity, more than half of the crude oil extracted from the ground is refined into fuel for vehicles, aircraft, and ships for transportation.

There is currently, however, a sharp discussion going on about the sufficiency of oil supplies in the future. Some describe oil production as having "peaked."[12] This does not mean that the world is "running out of oil," but rather that our ability to retrieve oil from the ground and bring it to market is shrinking, that supplies will not keep pace with global demand, and that prices are going to increase rapidly unless alternatives can be found.[13] We also can expect significant imbalances in the world energy trading regime now that the vast bulk of oil reserves are located in the Middle East and Russia, while the major consumers of oil—the United States, Europe, Japan, and China—rely on large-scale imports to meet domestic demand.

Oil trade is a major factor in the modern security environment. Russia uses its oil resources to expand its influence, while petroleum wealth in the Arabian Gulf region has been counted as a key source of funding for Islamic terrorism around the world. Securing the free flow of oil and natural gas from the Middle East was a central concern of U.S. foreign and strategic policy making throughout the Cold War, and gathered urgency after the 1979 Iranian Revolution, when the country with some of the largest known reserves of high-quality crude in the world suddenly went from being a close ally of the United States to an implacable enemy. Energy intensity, a measure of the units of energy burned per dollar of GDP, will likely become an important measure of efficiency as energy prices march higher and environmental concerns become more important. For both strategic and ecological reasons, inefficient, high-intensity users of energy will be challenged to lower the level of energy they expend per unit of GDP.

Water

Water, we are often reminded, is the foundation of all life and of human prosperity. Adequate, high-quality water supplies are indispensable for the growth and development of human social, economic, cultural, and political systems. Conversely, economic stagnation and political instability will persist or worsen in those regions where the quality and reliability of water supplies remain or are becoming more uncertain. Many parts of the world are facing a water crisis. Despite the fact that billions of tons of fresh water flow into the sea every day, over one billion people have no access to clean water, and over 2.6 billion live without adequate sanitation that could prevent water supplies from becoming polluted.[14] Furthermore, two regions with the highest levels of population growth—sub-Saharan Africa and North Africa/Middle East—are also regions that are chronically short of water.[15] The scarcity of water has been getting progressively worse despite the fact that this trend has been foreseen for decades. Unlike fossil fuels, there are no substitutes for water, and technology so far can do little to improve supply.

Lack of access to safe, clean water for drinking, sanitation, agriculture, and industry perpetuates poverty and is limiting viable development options in regions around the world.[16] Water scarcity and poor water quality increase the potential for domestic instability and heighten transnational tensions. History shows that in many regions around the world, water has been a source of considerable cooperation between nations that share water resources.[17] As populations in the driest parts of the world continue to increase, however, water scarcities may undermine international cooperation and encourage the use of military force to secure adequate supplies.

Future of Key Terrain

Geographic locations acquire strategic importance based on how humans use these locations. Rivers, mountain passes, canals, straits, overflight routes, air and sea points of debarkation, and spaceports are important to nations, and perhaps transnational competitors, as avenues to travel and choke points to be blocked. Nations have sought to control key geographic features to secure their borders, or to cut off the assault of a rival. During the Cold War, for example, a stretch of windswept ocean known as the GIUK Gap (for Greenland-Iceland-U.K.) was a central focus of the U.S. strategy to contain the Soviet Navy, prevent Soviet ballistic missile submarines from entering the Atlantic, and ensure that the U.S. Army could reinforce Germany in the event of conflict with the Warsaw Pact.

Strategic terrain will remain an important element in any understanding of the international environment in the future. For transnational terrorist organizations, ungoverned or ungovernable spaces will define the strategic terrain that they use as sanctuary from which to operate. Indeed, future non-state adversaries will attempt to "manufacture temporary autonomous zone (TAZ) sanctuaries as needed from any location that exhibits a vacuum of global order.

These places provide staging grounds for offensive operations in 'controlled' areas. The elimination of TAZs will be a long-run problem for nation-states."[18]

As sea ice retreats more and more rapidly from the Arctic, the region is becoming increasingly valuable for its possible undersea oil and other mineral resources; this and the opening of formerly ice-blocked sea-lanes are giving the region an increased profile in the security calculations of a number of states.[19] Russia, for example, claims the Lomonosov Ridge, which lies directly under the Pole, as part of its continental shelf, and thus part of Russian sovereign territory—including any oil and gas deposits that lie beneath the claim. Current economic exclusion zones recognize a 200-mile offshore limit; the Russian interpretation of the protocol would add 1.2 million square miles of territory to Russia if it is upheld by the United Nations.[20]

Strategic "terrain" is moving off-world as well, as specific locations in near-earth space become important to a variety of actors. Geostationary orbital slots that give owners the ability to communicate over wide areas of the earth are limited, while low-earth orbit—vital for Earth observation and navigation satellites—is fast becoming cluttered with dangerous debris.[21] In 2007, China destroyed one of its weather satellites in an ASAT (anti-satellite weapon) test, while in 2009 a defunct Russian satellite collided with and wrecked an American communications satellite.[22] "Lagrange points," areas of gravitational equilibrium that allow orbiting bodies to remain stationary with respect to the earth, moon, or other celestial object, may represent the ultimate "high ground" in the earth's gravity well.[23] Even the south pole of the Moon might be considered "key terrain," if its abundant, continuous sunlight and the potential availability of frozen water prove to be the key to establishing control over Earth's natural satellite.[24]

Identity Networks

States have traditionally held citizenship to be the highest order of identity or affiliation, but this claim to ultimate loyalty is being increasingly challenged by non-state entities. Emerging identity networks, in the form of political, religious, or social organizations, are rejecting the dominance of the state. As this trend progresses, states will feel pressure to assert their monopoly on violence and war, in an environment where leaders can no longer assume that citizens identify reflexively or exclusively with the physical territory on which they live. Identity networks constructed in cyberspace and community centers of various descriptions reach across national boundaries, allowing powerful transnational groups to coalesce and challenge state authority.

Identity networks of the future will be more likely to engage in governance, trade, taxation, and even warfare within and across state boundaries, much as Hezbollah does in Syria today. Some, like al Qaeda, are busily constructing affiliations and structures, and disseminating their myths and principles, across the global commons. Indeed, identity networks have

> the potential to cast the United States in the role that the Soviet Union held in the 1980s—a country driven to bankruptcy by a foe it couldn't compete with economically. We are staring at a future where defeat isn't experienced all at once, but through an inevitable withering away of military, economic, and political power and through wasting conflicts with minor foes.[25]

Thus, a key feature of conflict in this environment will be competition among networks, and between networks and hierarchies (usually those that underpin states). Events of the early twenty-first century have hinted at the disruptive nature of networks for hierarchies in economics and media, but this will become increasingly prevalent in military operations as well. Cyber and swarm attacks will be important tactics, as will any number of military operations classified as "irregular" in today's nomenclature. The "battle of the narrative" will expand into warfare in an emerging "cognitive domain," characterized by attempts to influence the place where "perceptions, awareness, beliefs, and values reside and where . . . decisions are made."[26] Conflict and war will evolve in a global order featuring national borders that are highly permeable to trade, human migration, and flows of information, knowledge, technologies, and money. In this world, more connections through communications technologies, trade, information media, and travel mean more avenues for ideas, memes, images, and concepts to propagate across the world.[27]

Dollars, Debt, and Defense

Many believe that globalization and deep economic interdependence minimize the impulse for war, and conversely, that the less states interact with one another economically, the more likely they are to go to war.[28] Others argue further that material production and financial resources can no longer be "captured" by aggressors because of global markets, and thus that economics is less a factor in conflict than it once was. Modern, rich states are less concerned with stocks of goods, but more with systems that direct the flows of goods and services.[29]

Global trade, the main driver of the world's economic growth for at least two decades, was on track in 2009 to record its largest percentage decline in over eighty years.[30] The recession that began in 2007 can be traced to a wider pattern of structural trade imbalances among creditor and debtor nations; improperly regulated financial markets; non-market (often politically motivated) considerations in lending practices; the opaque, unregulated securitization of debt; oil price volatility; and the collapse of home values in the United States and elsewhere around the world. Massive public and private debt in the United States, coupled with this severe economic downturn, resulted in high levels of mortgage default and the freezing of corporate bond markets. More problematic, many debt instruments were packaged and used to leverage further borrowing by investment banks, which resulted in massive defaults when nervous creditors called in their debts. The complexity of these instruments, coupled with the inability of markets to properly value them, discouraged banks and other financial institutions from lending to one another or anyone else, resulting in a powerfully negative environment for economic investment.

A period of de-globalization may take hold as high unemployment and social unrest, and the "dumping" of excess production capacity, are used to justify increased trade tariffs and controls over labor immigration. It was precisely this dynamic that made the Great Depression of the 1930s "great." In 2009, a report by the Economist Intelligence Unit assessed that there is a 10 percent chance that high levels of U.S. public, corporate, and private debt will lead to a collapse in the dollar as a global reserve currency.[31] The fear that the United States will inflate its currency to erode the value of its national, corporate, and personal debts has led China and Russia to work together on ways to limit their exposure to the dollar, and even replace it with a global (perhaps commodities-backed) currency not subject to the political and strategic dynamics of Washington.[32]   .

What then, might be the next steps in a full-blown global financial and economic unraveling? The initial impulse by investors has been to "flee" to the relative safety and security of U.S. treasury bonds. As economic growth regresses, however, even countries that traditionally invest heavily in dollar assets may not have available liquidity to purchase bonds. Currently, foreign governments and private investors hold some 40 percent of total U.S. debt. Furthermore, Washington is dependent on major exporter nations to fund government spending, because U.S. spending now exceeds revenue by $1.8 trillion dollars per year, or 13 percent of 2009's projected gross domestic product.[33] A key transition point will be reached should foreign buyers no longer participate in debt auctions held by the U.S. treasury. Market psychology can change quickly, and the danger for the United States is that some foreign buyers are beginning to fear that the U.S. government will no longer be able to service its debt as tax revenues collapse due to the weakening economy.[34]

The continuation of extreme financial and economic stress may have significant political and strategic implications, including

> economic collapse in Eastern Europe [that] could tear apart the European Union and create a new Iron Curtain. Further east, the slowdown in China's economy and the lack of political freedom is creating fertile ground for social turmoil. Millions of immigrant Chinese factory workers who returned to the countryside for the lunar New Year holiday had no jobs to return to.[35]

In addition to the threat of political and social instability around the world, massive failures in U.S. financial markets and government finances in a number of western countries, exacerbated by relentlessly aging populations, could mean that each will be less able to develop new military capabilities, or even maintain current expensive and capital-intensive capabilities.[36] These may include systems that are needed to maintain order in the Eurasian landmass, as well as naval, air, space, and cyber capabilities that secure the freedom to operate in the global commons. A western alliance tied down financially in this way may further encourage challenges around the world, as ambitious state and non-state actors attempt to carve out spheres of influence in the absence of U.S. or other allied power.[37]

Science, Technology, and Engineering

Constant scientific, technological, and engineering advances provide states and non-state groups with an ever-greater ability to modify and shape the world for their own purposes. Science, technology, and engineering are critically important to globalization because use of the global commons, especially space and cyberspace, is defined by the technical capabilities that a state or other actor can bring to bear in a conflict. Science, technology, and engineering were central to events in the later stages of the Cold War competition between the United States and the Soviet Union. U.S. investments in information technology provided the basis for later economic advances, and greatly increased wealth relative to the Soviets. A focus on new military technologies likewise allowed the United States to offset a number of the USSR's strategic capabilities, and threatened to negate Moscow's huge investments in air defenses, offensive ballistic missiles, and large-scale armored formations. The following provides an illuminating look at this dynamic:

> Precision provided a means to go from the many sorties needed to destroy a single target to a single sortie being able to destroy multiple targets. Stealth

would provide the means to negate the Soviet Union's massive investment in air defense and increase the element of surprise. Tactical ISR [intelligence, surveillance, and reconnaissance] provided the means to see targets deep beyond the front lines. Speed shortened the sensor-to-shooter times so that targets could be engaged as they were detected.[38]

Rapid advances in the science, technology, and engineering available to U.S. armed forces allowed for new concepts, such as Airland Battle or a direct precision attack against an enemy's leadership, that in turn dramatically changed the character and structure of U.S. forces.[39]

Adversaries are examining the U.S. way of war, and developing and assembling different technical capabilities to negate advantages. Already, terrorists have exploited technologies such as civilian aircraft and the internet as military assets, inflicting more casualties on U.S. soil during "9/11" than Imperial Japan was capable of in 1941. In the future, adversaries may not need to conduct kinetic attacks, as the potential exists to create and release weaponized organisms developed from data freely available over the internet.[40] Some state competitors are already in a race to develop a plethora of molecular manufacturing techniques that could provide economic and military advantage. Finally, new sources of energy, such as helium-3 used in fusion power reactors, or space-based solar energy collectors, may cause adversaries to seek control over places in which they are abundant (such as the lunar soil, or sun-synchronous orbits).

Accelerated information technologies will likely transform data management, the size and power of computer networks, and raw levels of processing power. Massive latent computing capacity resides in the millions of networked computers that could be linked for massive parallel-network computing. Indeed, botnets—networks of remotely-controlled computers used in spamming and distributed denial-of-service attacks by international criminals and perhaps states themselves—commandeer portions of a computer in a home office, making it the "sovereign territory" of a foreign power.[41]

We have already seen the use of "open source" technologies such as Google Earth to conduct surveillance against allied forces in Iraq, and against Indian citizens in Mumbai. Google Earth gives anyone on the internet free access to satellite imagery costing hundreds of billions of dollars that very few governments could afford to develop on their own. Emerging technologies such as Microsoft's Photosynth application mean that adversaries may not have to do surveillance now that near-real time immersive, ground-level imagery, meta-tagged and cataloged, can be browsed for free.[42] Likewise, a world embedded with computation and animated with robotic systems may be "hacked" and, like our commercial airliners, turned against us in ways that we have not yet foreseen.

Drivers for Engagement in the Commons

The following discussion is intended to further clarify the implications of these rather diverse trends for the future of engagement in the global commons. Taking the trends in their entirety, two major themes become evident: first, the United States and its allies command a shrinking portion of the world's economic, military, and ultimately, political power; and second, states themselves are ceding power in the commons to an array of non-state actors.

The first major driver that promoters of collective security in the global commons must accommodate is the idea that their power is becoming "smaller" relative to the rest of the world. Security arrangements that the United States forged between itself, Western Europe, Japan, South Korea, Latin America, and myriad other states around the world in response to Soviet power are the foundation of the even larger free market, open trade, investment, and security system generally termed *globalization*. Although the United States will likely maintain a larger economy and more sophisticated and powerful military capabilities than its nearest rivals over the next two to three decades, it is unlikely that it will grow faster than other state challengers around the world. In stark contrast to its post-Cold War position of near-global hegemony, over the next two decades the United States will "find itself in the position of being one of a number of important actors on the world stage."[43] For example, the U.S. population, though it is growing more quickly than any other developed country, will command an ever-smaller share of the total world population (from 5 to 4 percent) as the population of the developing world continues to explode. Echoing this trend is the fact that many of the United States' closest allies are in absolute demographic decline while some of the fastest growing nations on Earth (such as Yemen, which may have a population as large as Russia's by 2030) barely figure on today's world stage.

As new centers or poles of power emerge in the international arena, they will demand a greater say in how the seas, cyberspace, and outer space are used and governed. Competing views about the use and governance of exclusive maritime economic zones, for example, led to a series of naval encounters between U.S. and Chinese vessels in the South China Sea in 2009.[44] The Indian Navy, cutting through the legalistic restraints on piracy interdiction observed by the western powers, sank a pirate vessel off the coast of Somalia in 2008, upholding a more ancient standard of naval governance in the process.[45]

The second driver shaping the global commons of the future is the concern that states are losing influence to, and increasingly are in competition with, a number of non-state actors. The nation-state has been an enduring feature of the international environment for four hundred years. Today, however, the idea of state sovereignty and primacy is under challenge. Some states, such as members of the European Union, are delegating parts of their sovereignty upwards to international and supranational organizations. In many measures of power, such as the ability to command economic resources or political loyalty, some states are being overwhelmed by non-state actors that are extending control of territory and governance within their borders. Global networks, associations, and an array of interest-based nongovernmental organizations are challenging the state's legal and moral authorities, while some transnational groups and more local militias are gathering and building the capacity to pursue political interests independent of the state.

Armed groups that break the state's monopoly on the use of force are even seeking to impose their will on powerful states through the innovative use of information technology and "hybrid" modes of warfare. "Instead of separate challengers with fundamentally different approaches (conventional, irregular, or terrorist), we can expect to face competitors who will employ *all* forms of war and tactics, perhaps simultaneously."[46]

Western insistence on the positive relationship between international order and security and the need to respect basic human rights have formed the foundation of a world in which more individuals have a greater say in the way they are governed, and increased expectations about the span of their own personal autonomy—a phenomenon known as *liberty*. The so-called Westphalian system, founded in seventeenth-century Europe, encoded a number of rules about the authorities of states and their relations with one another in an "attempt to fashion a stable status quo and establish a mutually recognized set of rules and rights," covering "a broad range of religious, political, and territorial matters.[47] Many around the world, however, are dissatisfied with the present world order and do not recognize these same rules and rights. The result is a wider battle about the nature of relations within the international system and ultimately, that system's legitimacy.

For example, *political Islam* is a distinctly non-Westphalian mode of political development which strives for recognition in and use of the commons.

As one Muslim theorist put it, "The American war of ideas and the attack on our educational system began in the first decade of the twentieth century . . . there is a need to preserve the religious, intellectual, and cultural identity of the *ummah* and to sustain the thoughts of the Islamic awakening. . . ."[48]

Thus, globalization and liberty are the fundamental drivers shaping future engagement in the commons. Through the lens of our discussion of international trends, each of these drivers presents significant challenges and opportunities for the United States and its allies as they engage in the global commons going forward. Globalization is raising millions around the world out of abject poverty and giving them greater opportunities to improve their lives. At the same time, greater wealth translates to greater power and the emergence of possible competitors. Greater wealth also translates into greater stress on food, water, and energy supplies, causing higher prices and shortages that may translate into instability, civil conflict, and the failure of governments—as well as unsustainable debt and a fragile dollar. The world of liberty conceived by western democracies, if it is unbalanced by legally constituted governance and mechanisms to mitigate or resolve conflict, can result in failed states, refugee flows, and the rise of transnational groups that do not value domestic tranquility or the lives and prosperity of others.[49]

Conclusion: The Adversary Gets a Vote

> "The future is already here. It's just not very evenly distributed."
> *William Gibson*[50]

The United States and its allies have secured the global commons through an array of military, political, and technological capabilities and arrangements for more than fifty years. They have derived military and strategic advantage relative to competitors by their ability to translate technological innovation and industrial capacity into effective battlefield advantages. In response, adversaries are adapting military practices in an attempt to construct a mix of regular and irregular warfare, possibly with weapons of mass destruction, to extend their influence in the commons while deterring involvement by others in their affairs. Adversaries will blur the line between political conflict and open war, and place opposing forces in strategic dilemmas through hybrid modes of warfare that are designed to negate traditional technological advantages.

Transnational competitors will potentially develop around a set of ideas that are forged and disseminated within cyberspace, with the goal to disrupt state systems and carve out their own autonomous zones—not necessarily physical in nature. The specific goals of these groups are not important to this discussion, but it is possible that many groups with differing viewpoints or goals will share modes of operations, reaching a "critical mass" that overwhelms the ability of conventional, state-based militaries to innovate quickly enough to keep up in a "ecosphere of violence" against non-hierarchical foes that are utterly unconcerned with the forms, conventions, and rituals of state warfare.

Against this precarious backdrop, although the United States presently enjoys the largest concentration of economic and military power in the world, state competitors are shrinking its margin of superiority. Likewise, many European nations, along with Japan, Australia, and other liberal democracies, have significant demographic, social, and political concerns that blunt their ability to shape the commons around them. Because of the permeability of borders and flows of money and people, future conflicts will occur at least in part in the territories of these countries and the United States. As global financial markets and international trade link nations more closely to the wider global community, and as resource competition increases, the definition of "national interests" will further transcend borders. To defend these interests, allies must work together to address the increasing number of challenges and opportunities that cut across the global commons.

3 The Changing Security Environment

Dick Bedford

Introduction

The nature of decision making in 2030 will be little different from how it is today.[1] Those who act with alacrity and purpose will gain; those who fail to do so will lose. In the context of security, where costs are measured against interests, values, and public safety, every effort must be made to align functions and simplify decision making. This chapter is based in part on the research and analysis the author conducted in support of the Multiple Futures Project (MFP) team at NATO Allied Command Transformation.[2] It offers insights into the difficult choices associated with managing the risks involved in protecting the most vital element of society, our population, in light of increasing global complexity in general, and the interactions between states and non-state actors in particular.

Over the past thirty years, various groups and individuals have used systematic study of present trends as a means to explore different paths by which the future might unfold. Unfortunately, however, no matter how hard we try, the future will always be the province of the unknown. No single vision will be entirely correct, but elements of many will be present in whatever future unfolds. The problem of becoming wedded to a preclusive view is overcome by undertaking what may be called a "multiple futures" approach to evaluating possible outcomes. A collaborative evaluation of plausible futures eliminates the problems of a preclusive view of what the future may look like. This multi-level, what-if type analysis allows planners and practitioners to better understand enduring trends and take appropriate steps to minimize potential adverse implications. Peter Schwartz, in his book *Inevitable Surprises*, accepts the fact that the future is not foreseeable, but argues that with rigorous analysis and thoughtful planning it is possible to reduce potential vulnerabilities and minimize the impact of surprise:

> Sometimes you may be able to influence the outcome of a surprise. If it is a good thing, you can make more of it happen, and if it is a bad thing, you may be able to prevent it. Sometimes you may be able to take advantage of it, because you have developed relationships, products, financial resources, and information that put you in the right position when the time comes.[3]

It is incumbent upon every reader to do just that: identify and understand the range of possibilities the future holds. The goal, however, is not to get it perfectly right; rather it is to avoid getting it exactly wrong. To do so, one must be willing to think, discover, and innovate in ways that help illuminate and predict the hostile actions of our adversaries before they may occur, and where possible take steps to minimize the negative impact if they do occur.

Change and Challenges in a Complex World

As the first decade of the twenty-first century draws to a close, globalized nations and the highly integrated international system they inhabit are at a crossroads.[4] Central to this posture is the United States, as it moves from guarantor in a unipolar world to a multi-polar one where nations struggle to establish a balance between cooperation and competition, especially in the areas of economics and security. This world is marked by an uneasy equilibrium between developed nations that have a significant stake in globalization, and the power that comes with it, and determined state and non-state adversaries intent on degrading or reordering that power. Consistent with the recent past, opponents will work to undermine this tenuous balance by increasing their efforts to disrupt the global commons the modern world uses to communicate and interact. If this trend continues, the international system will be stressed and manipulated by forces of change the system is ill-designed to confront. Thus, the most significant challenge to the international system will be how to protect society while defending the global commons—the keystone of the globalized world. As Italian air strategist General Giulio Douhet warned in the run-up to World War I, "Victory smiles upon those who anticipate the changes in the character of war, not upon those who wait to adapt themselves after the changes occur."[5]

Over the coming decades, human ingenuity, governance, energy, and information technology will be significant factors in both protecting and disrupting the global system described in Chapter 1. The backbone of this system is composed of information, the flow of that information, and an educated, trained, and innovative population. Demographics, which are relatively certain for the next twenty years, will fundamentally define the character of the future world. When one focuses on Europe and North America, however, the decline in Europe's indigenous populations will particularly stress social structures and effective governance. Not only is Europe's overall population declining as a result of falling birth rates, its median age of 37.7 years in 2000 is projected to increase to 47 years by 2050.[6] The ageing of Europe, combined with competing ideologies and worldviews brought by immigration, will significantly impact the quality of governance as differing groups compete with and confront one another over relative values, religion, social/moral and ethical norms, culture, and geopolitical beliefs and perspectives. Nations that successfully integrate their indigenous and immigrant populations across this range of cultural, political, and ethical norms will have a significant advantage.

Advancing technology, information flows, and the energy that powers them have been the most dominant drivers in the cultural and economic advance of the human race over the past two hundred years. "Energy provides us with food, clothing and shelter; it transports goods and people; and protects us from our enemies. Energy is truly 'the master resource'—a truism that is often taken for granted."[7] The previous two hundred years have shown that our use of and demand for ever more efficient and effective sources of both information and energy are critical to the advancement of humankind. Over the next twenty years we will witness a rapid acceleration of this trend—one that will dwarf the advancements of the past century. During this period, a significant change in the global production and consumption of energy and the transmission and conversion of both information and knowledge will transform global markets, bringing both continuity and disruption to the political, strategic, and economic domains. Major innovations in nanotechnology, bio-engineering, and storage techniques will make the production and consumption of energy an increasingly individual, or in economic terms a micro, occurrence. This transition from macro to micro, from aggregate to individual, will give the soldier and citizen more power and convenience as the providers of energy shift from large-scale generation to an array of efficient, effective, renewable, and transportable technologies. Energy and technology are intimately related, and some believe that over the same twenty years the computational ability of machines will increase a million-fold in both performance and capacity; increases of this scale will inevitably bring significant changes to the globalized world.

Technology in and of itself nevertheless will not be the most significant change; rather this will come from the compounding effect of human ingenuity in the use of that technology, for good or bad, in the coming decades. History is replete with examples of human ingenuity gone wrong. This danger will continue as hostile state and non-state actors gain access to sophisticated, disruptive technologies that may be used to disrupt the global commons. One of the challenges to the international community will be how to develop and share the capability to detect, track, identify, and engage hostile actors intent on using these disruptive technologies, in particular nuclear and biological weapons.

These trends, combined with the increasing scarcity and misallocation of resources and weak or corrupt state governments, will remain at the heart of conflict and civil strife. In some culturally unique areas of the world, people are not only shaped, but to a large degree controlled, by their geography, values, and ideas, with little room to innovate, in what Robert D. Kaplan calls a "fusion of massed politics and shared paranoia."[8] States that lose the ability to control or at least rise to meet events will struggle to maintain even the semblance of order; in some cases they will fail. Using a geologic metaphor, Kaplan warns "artificial borders will crumble and become fissiparous, in essence crumbling like the Earth's crust. These 'shatter zones' threaten to explode or implode, or maintain a fragile equilibrium. And not surprisingly, they fall within the unstable inner core of Eurasia: the greater Middle East, the vast way station between the Mediterranean world and the Indian subcontinent that registers all the primary shifts in global politics."[9] While there is no easy answer for dealing with failed states, an important challenge for the international community over the coming decade will be how it addresses state weakness, especially in the volatile "shatter zone" of Eurasia.

No matter how prescient planners may be, the future will not develop as they envisage. Nevertheless, using trends like technology, information, demographics, state capacity, transnational terrorism, and irregular and hybrid warfare as a framework to think about potential futures is a useful guide for discussing risk. Risks refer to vulnerabilities and characteristics that not only physically endanger domestic populations and territorial integrity, but also threaten values and ideas. Territorial integrity includes the protection of national borders, domestic property, property abroad, and national resources claimed by the state. Today this interpretation can be expanded into the commons to include communications and computer networks using cyberspace, and satellites positioned in space. Values and ideas include the preservation and promotion of reason, discovery, innovation, and culture, the heritage of social norms, ethical values, traditional customs, and political systems that form the basis for civilization. The world of 2030 will differ little from the world of 1930 in the sense that people, their private property, civil rights, and national territory will remain the indisputable core responsibilities of the state to protect and defend. These responsibilities undoubtedly will influence national leaders across the coming decades as they balance risk and judge gain when making decisions that will affect the security of the global commons for decades to come.

Strategic Insights and Implications

This section will present a series of insights and associated implications that set the stage for succeeding chapters. The first insight addresses the increasingly unclear perception by the public regarding what constitutes an act of war. Defining "how" a sophisticated opponent might attack across geography, time, and space will foster a consensus as to what constitutes an attack (e.g., cyber attack, or denial of access to space or international straits), and eventually may suggest "where and when" an attack might be launched. The character of threats will continue to evolve and may be hybrid in nature: an interconnected and unpredictable mix of traditional and irregular warfare, terrorism, and organized crime.[10]

The second insight reflects the need to preclude or minimize conflict by acting outside traditional areas of engagement, whether singularly or in alliance with others, by promoting an integrated and comprehensive approach to the resolution of conflict. Such a comprehensive approach to security requires all international actors to contribute in a concerted effort, in a shared sense of openness and determination, based on their respective strengths and mandates.[11] Decisions on whether, and how, to act outside of traditional core missions may have to be made due to denial or disruption of access to the maritime, air, space, and cyberspace commons.

Increasingly, the security of the global commons will be affected by adversaries who seek to exploit national and global vulnerabilities. The third insight centers on the understanding that readily available, advanced technology will enable determined adversaries in new and unexpected ways. A mix of capabilities such as anti-satellite weapons, ballistic missiles, improvised explosive devices, and sophisticated cyber attacks in the hands of opponents can shut down economic markets and denigrate military command and control. Cyber assaults are known to have been used against Estonia and Georgia, for example, and are expected to continue. What is not known is what new and unexpected challenges the combination of advanced information networks, miniaturization, robotics, swarming, precision, and nanotechnology will pose. Some experts recognize that the space and terrestrial-based systems of communications that allied commanders in the field and police and fire chiefs in the street depend on to protect and defend society are complex and vulnerable.[12] As one analyst noted:

> To strategically impact our military, you have only to successfully attack one link in the chain, our satellites. Our homeland's complex infrastructure offers ever-increasing opportunities for disruption to enemies well aware that they cannot defeat our military head-on, but who hope to wage war asymmetrically, leapfrogging over our ships and armored divisions.[13]

In essence our enemies view the home front and the information systems that connect us to be one of our weaker links.

Furthermore, the proliferation of weapons capable of mass disruption, such as anti-satellite weapons, bio-engineered agents, and offensive cyber capabilities that can be used by individuals and small groups, must be considered. In due time, these types of extremely disruptive and destructive capabilities will be far more readily available, rendering adversaries more effective and lethal at greatly reduced cost and effort. The stark realities of these emerging threats to society, and in particular the global commons, will require changes to operational concepts, supporting capabilities, training, and the future alignment and structure of both security and military forces. Areas of strategic interest, present and future, include maritime security, the use and protection of space assets, and the development of cyber defense capabilities.[14]

The fourth insight is the *Battle of the Narrative*. Today's sophisticated adversaries are the masters of strategic communication and clearly understand the importance of dominating the media message. They know that in a strategic sense, perception can often be more important than reality, and since honesty and accountability are not compulsory they will always be first to manage perceptions. "Information has been, is, and will always be a strategic and political weapon and its power to influence will only increase as communications technology and the density of global media become more persuasive.[15] Shaping and managing perceptions, as we have seen in Afghanistan and Iraq, does not require a significant capital investment, yet for the savvy nation or non-state actor who understands the power of strategic communications, the return is immense.

If nations are to maintain public support and achieve a common understanding of the associated risk and gain in these environments they must develop the ability to anticipate, sense, discover, and communicate important developments and social movements to their national populations. Allies likewise need to be able to consistently and persuasively communicate their core values and ideas to the global community, especially those under direct assault: human rights, representative democracy, and rule of law.[16] The "voice of narrative" must pervasively and convincingly tell a positive story of enlightenment, from scientific and philosophical enlightenment to the continual quest for freedom, innovation, and self-expression. Dominating the narrative is and always will be a two-part process: first, create the message and second, transmit it in a timely and effective manner. In the past decade, technology has amplified the ability for a range of media savvy experts to disseminate their message.

Google, Twitter, YouTube, and Facebook have changed society by giving people the means to control the fidelity and frequency of the information they transmit and receive. Increasingly, those who prove the most agile and flexible at adapting to the opportunities of the twenty-first century will be the ones who shape and dominate the ways we communicate our values and ideas. Social networking sites have become vital forums for sharing and disseminating information, especially in countries where governments maintain strong controls over access to information, such as China, Iran, and Syria. The use of social networks as a vital conduit of information to the world during the protests that followed the 2009 Iranian presidential elections is well documented, as both sides competed across the internet and mass media to achieve their strategic and political aims.[17] In an increasingly interconnected world, leaders and citizens will interact more easily and directly, while the transmission of information, both good and bad, will be ubiquitous and near instantaneous, forcing people to evolve to meet a variety of unforeseeable and dynamic political, social, cultural, ethical, technological, and military developments.

Those who win this "Battle of the Narrative" will be prepared to better understand, shape, and react to the increasing technological, social, and economic interdependencies of the changing environment, and when confronted, respond quickly and persuasively to adversaries intent on disrupting access to the global commons.

Defense and Security: Two Sides of the Same Coin

Despite the ongoing danger to the international system from potential interstate conflicts in Africa, the greater Middle East, the Caucasus, and East and South Asia, large-scale, state-versus-state confrontation in the next twenty years is likely to be replaced by instability arising from fragile and failing states and competition over ungoverned spaces. Martin Van Creveld postulated in his ground-breaking 1991 book, *The Transformation of War*, that war would be fought to undermine the sovereignty of nations rather than to conquer territory, with conflicts forming along religious, ideological, social, and political lines.[18] These conflicts would not be waged by the armies of sovereign states, but by groups that today are labeled terrorists, insurgents, guerrillas, and criminals. "Their organizations are likely to be constructed on charismatic lines versus institutional ones, and to be motivated less by 'professionalism' than by fanatical, ideologically-based loyalties."[19]

Understanding the ideological composition of transnational groups, however, while important, is only the first step. We must also understand why they fight. This understanding is critical in a security environment framed by fragile and failed states led by radical groups that seek to subvert the globalized world. Going beyond Van Creveld's reasoning, in the knowledge that there is no preclusive view of war, it is clear that these challenges will be exacerbated by uncontrolled and illegal migration, radical demographic change, and friction within the international system caused by the inefficient allocation of resources. In this environment, adversaries will combine external attack with internal insurgency, in a hybrid assault designed to undermine the fundamental principles that bind a sovereign nation or alliance of nations. When Hasaan Nasrallah, the Secretary General of Hezbollah, was interviewed in 2006 after a confrontation with the Israeli Army, he referred to a new, hybrid form of warfare that Hezbollah's leadership was pioneering: "The resistance withstood the attack and fought back. It did not wage a guerrilla war either . . . it was not a regular army but was not a guerrilla in the traditional sense either. It was something in between. This is the new model."[20]

In Kaplan's unstable inner core of Eurasia, adversaries in the future may well achieve this "new model," externally by disrupting the global commons and internally by attacking national solidarity and civic values: the sanctity of life, individual liberty, and representative democracy based on the rule of law. These attackers would use both physical and psychological means to weaken our resolve and hasten our exit. In this race to deny and deter, nations "will confront new or heightened forms of competition in space and cyberspace, over the global commons around the world, and for the control of sources of scarce natural resources used to fuel growing economies and the choke points that link great nations to the world around them."[21]

As a natural extension of the phenomena outlined above, the use of advanced technology will increase both the breadth of vulnerabilities and the level of lethality that modern society will face. This availability of increasingly affordable and adaptable technology, especially the technology of nuclear and biological weapons, will require heightened vigilance, positive control, and close cooperation and consultation among the globalized nations at the international level. A single nation will not, regardless of the resources it expends or the attention it applies, be able to control this almost certain proliferation. The acquisition of nuclear and biological weapons by regimes hostile to democratic states will increase the potential that these weapons will be used to gain regional hegemony and disrupt the strategic balance. Combating these weapons will require an integrated international capability to detect, track, identify, target and engage those who threaten use of weapons of mass destruction or mass effect.

Whether the motives of the opposition are based on an assertion of power, religious extremism, rejection of equal rights, or envy of or aversion to an accumulation of national wealth and resources, they will work to subvert and undermine by attacking the fundamental principles of a free society. In the future, attacks will be interconnected and unpredictable, combining traditional with irregular and psychological warfare, terrorism, and organized crime. In the future, one of the weapons in this assault will be the instantaneous connectivity of an increasingly effective mass media that our adversaries will use to erode, reshape, and corrupt the liberal values, ideas, and markets that characterize the free nations of the west. As one analyst notes:

> These dramatic changes in the information dynamic have created what can be characterized as not just a Tyranny of Real Time but a Tyranny of the Time Line. At this critical information juncture, the time lines of media action and institutional reaction are increasingly out of sync. The moment any crisis in-

cident takes place there is an imperative to fill the resulting information space within not hours but minutes, and if possible to dominate it. But the competition is ruthless and unforgiving. The new breed of "information doers" enters that space immediately and relentlessly, first to bear witness digitally and then to transmit both the impressions and recorded material. And increasingly they do so overwhelmingly and more effectively.[22]

Sadly, few decision-makers today fully embrace this new dynamic, resulting in a reactive, tardy, non-compelling, and inadequate narrative. By 2030, we will enter the third generation of "information doers" who will shape information and perceptions in ways that today are unimaginable. To prepare for that future, leaders and decision-makers need to be agile in their ability to actively shape the information space—before, during, and after the event. In his book *The Pursuit of Glory*, Tim Blanning quotes Christian Wolff, one of the most perceptive philosophers of the eighteenth century, who would have innately understood the importance of shaping the "information space." He wrote in 1780: "Philosophers should be the teachers of the world and the teachers of princes. They must think logically and we must act logically. They must teach the world by their powers of judgment, we must teach the world by our example. They must discover, and we must translate their discoveries into practice."[23] Thinking, discovering, and translating will be critical responses to those who seek to disrupt and/or deny access to our centers of commerce and our integrated economy, including our social networks and the facilitating, but increasingly vulnerable, global commons that foster the connectivity and prosperity of the globalized nations.

Planning today to protect the global commons of tomorrow, to safeguard our property, territory, and economic interests, is the paramount work of government. To respond effectively in this environment of offense, defense, subterfuge, and deception, the capabilities of free nations, not solely military but across the range of integrated and comprehensive responses, will need to be flexible, adaptive, and innovative. The future by design will not favor one nation or non-state actor over another. For those nations whose citizens are able to think, discover, and translate thought into action, there will be ample opportunity to take the initiative and positively influence ideas, values, events, and capabilities. Such nations must, however, work in concert to improve their ability to respond to unpredictable and complex challenges.

The most serious future threats will not be super-empowered individuals or groups who overwhelm society with remarkable new capabilities. Adversaries are more likely to combine known capabilities and technologies in unique ways, as noted analyst Colin Gray pointed out: "The fundamental reason why we can be surprised tends not to be the sudden emergence of novel factors of menace— but rather the consequences of known trends that interact in unexpected ways, resulting in unanticipated consequences."[24] This novelty, when coupled with a lack of will for prompt and forceful action, would be a recipe for disaster. Thus Winston Churchill, addressing the British House of Commons on 2 May 1935, castigated the government for such a failure of will: "Want of foresight, unwillingness to act when action would be simple and effective, lack of clear thinking, confusion of counsel until the emergency comes, until self preservation strikes its jarring gong—these are the features which constitute the endless repetition of history."[25] Using Churchill's logic, arguing about the utility of defense over security or security over defense is simply a fool's errand. Nations will inherently wish to defend their populations and territory from foreign invasion. In the complex world of the twenty-first century, they will also work to secure their strategic interests as part of the global commons no matter where those interests might reside.

Deterrence in a Complex and Changing World

In the face of these unpredictable and complex threats, it is essential that influential nations and alliances continue to demonstrate strength and resolve. The universal requirement of any government is to ensure the safety and security of its society. All liberal democratic governments must be informed and vigilant as to the means, methods, and capabilities of their opponents. Using NATO as an example, it is illustrative that the Alliance was founded in 1949 by a treaty that reaffirmed the purposes and principles of the recently formed United Nations. In the wake of World War Two, the twelve plenipotentiaries who signed the treaty understood the importance of an alliance of nations whose steadfast purpose was the protection of the fundamental values and ideas upon which these societies were founded. In the words of the treaty, "[T]hey are determined to safeguard the freedom, common heritage and civilization of their peoples, founded on the principles of democracy, individual liberty and the rule of law."[26] Nations that share strategic interests and choose to ally themselves fare better and promote stability in the international system. While there may be times when a single nation may elect to go it alone; history will not be on its side. The long-standing lesson of the conflicts in Afghanistan and Iraq is that one nation, no matter how powerful, simply cannot resolve the many problems resident in the complex and changing world of today and tomorrow.

The trends of today, the complexity, the dangers, and the opportunities, some of which this chapter presents, will continue. By 2030, that environment may be so complex that like-minded nations may very well find that banding together, politically, militarily, and economically is the only way to send a clear signal of solidarity and resilience to their opponents, in essence a clarion's call that there will be strength behind the response to any attack, whether territorial or not. To effect this deterrence, nations may elect to adopt a comprehensive approach, developed in concert with international organizations such as NATO, the European Union, the African Union, and the United Nations, whereby they agree to the coordinated use of all levers of power—political, military, economic, and civil—to provide mutual security and defense. It is important to keep in mind, however, that the more comprehensive the approach, the more engagements will be affected by a range of actions and events, some of which exist outside the geographic boundaries that shape the strategic interests of nations. To be effective, representatives of nations must develop better partnerships, leverage mutually supportive relationships, improve the integration of military and non-military elements of government, and work more closely with international organizations. In preparing for operations in this increasingly complex environment, "we must respect and develop service cultures, shape and prepare our civilian workforce for new roles, convince our inter-agency partners of the benefit to their respective missions, and reassure our multinational partners of our commitment to partnering with them."[27]

While every nation of the globalized community may not be able to acquire the necessary capabilities and training for every contingency on its own, all must at a minimum agree to a coalition or alliance of nations and like-minded organizations that prepare its members to deter and confront foes and dangers alike in the coming decades. Coalition or allied forces must be flexible, adaptable, well-trained, well-equipped, deployable, and sustainable. They will require a comprehensive command structure that is able to integrate and work effectively with other institutions. Forces must be able to conduct a full range of operations and missions concurrently, ranging from collective defense to stabilization and reconstruction operations, and from security sector reform to large-scale high-intensity combat operations. These forces must assure access to and unencumbered use of the global commons, a pivotal factor for all successful operations.

Developing the necessary capabilities and generating the required forces for these operations and missions will remain a core responsibility of individual nations. They will need to create new or dedicated capabilities to protect major communication nodes and associated infrastructure. History shows that humans have at one time or another fought for dominance over every medium that contributes to commerce. Space, as a global common and increasingly important venue for commercial activity, may well be no different. As such, it is vital to protect and assure access to commercial and military space systems.[28] As the globalized world increases its dependency on information transmitted across space-based and terrestrial technologies, it is important to note that adversaries, both state and non-state, will not have to dominate the spectrum—a simple strategy based on denial and disruption will be sufficient.

As military and security forces contemplate the series of complex tasks that missions of tomorrow will demand, such as adapting to the demands of hybrid threats, operating with other, often civilian, organizations, developing a comprehensive approach, countering proliferation, building expeditionary forces, and winning the battle of the narrative, it will be incumbent that nations invest in training and set the highest standards of professional excellence for their civilian and military forces. Present and future demographic trends, however, suggest that it will be increasingly difficult for western nations to recruit, educate, train, and retain a professional force of the highest caliber that is able to conduct operations in a complex and austere environment. One study warns: "[Europe's] declining population cohort could affect their ability to meet planned force levels, and make it more difficult to modernize their smaller, more expensive professional forces, particularly when faced with mounting health and social costs for its ageing population. Some European allies may have to address the question of whether they will be able to sustain a viable military capability."[29] Over the past 200 years, western civilization has relied on human ingenuity as an X-factor in building economies and winning wars. To maintain that edge it is imperative that nations cultivate a stable, prosperous and educated population; to do otherwise is to commit national suicide.

Conclusion

By evaluating the strategic trends and evolving threats in a changing world, it becomes apparent that the unpredictability and complexity of the future security environment will strain a nation's citizenry to the core, putting at risk the preservation of values and ideas that embody western culture. No nation can meet the challenges alone, and history shows that when confronted by a determined foe, allies or coalitions fare better when they coordinate their efforts. To accomplish this goal, it will be essential that nations achieve a common understanding of what constitutes an attack, whether territorial, physical, or virtual, and just as importantly, reach consensus, both internally and externally, on how to respond.

A comprehensive approach, developed in concert with international organisations, will be fundamental to national security. It goes without saying that the more comprehensive the approach, the more engagements will be affected by actions outside of national boundaries. To be effective in this environment, nations must develop better partnerships, leverage relationships, and work with other international actors to improve both the deployability of forces and the transparency of decision making. Success will depend on the ability to manage conflict effectively and mitigate the consequences that spring from subversive activity and unanticipated tactics. Burgeoning technological developments will contribute to the breadth of both alliance capabilities and vulnerabilities, and to the ingenuity of adversaries as they seek to use advanced technology to disrupt society.

"Historically, every military organization that has transformed successfully has done so by identifying specific military problems that need to be addressed."[30] To this end, nations will have to maintain and improve existing capabilities, and in some cases develop new ones, to address problems found in emerging security challenges. In the following chapters, the contributors to this book will present frameworks that nations can use to counter adversaries that threaten the global commons. The authors' analyses and ideas are intended to stimulate dialogue and inform decisions on what needs to change. Furthermore, their findings will support the development of good public policy as a foundation for improving a nation's, or an alliance's or coalition's, ability to protect their populations and the global system on which they depend.

Foretelling the future is always risky, as trends invariably change in magnitude and direction. We must not lose sight of the fact that, no matter how hard we try, the future is not foreseeable, and we will be surprised. Although changes to the cultural and geopolitical context, and the introduction and use of new technologies, will alter the conduct of war, war always has been and always will be a human endeavour. When it comes to defense and security, the alliances of liberal democracies must be supreme—and in the case of war, that means winning, period. Parties that go to war will use all means at their disposal to achieve victory, and, as Ralph Peters reminds us, when fighting to preserve one's way of life, "to fail is to nourish monsters."[31] The men and women who serve in their countries' militaries must receive the very best training, education, material, and support that society can provide if allied and coalition nations are to be successful in their mission—to protect and defend the populations of modern civilization.

4 Indistinct Legal Regimes

James Kraska

International Law

Global legal regimes provide stability and predictability in international affairs, and provide a minimum basis for the maintenance of world public order. International law is that body of rules and regimes that bind nations in legal and political relationships. Modern concepts of international law spring from the Greek and Roman traditions, in particular the principles of *jus gentium*, which reflected the basic tenets of equity and natural law recognized by civilized nations.[1] These ideas were carried into the Middle Ages by natural law theologian-scholars, who cultivated the "Just War" doctrine, the precursor to laws of armed conflict. Frederick III, German emperor from 1440–1483, was the last of the emperors crowned in Rome by the pope, and the weakening of the ecclesiastical order, accelerated by the Reformation, encouraged the development of a new source of authority for the rules governing nations.[2]

Cooperation among the states of the Hanseatic League, founded in the thirteenth-century German lands, and the Italian city-republics, provided the impetus to develop diplomatic conventions and mutually-accepted rules. The Bourbon and Hapsburg rivalry engulfed central Europe in the Thirty Years' War (1618–1648), constituting the first "world war." The devastation wrought by the conflict inspired Dutch jurist Hugo Grotius (1583–1645) to develop a law of war, continuing the work of Alberico Gentili (1552–1608), an Italian doctor of civil law who wrote pioneering works on the relations between states for Elizabeth I of England. Regarded as the father of modern international law, Grotius was a rationalist who derived law from evidence in nature as well as universal reason. He believed legal regimes could be derived from the application of strict logic, producing a coherent system of law. The Peace of Westphalia, ending the Thirty Years' War in 1648, included the Treaty of Westphalia and the Treaty of Münster, which together codified the notion of the inviolability of state borders on land. Epochal documents, these treaties also recognized sovereignty over land areas under individual autonomous rulers, ushering in the era of the modern nation state. Whereas the complex treaties recognized that states exercise complete authority over and are responsible for maintaining security inside their borders, it was manifest that no nation could exercise sovereignty over the oceans.

Contemporary legal regimes provide rules for not only the oceans, but other shared commons as well, including international airspace, outer space, and—recently—cyberspace. The sources of these laws include customary international law, or the practice of states combined with a sense of legal obligation; international treaties and agreements, which reflect the positivist approach to law and require specific consent by nations; the judgments of international judicial bodies; and general principles and the opinions of respected legal scholars. This chapter will explore how the legal aspects of the global commons are both established and evolving, having a distinct set of rules, but with an indistinct trajectory toward the future.

Law of the Sea

Since its inception in 1945, the essential treaty framework for world order has been the United Nations Charter, which governs relations among all member states. After the UN Charter, the most comprehensive agreement in existence is the 1982 UN Convention on the Law of the Sea.[3] With more than 155 state parties, this Convention has become a "constitution" for the world's oceans. Moreover, since the agreement is an "umbrella" treaty, it provides the essential rule-set for a multitude of supporting practices and treaties to regulate international conduct at sea and in the air. Consequently, the Law of the Sea (LOS) Convention is the essential point of departure for understanding the law of the global commons.

The LOS Convention prescribes rules for activity on, over, and under the world's seas, and many of its provisions reflect the principles of customary international law that developed both prior to Grotius and subsequent to the publication of his treatise, "On the Law of War and Peace," in 1625. Interlocking, complementary regimes set forth in the LOS Convention delineate navigational rights and freedoms that may be exercised by nations that operate vessels, which are called "flag states." Nations geographically situated on the sea are "coastal states," and they may assert sovereignty, or certain designated sovereign rights or jurisdiction, in that ocean space adjacent to their coastline. Coastal states also may elect to develop areas of their shoreline to accept international shipping commerce, thereby acquiring the status of a "port state," to which inure the associated legal obligations and duties of operating shipping and port facilities.

Because the Convention balances the rights and duties of flag, coastal, and port states, the entire architecture of oceans law represents a "package deal," in which states are required to accept all of its provisions, enjoying rights and fulfilling concomitant responsibilities. This careful balance between the rights and duties of flag and coastal states represents a grand bargain that unfolded during the negotiation of the Convention. Today the compromises in the Convention are the bedrock of global oceans law and policy. This narrative on the importance of international law at sea is at odds with much of the conventional wisdom that characterizes the oceans as an ungoverned legal vacuum.

The global order of the oceans springs from the architecture of the international law of the sea and of the supplementary treaties, codes, and guidelines produced by member states of the International Maritime Organization. The 1982 LOS Convention was the first, and remains the foremost, international instrument to formalize collaborative approaches to oceans security. Previous attempts in 1930, 1958, and 1960 to develop a widely accepted multilateral framework on oceans law either ended in utter failure or achieved only modest gains. In contrast, the 1982 LOS Convention was a breakthrough in the resolution of long-standing issues. The agreement contributes directly to international peace, prosperity, and security by replacing abundant conflicting maritime claims with universally accepted limits on coastal state sovereignty and jurisdiction. It is anchored in a set of navigational regimes that establish mutual expectations by delineating the rights and duties of flag, port, and coastal states, and providing the means to adjudicate disputes.

Historically, the oceans were divided between internal waters, territorial seas, and high seas. In the latter half of the twentieth century, new concepts evolved, including the contiguous zone, the exclusive economic zone (EEZ), the extended continental shelf, and archipelagic waters, in which coastal states may exercise functional sovereignty, or sovereign rights or jurisdiction over vast areas of the oceans. For the purpose of exploring legal regimes related to the global commons, it is important to note that all water seaward of the outer limits of the territorial sea (defined below)—including high seas, exclusive economic zones, and contiguous zones—constitute "international waters." All nations enjoy high-seas rights and freedoms of navigation and overflight in international waters. Even in "national waters," however, foreign-flagged vessels may exercise the regime of innocent passage in territorial seas, while the regime of transit passage or innocent passage may apply even in internal waters in some cases. Consequently, a clear understanding of the legal framework of the global commons begins with an explanation of the legal character and navigation regimes applicable to "national waters," and then sets forth the broad navigational regimes applicable to "international waters." The point of departure for this analysis is the concept of the "baseline."

All of the various regimes in the LOS Convention are measured from the baseline of the coastal state, which is an imaginary line that normally traces the low-water mark along the shoreline, as marked on the nation's official large-scale charts. In certain limited instances, where the coastline is deeply indented and cut into, or where there is a fringe of islands along the coast, coastal states may deviate from the low-water mark convention and instead draw straight baselines. Straight baselines nevertheless must not depart from the general direction of the coast, and the sea areas they enclose must be closely linked to the land domain.

Coastal states may be entitled to enclose limited parts of the oceans as "historic internal waters," but the test for doing so requires the acquiescence of other nations and is notoriously difficult to meet.[4] Lakes, rivers, some bays, harbors, some canals, and lagoons are examples of internal waters, which lie landward of the baseline. Coastal nations exercise the same jurisdiction and control over their internal waters and superjacent airspace as they do over their land territory. Because ports and harbors are located landward of the baseline, entering a port ordinarily involves navigation into internal waters and the consent of the port state. There is no right of innocent passage in internal waters, and, unless in distress, foreign ships and aircraft may not freely enter the areas.

Immediately seaward of the baseline lies the territorial sea. The territorial sea is a belt of ocean that may extend a maximum of twelve nautical miles from the baseline of the coastal nation, and the area is subject to the sovereignty of the coastal state. Ships of all nations, however, enjoy the right of innocent passage in the territorial sea, although aircraft are not entitled to assert a similar right to overfly the territorial sea. The right of innocent passage means continuous and expeditious traversing of the territorial sea, and may even include stopping and anchoring, but only insofar as incidental to ordinary navigation, or as rendered necessary by force majeure or by distress. All civilian vessels and warships enjoy the right of innocent passage, which cannot be conditioned on consent or notification by the coastal state. Generally, passage is innocent so long as it is not prejudicial to the peace, good order, or security of the coastal nation. The LOS Convention contains an exhaustive list of such prejudicial activities deemed inconsistent with innocent passage, and these include any threat or use of force against the sovereignty, territorial integrity, or political independence of the coastal state.

A coastal nation may enact certain reasonable and necessary restrictions upon the right of innocent passage for purposes of resource conservation, environmental protection, and navigational safety. Such restrictions, however, may not have the practical effect of denying or impairing the right of innocent passage, and they may not discriminate in form or in fact against the ships of any nation, nor can they prohibit the transit rights of nuclear-powered sovereign warships. Oman, for example, purports to require prior permission for innocent passage for warships and nuclear-powered vessels, and vessels carrying dangerous substances. The coastal nation may designate sea-lanes and traffic separation schemes, and even temporarily suspend innocent passage in cases in which it is essential to do so for security. Beyond the territorial sea, coastal states are entitled to claim a contiguous zone, extending seaward from the baseline up to twenty-four nautical miles. Within the contiguous zone, the coastal state may exercise the control necessary to prevent or punish infringement of its customs, fiscal, immigration, and sanitary laws and regulations that occur within its territory or territorial sea. Ships and aircraft of all nations, however, enjoy high seas freedoms, including overflight, in the contiguous zone.

International straits are those areas of overlapping territorial seas that connect one area of the high seas or EEZ to another area of the high seas or EEZ, and that are used for international navigation. These waters are simultaneously territorial seas and constitute an international strait; because of the dual nature of the waterway, the regime of transit passage, rather than the rules of innocent passage, applies to foreign-flagged vessels and aircraft. Transit passage, which permits continuous and expeditious transit by surface ships, submarines, and aircraft, exists throughout the entire strait (shoreline-to-shoreline) and not just the area overlapped by the territorial sea of the coastal nations. Unlike innocent passage, transit passage may not be suspended. Vessels and aircraft may transit in the "normal mode," meaning that submarines may travel under the water and aircraft may overfly the strait. While conducting transit passage, ships may conduct formation steaming and launch and recover aircraft and other devices. There are more than 125 international straits throughout the world. The Strait of Hormuz separating Iran and Oman is an example of an international strait with particular strategic importance. The passage is only twenty-one miles wide at its narrowest point.[5]

Coastal states may claim an exclusive economic zone, a resource-related zone adjacent to the territorial sea in which a coastal state may exercise certain sovereign rights and jurisdiction, but not sovereignty, out to a distance of 200 nautical miles from the baseline.[6] Ships and aircraft of all nations, including warships and military aircraft, enjoy complete freedom of movement and operation on and over and under the waters of the zone. Unlike sovereignty over the territorial sea, however, the scope of sovereign rights in the EEZ apply only to living and nonliving resources of the water column, seabed and subsoil, and to jurisdiction over artificial installations, marine scientific research and, marine environmental protection.[7]

The LOS Convention recognizes the sovereign rights of a coastal nation to prescribe and enforce its laws in the exclusive economic zone for the purposes of exploration, exploitation, management, and conservation of the natural resources of the waters, seabed, and subsoil of the zone, as well as for the production of energy from the water, currents, and winds. Coastal nations may exercise jurisdiction over the establishment and use of artificial islands, installations, and structures having economic purposes; over marine scientific research; and over some aspects of marine environmental protection (including implementation of international vessel-source pollution control standards). In the EEZ, all nations enjoy the right to exercise the traditional high seas freedoms of navigation and overflight, of the laying of submarine cables and pipelines, and of all other traditional high seas uses by ships and aircraft that are not resource related.

Codification of the EEZ has brought nearly one-third of the high seas under some form of national administration.[8] Unlike the territorial sea, however, the balance of rights and interests in the EEZ inures to the international community, so ships and aircraft of all nations enjoy the rights and freedoms associated with the high seas, including the right of overflight. Naval forces may conduct task force maneuvering, flight operations, military exercises, surveillance, intelligence-gathering activities, and ordnance testing and firing in the EEZ. Despite the fact that coastal nations lack the authority or competence to restrict or impede the exercise of high seas freedoms in the exclusive economic zone, on numerous occasions China has interfered with foreign military activities in the EEZ off the Chinese coastline.[9]

Most rules for navigational safety governing surface and subsurface vessels, including warships, are contained in the 1972 International Regulations for Preventing Collisions at Sea, known as the "72 COLREGS" or the "International Rules of the Road."[10] These rules apply to all international waters (i.e., the high seas, exclusive economic zones, and contiguous zones) and, except where a coastal nation has established different rules, in coastal nations' territorial seas, archipelagic waters, and inland waters as well. Any nation may declare a temporary warning area in international waters and airspace to advise other nations of the conduct of activities that, although lawful, are hazardous to navigation and/or overflight. Notice of the establishment of such areas must be promulgated in advance. States may provide notice in the form of a special warning to mariners, notice to mariners (called a NOTMAR), notice to airmen (NOTAM), or by satellite and radio communication message through the Global Maritime Distress and Safety System. Ships and aircraft of other nations are not required to remain outside a declared warning area, but are obliged to refrain from interfering with activities therein.

An archipelagic nation is a nation that is constituted wholly of one or more groups of islands (e.g., Indonesia). Such nations may draw straight archipelagic baselines joining the outermost points of their outermost islands, provided that the ratio of water to land within the baselines is between 1:1 and 9:1. The waters enclosed within the archipelagic baselines are called archipelagic waters. The archipelagic baselines are also the baselines from which the nation measures seaward its territorial sea, contiguous zone, and exclusive economic zone. These island nations may designate archipelagic sea-lanes through their archipelagic waters suitable for continuous and expeditious passage of ships and aircraft. All normal routes used for international navigation and overflight are to be included.

If the archipelagic nation does not designate such sea-lanes, the right of archipelagic sea-lanes passage may nonetheless be exercised by all nations through routes normally used for international navigation and overflight. All ships and aircraft, including warships and military aircraft, enjoy the right of archipelagic sea-lanes passage while transiting through, under, or over archipelagic waters and adjacent territorial seas via all routes normally used for international navigation and overflight. The right of archipelagic sea-lanes passage is substantially identical to the right of transit passage through international straits. Outside of archipelagic sea-lanes, all ships, including warships, enjoy the more limited right of innocent passage throughout archipelagic waters just as they do in territorial seas.

The juridical continental shelf of a coastal nation consists of the seabed and subsoil of the submarine areas that extend beyond its territorial sea to the outer edge of the continental margin or to a distance of 200 nautical miles from the baseline used to measure the territorial sea, where the continental margin does not extend to that distance. Although the coastal nation exercises sovereign rights over the continental shelf for purposes of exploring and exploiting its natural resources, the legal status of the superjacent water is unaffected. Moreover, all nations have the right to lay submarine cables and pipelines on the continental shelf. Generally, when two nations are within 200 miles of one another, an equidistant line separates their respective zones.

Of special note, the waters, ice pack, and airspace of the Arctic region beyond the lawfully claimed territorial seas of littoral nations have international status, and are open to navigation by the ships and aircraft of all nations. Canada, for example, has claimed sovereignty over the Arctic on the basis of discovery, historic internal waters, contiguity to the continental landmass, or through the so-called "sector" theory, but none of those claims are recognized in international law. Accordingly, all ships and aircraft enjoy the freedoms of high seas navigation and overflight on, over, and under the waters and ice pack of the Arctic region.

The 1959 accord governing Antarctica provides the continent "shall be used for peaceful purposes only," and that "any measures of a military nature, such as the establishment of military bases and fortifications, the carrying out of military maneuvers, as well as the testing of any type of weapons" shall be prohibited. The treaty does not, however, affect in any way the high seas freedoms of navigation and overflight in the Antarctic region.

As a general rule, international law does not recognize the peacetime right of any nation to restrict the navigation of foreign warships and overflight of military aircraft beyond the outer limits of the territorial sea. Although a number of coastal nations have asserted claims that purport to prohibit warships and military aircraft from operating in so-called security zones extending beyond the territorial sea, such claims have no basis in international law in time of peace.[11]

All nations may establish temporary maritime zones for a variety of lawful purposes, such as to provide warning of naval exercises, to facilitate the conduct of military operations, or to exercise the belligerent right of approach and visit in time of war to determine the friendly or enemy character of merchant vessels.

Law of Airspace

Under international law, airspace is classified as either national airspace (that over the land, internal waters, archipelagic waters, and territorial seas of a nation) or international airspace (that over contiguous zones, exclusive economic zones, the high seas, and territory not subject to the sovereignty of any nation). Subject to a right of overflight of international straits and archipelagic sea-lanes, each nation has complete and exclusive sovereignty over its national airspace. The aircraft of all nations are free to operate in international airspace without interference by other nations. The rules for air navigation in international airspace applicable to civil aircraft are located in Annex 2 (Rules of the Air) to the International Convention on Civil Aviation (ICAO), of 1944.

A Flight Information Region (FIR) is a defined area of airspace within which flight information and alerting services are provided. FIRs are established by ICAO for the safety of civil aviation and encompass both national and international airspace. Under article 3 of ICAO, state aircraft have sovereign immune status. This means that all military aircraft and government spacecraft, commanded by a member of the armed forces and manned by a crew subject to regular armed forces discipline, plus unmanned aerial vehicles, are immune from arrest or search, whether in national or international airspace. Consequently, state aircraft not intending to enter national airspace are not required to identify themselves or otherwise comply with FIR procedures. Although many air forces comply with ICAO procedures as a matter of policy for routine and point-to-point flights, there is no requirement to do so, and aircraft conducting military contingency operations, classified or politically sensitive missions, and routine aircraft carrier operations or other training activities would not be expected to file a flight plan. All aircraft, including military aircraft, however, have an obligation to navigate with "due regard" for civil aviation safety.

International law does not prohibit nations from establishing air defense identification zones (ADIZ) in the international airspace adjacent to their territorial airspace. The legal basis for ADIZ regulations is the right of a nation to establish reasonable conditions of entry into its territory. Accordingly, an aircraft approaching national airspace can be required to identify itself while in international airspace as a condition of entry approval. A coastal nation may not apply its ADIZ procedures to foreign aircraft not intending to enter national airspace. In the case of imminent or actual hostilities, however, a nation may find it necessary to take measures in self-defense that will affect overflight in international airspace. For example, if military aircraft flying in international airspace commit a hostile act, or demonstrate hostile intent, against a coastal state, the coastal state may respond to the threat without waiting for the military aircraft to actually cross into national airspace.

Outer Space Law

While each nation has exclusive control over the use of its national airspace, the upper limit of airspace subject to national jurisdiction has not been authoritatively defined by international law. Numerous proposals for designating such a boundary have been presented in international forums such as the UN Committee on the Peaceful Uses of Outer Space, but no agreement has been reached.[12] Indeed, states have not been able to agree on whether a boundary is even necessary. State practice, however, generally recognizes the rule that national airspace terminates and outer space begins at the point at which artificial satellites can be placed in orbit without falling to earth. Man-made satellites and other objects in earth orbit may overfly foreign territory freely.

The body of international law solely dedicated to space activities is relatively small, consisting of broad principles. After the launch of the Soviet Sputnik satellite in 1957 and the U.S. Explorer I satellite the following year, there emerged recognition that nations should define what constitutes the threshold between airspace and outer space. Furthermore, general rules governing human conduct in space had to be developed. In 1961, the UN General Assembly adopted Resolution 1721 (XVI), which proclaimed that, "outer space and celestial bodies are free for exploration and use by all States in conformity with international law and are not subject to national appropriation."[13] These principles were reaffirmed in General Assembly Resolution 1962 (XVIII) of December 1963, which proclaimed that outer space and celestial bodies are free for exploration and use by all states on a basis of equality and in accordance with international law, and that outer space and celestial bodies are not subject to national appropriation by claim of sovereignty by any state.[14]

Unlike the law of airspace, treaties governing outer space typically do not exempt military spacecraft and space activities. International law, including customary international law and the UN Charter, applies to outer space, which is open to exploration and use by all nations. Outer space is not, however, subject to national appropriation by any state, and it must be used for peaceful purposes. The term "peaceful purposes," however, does not preclude military activity. While acts of aggression in violation of the UN Charter are precluded, space-based systems may lawfully be used to perform essential command, control, communications, intelligence, navigation, environmental, surveillance, and warning functions to assist military activities on land, in the air, and on and under the sea. As in international airspace, users of outer space must exercise "due regard" for the rights and interests of other users.

Freedom of space is the cornerstone of space law and the space legal regime, and includes the right to free overflight in and through outer space and the right to conduct such non-hostile activities as reconnaissance and surveillance from space. The principal international agreement applicable to outer space is the Outer Space Treaty of 1967.[15] The preamble affirms that mankind has an interest in maintaining the exploration of space for peaceful purposes. Article I of the Treaty assures all parties freedom of access to and exploration of, all regions of outer space, the moon, and other celestial bodies; and freedom to use outer space, the moon, and other celestial bodies on the basis of equality. Article II of the Treaty prohibits the appropriation of outer space, the moon, or other celestial bodies by claim of sovereignty, by means of use or occupation, or by any other means.[16] Finally, article III requires that all activities in outer space and on the moon and other celestial bodies be conducted in accordance with international law, including the U.N. Charter.

The law of armed conflict applies in outer space, including the principles of the inherent right of self-defense in article 51 of the UN Charter, and the prohibition on armed aggression contained in article 2(4). While under both customary and treaty law a right of passage concept for orbiting satellites and manned spacecraft in outer space has developed, there is no corresponding right of innocent passage for spacecraft through foreign national airspace en route to or from outer space. There have been occasions when space objects crossed foreign airspace. For example, in 1978, pieces of the disintegrating, deorbiting Soviet satellite Cosmos 954 fell throughout uninhabited parts of Canada. Ottawa characterized the cause of the resulting damage in part as an "intrusion" into Canadian airspace.[17]

Article IX of the Treaty adopts the same "due regard" provision that is a feature of the law of international airspace. States also are required to avoid activities that would be harmful to the environment of the earth or to celestial bodies, and to initiate international consultations before proceeding with a space activity that could cause potentially harmful interference with the space activities of other parties.

Nuclear or other weapons of mass destruction may not be stationed in outer space and nuclear explosions in outer space are prohibited. Article IV of the Treaty reserves the moon and other celestial bodies exclusively for peaceful purposes, but the term is not well defined. A small number of nations suggest the provision effectively "demilitarizes" outer space and celestial bodies, and therefore, a military presence on them is limited to scientific research and similar peaceful purposes. A majority of states, however, do not accept the view that "peaceful purposes" means "non-military," and instead have adopted the position that "peaceful purposes" means "non-aggressive."[18] Consequently, the term "peaceful purposes" does not preclude military activity in outer space, and space-based systems are lawfully deployed to conduct command, control, communications and geo-spatial intelligence. The requirement to reserve outer space for "peaceful purposes" also does not prohibit using space as for purposes of self-defense, although whether weapons lawfully may be positioned in outer space is still an open question.

Cyberspace Law

There is no universal definition of "cyberspace," and even within individual countries, competing definitions flourish. Cyberspace typically includes the global domain of electro-magnetics used to connect information technology infrastructures and telecommunications systems, and often is used as a synonym for the internet. Science fiction author William Gibson coined the term "cyberspace" in his landmark 1984 book, *Neuromancer*.[19] The novel introduced the world of literature to the "cyberpunk" genre, and the concept of "cyberspace" has since become ubiquitous.

The key problem with governance of the internet is that despite virtual global connectivity for the purposes of information sharing, sensors, communications, directing actions, and controlling public and private sector functions, for the most part cyberspace activity is regulated through the laws of individual states. Consequently, while information travels seamlessly in metaphorical "space" between two locations or among numerous nations, the applicable law is derived from domestic legal systems. National laws vary greatly, and criminals and even some states have been able to capitalize on the exploitation of regulatory and governance seams to disrupt or deny the legitimate use of cyberspace. For example, the Canadian cyber research firm SecDev traced a vast "Ghostnet" of coordinated computer intrusions in over 100 nations, all of them orchestrated from China.[20]

One of the principal international legal authorities that provide a measure of global governance over some aspects of cyberspace is the International Telecommunication Union (ITU), which is part of the UN system. The 191-nation ITU is responsible for administering the assignment and allocation of the radio frequency spectrum and satellite orbits, and provides guidance on its use. Article 44 of the ITU states that the radio frequency spectrum and geostationary orbit are limited natural resources that must be used in accordance with the Radio Regulations issued pursuant to the ITU Constitution.[21] The Radio Regulations detail the allocation of frequencies among various services (e.g., broadcasting, land-mobile satellite, radio navigation, and space operation), and the assignment of frequencies to states. New radio stations, for example, may be established and operated, but may not cause harmful interference with the radio services or communications of other users of the spectrum. Member states retain the freedom to operate military radio installations, but even these must, so far as possible, avoid harmful interference.

The Regulations also establish procedures for states to register frequencies and positions on the geostationary orbit. Registration entitles a country to the indefinite use of the frequency and orbital slot, but this status does not equate to ownership of the orbit, which is considered a natural resource of outer space. Although the Radio Regulations have the force and effect of a treaty and are binding on states' parties, neither the ITU Constitution nor the Radio Regulations delineate sanctions for violations.

Military forces should observe, as far as possible, the prohibitions on causing harmful interference with another's use of the radio frequency spectrum. These provisions do not apply among belligerents in time of armed conflict, however, but they still would apply between belligerents and neutral countries that are not party to the conflict. Attacks in cyberspace may be conducted using either kinetic attack that relies on direct physical impact to achieve an effect, or non-kinetic attack, conducted solely in the electromagnetic spectrum. Either way, cyberspace activities are subject to the prohibition against the use of armed aggression contained in Article 2(4) of the UN Charter, and may be repulsed through the inherent right of self-defense reflected in Article 51. Rather than focusing on the means used to conduct an attack, the determination of an appropriate response should focus on the effect of the attack. If the consequence of cyber attack creates an effect like that which could have been achieved by a kinetic attack, then a state has suffered as a victim of armed aggression and may exercise the inherent right of self-defense.[22] The principles of the traditional law of armed conflict apply in such cases, including military necessity, distinction, and proportionality, and the obligation to minimize collateral damage. It is less certain, however, exactly where the threshold for the "use of force" is situated, and activities that disrupt or deny the use of cyberspace to other users, like distributed denial of services attacks, may have a more ambiguous legal status.

Developing New Regimes

The origins of the law of the global commons began on the seas. The ancient trading civilizations throughout the Eastern Mediterranean understood that the seas were open to all. Later, Christian legal-theologians imported this understanding into the law of nature, where it evolved into an accepted norm. All the while, some coastal states also have laid exclusive claim to parts of the oceans to secure military or economic advantage. For the most part, however, the liberal world order of the oceans has held sway, and it has been adopted as the prevailing legal model for the other domains that constitute the global commons: airspace, outer space, and cyberspace.

The growth in oceans law has continued apace, and the breakthrough 1982 Law of the Sea Convention is the umbrella under which international oceans policy is developed and implemented. One of the principal agreements is the 1974 International Convention for the Safety of Life at Sea (SOLAS), which is the cornerstone for cooperation regarding merchant fleet security. The treaty applies to 98 percent of world shipping, and it reflects comprehensive safety standards for the construction, design, equipping, and manning of vessels. Ship subdivision and design safety, fire protection, lifesaving appliances and arrangements, radio communications, safety of navigation, carriage of cargoes and dangerous goods, and safe management practices are all part of the package. In 2002, in the wake of the attacks against the United States on 11 September 2001, the International Maritime Organization convened a diplomatic conference to adopt amendments to Chapter XI of SOLAS, called the International Ship and Port Facility Security Code. This Code launched a worldwide public-private partnership for maritime security, designed to enable national governments to develop better oversight of their commercial shipping and port industries.

Over the past two decades, international maritime law has evolved from a set of rules designed to avoid naval warfare by keeping maritime powers apart, toward a new global framework designed to facilitate maritime security cooperation by bringing naval forces together to collaborate toward achieving common goals. The emerging global maritime security regime is inclusive, multilateral, and consensual. Ensuring maritime security requires a concerted effort among littoral and coastal states, landlocked and port states, and especially flag states, working in conjunction with international organizations and the maritime industry. Nearly every maritime security scenario involves multiple states and stakeholders, all with an interest in collaborative decision making. A vessel hijacked by pirates or engaged in smuggling most likely is registered in one nation (such as Greece), owned by a corporation located in another nation (perhaps South Korea), and operated by a crew comprising nationals of several additional countries (such as the Philippines and Pakistan). Furthermore, the vessel may well be transporting either containerized cargo or bulk commodities owned by companies in one or more additional states (like Singapore). Finally, port officials, or naval forces from several nations, may be involved in searching or seizing a vessel, and each operates within distinct national rules of law enforcement and the use of force. Any nation may assert jurisdiction over captured pirates; Kenya, for example has entered into agreements with the United Kingdom, United States, and European Union to criminally prosecute many of the pirates seized by warships off the coast of Somalia.[23]

An adjunct of the international Law of the Sea, airspace law shares the same intellectual space as oceans law. Just as no nation owns the oceans, no nation owns the airspace. With the advent of space flight, the existing liberal regime was refashioned to shape the law of outer space. In each of these geophysical domains, a liberal order was successfully adopted to facilitate commerce, mutual security, and international cooperation. Consequently, international law constitutes the "language and logic" for facilitating cooperation among stakeholders.[24] In just over a decade, the regime of cyberspace has followed the same path, generating a social-economic boom and ushering in the Internet Age. Throughout the global commons, however, the liberal order is continually being challenged by states, rogue non-state organizations and individuals, which cast some doubt on whether freedom in the global commons will remain secure.

PART II
CHALLENGES TO FREEDOM

5   Maritime Security

Jeff Kline

The Oldest Common

The oceans are the world's oldest international common. As discussed by James Kraska in Chapter 4, international recognition of a "freedom of the seas'" doctrine is traced to Hugo Grotius' 1609 publication of *Mare Libernum*. Grotius' thesis, primarily a dissertation on the Dutch East India Company's right to participate in the East Indian trade, reflected earlier Roman and Asian free maritime trade practices and became the cornerstone for the body of international law that recognizes international waters as a common.[1] Today, this tradition is formalized in international agreements such as the United Nations Convention on the Law of the Sea (UNCLOS) and the International Convention on the Safety of Life at Sea (SOLAS).

The common good derived from freedom of the seas doctrine is difficult to overstate. International waters that comprise the maritime commons are the backbone of global trade. Over 90 percent of all raw commodities and merchandise is conveyed by ship. In 1970, 2.6 billion tons of goods crossed the seas; by 2006 this had grown to 7.4 billion tons.[2] The oceans are also a growing source of food, energy, and mineral resources. Between 2000 and 2006, worldwide fisheries' capture is reported to have been between 90 and 95 million tons each year. Ocean fish is the protein most widely consumed by humans.[3] Undersea resources are increasingly being tapped as new technology allows for deeper undersea mining and drilling. Undersea cables provide the infrastructure for transcontinental information exchange. Thus the oceans are the critical link in the world's shipping and logistics networks; connecting the nodes of manufacturing centers, oil platforms, and fishing grounds to consumers through port cities, rivers, inland waters, and territorial seas.

The maritime commons' adjacency to the sovereign legal regimes of territorial waters is both an inherent characteristic of the trade network and a challenge to its safety. Pirates, terrorists, smugglers, poachers, and polluters can operate from havens of ungoverned spaces, while the international community is hindered from collecting information and taking defensive action to stop them. At a time when international agreements are being developed to allow for legal action against these threats, the newer commons of air, cyberspace, and outer space are already enhancing maritime information collection, fusion, dissemination, and response networks to defeat them. The air domain provides a venue for surveillance and deterrence over large water spaces; satellites collect information on ocean traffic and relay maritime information worldwide; and cyberspace provides the medium for collecting, fusing, and disseminating information to a broad range of maritime users. Effective maritime domain awareness is dependent on this complex network of overlapping commons, and therefore also dependent on their security.

This chapter will explore the various threats to security in the maritime commons, the international community's requirements to effectively counter these threats, and a template for meeting these requirements. The health of mankind's future relies on our ability to maintain free access to and secure use of the maritime commons.

Threats to Freedom of the Seas

Threats to maritime security fall under three broad categories: natural weather phenomena such as hurricanes, tsunami, giant waves, and storms; active sea denial executed by states during times of conflict; and the activities of non-state actors like terrorists, pirates, smugglers, poachers, polluters, and illegal immigrants.[4] State actors' sea control and sea denial activities are addressed by Thomas Bowditch in Chapter 10. We focus here on the natural and non-state actor threats.

Naturally occurring events that threaten use of the maritime commons, and responses to them, deserve some discussion as they may provide insight into a system to counter human-made threats. Given the importance of timely arrivals to meet "just in time" manufacturing models and the increasing size of tanker and container ships and hence their cargos, weather can significantly impact global business and trade as well as the safety of merchant crews. To mitigate these dangers, the international community has improved global and local awareness of current and impending weather conditions through the use of space surveillance and better prediction models. Maritime safety has been dramatically enhanced with reports from local sensors and human observation, worldwide communications and warnings, improved international ship safety standards, and ship routing recommendations. Of all ships operating under the International Maritime Organization convention—a set of standards for safe navigation and reporting—less than 0.2 percent have been lost annually between 2001 and 2007.[5] International recognition of the importance of providing mariners with weather reports, warnings, and suggested routings on a global scale provides an inspirational template for countering human-made threats to the maritime domain.

There are two broad categories of non-state actors that disrupt the use and health of the maritime commons. There are those that threaten the safe and free passage of vessels on international waters, such as terrorists and pirates, and those that use the maritime commons for illicit ends. The latter category includes smugglers of drugs, weapons, and humans; illegal seaborne migration; polluters; and poachers of natural resources. This chapter addresses each in turn.

As described by Scott Jasper in Chapter 1, piracy is an act of violence, or the threat of violence, against a ship in international waters with the intent to commit crimes such as theft, hijacking, murder, and kidnapping. Piracy is distinguished from sea robbery by location: piracy occurs in international waters beyond any state's geographic sovereignty, while sea robbery occurs within the territorial waters of a sovereign state. This is an important distinction because, in addition to manpower and boats, pirates need ungoverned territorial seas to gain access to international waters, and ungoverned land to establish a safe haven ashore.[6] The international community is constrained in targeting those portions of a pirate network that fall within sovereign territory, whether it is effectively governed or not.

The threat to commercial shipping from pirates is undisputed, particularly in such densely traveled maritime passageways as the Gulf of Aden, the Gulf of Guinea, and the Malacca Straits. The International Chamber of Commerce's International Maritime Bureau Piracy Reporting Center logged a total of 293 incidents of piracy in 2008, up 11 percent from 2007. In 2008, 889 merchant crewmembers were taken hostage, more than any year since data collection began in 1995.[7] Yet the actual impact of piracy on global trade is debated. A recent RAND report on maritime security cites figures that indicate the cost of piracy to the international shipping community may be at most 2 percent of maritime commerce's eight trillion dollars in annual value.[8] Some argue that simply paying ransom—only $30 million for all of 2008 to the Somali pirates who were making international headlines—is more cost effective than preventive measures.[9] The financial cost to individual shippers, however, (for example, the insurance rate for a container transiting through the Gulf

PHOTO 5.1 Piracy in the Gulf of Aden 02/12/2009—Visit, board, search, and seizure teams aboard rigid-hull inflatable boats from the guided-missile cruiser USS *Vella Gulf* (CG 72) close in to apprehend suspected pirates 12 February 2009, in the Gulf of Aden. Nine suspected pirates were apprehended and brought aboard *Vella Gulf,* the second group of suspects apprehended in a 24-hour period. *Vella Gulf* is the flagship for Combined Task Force 151, a multi-national task force conducting counterpiracy operations in and around the Gulf of Aden, Persian Gulf, Indian Ocean, and Red Sea.

SOURCE: U.S. Navy photo by Mass Communication Specialist 2nd Class Jason R. Zalasky; http://www.defenselink.mil/multimedia/. Reprinted with permission.

of Aden went from \$900 in 2007 to \$9,000 in late 2008) and the real human cost inflicted on the crews who are piracy's victims must be taken into account when considering whether preventive actions are worthwhile.[10]

In addition, unchecked piracy has a cancerous effect by encouraging corruption in government, and among shipping officials who accept pirates' bribes for access to information or other clandestine support.[11] Piracy could also become a larger threat to world energy supplies, as evident in the 2008 hijacking of the oil supertanker *Sirius Star* and frequent oil thefts in the Gulf of Guinea. Finally, fueled by ransom money, the impact of unrestrained piracy on worldwide commerce may grow as pirates make more sophisticated use of Global Positioning System (GPS) technology, satellite phones, and Automatic Information System (AIS) intercepts. The unsuccessful hijacking of the U.S. flagged MAERSK ALABAMA about 350 miles off the Somalia coast in 2009 demonstrates piracy's extending reach offshore.[12] And as has long been the case with narcotics cartels operating in the Gulf of Mexico and along the Pacific Coast of Central America, dirty money can be used to compromise government and commercial officials and thus improve maritime domain awareness for nefarious organizations.[13] Finally, and perhaps most important, piracy is a threat to freedom of access to what is recognized as a global common. As Martin Murphy puts it, "Freedom of navigation is a fundamental interest to all countries for trade and defense. It is a freedom that needs to be defended vigorously."[14]

Terrorists differ from pirates primarily by motivation; their political agendas harbor an even greater potential than piracy for disrupting stability in the maritime common. Although most maritime terrorist attacks take place in the ports or waterways under sovereign state jurisdiction, they still disrupt access to international waterways and affect the transport of goods, services, and people in the larger maritime trade network. Terrorists target ships using small boats as rams or by actual boarding, like the 1985 attack on the cruise ship *Achille Lauro*, the 2000 attack on the USS *Cole*, and a 2002 attack on the oil tanker MV *Limburg*. They may also raid ports, as they did in a suicide attack on Israeli's Port of Ashdod that was delivered by shipping container. There is evidence that the sophistication of these operations may increase to include underwater attacks: in June 2003, a Philippine-based terrorist group kidnapped a resort maintenance man, who, on his release, claimed he was targeted for his SCUBA skills. This parallels a statement made by al Qaeda operative Omar al-Faruq in June 2002, who confessed to a plan to attack U.S. warships using SCUBA gear.[15]

Terrorists also use the maritime commons as a logistics transportation venue to move their own weapons, supplies, operatives and hostages, masking these operations within complex systems of trade, fishing, and pleasure boating. Custom-built containers outfitted to house terrorists are known to move on al Qaeda-operated freighters.[16] This level of impunity makes the clandestine movement of nuclear, biological, or chemical agents across the maritime common a viable threat. The terrorists who executed the 2008 attacks on Mumbai infiltrated India via the sea, highlighting concerns about small-vessel security for all coastal states.[17]

Since ancient times, the intent to evade customs and excise taxes and other regulatory provisions has driven smuggling enterprises in every maritime environment. As addressed in Chapter 1, trafficking in narcotics, weapons, and humans is profitable enough now to employ semi-submersible craft, high-speed boats, aircraft, and disguised shipping containers to move contraband across the oceans and political boundaries. Global criminal networks leverage access to the maritime common to conduct their business, and benefit from its complexity to avoid sovereign nations' efforts to collect customs and inspect those transiting borders and ports. Countries with long coasts are particularly vulnerable to illegal seaborne migration. People using the seas to gain access to southern Europe from West and North Africa, or to the United States from the Caribbean, place high demands on state assets to both discourage the practice and provide safety for those illegal immigrants who have embarked on unseaworthy craft.

The maritime common also provides a major source of protein for much of the world's population. Poaching and polluting have serious impacts on the health of fish populations, and thus the sustainability of this resource. For example, the United Nations reports that as much as 70 percent of world fish stocks are fully fished out, over-fished, or depleted; the illegal, unreported, and unregulated fishing of the most vulnerable species is helping drive them to collapse. One quarter of the coral habitats that support many fish species have been destroyed by human influence, particularly pollution, and a large portion of the remainder is declining.[18] The cost in lost catch to legitimate fishers and uncollected revenue to governments from illegal activities is estimated to be about $15 billion a year.[19] As the world population grows and turns even more toward the seas for food and other resources, poaching and polluting also pose a serious threat to access and use of the maritime common.

The vast space involved, number of craft on the seas, differing legal regimes, mistrust between states, and limited resources all challenge the international community's and individual states' efforts to counter these threats. Nevertheless, just as there has been a successful global response to mitigate the effects of natural weather events on use of the maritime commons, so too can the world make a coordinated effort to limit the non-state actors who threaten security in the maritime common.

Response to Maritime Threats

There are three requirements for an effective response to maritime threats: knowledge, platforms, and law. A program to provide maritime security must have an information system that can collect, analyze, and disseminate intelligence in a timely enough manner to deter or respond to attacks; adequate ships, aircraft (fixed wing and helicopter), and personnel to use the intelligence to deter or respond to attacks; and a strong legal regime and infrastructure to apprehend, hold, prosecute, and punish offenders.[20] This section will address each of these key components for maritime security.

The National Plan to Achieve Maritime Domain Awareness, one of eight plans that support the U.S. National Strategy for Maritime Security, defines maritime domain awareness as "the effective understanding of anything associated with the maritime domain that could impact the security, safety, economy, or environment of the United States."[21] This definition is equally applicable to the global community. The complexity of collecting, compiling, analyzing, and disseminating information to meet this task on a global scale is daunting, but not impossible. Weather forecasting and warning systems already use the outer space, cyberspace, and air commons to collect information and disseminate it to a global audience. And, as maritime information becomes increasingly ubiquitous, the resulting transparency may in itself deter nefarious actors. There are both catalysts for and challenges to achieving this deterrent effect in maritime domain awareness systems. A global maritime information system must collect, fuse, interpret, display, and then share information to be effective, each component having its own abilities to benefit from the newer commons of outer space, cyberspace, and air.

Our present ability to collect information is unparalleled in history. Various nations field different levels of technological capabilities from satellites, air forces, and surface and land radars, to underwater sensor networks. The European Union-funded Sea-Horse satellite system is an example that combines outer space and cyberspace to collect information to counter seaborne illegal migration. Capable of tracking movements between Africa and the shores of Spain and Portugal, the system combines overhead imagery with a high-speed communications and data network that links the police forces of these countries so they can find, track, and if necessary, intercept both human and drug smuggling.[22] On the other end of the technology spectrum, citizen participation in helping collect information for authorities is on the rise. The U.S. Coast Guard's 13th District has formalized local monitoring of the U.S. northwest shoreline, bays, and waterways through the Citizen Action Network, a program that enrolls volunteers living on the shore to report suspicious activity or call for emergency rescue.[23]

State and international regulatory measures such as the U.N.'s SOLAS requirement for all commercial vessels over 300 tons to carry AIS, a 96-hour-prior arrival notice required by many states, and mandatory reporting for shipping container manifests, also aid information collection. The commercial community of shippers, port operators, wholesale customers, and suppliers maintain shipping manifests, port schedules, and shipping schedules that are another potential source of information.

The volume of information that awaits gathering, however, introduces severe challenges. The sheer number of seagoing vessels, the oceans' vastness, and the data gaps left by ungoverned maritime areas where states have the authority, but not the ability, to monitor coastal traffic, are examples of the information-collection issues that must be addressed. SOLAS only requires vessels greater than 300 tons to be equipped with AIS. This leaves the majority of vessels with no automatic identification requirement. Monitoring, identifying, and potentially tracking smaller vessels are complicated further by the vast water area they transit and complex weather patterns that degrade the effectiveness of sensors. The resources to collect AIS information are not available to many coastal countries, nor are the requisite numbers of aircraft and ships to patrol their waters effectively. Even with a functioning national government, there are many unwatched spaces in territorial waters and exclusive economic zones adjacent to the high seas.

The problems do not end with monitoring. Once the means to get the information are in place, some organizing entity or intelligence center must collect the data, store it, analyze and make some sense out of data from different sources, then display and/or disseminate the fused information for potential action. These operation centers may be local, national, or regional in nature.

One model is the International Maritime Bureau (IMB) Piracy Reporting Center in Kuala Lumpur, a 24-hour information center that receives reports on piracy and suspicious craft movements, collates and analyzes the information, then broadcasts status reports via the INMARSAT-C satellite communication system. This center is funded through contributions from the shipping industry via the IMB, and data displays on pirate attacks are available on the International Chamber of Commerce website.[24] At the U.S. national and state level, Project Sea Hawk, an interagency and inter-governmental collaborative operations center, coordinates over fifty federal, state, and local law enforcement agencies involved in providing security for the Port of Charleston, South Carolina, and its surroundings.[25] This center relies on the U.S. government to provide the means for continued operations. At the regional level, the North Atlantic Treaty Organization (NATO) Maritime Component Commands at Northwood, England, and Naples, Italy, each have a Surveillance Coordination Center that builds a comprehensive picture of everything associated with the global maritime environment that could influence the safety, security, or economy of alliance member nations and partners.[26] Likewise, the Information Sharing Center in Singapore, formed by the sixteen-nation Regional Agreement on Combating Piracy and Armed Robbery (ReCAAP) in 2004, is a maritime fusion and sharing center to combat piracy and armed robbery.[27]

To be effective, any new information center will have to be able to receive, store, and process data from diverse sources and from various kinds of databases. These data sources, furthermore, may be protected by different security classification and access levels that address commercial, legal, and national sensitivities. Automatic data fusion and anomaly detection technology currently in development will make it easier to analyze and display useful information, and generate alerts as needed. While information sharing and dissemination technologies can use cyberspace for the fast, reliable, and accurate exchange of information, national, legal, and bureaucratic barriers remain a complicating factor.

The final element necessary for effective maritime domain awareness is the dissemination of information to another operations center, a community of interest, or to a specific response platform. The U.S. Naval Studies Board of the National Research Council highlights the importance of information sharing for maritime security, because it establishes trust between countries, agencies, and commercial entities that share a common interest in protecting the maritime common.[28] The foundations for mutual trust can be built through the development of symposia for communities of interest, bilateral agreements, regional partnerships, and international standards. For example, the 2008 Global Maritime Information Sharing Symposium, organized by the national Office of Global Maritime Situational Awareness and sponsored by the U.S. Department of Homeland Security and U.S. Department of Defense, brought together various law enforcement, defense, and commercial organizations. The Global Maritime Domain Awareness Conference, hosted by the Director General of the Chilean Maritime Territory and Merchant Marine, attracted worldwide attendance that same year.

Cyber technology is helping to enhance mutually advantageous information sharing. As mentioned earlier, the IMB provides updated information from the Piracy Reporting Center via the International Chamber of Commerce website. In addition to free-access websites, dedicated systems share controlled information among partners at various levels of access. Examples include Combined Enterprise Regional Information Exchange Systems, a classified information network shared by seventy-seven nations; the Regional Maritime Awareness Capability, an internet-based AIS and radar sensor exchange system offered by the U.S. European Command; the Maritime Safety and Security Information System, shared by nearly sixty countries worldwide to exchange AIS information via the internet; and the Long-Range Identification and Tracking system, sponsored by state members of the International Maritime Organization, which allows members to exchange shipping information over long ranges.[29]

Despite the growth of these information-sharing measures, however, there remain obstacles to the universal exchange of maritime security information. Not all coastal countries have sufficient resources to establish inter-agency fusion centers or the associated technology to receive and/or communicate information. While international aid may be able to fill resource needs, participants must also overcome the lack of trust and bureaucratic barriers that constrain them from sharing information. For example, security and legal obstacles within a country's borders may prevent the free exchange of information between the defense and law enforcement agencies. In addition, there are issues of mistrust between countries or groups of countries concerning the levels of information to be provided. To illustrate, if Nigeria shares all its sensor data with the United States, how can it be assured the United States will share an equivalent amount of information, particularly in light of the relative difference between each nation's potential to collect information? Both parties will need to agree on initial steps of good faith to begin a program of information sharing.

In addition to sensors that collect information in support of maritime domain awareness, the second element of effective maritime security is seaborne
and airborne platforms that provide visible deterrence and are capable of responding at need. Patrols do act as a deterrent: pirate attacks in Indonesian
waters decreased from one hundred twenty-one in 2003 to only twenty-eight
low-level incidents in 2008, a mere two of which occurred in the Malacca Straits.
This dramatic decrease is attributable in part to increased littoral patrols.[30] In
March 2009, the head of U.S. Central Command's Naval Forces, Vice Admiral
William Gortney, credited an increased naval presence off Somalia with halv-
ing the rate of pirate attacks in the Gulf of Aden and off the eastern Somalia
coast.[31] This "cop on the beat" effect can be reinforced by sharing maritime
surveillance information with the international community, broadcasting the
message that the world is watching and able to act.

The allocation of sufficient resources for effective patrols usually requires
cooperation between the law enforcement agencies and national defense forces
where these two functions are separate. The U.S. Maritime Operational Threat
Response plan, another of the Maritime Security Supporting Plans, provides
a process for coordinated responses by various U.S. agencies to a maritime
threat, and may provide a template for internal agency coordination in other
nations. In the waters adjacent to high-traffic international straits and archipelagos, cooperation between bordering coastal states will boost information
collection and facilitate coordinated patrolling, as demonstrated by the increased cooperation between Malaysia, Indonesia, and Singapore to improve
safety and security in the Malacca Straits.[32]

Different platforms perform complementary roles to meet maritime security needs. Long-range maritime patrol aircraft, for instance, fly at higher
altitudes for surveillance and lower altitudes for identification and deterrence.
Helicopters search in high-clutter environments to identify contacts, prevent
attacks, and provide quick response. And ships of various sizes deter, intercept, board, detain, and transport prisoners. When added to the cost of sensors,
AIS land-based receivers, command centers, and information-sharing systems,
however, these platforms represent a major capital investment for a coastal
state. The lack of resources to obtain adequate forces, combined with national
sovereignty that does not willingly cede responsibility for security within territorial waters, creates ungoverned maritime spaces that foster threats.

Even when sufficient maritime domain awareness and response forces are
present, domain security demands a legal regime that allows data collection,

supports response, and provides a venue to prosecute infractions. The U.N. Convention on the Law of the Sea sets a legal framework applicable to fighting piracy. In the case of Somali pirates, the U.N. recognized the transitional Somali government's inability to enforce law in its own territory. At Mogadishu's request, on 16 December 2008 the Security Council adopted Resolution 1851, authorizing the international community to fight piracy ashore if necessary.[33] Yet, obstacles to bringing pirates to justice still exist. No international court is set up to handle piracy suspects, which means individual countries must agree to accept pirates caught in international waters into their court and prison systems for prosecution and punishment, and bear all the attendant costs. In 2008, Kenya agreed to accept Gulf of Aden pirates from the United States,[34] but difficulties with collecting evidence to meet rigorous legal requirements led the U.S. Navy to release nine suspected Somali pirates in March 2009 by turning them over to the Somali Coast Guard, due to the lack of enough evidence to try them in Kenya.[35] Similar legal issues exist for the other security threats to the maritime commons.

To summarize, maritime domain awareness, platforms to deter and respond, and a legal regime that supports interception, arrests, and prosecutions are the key elements of maritime security. Technology aids in the establishment of effective information and response systems, but restrictive legal domains, competing interests that breed mistrust, nationalism, lack of resources, and the physical and economic complexity of the maritime domain remain challenges to be overcome if the global community is to achieve effective security. World leaders must continue to address these obstacles to assure freedom in the maritime common.

The Way Ahead

"We must evolve and establish international relationships to increase security and achieve common interests in the maritime domain."
Admiral G. Roughead, U.S. Navy, Chief of Naval Operations[36]

A strategy for more effective maritime security seems to be emerging, and should be endorsed by the international community, world leaders, and commercial interests. This three-fold strategy promotes the universal value of maritime safety and security, fosters trust between potential international and commercial partners, and develops resources at the regional level, and establishes legal standards at the international level.

UNCLOS, SOLAS, and various national policy statements all underscore the importance of the maritime domain for the common global good. The U.S. National Strategy for Maritime Security states:

> Because the economic well-being of people in the United States and across the globe depends heavily upon the trade and commerce that traverses the oceans, maritime security must be a top priority. Maritime security is required to ensure freedom of the seas; facilitate freedom of navigation and commerce; advance prosperity and freedom; and protect the resources of the ocean. Nations have a common interest in achieving two complementary objectives: to facilitate the vibrant maritime commerce that underpins economic security, and to protect against ocean-related terrorist, hostile, criminal, and dangerous acts. Since all nations benefit from this collective security, all nations must share in the responsibility for maintaining maritime security by countering the threats in this domain.[37]

It is not enough, however, for world leaders like the United States to act to secure the maritime domain; the United Nations must reinforce the message to coastal states that they need to make resource decisions that will give them the capability to contribute to maritime security. The United States recognizes the necessity for collaboration in its International Outreach and Coordination Strategy, a part of the National Strategy for Maritime Security, by setting as a goal, "Enhanced outreach to foreign governments, international and regional governments, private sector partners, and the public abroad to solicit support for improved global maritime security."[38] Global maritime security, however, may best be achieved by first achieving regional security.

Focusing efforts at the regional level to inspire local cooperation in information collecting and sharing may be more effective than attempting to achieve global cooperation. Regional conferences—best led by a regional nation—can highlight the common interest in maritime security and identify common threats, and can build a base of trust from which to move forward to information sharing and response cooperation. In addition to inspiring these conferences, world leaders need to recognize positive emerging patterns and trends for potential transplant to other areas.[39] A specific example is the proposal for the International Maritime Organization to create new 24-hour pirate information centers in Yemen, Kenya, and/or Tanzania, patterned after the successful Pirate Reporting Center in Malaysia.[40] The international political and commercial communities can provide a structure by which to develop standards for

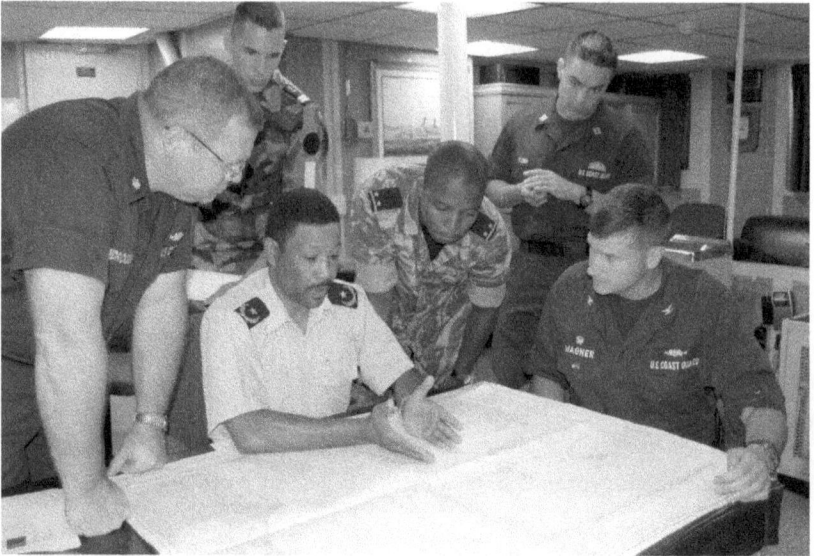

PHOTO 5.2 Local Cooperation for African Maritime Security 06/07/2008—U.S. Coast Guard Capt. Robert Wagner, right, commanding officer of the high endurance cutter USCGC *Dallas* (WHEC 716), and law-enforcement officers from several African nations discuss tactics during an operational brief aboard *Dallas*, near Mindelo, Cape Verde, 7 June 2008. *Dallas* is deployed under the direction of Commander, U.S. Naval Forces Europe, 6th Fleet, supporting Africa Partnership Station, an initiative aimed at strengthening global-maritime partnerships through training and other collaborative activities in order to improve global maritime safety and security.

SOURCE: U.S. Coast Guard photo by Public Affairs Specialist 1st Class Tasha Tully; http://www.defenselink.mil/multimedia/. Reprinted with permission

safety, legal regimes, and information sharing, but effective action will work best if it emerges from regional agreements and practices. The success of a regional approach is evidenced by ReCAAP's International Sharing Center (ISC) 2009 Half Year Report (January–June 2009). The Singapore ISC report claims a decrease in reported piracy and sea robbery-attempted incidents the first half of 2009 as compared to similar periods from 2005–2008.[41]

Another example of a regional approach to global security is the concept of building maritime partnerships embedded in the joint U.S. Coast Guard, U.S. Navy, and U.S. Marine Corps document, "A Cooperative Strategy for 21st Century Seapower," which pledges to: "Foster and sustain cooperative relationships with more international partners."[42] Operation Active Endeavour, in which NATO ships patrol throughout the Mediterranean, monitor shipping, and help to detect, deter, defend, and protect against terrorist activity, epitomizes that mandate. Through the sharing of data gathered at sea, Active Endeavour has increasingly become an information and intelligence-based operation that deploys surface forces as direct-reaction units to track and board selected vessels. In addition to the benefits of maritime security, the operation has become a useful tool to increase practical cooperation and interoperability among NATO allies and partner countries.[43]

Where resources in sensors, communications, and seaborne platforms are lacking, wealthier nations might offer local aid and guidance, which could in turn act as a catalyst for countries to participate. With communication systems in particular, it is important to give recipient countries resources that are compatible with existing international standards where possible, to enhance cooperation. Providing Nigeria with the resources to establish the Maritime Safety and Security Information System and its own AIS stations to bolster Gulf of Guinea security is one example.[44] Another example of building partnerships for improving maritime security is the deployment of the Africa Partnership Station in the Gulf of Guinea, supported by the USS *Nashville* (LPD 13).[45]

This strategy relies on local efforts to promote maritime security, while international standardization provides guidance. One example of this bottom-up regional development and top-down standardization is the U.S. Maritime Administration's contribution to the Organization of American States' (OAS) port security assistance program, which provides aid to OAS members to comply with the International Maritime Organization port security standards. Another is the International Ship and Port Facility Safety Code, an element of SOLAS that promotes bilateral and multilateral exchanges of law enforcement requirements for international maritime security standards between nations. The U.S. Customs and Border Patrol's outreach to individual countries to participate in the Container Security Initiative is yet another bilateral approach with global benefit.[46]

To gain acceptance from regional partners, international agencies should address those countries' regional concerns as well as global interests. The mandatory registration of fishing vessels and fish processing ships, and a regulation that they adhere to the SOLAS AIS requirements regardless of tonnage, would enhance the ability of coastal countries to enforce fishing regulations in their exclusive economic zone, a major concern for African nations.[47]

International standards for the use of cyberspace communication links are necessary to establish effective maritime awareness systems. Finding a common database structure, or agreeing on a communication architecture that allows information exchange without restricting hardware choices, is more a job for international policy than technology.

Dependent on the other global commons for its security and health, the maritime commons is critical to the world's ability to transport food, goods, energy, and services. Some non-state actors threaten safe access to the maritime commons, and use the oceans for their own illegal ends. To counter these threats, a system that provides for maritime domain awareness, seaborne and airborne platforms to deter and react, and a legal regime to enforce and prosecute is essential. These three elements require national, regional, and international cooperation. The path to better domain security and health begins with the current strategy of promoting trust through bilateral, multilateral, and regional agreements, while setting international safety and security standards to be followed by nations, fishers, shippers, ports, maritime security agencies, and other mariners. Major maritime nations like the United States must continue to inspire, provide resources where necessary, and if invited, participate in bilateral, multilateral, and regional agreements and patrols, to achieve worldwide maritime security.

6 Cyberspace Control

Steven H. McPherson and Glenn Zimmerman

Cyberspace: A New Domain of the Global Commons

The history of humankind is a continuing story of exploration and advancement into new frontiers and emerging domains. The historical record shows that as we strive to master any domain, we maximize our activities' value and gain through a system of transportation, communications, and control networks that reach across all available domains. This requires sufficient wherewithal to harness the fundamental physical properties and develop the unique skills that will enable us to apply technological capabilities specific to each domain. This history of exploration and advancement began with the wheel and a network of roads, and continued with ships and a network of sea-lanes, the airplane and a network of air routes, and electrical wiring and the electronic network. Connectivity is fundamental to civilization, and drives human expansion into new domains regardless of the physical challenges and any perceived limitations. The ability to connect, communicate, and control is inherent to the human experience.

While the twentieth century was the culmination of the mechanical era and produced the giants of the industrial age, the twenty-first century promises to usher in a post-mechanical electronic age as the lever, the pulley, and the incline plane—the fundamental tools of the mechanical processes and methods—give way to the transistor, capacitors, and semi-conductors as the fundamental tools of electromagnetic invention. Cyberspace is the frontier of the twenty-first century—the latest domain of commerce and globalization to emerge as a global common.

The gestation and birth of this electromagnetic expanse has, often seren-
dipitously, followed revelation and new scientific discovery. The cyberspace
domain continues to evolve through advanced applications shaped by engineering and technology; ultimately to achieve the goal of connectivity, communication, and control across what once was a vast untapped frontier. The
reason for this persistent evolution is because what differentiates humans from
other animals is the impulse to be in constant communication with our fellow
beings. There is no other animal for which this desire, or rather this necessity,
for communication is the guiding motive of its whole life.

This observation is a fundamental principle in the science of cybernetics.
Norbert Wiener, a pioneer of cybernetics, recognized that what makes the
human being unique is the innate drive to pursue communication and connectivity regardless of the environment.[1] Key to the evolution of the species,
advances into a new domain are quite rapidly expressed by connectivity and
communication achieved in that domain. This has proven true for the exploration of land and sea, and the same pattern can be detected in the emergent
domains of air, space, and the electromagnetic environment we are now calling
cyberspace.

Cyberspace, from the Greek Κυβερνήτης (kybernētēs: steersman, gov-
ernor, pilot, or rudder), is the global domain of electromagnetics accessed
through electronic technology, and exploited through the modulation of
electromagnetic energy to achieve a wide range of communication and control
system capabilities. Through its electromagnetic nature, cyberspace integrates
a number of entities (sensors, signals, connections, transmissions, processors,
controllers), and generates a virtual interactive experience for the purpose of
communication and control regardless of geographic location. In pragmatic
terms, cyberspace enables interdependent information technology infrastructure networks and telecommunications networks—such as the internet, computer systems, integrated sensors, system control networks, and embedded
processors and controllers—that are common to global communication and
control systems.

Cyberspace is the global "center of gravity" for all aspects of national power,
spanning the economic, financial, technological, diplomatic, and military capabilities a country might possess, and as such, to cite Clausewitz, is therefore
"the hub of all power and movement on which everything depends."[2] As we
have gone from using physical devices and activities, such as writing with pen
and paper or exchanging coins and paper bills, to convey information or con-

duct transactions, to moving digital representations of both information and wealth through cyberspace, the criticality of this domain has increased exponentially. Fifty years ago, the loss of access to cyberspace would have been an inconvenience to a few, at the worst. Today, such an event would literally bring globalized nations to the edge of collapse as communication systems, financial markets, transportation, power generation facilities, medical services, and so on would simply fail as they became isolated or corrupted without access to cyberspace.

This chapter will explore all aspects of the electronic domain of cyberspace within the historical context described by Alfred Thayer Mahan, who saw "the global commons" as a means to advance commerce through a secure, networked infrastructure that connects global enterprise across the commons.[3] Security for the global commons includes the requirements to defend that enterprise and protect it from the perils of what Mahan would call "commerce-destroying warfare." The chapter also will describe the wide range of enemy actors operating within cyberspace and the devious methods, which can at times seem daunting and unstoppable, they use to interfere with global enterprise in a modern application of "commerce-destroying warfare."

Lanes of Communication: From the Sea to Cyberspace

Alfred Thayer Mahan, in his most well-known work, "The Influence of Sea Power Upon History," described the sea as a "great highway" passing in all directions, a domain of trade and international communication with tremendous social and political importance.[4] Mahan observed that certain lanes of travel, sea-ports, and communication routes will inevitably be preferred over others, and become recognized as "trade routes," which over time can have a significant influence on national and international commerce, and the course of history.[5]

Mahan made clear that the driving motivation to operate in the commons is to conduct and expand opportunities for trade, and that an increasing number of participants will be drawn to use the commons by a prevailing ease of timely and secure operations at reasonable cost. The selection and utility of any of the commons for trade over time will come down to the one that offers the ideal cost to transport the ideal product. The land and sea networks, for example, are best suited to ship raw materials, which move in massive quantities and are not pressured by constraints of time, to minimize costs and maximize profits. By contrast, highly perishable goods, which tend to be in relatively limited quantities and have tight time constraints, are better moved across the air networks. This principle also holds true of electronically generated products like software and music, and general commerce in the electro-magnetic networks, where shipment, transport, and delivery of products can correspondingly be maximized to optimize net commercial gain.

To maintain a vibrant global enterprise and ensure the profitable delivery of goods and services in any domain, however, an efficient infrastructure for transportation and communication across the commons must be in place, such as the eighteenth- and nineteenth-century infrastructure of shipping ports, sea-lanes and trade routes, and distant ports of exchange across the globe as described by Mahan. The needs of commerce in those centuries, however, could not be met if safety was not secured. The voyages were long and dangerous, and often beset with enemies. In these centuries, a level of lawlessness prevailed on the seas that is hard for us to grasp, and the periods of settled peace between maritime nations were few and far between. The maritime infrastructure of today remains a critical part of the networked global enterprise, all of which depends on a minimal level of security to assure its effectiveness and vigor.

Mahan called the irregular warfare operations of the pirate, the privateer, or the highwayman, directed against peaceful merchants operating within the commercial infrastructure, "commerce destroying warfare":

> To attack the commerce of the enemy is therefore to cripple him, in the measure of success achieved, in the particular factor which is vital to the maintenance of war, moreover, in the complicated condition of mercantile activity no one branch can be seriously injured without involving others. This may be called the financial and political effect of commerce destroying warfare. It is strictly analogous to the impairing of an enemy's communications, of the lines of supplies connecting an army with its base of operations, upon the maintenance of which the life of the army depends. . . . [Commerce] is the life of war; lessen it, and vigor flags; destroy it, and resistance dies.[6]

The goal of securing the global commons is to give operators enough confidence in the success of the global enterprise to continue the system of commerce, which must go well beyond the value of secure infrastructure and secure operations. The strategic value lies in the unimpaired ability to conduct all of a state's critical functions—not just commerce, but also transportation, communications, command and control, and so on. Failure to achieve this objective will erode the confidence of commercial participants, and risks forfeiting the commercial lanes and thus the gains of trade. The strategic objective at the macro level is to secure the means to advance the gross national product and thus the well-being of the nation.

A nation's system of international commerce and the ability to operate that system without interference are fundamental to that nation's security. In direct correlation, the ability of globally active nations to freely operate in an interconnected system of global commerce is critical to a stable international environment. The security of the global commons underlies the importance of a security posture in which international agreements and alliances will address the security of trade across all commons.

Admiral Arthur K. Cebrowski, who first articulated the tenets of network-centric warfare as a distinct concept in the late 1990s, drew on Mahan's concept of the sea as a wide strategic commons for trade and international communication to think about cyberspace. He not only advocated that space and cyberspace be added to the list of strategic domains that must be controlled to maintain global freedom of movement and freedom of commerce, but maintained that cyberspace is becoming the preeminent domain of political victory or defeat.[7]

Critical to any nation's security is the ability to function freely in commerce, transportation, communication, and command and control. One of the recognized barriers to becoming a global hegemonic power is the ability to operate in and control the strategic commons. Therefore, nations with hegemonic aspirations would be expected to erode an adversary's ability to operate effectively in these commons, and to achieve the ability to control the commons for their own freedom of movement.[8] The United States and its allies are now realizing how critical security and freedom of maneuver are in the electromagnetic domain.

The Growing Threat of Cyber Intrusions

The electromagnetic environment is emerging as a medium on a par with the land, sea, air, and space domains. Throughout the eighteenth century, military forces were organized for the most part around land-based armies. In the nineteenth century, naval forces became predominant. The twentieth century saw the rise of air forces as a major weapon of war, while the twenty-first century will be dominated by electronic innovation.[9] Hence, effective operations in the electromagnetic environment will be the primary commerce and security challenge of this century.

What sets cyberspace apart from the other domains is the departure from the mechanical to the electronic, and the resultant transition away from the capital demands of the industrial complex. Due to the ubiquitous appeal and proliferation of cyber technologies, the mass market and economies of scale result in a prevailing lower cost of entry for the enterprising user. Many sophisticated tools and capabilities are available at little to no cost to the motivated individual or group. A casual Google search yields thousands of websites providing toolsets to hack networks, spoof email addresses, hide one's surfing and file access activities, and so on. Gaining access to the domain is often quite simple and inexpensive. A laptop computer with a wireless networking card, or even a smart cell phone, can provide both access and the means to exploit the domain for a variety of purposes.

The highly asymmetric nature of cyberspace allows the exploiter to create effects from the local to the global level using readily obtainable tools and devices. For intervention in civil, commercial, or military operations, the high cost and complexity of engagement in the air or sea domains makes cyberspace an especially attractive and valuable playing field or battleground for those who seek to interfere with commerce and communications. Based on current trends, the level of negative, commerce-destroying activity, by both civilian (terrorists, criminals, etc.) and military (insurgent, state, etc.) enemy actors in cyberspace, promises to grow just as quickly as will positive and constructive components.

While all of the domains of the global commons provide a medium for civil and commercial as well as military operations, cyberspace is unique in that all military operations depend almost entirely on civilian-run systems and providers. This extremely tightly woven and unparalleled level of integration extends to virtually every aspect of the cyber domain, beginning with communication networks. Telecommunication providers create the foundation for military, civil, and commercial voice and data systems spanning the globe. These networks, operating over copper or fiber optic cables, microwave relays, and satellite links, form the vast, dauntingly complex linkages we take for granted in cyberspace. The multiple cell towers, switches, satellite relays, and undersea cables of these linkages represent the pervasive nature of cyberspace.

As various technologies have converged, the demarcation between voice and data transfer has become increasingly blurred and is for all practical purposes now nonexistent. While simplifying the creation, maintenance, and operation of multimodal networks through which all forms of communication—voice, video, data, and even high-definition movies—can move, cyber technologies simultaneously have opened up a shared vulnerability for all of these forms of information transfer. For example, the shift from closed, proprietary financial data networks to internet banking transactions has facilitated access and enhanced customer service, while also creating new and readily exploitable risks to both the financial institution and the individual user. Almost every user of online banking services has been the unwelcome recipient of a "phishing" email purporting to be from their bank and requesting help in "securing" their online banking access. Annoyance events like this, coupled with the explosive rise of identity theft, are evidence of the fact that technology not only has transformed banking into a universally available service, but also has freighted it with very real risk.

Although the true nature and extent of cyber intrusions and thefts within the financial sector may not be known, primarily due to the traditional "cone of silence" imposed to shield reputations and corporate goodwill, it is inevitable they will only get worse. One need only look briefly at those stores moving from the traditional brick and mortar paradigm to an online presence to see the risks and consequences involved. Well-publicized denial-of-service attacks on eBay and Yahoo are but a few of the better known incursions against online entities.[10] The compromising of online stores such as SalesGate and CD Universe, where thousands of credit card numbers were stolen from database servers, highlight just how serious the challenges are when moving into cyberspace from the traditional storefront.[11]

Nonetheless, this is definitely the wave of the future. The ever-increasing economic value placed on the electronic domain follows a pattern similar to that experienced in the other mediums of the global commons. Just as trade over land, sea, and air drove the need to secure freedom of operations, so the electronic domain is experiencing a similar evolution. In 1999, the United States Department of Commerce first began tracking online retail sales in the business-to-consumer category. From a baseline of less than $5.2 million during that first quarter of tracking, online retail sales grew to over $8.7 *billion* dollars one year later.[12] While this initial growth was explosive, it heralded a more restrained but sustained trend. By 2006, U.S. e-commerce retail sales had reached $107 billion, and over $127 billion dollars in 2007.[13] This transactional level pales in comparison to online transactions between businesses, in which manufacturers experienced online sales growth from $1.5 to over $1.8 *trillion* between 2006 and 2007.[14]

Global transactions by all nations experienced similar growth during these years. The first figures Canada published for its online retail sales, in mid-2000, indicated transactions of approximately C$660 million (roughly $444 million U.S.). By the end of 2000, Canadian online sales had surpassed C$1.149 billion ($774 million U.S.).[15] Japanese online business-to-consumer transactions grew by 28 percent from 2003 to 2004, from 4.375 trillion to 5.6 trillion yen ($37 billion to over $52 billion).[16] European Union member countries saw online transactions grow as well but in a less consistent fashion, as countries with more robust infrastructure logically tended to experience more rapid and sustained growth. Germany, England, and France led the EU with $1.2 billion, $1.04 billion, and $345 million dollars respectively in online sales in 2000.[17] While even in the aggregate these levels of economic impact may seem small when placed against all nations' GDPs, the key point is how rapidly economic value has been transferred to this newest domain of the global commons. Additionally, the concept of value takes on a more expansive construct in cyberspace, which can best be encapsulated in an objective fashion by depicting value via Beckstrom's Law, developed by Rod Beckstrom, former director of the National Cybersecurity Center at the U.S. Department of Homeland Security.

Beckstrom's Law: A Transaction-Based Network Valuation Model[18]

Put in economic terms, the net present value (V) of any network (j) to any individual (i) is equal to the sum of the net present value of the benefit of all transactions less the net present value of the costs of all transactions on the network over any given period of time (t), as shown in the following equation.

$$V_{i,j} = \sum_{k=1}^{n} \frac{B_{i,k}}{(1+r_k)^{t_k}} - \sum_{l=1}^{n} \frac{C_{i,l}}{(1+r_l)^{t_l}}$$

Where

$V_{i,j}$ = net present value of all transactions of $k = 1$ through n to individual i with respect to network j

i = one user of the network

j = identifies one network or network system

$B_{i,k}$ = the benefit value of transaction k to individual i

$C_{i,l}$ = the cost of transaction l to individual i

r_k and r_l = the discount rate of interest to the time of transaction k or l

t_k or t_l = the elapsed time in years to transaction k or l

To simplify subsequent derivations of the equation, the net present value benefit and cost terms will be simplified. Thus the equation is simplified to:

$$V_{i,j} = \sum B_{i,k} - \sum C_{i,l}$$

Valuing an Entire Network

The above equation represents the value of the network to one user. The value of the entire network Nj is the summation of the value of that network to all individuals or entities, i through n, engaged in transactions on that network. Thus a summation term is now added before $V_{i,j}$.

$$\sum_{i=1}^{n} V_{i,j} = \sum B_{i,k} - \sum C_{i,l}$$

The Sum Value of All Networks

Similarly, to value all networks to all users in the world simply requires a summation of all networks j = 1 through n.

$$\sum_{j=1}^{n} \sum_{i=1}^{n} V_{i,j} = \sum B_{i,k} - \sum C_{i,l}$$

It took decades, and even centuries, for the levels of commerce across land, sea, and air to reach the level of pervasiveness and access that cyberspace has brought to the world in a matter of years. Unlike the typical barriers of time, distance, and cost that limited access to and control of a domain to those relative few with the requisite capital and resources, the electronic domain has transcended much of the past to bring commerce to the front door, desktop, or lap of anyone with access to a computer. What is more critical, however, is the underlying value that trade creates for all people everywhere: those who conduct trade establish relationships that can withstand the distractions of conflict and unfamiliarity. Cyberspace has increased these enduring kinds of relationships exponentially across the globe in a remarkably short time.

In addition to tightly integrated commerce systems under threat of destruction by cyber actors, public utilities are also at risk of cyber exploitation.

For years, the operation of the core infrastructure that makes up utility grids required physical access to a control system at a given location to accomplish anything. Take, for example, the Grand Coulee dam in Washington State, which generates a significant percentage of the electrical power for eastern Washington State. Fifteen years ago, the only way to adjust spillway release levels was to be in the control room at Grand Coulee and enter the necessary instructions directly into the control system. Today, the same operation could potentially be accomplished using a small Java applet on a Blackberry. This evolution toward anytime, anywhere access to critical utility systems was initially seen as a timesaver and quantum leap in responsiveness. Unfortunately, few thought about the more insidious opportunities such readily available and off-the-shelf systems could provide.

Sophisticated Enemies on Multiple Fronts

The nature of enemies in cyberspace spans the gamut from low-level vandalism by bored teens or disgruntled employees to serious invasions by terrorists, criminals, and formal state-sponsored entities. Each demands a response tailored to the threat, and therefore a clear understanding of what each threat entails. Insider threats, which can range from accidents and poor practices to intentional malicious acts, make up a sizeable number of cyber events. These can result in minor issues such as erased files or missing printouts thanks to inattention, or major ones such as crippled systems and significant financial impact from an act of vengeance. Hackers are the flipside of this kind of threat, as they operate externally but generally seek the thrill or status they get from compromising systems to which they do not have authorized access. For many years, hackers were more of an irritant than a real threat, but recent events have seen an increase in sophisticated methods bankrolled by criminal and terrorist organizations that have considerably greater objectives than simply gaming the system. "Ransomware," which holds one's data hostage by locking documents until payment for a decryption key is made, is just one example of the evolving role of crime in the hacker community.[19] Likewise, terrorist organizations may seek to create panic and disruption through the destruction of critical data, and by compromising "secure" systems that govern traffic, finance, and energy production and transfer nodes.

The final category of hacker threat takes the form of the state-sponsored "cyber warrior." While virtually all modern nations deploy some form of cyber capability, the Russian Federation and the People's Republic of China are the most aggressive in training for, developing, and executing cyber activities. These activities can take the form of traditional computer network attacks or far more subtle assaults such as the formation of "smart mobs," which serve as *ad hoc* proxies to accomplish the aims of their state sponsor. Russia appeared particularly effective in this respect, using online real-time recruiting for denial-of-service attacks during its brief war with Georgia in 2008. Thousands of websites sprang up with entreaties to patriotic Russians to join as cyber warriors against the networks of the enemy. These websites provided basic tools and instructions that permitted complete novices to join the fight with little more than a few clicks of the mouse.[20]

Attack Vectors

The wide variety of methods for cyber exploitation or attack depends on an array of technologies, but quite often the most successful attacks use some of the most technically simple approaches. While an in-depth analysis of all available cyber attack methods is beyond the scope of this chapter, it is worth taking a look at some of the more common technologies and methods. One of the more popular types of attack uses "malware" (a contraction of the phrase "malicious software") or other penetration-type approach to spread program code designed to corrupt, co-opt, or otherwise interfere with a system it breaches. This breach can take the form of a computer virus, Trojan, or worm, but in the end, the intended result is generally the same: to damage, or at least degrade, the targeted system(s).

Another popular method, typically used by criminals to extort money, involves the online manipulation of individuals, through the crafting of fake emails, websites, and instant messages intended to entice the recipient to provide protected information such as bank account numbers, user IDs, and passwords. This vector is known as a "phishing" attack when used against a large, general audience of users, and a "spear phishing" attack when targeted against a specific, narrow audience. In each of these cases, the websites and messages are designed to mimic legitimate sites and entities, but the unwitting user who responds winds up handing over highly sensitive information to any number of unscrupulous actors.[21]

The distributed denial-of-service attack is a well-known and frequently used means of bringing down or severely degrading a targeted website or websites. In its most basic form, this approach simply overloads a given target with large amounts of traffic, which prevents the system from responding to legitimate user requests. In many ways, it can be likened to having thousands of people call into an office to tie up all the phone lines, or piling large numbers of overfilled trash bags against the doors of a building to prevent anyone from entering or leaving. This type of attack is not particularly elegant or sophisticated, but it is quite often effective, as was seen in denial-of-service attacks against eBay and Amazon.com in 2000.[22] Examples at the state level include the so-called Cyber Riot in Estonia, which took place over several weeks in April–May 2007, and a preemptive effort by Russian actors to shut down Georgia's government websites before and during the 2008 South Ossetia offensive.[23]

An often overlooked vector lies in the vulnerability of the supply chain for semiconductors used in commercial and military systems. Now that the manufacture of these critical components is almost entirely outsourced to Asia, it is impossible to ensure no malicious instructions are introduced into the devices at time of manufacture. In theory, an integrated circuit or microprocessor could contain instructions buried deep within, that could be activated remotely using a predefined signal, time index, or other initiator. These instructions could conceivably disable a critical system of an aircraft in flight, shut down a security system, or even introduce phantom images into air traffic control radar. The possibilities are almost endless, but little if any effort has yet been made to address this very real threat.

Perhaps the two least known and yet most destructive attack vectors in a potential adversary's portfolio are the ability to manipulate data without the owner's knowledge, and direct electromagnetic attack. Data manipulation can range from the complete substitution of entire databases with false data, to far more subtle adjustments in specific data elements. Take for example the theoretical case of a high profile patient at a hospital. Infiltrating the patient database, a potential attacker could alter the dosage of a medication, or even change the prescription to one that will be fatal to the patient due to an allergic reaction. This scenario might seem entirely too farfetched for the average person to consider, and yet it is a very real threat.

Direct electromagnetic attack, by contrast, is the closest to a kinetic-style effect that can be generated in cyberspace. A sudden spike across the spectrum, such as an electromagnetic pulse (EMP), causes a massive surge in electromagnetic activity that destroys all unprotected electronic devices within a large range. Ironically, older analog technology is more likely to survive, while more advanced and low-power systems are the most vulnerable to such an event. The original way to generate EMP was the atmospheric detonation of a nuclear device at medium to high altitude. Today, EMP can be generated by such means as an explosively pumped flux compression generator, which essentially uses a controlled high explosive to transfer energy to a directed magnetic field.[24]

Recent International Events

The highly publicized 2007 Cyber Riot on Estonia, the most heavily networked nation in Europe, was, in real terms, not a significant military event nor even a sophisticated form of cyber assault. While newspapers, blogs, internet sites, and news networks trumpeted the onslaught of the first cyber war, the government of Estonia was busy dealing with a rather mundane large-scale distributed denial-of-service attack. The impact was certainly visible, but while frustrating, it did not result in any long-lasting effects.[25] It did, however, bring to the forefront some important policy considerations that had not previously been addressed.

First, should this cyber event be defined as an attack? Second, if it was an attack, would article V of the NATO treaty apply? In other words, if Estonia, as a NATO member, were declared under attack, would the other members be obliged to come to Estonia's aid with armed force? These questions led to the most important follow-on initiative of the entire event, namely the ongoing effort to codify what truly constitutes an attack in cyberspace.[26] Much to the world's dismay, however, the answer still has not been satisfactorily established either for Estonia or in general.

In a different context, the cyber attack mounted by Russian sources as a prelude to a traditional military land invasion in the South Ossetia region of Georgia was meant to be an aspect of military action.[27] While in the case of Estonia there was a pervasive and significant level of advanced networking and infrastructure to assail, less than 20 percent of Georgian citizens, by contrast, have any measure of internet access. The defacement of a few key government websites was not even known to most of those directly involved in the conflict itself, and was a far bigger issue for those watching from outside the borders of the nation. In short, the first inarguably true cyber attack has yet to manifest itself. Yet, the question still becomes one of when rather than if.

Enemy Exploitation

Cyberspace provides a uniquely pervasive level of connectivity unlike any other domain of the global commons. The ease of exploiting this fundamental characteristic yields several low-investment but high-return capabilities for those committed to transnational terrorism or criminal activity. Using a commonly available cellular phone to detonate an improvised explosive device is just one example of how to transform an innocuous form of access to the electromagnetic domain into an effective weapon.[28] Nonetheless, not every form of exploitation relies on a violent kinetic result. In fact, the most common way to exploit cyberspace is by using it to export one's message to audiences that would be otherwise unreachable. In the context of jihadist websites, criminal forums, and warez (illegal software) sites, the ability to recruit, covertly exchange messages and instructions, and even conduct financial transfers and payments in itself constitutes a form of attack against legitimate entities.

Robert Steele, a former clandestine case officer for the CIA who works in open-source intelligence, that is, building intelligence by monitoring and trolling public information sources like the internet, said one-third of the jihadist websites operating today are used to incite violence, one-third raise funds for organizations that fund terrorists, and another third indoctrinate through theology and intellectual discourse. They are all growing in popularity.[29] Although laws exist in the United States and other countries against websites that directly incite violence, the U.S government has had a tough time monitoring and shutting those sites down. Jihadist sites are typically not in English, can be posted and removed quickly, and utilize servers scattered across different countries around the globe.

Cyber Attack Attribution

Due to the integrative and connective nature of cyberspace, there are multiple synergies that can accrue in concert with the other global commons. Communication through cyberspace overlies every other form of transport available today. Whether we move goods, services, or information via roads, sea-lanes, air routes, or by satellite, the ubiquitous nature of cyberspace pervades each transaction. This ready availability conveys great ease of access, but makes reliable attack attribution far more challenging.

If one were to be robbed at gunpoint, for example, it would be a relatively straightforward matter to identify at least a few critical characteristics of the attacker. A cyber mugging, by contrast, might consist of someone stealing your identity from your home computer remotely, and then proceeding to empty your bank accounts. You may not even realize anything has occurred, let alone who is responsible, until you attempt to withdraw money from an ATM only to find your balance is zero. The anonymity granted by cyberspace provides a safe forum for those otherwise too intimidated to advance their perspective, but it also grants those engaged in nefarious activities the veil of non-attribution.

While the denial-of-service attacks against Estonia and Georgia are known to have originated at least in part from Russian websites, the actual organizers remain anonymous. Nor is there clear evidence the Russian government played a role in organizing the attacks. Even if individual identities were to be uncovered or such evidence were to emerge, however, international law, as mentioned above, has yet to resolve the issue of how to classify, much less prosecute, such acts.[30]

Even when the source of an attack can be narrowed down to location X in country Y, it is virtually impossible to say with certainty who is responsible. In early 2009, security researchers in Canada were asked by a Tibetan exile group to investigate an apparent breach of their computer network. Over several months, the investigators uncovered an espionage cyber-network, spread across 103 countries and infecting more than a thousand government-run computers, that used malware to trick recipients into opening attachments. The attachments carried "Trojan horse" code that, once downloaded, "provided near-complete control over the victims' computers. Attackers could steal files, capture passwords, and even activate a Web camera."[31] Although these attacks were traced to computers located on the Chinese island of Hainan, and evidence pointed to official Chinese complicity, no one has been held accountable.[32]

Conclusion

While the physical basis for the newest and most expansive domain, the electromagnetosphere, has existed since time began, interest in, and more importantly the use of, this domain in the form of cyberspace has only recently begun to reach truly global proportions. In the nineteenth century there were no televisions, airplanes, computers, or spacecraft, nor were there antibiotics, credit cards, microwave ovens, compact discs, or mobile phones. There was, however, an internet.[33] The telegraph was the initial technological leap into the electronic common. The post-Gutenberg era of information distribution had dawned, and with it a new wave of commerce and globalization.

By 1847, the St. Louis *Republican* had declared "the telegraph has become one of the essential means of commercial transactions." Businessmen in the mid-nineteenth century were communicating and controlling the delivery of goods and services at a rate previously unimaginable. The result was a complete realignment of seasonal business calendars, re-stock and distribution schedules, and manufacturer-distributor-customer relationships. The impact of this high-speed, interconnected activity on trade, as inventory requirements decreased, delivery times were reduced and, prices became more competitive, created a more favorable commercial environment.

The means of controlling commerce began to change significantly, as the new-found relationship between trains and the telegraph illustrates. A large portion of the railroad infrastructure operated on a single-track architecture, which raised the risk of collision if engineers did not strictly monitor their travel rates between stations, or dispatchers did not keep a clockwork adherence to schedules. This risk was greatly reduced when telegraph operators became a part of the manpower pool in the train depot. The integrated operation of train and telegraph provided what was essentially real-time monitoring and control of the entire rail transportation network, thus increasing the timeliness and safety of the rail commerce system. It was not long before the telegraph connected countries across the oceans, and the benefits of global connectivity for global commerce via electronics were realized.

From the telegraph to radio to satellite communications and the ubiquitous connectivity we enjoy today, cyberspace has matured into a global commons worthy of protection to ensure its productive use by all. Just as with every other domain of the global commons, cyberspace faces threats in the form of multiple civilian and military "bad actors" employing complex and constantly evolving techniques. Irrespective of whether their motivations are criminal, ideological, or economic, all nations must recognize the need to counter the threats these actors pose, and secure the freedom of cyberspace for all legitimate purposes.

7 Space Assurance

Mike Manor and Kurt Neuman

A New Strategy for a New Reality

> "Many decades ago space was thought of as a sanctuary. We are
> entering into a new era where space is a contested environment."
>> *Colonel Sean D. McClung,*
>> *Director of Air University National Space Studies Center[1]*

On a clear night, the moon's Sea of Tranquility remains a visible reminder of a time when manned spaceflight captivated the imagination and gave hope to humankind. President John F. Kennedy's bold ambition to land a man on the moon by the end of the 1960s rallied the scientific community and much of the free world during the height of the Cold War's battles for ideological influence and prestige. Despite the successful conclusion of this epic struggle and ensuing cooperation in space between its main protagonists, the current global space environment is marked by instability and uncertainty rather than peaceful security. As the world has become inextricably reliant on space for its communications networks, terrestrial globalization has spawned a rapid "population growth" of both space objects and space players, along with the associated personal and political agendas. This growth, combined with the inherent vulnerabilities of space assets and advances in anti-space technologies, now poses significant dangers to peaceful, uncontested space activities.

To address these realities, the United States, as the leading space power among its allies and partners, requires a new strategy that will allow it to sustain preeminence in space over adversaries, while simultaneously cultivating inclusive, diplomatic mechanisms to establish an orderly, cooperative, and peaceful space environment. This strategy will help assure allies and partners unhindered access to the increasingly vital global common of outer space.[2]

A Global Community Reliant on Space

Access to and freedom of action in space are vital across the globe for security and prosperity. Space capabilities integrate tightly with everyday activities in the lives of individuals, commercial enterprises, and real-time military functions. In allied and coalition military operations, space effects are an indispensable asset for joint forces at every level.

In 2002, U.S. President George W. Bush directed a review and update of national space policy that resulted in several new National Security Presidential Directives (NSPD), including the overarching National Space Policy (NSPD-49) issued in August 2006. This document states that space capabilities, including both ground and space segments and their supporting links, are "vital to [our] national interests." It goes on to say that "Freedom of action in space is as important to the United States as air power and sea power."[3] Reflecting the principles of the 1967 Outer Space Treaty, NSPD-49 commits the United States to support the exploration and use of outer space by all nations for peaceful purposes and the benefit of all humanity. It expands on this position, however, by adding that "peaceful purposes" allow U.S. defense and intelligence-related activities in pursuit of national interests.

The entire world has become so reliant on space assets that having their use interrupted or denied would affect people in ways yet unimagined. The unexpected loss of the Galaxy IV communications satellite in 1998 temporarily affected over forty-five million users, ranging from medical workers and on-call doctors, who could not be contacted via their pagers, to gas station owners who lost pay-at-the-pump functions.[4] If such consequences result from the untimely demise of a single satellite, imagine the impact the loss of multiple satellites would have. A major disruption in space-based communications and financial transaction capabilities would severely affect worldwide commerce and the global economy.

Recent studies have begun to look at the impact of a "day without space." Consider the consequences of this scenario as described in 2002 by Lieuten-

ant General Joseph Cosumano, Jr., then Commanding General U.S. Army
Space and Missile Defense Command/Commanding General U.S. Army Space
Command:

> Take a few moments with me now to sit back and think what a day with-
> out Space would mean to our nation, and to our military. First, most pagers,
> phones, personal data devices, radios and televisions would become silent. . . .
> All land, sea and air vehicles leveraging the Global Positioning System (GPS)
> for precise location and navigation would have to come up with another
> means to determine their exact location and navigate from where they are to
> where they want to go. . . . In many cases it could mean the difference between
> life and death (e.g., if you cannot contact emergency responders such as the
> police, fire department and ambulance services in life threatening situations; if
> you cannot receive warnings of hurricanes, tornados, floods, and forest fires).
> Additionally, the impact to our nation's economy could be devastating, not
> only from business losses but also from the chaos resulting from disruption to
> international monetary transactions.
>
> From a military perspective, a day without Space would mean we would
> have no effective long-haul communications, thus precluding direct command
> and control with our joint and coalition partners and ensuring a limited reach-
> back capability. Without Global Positioning Systems we would have no beyond-
> line-of-site Blue Force Tracking capability; . . . we would have to navigate using
> maps and lensatic compasses; . . . and we would probably see increased col-
> lateral damage as we return to the days of "dumb" and laser-guided bombs.
> Our intelligence, surveillance and reconnaissance capabilities would be severely
> limited. . . . Early warning of ballistic missile launches would be minimal and
> tracking of these missiles would be almost non-existent.[5]

Challenges to Space Access and Peaceful Use:
The New Reality

The fundamental meaning of "space assurance" has changed within the context
of a globalized world. In the earliest period of space exploration, assurance
described the physical hazards associated with reaching and surviving in the
space medium. Globalization has introduced several new issues regarding access to and freedom of action in outer space, the essential elements of space
assurance in the present day.

Global and National Arrangements

Management and governance of the global space commons for mutual protection is one significant challenge. There are avenues available to address this concern, yet no globally recognized organization has been able to effectively resolve the critical issues relating to the governance and protection of the space commons.

Outer Space Treaty   As the United States and Soviet Union moved toward nuclear stalemate in the Cold War, space became the only reliable medium for verifying that neither side was threatening the already tenuous situation. Since these were the only two significant space powers at that time, it was in the best interests of both parties to allow the other to use space for treaty verification. The importance of space to maintain the status quo, as well as a fear that space might become the next battleground, led the United Nations to broker the Outer Space Treaty in 1967.[6] Based on the concept of a global commons, this treaty established basic requirements for responsible behavior in space. For example, it banned nuclear or any other weapons of mass destruction from being placed in orbit around the earth and declared that the moon and other celestial bodies shall be used exclusively for peaceful purposes. Ultimately, the Outer Space Treaty provided the protective umbrella under which each nation could pursue access to the space medium.

Despite agreements such as the Outer Space Treaty, some countries have created competition for unfettered access through the development of counter-space capabilities that could degrade the effectiveness of satellite systems. For instance, China publicly displayed a potential counter-space capability when it used a laser to illuminate a U.S. intelligence satellite in 2006,[7] and in 2007 destroyed a domestic weather satellite in orbit using a ballistic missile-launched kinetic anti-satellite weapon.[8] The growing dependence of U.S. allies and partners on space assets for their security and economic well-being make these emerging threats all the more dire. It is clear that the perception of space as a sanctuary for peaceful use no longer applies in today's globalized world. The Outer Space Treaty alone cannot ensure any nation's unhindered access to space.

United Nations   While the UN was able to broker the Outer Space Treaty, power distribution policies hamper its effectiveness as the governance body for space. Currently, the UN Committee on Peaceful Uses of Outer Space (UNCOPUOS) leads the participating nations and acts as a clearing house for global space issues. UNCOPUOS regards inclusivity as a priority, so any resolution requires a consensus vote, something nearly impossible to achieve because all sixty-nine voting members have wide-ranging equities. The search for consensus drives solutions to the lowest common acceptable denominator and places the interests of a small, non-space-faring nation such as Burkina Faso on equal footing to that of a large space power such as the United States. The weakness of this arrangement was demonstrated in 1976, when eight equatorial nations attempted to lay claim to the geostationary belt positions directly overhead, in a move called the Bogotá Declaration.[9] The most powerful space-faring nations, the United States and the Soviet Union, simply disregarded it, leaving the UN with little recourse.[10]

Mancur Olson, the noted political economist, explains that these kinds of dynamics are not uncommon in large groups that attempt to provide some measure of public good. Olson concluded that members of large groups "will not act to advance their common or group objectives unless there is coercion to force them to do so, or unless some separate incentive, distinct from the achievement of the common or group interest" is offered to all members.[11] The current UN-led space authority provides neither coercion nor incentives for member nations to solve issues in the global space commons, and thus, consensus and the maximum public interest remain unattainable. Nations with more interests in space bear the cost of providing such things as security in the space commons for other nations, because they would rather pay those costs than go without the significant benefits.

National Security Space   On the national level in the United States, another space entity has similar problems. Within the U.S. Department of Defense (DoD), the National Security Space (NSS) enterprise is a closely interwoven and interdependent group of commercial, civil, military, and intelligence organizations that are engaged in space activities.[12] Although its members remain a collection of disparate organizations with different mission priorities, goals, and interests, they provide each other with mutually supportive capabilities to collectively maintain the U.S. strategic advantage in space. Such collaboration is critical, because no single entity has the ability to sustain itself without the aid of others: infrastructure, research and development, personnel, and operations all require substantial investment. Additionally, many entities working together can provide the overlapping capabilities needed to satisfy user demands in a way no one organization could manage. Unfortunately, without a single authority to guide space policy, this diverse and complex enterprise is prone to bureaucratic competition over policy, programs, and budgets.

More than other nations, the United States tends to draw a line of distinction between the various sectors to which its space organizations belong. Countries such as Russia and China, by contrast, make no distinction between civil and military programs, meaning that advances in civil space capabilities are easily fed into their military space programs. The eighteen member nations of the European Space Agency (ESA) jointly conduct civil space activities, but ESA also runs satellite programs with military application, such as the Galileo navigation constellation. Tighter integration of military, intelligence, civil, and commercial space sectors affords a greater level of resource sharing, but broad applicability could sacrifice the advanced development of capabilities that would satisfy the specific requirements of a single sector.

Intrinsic Vulnerabilities

As with most growing communities, space is dealing with the problem of increasing pollution. Michael Krepon of the Henry L. Stimson Center put it succinctly: "Space debris poses a common threat to all space-faring nations."[13] As evidence, he cites how a piece of debris the size of a marble could strike a satellite with approximately the same energy as a one-ton safe dropped from a five-story building. Although the space medium of near-earth orbit is relatively large, the maneuver space that systems have enjoyed in the past appears to be shrinking. Space systems are now flying in closer proximity to each other and to debris, and collisions have happened.

Lack of Organizational Coordination and Oversight   A key vulnerability in the space commons is a lack of organizational coordination in the conduct of space traffic control functions, as well as a common picture of what is happening in the medium. These factors contributed to the unexpected collision between Motorola's Iridium 33 and a decommissioned Russian communications satellite, Cosmos 2251. This event resulted in over 2,000 pieces of hazardous debris in orbit that will have to be tracked and avoided by other spacecraft for decades.[14]

The U.S. NSS enterprise lacks the mechanisms to share timely information between disparate players and international partners with national space interests. "United States Strategic Command tracks more than 18,000 orbiting space objects, but it lacks the manpower to provide warnings of possible collisions to all except manned spacecraft and the most crucial United States military satellites."[15] In addition to providing collision avoidance data, a warning of a deliberate attack would need to be disseminated quickly. An attack on a military satellite, however, may be difficult to discern and may not trigger the timely notification of other intelligence, civil, or commercial groups, possibly leaving them exposed to a similar attack. The complexity of notification channels is increased if the initial attack is on a commercial, civil, or allied space system.

Lack of Space Situational Awareness   Space systems are inherently vulnerable because they operate in predictable orbits over potentially hostile areas without escort. In many cases, there is no ability to monitor the current status of a vehicle when it is out of line-of-sight contact with operators, while other actors have the capability to track and target space vehicles from multiple locations around the globe.

The prevailing lack of situational awareness in space may prevent the detection, identification, and attribution of, and response to, an attack on space systems.[16] Operators may not immediately know whether a satellite malfunction is due to hardware or software failure, or a hostile attack, which in turn will make it extremely difficult to attribute an attack on a space system to a specific perpetrator. This task is even more complex in the case where cyberspace capabilities are used to attack software functions, as it is easy to use third-party (proxy) computers to disguise the true origin of the attack. In essence, an attacker could damage a space system without fear of blame or reprisal.

Lack of Redundancy   Space capabilities may also be vulnerable due to a lack of redundancy. Not only are the space systems limited in numbers, but also in their corresponding ground architecture. The significant cost of building, maintaining, and operating ground facilities often drives the decision to centralize the operations of multiple space systems into consolidated centers, a decision that may decrease costs but sacrifice survivability and increase susceptibility to attack.

Performance over Protection   Historically, mission protection has been consistently traded for improved performance and cost savings in the development and use of space systems. These investment decisions increasingly focused on performance because of the prevailing expectation that threats would diminish as part of the post-Cold War peace dividend. Reality has proven these assumptions wrong, as global reliance on space assets has grown at a time when nations and non-state actors are developing more anti-space capabilities.

The combination of growing reliance, little investment in protective measures, and increasing anti-space threats contributes to a condition of instability across the space commons. Additionally, there has been little emergency planning or exercise of contingency plans to maintain essential functions without the benefits of space assets. The full extent to which space systems are utilized in global security and commerce, as well as what would be done should a hostile actor deny or disrupt those systems, remains uncertain.

Foreign Competition   Reliance on foreign parts suppliers may create a situation of increased risk to national security objectives. For example, the supply of Russian rocket motors for the Atlas V launch vehicle could be a potential vulnerability, as any degradation in state relations could disrupt the United States' ability to acquire needed parts. Free market forces that drive competition also can take business away from national defense industries and strengthen foreign competition.

Disruptive Purposes

The global community faces an increasing number of anti-space threats from state, non-state, and even individual actors as the space domain becomes more accessible to those who seek to disrupt space operations and contest freedom of action.[17] These threats are evolving to include traditional and non-traditional dimensions of warfare.

Strike on Space-related Ground Architectures   An attack on space assets need not entail anti-space weapons, and could be executed using terrestrial-based forces. Because on-orbit space assets are essentially tethered to their corresponding ground architectures, an adversary can render them helpless by striking launch facilities, command and control facilities, communications antennas, and relay stations.

Terrestrial-based weapons delivered from air, land, sea, and possibly cyberspace, all can reach ground-architecture targets. Because these conventional weapons are already part of the global strategic calculus, their use will not result in treaty disputes, thus possibly increasing the likelihood of their use. NATO forces conducted these types of conventional strikes in the Serbia-Kosovo war (1998–1999) by using aircraft against Serbian satellite broadcast facilities and antennas[18] during Operation ALLIED FORCE (March–June 1999), in an effort to eliminate broadcasting.[19]

Ground-Based Strike on Space Objects   Scaled operations against space objects are a far cry from the Cold War threat of a nuclear blast in space that would destroy all satellites in low earth orbit (LEO). Although the electromagnetic pulse from such a blast would have far-reaching consequences, the likelihood of a nuclear detonation in space is minimal. Any nation willing to launch a nuclear weapon into space would escalate a confrontation to the point where global condemnation and retaliation would be a near certainty.

There are other ways to strike objects in space without resorting to high-altitude nuclear detonations. Ground-based systems such as anti-satellite (ASAT) missiles can strike and destroy a satellite on-orbit. Although the world has yet to see one nation destroy another nation's satellite during hostilities, the United States, the former Soviet Union, and China have each demonstrated this capability by destroying one of their own satellites.[20]

China, which has devoted considerable resources to developing its space control capabilities, now stands at the top of the growing list of state-actors that have the potential capacity to threaten others' space assets.[21] Chinese capabilities extend from the development of highly capable micro-satellites to a provocative direct-ascent ASAT demonstration in early 2007 that destroyed one of their FY-1C weather satellites in LEO.[22] This action showed that China has the ability to target other satellites, such as intelligence systems, if within reach of their ASAT network.

In addition to the ASAT weapons, the Chinese have also developed directed-energy space capabilities. In September 2006, Dr. Donald Kerr, then Director of the National Reconnaissance Office, confirmed a Chinese weapon temporarily "blinded" a U.S. reconnaissance satellite.[23] This incident confirmed the Chinese have the ability to find, fix, track, target, and place a laser with great precision on a satellite in orbit.

In-Space Object Strike on Space Object   Developments in the areas of nano technologies, artificial intelligence, cyber, and co-orbital capabilities have the potential to provide further advantages over a potential adversary in space. Futurists such as Ray Kurzweil claim that significant technological innovation is within reach, and predict that computers will soon have the processing capacity of the human brain.[24] Although visions of that action-movie menace, the "Terminator," in space remain far-fetched, the idea of space systems that are both self-aware and autonomous has not been lost on major space-faring entities. The U.S. Defense Advanced Research Projects Agency recently demonstrated the ability to robotically repair a satellite on-orbit in an experiment called Orbital Express. In this demonstration, the "repair" satellite autonomously docked with its experimental target satellite, replaced the batteries, re-inserted a space flight computer and transferred propellants.[25] In addition, both NASA and the U.S. Air Force have demonstrated the ability of a satellite to autonomously rendezvous and inspect other objects in space.[26] While the

United States supports using this technology only for non-aggressive purposes, these satellites highlight the difficulty in defining the term "space weapon." A slight modification to the repair satellite's orbital flight path could turn these systems into a battering ram, or turn the grappling devices used to repair satellites into weapons capable of dismantling or destroying another space object.

Unconventional Approaches   Several trends also illustrate a growing risk of future disruption in space from non-traditional types of threats. The rise of piracy in other domains, for instance, indicates the likelihood that the same threat will arise in the space domain.[27] Space piracy will likely take the form of stealing satellite communication bandwidth or jamming a communication signal, and have the potential to inflict heavy costs on commercial providers; furthermore, just like pirates at sea, space pirates could extort ransoms from companies to stop the attacks. Although these scenarios may appear fanciful, the proliferation of low-cost technologies and the knowledge to use them in a potentially harmful manner make space piracy a real possibility.

Non-state actors or individuals can build GPS and mobile satellite communication jamming devices for $7,500 or less from components on the open market. Celestial observation technology, such as adaptive optics, have declined in price to the point that casual astronomers can track and view satellites in LEO.[28] Despite being benign on the surface, such technology makes it possible for adversaries to gain critical information on satellite construction, materials used, operating capabilities, and potential vulnerabilities.

Interference or inadvertent disruption in the space commons is also quite possible. In 2003, the U.S. State Department discovered an unknown source was jamming the transponder on the commercial communication satellite, TELESTAR-12, which the State Department leased for its Voice of America broadcasts to Iran.[29] After a few weeks, the source of the jamming was isolated to a dish located on the Iranian Embassy's roof in Cuba.[30] The Iranian government had attempted to jam an unrelated anti-Iranian broadcast on the same satellite, but the jamming effects bled over onto the U.S.-leased transponder.

Disrupting and controlling the space commons will not be an end in itself, but rather part of a larger operation. Anti-space capabilities will most likely be synchronized with other military assets and launched at a specific time and place to gain local control, rather than to control the entire space commons. For example, a competitor could conceivably laze or jam allied intelligence satellites as a precursor to launching a surprise attack on another nation.

Overcoming Access Challenges: The New Strategy

The new reality of a contested space environment dictates that the United States develop a feasible strategy to secure freedom in the global common of outer space. This strategy should embrace measures and opportunities for cooperation with other nations, so they may prepare for the worst while still pursuing courses of action that are in the best interest of all nations. A balanced and realistic strategy will emphasize diplomatic solutions and effective deterrence first, but also promote contingency planning along with advances in protection and situational awareness capabilities.

Diplomacy

The United States must build strong partnerships on the home front by bringing together, formalizing, and strengthening the disparate groups of players that comprise U.S. space operations, while also strengthening its external partnerships. Prussian philosopher Immanuel Kant (1724–1804) suggested that although the natural state of man is war, a state of peace can be established if nations pledge peace to each other.[31] Kant conceived that such pledges would take the form of disseminating democratic principles, creating economic interdependence, and establishing international organizations.[32] Likewise, peace in the space commons can be achieved through similar diplomatic mechanisms.

Organization/Governance   Governance of U.S. space activities is currently fragmented, with authority dispersed across multiple agencies, including the DoD, State Department, intelligence community, and Department of Commerce. The National Security Space Office presently is chartered to promote unity of effort, but its jurisdiction is only across the DoD and the intelligence community.[33] In addition, its authorities and span of control have been greatly diminished over the past several years. To address this fragmentation of governance, the U.S. must establish clear and coherent authority for space policy, programs, budgeting, and execution, and consider revising the various participants' traditional insistence on creating and keeping control of singular, proprietary space architectures. These steps would help to align currently fragmented roles, responsibilities, and authorities for greater clarity, efficiency, and effectiveness.

Given its reliance on space capabilities for all aspects of communications, commerce, and defense, the United States must reconcile growing anti-space threats with the need to depart from established traditions in space planning and operations. Although no single nation has the authority or ability to ensure the global common of space is accessible to all, the United States might be the only nation capable of establishing acceptable rules of conduct and appropriate behavior, and thus charting an acceptable course for all others.[34]

A new space organization, involving a governing body made up of a limited number of space-faring nations, is one such diplomatic mechanism. For general membership, a nation would have to possess the ability to launch, operate, and maintain systems in the space commons; commercial and civil space entities would fall under the nation's flag they claim upon launch. In Kantian terms, this new international space organization would provide a forum to "pledge peace" by offering participants a mutually agreed means to resolve shared issues in the space commons. This forum would also help further economic interdependence by creating opportunities for joint space ventures.

As Mancur Olson explained, smaller groups succeed where large groups fail, because each member of a smaller group shares a larger portion both of the burden and the benefit of the good, and the actions of one member will have a noticeable effect on the others.[35] A forum of space-faring nations as described above will have the most to gain from the institutionalization of space activities, and thus the incentive to see their issues resolved. These powers will in turn provide the public with space-based "goods," such as enhanced global security. Additionally, enforcement of any group decision will be shared among the members. The failure of the Bogotá Declaration to influence great-power policymaking illustrated that a realistic enforcement mechanism for space policy will be achieved only through the buy-in of the dominant space-faring nations. The formation of a smaller organization of space-faring nations will go a long way toward achieving consensus on decisions, as well as formalizing the ability to enforce these decisions.

Interdependence/Cooperation   There are many non-organizational diplomatic measures that would also help ensure freedom in the space commons. Cooperative defense measures that increase transparency would enhance stability by raising the cost and lowering the benefit of hostile actions. Sharing space situational awareness data that builds a common operating picture for all nations would decrease a potential adversary's ability to take hostile action without being identified. The likelihood of attribution, based on an accepted standard of conduct for responsible activities in space, would make it less profitable for a nation to attack another's space assets. Mutually agreed-upon standards of conduct for space systems should cover safety concerns for navigation and command and control; monitoring of dual-use technologies such as micro-satellites; prevention of space debris; and system disposal methods.

Program co-dependencies and collective defense measures are another means to help ensure freedom in space through cooperation. For example, the United States and Australia are currently partnering on the wideband global satellite communications (SATCOM) program, to increase shared communications bandwidth between the two nations.[36] Similarly, Washington and Brussels have partnered to make the GPS and Galileo navigation constellations compatible.[37] These types of cooperative activities improve stability by expanding the number of nations the attacker would have to contend with in the aftermath, and thus raising the potential cost and lowering the likely benefit of an attack. Additionally, allied and partner nations can attempt to limit an adversary's access to space through methods such as diplomatic alliances and economic sanctions that curtail the proliferation of space technologies and assistance. Such actions serve to isolate an adversary, and help prevent it from acquiring permanent as well as more temporary means of access to the space domain. A co-dependent international cooperative partnership could provide leverage to quell potential conflict, communicate the consequences of irresponsible behavior and demonstrate a credible threat of repercussion.

Deterrence

Deterrence is an indispensable part of the new strategy; it "is both exquisitely simple and devilishly complex. In its purest form, it's nothing more than a rational calculus of costs and benefits reinforced by the threat of punishment."[38] Traditional deterrence theory from the Cold War era, however, will have to be rethought. The breakdown of bi-polarity and subsequent dispersion of global power centers, which includes the rise of new non-state actors, has multiplied both the objects and the mechanisms of deterrence. While the essence of deterrence has not changed—it is still the product of capability, will, and perception[39]—the new variables have rendered old strategies aimed solely at nuclear-armed national actors inadequate, especially in space.

A more holistic approach is necessary, one that leverages the complete set of national capabilities—economic, diplomatic, legal, social, technical, and conventional military forces—for space deterrence across the entire spectrum of threats, from nuclear-armed states to radical sub-national actors. The challenge in deterring attacks on space systems is to discern both the actor's rationale and the correct mechanism to use against it. As Dr. Lani Kass explains, deterrence is a matter of finding the right pressure points and then applying the appropriate capabilities, coupled with manifest intent, to these pressure points to create a perception in the mind of the actor that costs outweigh benefits.[40]

To deter an adversary from attacking space systems, options that encompass the whole of a target government's assets and capabilities must be at the disposal of the national leadership to provide a "best fit" deterrent option. This "whole-of-government" deterrence strategy for space would closely resemble a counter-value concept. Simply put, this means finding an adversary's pressure point: the level of cost that actor would face in a retaliatory strike, equal to the value the potential target assigns to space. To be effective, this course of action must be clearly articulated to both the enemy and the international public, so that the former is convinced the targeted state would take action.

Contingency Planning

Internal contingency planning is critical to lowering risk should diplomatic efforts fail. This includes instituting protective measures, enhancing space situational awareness (SSA) and emergency responses, and improving competitive advantages.

Protective Measures   The U.S. administration must expand its focus from simply launching assets to protecting them and preserving the capabilities they provide, including improvements to the survivability of space capabilities if they are attacked. To this end, the administration should introduce minimum space-system survivability standards, such as improved maneuverability capabilities, hardening, and encryption, as well create a mechanism to monitor and enforce these standards.

SSA and Emergency Responses   The United States and its allies should also improve its space situational awareness capabilities. SSA—knowing what is going on in space—would help protect both government and commercial vehicles against collisions, as well as attacks. The natural progression from understanding what is happening in space is to then codify and coordinate emergency response activities. Once the situation is defined, prescribed measures should inform responders how to react to a given situation. These measures include cross-organizational coordination between the various space-faring entities (governmental, military, commercial, and allied), to disseminate warnings and protect space systems.

Additionally, allied nations could develop a rapid surge and reconstitution capability to launch replacement satellites. Such a capability could work alone or in tandem with a "virtual armada" of allied space systems. This armada could complicate an adversary's targeting problem sufficiently to discourage space warfare. Such a plan would also involve building redundant capabilities into the other mediums of air, land, and sea.[41] For example, contingency communications bandwidth could be provided by unmanned aerial vehicles (UAVs). While not globally available like a satellite constellation, UAVs could provide a regional backup that would ensure continuity of service until SATCOM was restored. Being unable to disrupt services at critical junctures would lower the benefit for a potential attacker and dissuade adversaries from investing in counter-space capabilities.

Competitive Advantages   One important way space-faring nations can ensure future access to space is to improve their competitive advantage. Less obviously protective activities include strengthening their industrial base, encouraging students to pursue space expertise and engineering, and establishing policy that facilitates the growth of commercial space capabilities. Each of these activities strengthens a nation's ability to compete in the global environment by ensuring it maintains the ability to produce its own space systems.

The U.S. defense and intelligence sectors rely on private, commercial capabilities in the areas of launch, SATCOM, and imagery. In fact, it is estimated that eighty percent of DoD's SATCOM bandwidth during Operation Iraqi Freedom (begun in 2003) was via commercial sources,[42] including international companies such as Globalstar (headquarters in California), Inmarsat (London), Intelsat (Bermuda), Iridium (Maryland), and Thuraya (United Arab Emirates).[43] The intelligence community also relies on commercial capabilities provided by such assets as DigitalGlobe's (Colorado) Quickbird satellite to satisfy a growing requirement for imagery intelligence.[44] The government's use of commercial systems has grown because it can lease or purchase the desired capabilities on an as-needed basis instead of developing, fielding, and operating an entire system, thus making the private option convenient and cost-effective. This trend may not be sustainable, as industry will not always be able to surge when and where the government needs it most. This highlights the need for stable investment in commercial systems to ensure critical capabilities are available when needed.

Conclusion

The fundamental meaning of "space assurance" has changed within the context of a globalized world. As more and more actors develop or otherwise gain access to satellite technology and other space assets, the domain of space is increasingly characterized by instability rather than peace. This new reality demands leadership, and the United States, as the leading space power among its allies, must move beyond go-it-alone strategies to engage in cooperative development and security with friendly space-faring nations. These nations must seek a strategy of diplomacy if they are to preserve freedom of access and use of the global common of outer space, while planning ahead to take protective action and maintain plausible deterrence capabilities.

8 Ballistic Missile Defense

Will Dossel

The Mandate

The continued proliferation of ballistic missiles throughout the world, and consequent greater potential for the use of weapons of mass destruction (WMD), mandates an examination of the role and capabilities of ballistic missile defense in securing the freedom of and access to the global commons. It is not the advent of the ballistic missile, nor the fact that nuclear-capable missiles exist, that is new. What has changed in the intervening years is the panoply of state- and non-state actors that now possess the capability to deploy ballistic missiles, and the magnitude of disruption they may cause owing to WMD proliferation. This chapter will outline the nature of the threat, define and detail what constitutes ballistic missile defense (BMD), and identify areas of opportunity for the utilization of BMD in global and regional contexts to secure the commons.

The Threat

Since the close of the Cold War, ballistic missiles have become a growth industry. This situation has evolved despite legalized control regimes that seek either to outlaw an entire class of weapon (e.g., the Intermediate-Range Nuclear Forces Treaty)[1] or control the international flow of technology, knowledge, and material related to the design, development, and production of ballistic missiles (e.g., the 1987 Missile Technology Control Regime).[2] Indicative of this growth is the near tripling of ballistic missile-capable nations from nine in 1972 (Table 8.1) to twenty-three in 2007 (Table 8.2).

The use of ballistic missiles by these actors falls generally into two categories: as a coercive force or as a means of asymmetric attack.

Coercive Force

The coercive deployment of ballistic missiles usually frames them as a weapon of terror, or through their implied use, a weapon of deterrence. An actor that brandishes the missiles as terror weapons usually seeks to enforce a set of conditions or terms vis-à-vis the targeted actor for a particular end, typically to terminate a war, and generally targets civilian and other non-military target sets, as was the case, for example, during the latter stages of World War II in Germany's seven-month *Operation Penguin* campaign. Launching over 3,000 A4/V-2[3] ballistic missiles at targets ranging from southern England to the freed territories on the continent, Germany sought through what was primarily a psychological campaign to win back the initiative in the war and offset the Allies' successes in the air and on the ground following the Normandy invasion.

TABLE 8.1 Ballistic Missile States (1972)

Country	System	Country of Origin	Nuclear State
Bulgaria	SS-1C SCUD B (SRBM)	USSR	No
China	CSS-1 (MRBM); CSS-2 (MRBM)	China	Yes
Czechoslovakia	SS-1C SCUD B (SRBM)	USSR	No
France	SSBS S-2, MSBS M-1 (MRBM)	France	Yes
GDR (East Germany)	SS-1C SCUD B (SRBM)	USSR	No
Poland	SS-1C SCUD B (SRBM)	USSR	No
United Kingdom	Polaris A-3 (IRBM)	US	Yes
US	Minuteman I-III, Titan II, Poseidon (ICBM); Pershing I (MRBM); Lance (SRBM)	US	Yes
USSR	SS-1 SCUD B (SRBM); SS-4 SANDAL, SS-5 SKEAN, SS-6 SAPWOOD, SS-7 SADLER, SS-8 SASSEN, SS-9 SCARP, SS-11 SEGO, SS-12 SACLEBOARD, SS-13 SAVAGE (ICBM); SS-N-5 SARK, SS-N-6 SERB (MRBM)	USSR	Yes

NOTES: SRBM: < 1,000 km; MRBM: 1,000 – 3,000 km; IRBM: 3,000 – 5,500 km; ICBM: >5,500 km

SOURCE: http://www.missilethreat.com/missilesoftheworld/

TABLE 8.2 Ballistic Missile States (2007)

Country	System	Country of Origin	Nuclear State?	MTCR Member?
Belarus	SS-1C SCUD B, SS-21 (SRBM)	USSR	No	No
China	CSS-2, CSS-3 (IRBM); CSS-4, JL-2, DF-31 (ICBM); CSS-5, CSS-N-3 (MRBM); CSS-6, CSS-7 (SRBM)	China	Yes	No
Egypt	SS-1C SCUD B (SRBM)	USSR	No	No
France	M-45 (ICBM)	France	Yes	Yes
India	Prithvi I/II, Dhanush, Agni 1 (SRBM); Agni 2, Agni 3 (IRBM)	India	Yes	No
Iran	SS-1C SCUD B, Fateh 110, CSS-8 (SRBM); Shahab 3 (MRBM)	USSR, China, DPRK	No	No
Israel	Jericho 1 (SRBM); Jericho 2 (MRBM)	Israel	Yes	No
Kazakhstan	SS-1C SCUD B, SS-21 (SRBM)	USSR	Yes	No
Libya	SS-1C SCUD B (SRBM)	USSR	No	No
North Korea (DPRK)	SS-1C SCUD B, SS-1D SCUD C, SS-1E SCUD D (SRBM), No Dong (MRBM), Taepo Dong 1 (MRBM); Taepo Dong 2 (ICBM)	Egypt, China, DPRK	Yes	No
Pakistan	Hatf-2, Ghaznavi, Shaheen I (SRBM), Shaheen II (MRBM), Ghauri (IRBM)	China, Pakistan	Yes	No
Russia	SS-1C SCUD B, SS-21, SS-26 (SRBM); SS-18, SS-19, SS-25, SS-27, SS-N-8, SS-N-18, SS-N-20, SS-N-23 (ICBM)	Russia	Yes	Yes
Saudi Arabia	CSS-2 (IRBM)	China	No	No
South Korea	NHK-1 (SRBM)	South Korea	No	No
Syria	SS-1C SCUD B, SS-1D SCUD C, SS-1E SCUD D, SS-21 (SRBM)	USSR	No	No
Turkey	Project J (SRBM)	China	No	Yes
Turkmenistan	SS-1C SCUD B (SRBM)	USSR	No	No
Ukraine	SS-1C SCUD B (SRBM)	USSR	No	Yes
United Arab Emirates	SS-1C SCUD B (SRBM)	DPRK	No	No
United Kingdom	Trident D-5 (ICBM)	US	Yes	Yes
United States	Minuteman III, Trident D-5 (ICBM)	US	Yes	Yes
Vietnam	SS-1C SCUD B (SRBM)	USSR	No	No
Yemen	SS-1C SCUD B, SS-21 (SRBM)	USSR	No	No

NOTES: Italicized = new to list, post-1972. SRBM: < 1,000 km; MRBM: 1,000 – 3,000 km; IRBM: 3,000 – 5,500 km; ICBM: >5,500 km

SOURCE: http://www.missilethreat.com/missilesoftheworld/

In similar fashion, Iraq, late in the Iran-Iraq war (1980–88), launched a pro-longed series of ballistic missile attacks against major Iranian cities, including Teheran, at one point forcing up to one-third of the populace to flee the city. Though the warheads carried conventional high-explosives, Iraq's frequent use of chemical weapons in combat elsewhere led the Iranians to believe attacks with WMD-laden missiles would be forthcoming, and eventually compelled them to seek a peace on less than equitable terms.[4] Most recently, demonstrating the extent to which missiles and technology can proliferate, Hezbollah in 2006 and Hamas in 2008 launched thousands of battlefield (Katyusha) rockets and a smaller number of short-range (Qasam) missiles from their strongholds in Lebanon and Gaza into Israel, as part of a campaign to de-stabilize the Israeli government and exact revenge for Israeli strikes against Hamas and Hezbollah forces and leaders.[5]

Deterrence as a form of coercion relies on the ability of one state to threaten to impose sufficient damage on another, such that the calculation of costs by the latter compels it to forgo a particular course of action. The introduction of large fleets of land- and sea-based thermonuclear-armed ballistic missiles, beginning in the 1960s, gave credence to U.S. and Soviet threats of annihilation literally within minutes. As the Cold War unfolded, the ability of the two protagonists to avert the possibility of a nuclear first strike with the promise of an equally annihilating response, or second strike, evolved into the doctrine of mutual assured destruction (infamous by its acronym—MAD).[6] Two factors are important in this scenario: the credibility of a nation's deterrent (i.e., its ability to survive a first strike and deliver an effective response), and its level of tolerance for damage from even limited strikes. While the balance in the Cold War rested between two actors with roughly equal means of destroying the other, and who shared an understanding of "the rules of the game," that precarious balance has been disturbed by the relatively recent appearance on the scene of several proto-nuclear and nuclear-capable states that challenge the traditional calculus of nuclear deterrence.

When one WMD-enabled actor comes to believe that another may have a low tolerance for, or ability to absorb, damage, this situation provides the rationale for minimal deterrence theory. In this case, a lesser actor, a regional power for example, who has the resources to build and deploy a small force of nuclear-armed missiles, seeks to deter a more powerful state from taking action against it on the assumption that the stronger state would view the domestic death and destruction from even a very limited attack as being far worse than the consequences of not intervening against the presumably weaker regional power.[7] The widening proliferation of ballistic missiles with greater range, when combined with the spread of WMD in a globalized environment, has served to magnify the standing and relative importance that possession of this capability imputes to regional powers. This is particularly the case with those nations harboring dangerous aspirations and designs on the global commons, as they come to regard their smaller arsenals as equivalent with those of the traditional great powers in the ability to deter intervention and enable the owners' regional aspirations.

Asymmetric Attack

Ballistic missiles provide an asymmetric means of response for an actor that faces an otherwise overwhelming array of forces or capabilities. Regional or near-peer powers are finding that ballistic missiles allow them to project striking force over longer ranges, and with increasingly greater accuracy, putting opponent's critical operational nodes and forces at risk without the cost in time and money to build and maintain air forces with commensurate capability.

Conventionally armed, highly accurate, and mobile-based missiles offer near-peer nations the ability to exercise sea denial,[8] offset opponent's attempts at air superiority, hold forward-airports and -seaports hostage, or conduct strikes with or in support of conventional forces. During the Cold War, in the event that it perceived an imminent attack, the Soviet Union planned to use its numerically superior ballistic missile forces, deployed throughout the Warsaw Pact nations, to preemptively strike NATO's qualitatively and quantitatively superior anti-armor tactical- and long-range nuclear strike air forces before they had an opportunity to get airborne. Sufficient damage was expected such that Pact air forces would be able to deal with the remnant, thereby ensuring local air superiority for the forward advancement of Pact armored forces.[9]

The net effect for preemption in this case is to sufficiently change the initial conditions such that subsequent operations are on a footing more favorable to the preemptor. NATO and other allied/combined air operations in Kosovo, Serbia, and Iraq since the 1990s confirmed this understanding, convincing China to embark on its own ballistic missile development and deployment program.[10] To underscore the point, China's heavy investment in ballistic and cruise missile systems is explicitly cited in a 2009 U.S. Department of Defense report on Chinese military power, which details China's anti-access/denial strategy that integrates conventionally armed anti-ship ballistic missiles based on the CSS-5 (DF-21) with extensive C4ISR (command, control, communications, computers, intelligence, surveillance, reconnaissance) to locate, track, target and home, using onboard guidance systems, on large ships such as aircraft carriers.[11]

Proliferation of Ballistic Missiles

The rise to prominence of ballistic missiles as a threat is directly linked to the widespread proliferation of technology, subcomponents, and even complete systems. A textbook example of the wide-ranging effects of proliferation and the way it can influence regional security is found in Iran's development of an indigenous missile production industry. Iran made limited attempts at obtaining ballistic missiles prior to 1984, the most noteworthy being an exploratory outreach to Israel by the government of Shah Mohammed Reza Pahlavi in 1977.[12] Construction of a missile development center at Shiraz began in 1978, but that effort ended when the Shah was overthrown the following year. Iranian interest in acquiring ballistic missiles was rekindled, however, as a direct result of the Iran-Iraq War. Lacking its own arsenal, Iran came under Iraqi ballistic missile attack, first with battlefield rockets like the FROG-7 and later the SCUD, which was used in volume against Iranian cities.[13] The toll, both psychological and in terms of actual casualties, was such that Iran undertook to both develop its own missiles and seek to acquire them from another state.

Access from another state, however, was problematic. At this point, the Soviet Union was the only state exporting the SCUD, and since Iraq was already a client, Iran would not be able to procure any from that source. Additionally, the Soviets had agreements with client states that they would not export the missiles to a third country. Iran nevertheless entered into secret negotiations with Libya and Syria, and eventually got Libya to agree to the sale of a small number of complete systems—missiles, transporters and associated equipment—which were delivered via Turkey in late 1984.[14] With training assistance from the Syrians, Iran launched its first long-range attack in March 1985 against the Iraqi city of Kirkuk. From 1985 to 1987, this "War of the Cities" seesawed back and forth between Iraqi SCUD attacks and Iranian responses.

Early in the operation, Iran also sought assistance and missiles from North Korea (the DPRK) who supplied their indigenously produced SCUD-B (named the *Hwasong* 5) during the second round of conflict, generally ascribed to the period 1986–87.[15] As Iranians gained experience assembling "kits" supplied by the DPRK, they were simultaneously working on reverse engineering to facilitate their own fabrication and assembly capability. Again, the DPRK assisted in this effort by helping Iran establish a SCUD B production facility in 1987.[16] Over the next five years, the DPRK alone would sell 200 to 300 SCUD B missiles to Iran, enabling Iran to mount increasingly larger missile attacks on Iraqi cities, with seventy-seven missiles launched in the fifty-day period between 1 March and 20 April 1987.[17]

Over time, Iran's missile production complex has grown, comprising a network of facilities centered on the Fajr Air Base east of Tehran and a Chinese-built ballistic missile test range.[18] Twenty-five years after the initial surreptitious purchase of SCUD Bs from Libya, Iran now boasts the ability to deploy ballistic missiles against any nation in the region, including Israel, and, with the successful launch of the Safir-2 space launch vehicle (SLV) in 2009, can demonstrate a notional intermediate-range missile capability.[19] Taking advantage of a network of proliferators, both state-sponsored and private, it has built an indigenous production capability for a variety of rockets and missiles with conventional or WMD-dispersal warheads.

Similarly, the DPRK is meeting its own goals of establishing a significant, if not regionally dominant, missile threat. The revelations of North Korea's missile capabilities have tended to come as a surprise to its neighbors and their allies in the region. A classic case was the 1998 launch of a presumed space-launch vehicle, the Taepodong-1 (TD-1), which flew over Japan without prior notification or warning. The launch, coupled with the release of then-Secretary of Defense Donald Rumsfeld's report to the U.S. Congress, served as a stimulus to missile defense programs in the United States and Japan.[20] A subsequent attempt at launching a longer-range variant in 2006 (the TD-2), coincident with a number of short- and medium-range missiles, failed approximately forty seconds into flight. According to a defector from the lead production facility, President Kim Jong-Il is alleged to have given the go-ahead for TD-2 production himself, saying "If we can develop this we have nothing to fear. Even the American bastards won't be able to bother us. Whether we live or die, we must quickly develop the Hwasong-6 [another name for the TD-2]."[21]

Clearly signaling their intent to fulfill Kim's ambition despite international protests and UN Security Council resolutions against them, the DPRK attempted another TD-2 SLV launch in April 2009.[22] Unlike in 1998 or 2006, the North Korean government declared that this was a space launch intended to place a small communications satellite in orbit. In doing so, they followed the protocols of space-faring nations by adhering to the provisions of the Outer Space Treaty and publicizing hazard areas where booster stages were expected to drop along the path of flight. This time the missile completed almost two-thirds of its flight before a malfunction in the third stage sent the remainder into the waters of the mid-Pacific. Although the failure indicated how far the North Koreans still have to go to build and field an ICBM force, it has become obvious that mere condemnatory rhetoric and UN resolutions that carry no significant penalties for the government in Pyongyang have little deterrent effect.[23] The fact that the first two stages evidently functioned successfully will encourage sober assessments of North Korean missile capabilities by the global community. The final piece of a fully capable system—the ability to weaponize nuclear warheads and mount them on missiles—remains to be demonstrated, although underground nuclear testing by North Korea continued in May 2009 with a blast of approximately four kilotons near the town of Kilju,[24] followed by defiant test-firing of five short-range missiles into the sea opposite Japan, further rattling nerves in the region.[25]

As was the case with Iran, the DPRK has been able not only to develop an indigenous family of missiles from battlefield to intermediate range, but also to export the technology, skilled labor, scientists, and even entire systems to other countries. All of this was possible despite UN resolutions and non-proliferation accords to the contrary. At best, those and similar institutions only served to delay rather than deny. As more nations seek their own means for access to space, the difficulty of controlling missile proliferation will correspondingly grow as access to dual-use technology and materials becomes more widespread, in spite of non-proliferation regimes like the International Code of Conduct against Ballistic Missile Proliferation (2002).[26] Concurrent WMD programs, especially those that are either covert or lack international monitoring, will serve to enhance the desirability of ballistic missiles as the preferred means of delivery. Absent effective controls on the production of ballistic missiles by potential adversaries, a solution must be developed to counter or degrade their operational use.

Three Pillars of Missile Defense

Three elements or so-called "pillars" characterize ballistic missile defense: offensive operations, passive defense, and active defense, all supported by command, control, communications, computers and intelligence (C4I). Individually, each has its own advantages, obstacles, and measured successes in application. It is not until they are integrated with air and cruise missile defense, however, that the full benefit of BMD is realized.

Offensive Operations

Historically, defense against ballistic missiles has depended on offensive operations. These are actions taken to strike at ballistic missiles before they are launched—to wit, disabling or destroying their supporting production and launch infrastructure, or destroying the missiles themselves before they can take flight, through offensive counterair (OCA) operations.[27] The reality of the historical record for this approach is not encouraging.

Typically, offensive operations using OCA have expended a disproportionate amount of attack assets for benefits realized. For example, between August 1943 and May 1945, a significant portion of the British and U.S. strategic bombing force was diverted from Operation POINTBLANK, the strategic bombing campaign directed at the German industrial heartland, to the aerial campaign against Germany's V-1 and V-2 rockets, called Operation CROSSBOW. From December 1943 to June 1944 alone, more than 25,000 sorties were flown and 36,000 tons of bombs dropped in support of CROSSBOW.[28] Yet despite this and the Normandy invasion in June, the V-1 raids continued and the first V-2s struck Paris and London that September.

Similarly, during Operation DESERT STORM in 1992, one-third of the over 2,000 daily air sorties were diverted to SCUD hunting. As part of that effort, a dedicated A-10 Thunderbolt II was kept in each air patrol zone for twenty-four hour attack coverage. Additionally, Special Forces units were inserted into Iraq to search for mobile launchers. Despite the extraordinary level of effort, only a handful of fixed sites were destroyed, but no mobile launchers or missiles.[29]

Another offensive option against ballistic missiles is the invasion of denied territory by ground forces in an effort to locate and destroy the base of the threat. Israel faced this choice twice in the period 2006–08, when confronted with significantly increased daily Qassam rocket attacks by first Hezbollah and then Hamas; since 2001, there had been over 2,300 such attacks in and around the western Negev settlements.[30] The widespread use of Israeli airstrikes and mechanized infantry in heavily urbanized, densely populated areas, to try to stop the rockets, resulted in civilian deaths and infrastructure damage that received wide play in Arab media, despite the damage and death caused by Hezbollah- and Hamas-launched rocket attacks.[31]

The key to successful offensive operations is access to persistent, actionable intelligence. Such intelligence provides not only real- or near-real-time indications and warnings of launch, but also of force disposition, configuration, vulnerabilities, and—when combined with strategic intelligence—capabilities and intent. In each of the cases cited above, intelligence shortcomings were a major factor in the poor results that were obtained despite the commitment of significant forces to the fight. In Operation CROSSBOW, sorties were misdirected against numerous but empty launch ramps throughout the north of France and the Low Countries, to the detriment of the campaign against fuel production and other supporting infrastructure. In Operation DESERT STORM, planners clung to an assessment that it took thirty minutes for a SCUD launcher to uncover, launch, and reset, despite the insistence of Egyptians that it could be accomplished in one-fifth the time, based on their own operational experience. This mistake was compounded by a lack of persistent surveillance and the means to counter Iraqi camouflage/concealment capabilities. In the case of the Israelis, once again, the lack of persistent surveillance backed up by rapid, precise strikes forced what was perceived to be a disproportionate response to the high-frequency but relatively low-casualty Qassam rocket attacks.

Passive Defense

Passive air defense entails all measures taken to minimize the effectiveness of hostile air and missile threats against friendly forces. These measures include camouflage, concealment, deception, dispersion, reconstitution, redundancy, detection and warning systems, and protective construction.[32] For example, the Defense Support Program[33] constellation of early warning satellites proved effective during DESERT STORM when it detected the launch of Iraqi SCUD missiles and provided warning to civilian populations and coalition forces in Israel and Saudi Arabia.[34] In this current age, counter-proliferation efforts such as the Proliferation Security Initiative and cyberspace protection and exploitation may also be construed to be passive defenses.[35]

Active Defense

When offensive operations and passive defenses fail to thwart ballistic missile attack, a third option, active defense (i.e., missile interceptors), is now available. In the past, active measures to solve the ballistic missile defense problem have proved exceedingly complex and technologically challenging.[36] To a large degree this has been because most efforts have concentrated on the final phase of ballistic flight. Each phase of flight, however, offers potential for active defenses.

The boost phase of flight is the period of greatest vulnerability for a ballistic missile, as it is still accelerating and thus easier to identify and localize by orbital early warning assets.[37] Additionally, because of the stress on the airframe while in the atmosphere, any damage to the missile body is likely to cause subsequent catastrophic failure and breakup of the airframe. Factors that complicate boost-phase intercept technically as well as operationally are that the period tends to be short in duration, launches are typically unannounced, and launch areas tend to be deep in denied territory. Boost-phase intercept systems must thus, by definition, be able to dwell for extended periods of time on threat-launch areas of interest and then quickly react with weapons that can rapidly cover the distances involved. On the downside, these systems must, perforce, be forward-deployed and ready to operate in high-threat environments close to denied territory, where they themselves become "high-value targets" with a corresponding demand for protection by other assets. Finally, they must face down additional difficulties from weather and other atmospherics as they attempt to solve the intercept equation.

The mid-course phase has its own unique set of opportunities and difficulties for active defense. It is the longest phase for decision making and actual intercept, but also, under certain conditions, presents some of the greatest obstacles. Among these is how to identify and pinpoint the warhead(s) within the target complex (which can include deployed countermeasures, upper stages, and associated debris) using tracking sensors and interceptors. Most sensors for the midcourse phase therefore will be high-powered ground- or sea-based radars, whose signal characteristics can distinguish specific targets from the clutter of the target complex. At endgame, interceptors, updated by ground- and sea-based sensors, rely on onboard terminal infra-red seekers to engage the identified target against the cold backdrop of space.

In the terminal phase, decoys and debris are stripped away by the atmosphere and the warhead is clearly visible to a range of sensors, simplifying the identification portion of the targeting solution. In this phase, a wider range of weapons may be used, including so-called "near-miss" weapons that use blast-fragmentation warheads as a kill mechanism.[38] Complicating matters, though, are the very short period of time between initial reentry and impact or detonation (especially for high-altitude nuclear bursts), and cross-range, track-angle, and transient speeds that induce major stress on command and control, tracking, and fire-control systems.

The inherent flexibility of BMD forces allows their capabilities to be scaled to the threat, given the set of variables presented by the three phases of flight. Where ICBMs (inter-continental ballistic missiles), for example, present the greatest stress in their general inaccessibility before launch (in either hardened silos or concealed mobile launchers deep in denied territory), ability to lift large payloads of warheads and countermeasures, and the high terminal speeds of their re-entry vehicles, the mid-course phase of flight presents the best opportunity for intercept. Since the flight time for an ICBM is typically fifteen to thirty minutes, it provides an expanded engagement- and corresponding decision-space for intercept. Conversely, for shorter-ranged missiles, defenses are stressed because the engagement- and decision-space are compressed by the tyranny of distance and time, and target numbers that are correspondingly high. At the same time, defenses can take advantage of slower re-entry speeds and a smaller probability of penetration aids owing to payload restrictions on smaller missiles, plus the fact that many such systems remain unitary throughout flight (the warhead remains mated to the airframe, like the SCUD) all of which favors intercept in the mid- and terminal phases of flight. The key for complete coverage is to balance risk and scale capabilities to the threat.

Today, the United States is developing and deploying a BMD system that addresses both the shortfall in defense against short- and medium-range ballistic missiles and the threat posed by nations seeking longer-range missiles.[39] At the end of 2008, the U.S. system consisted of the following elements:

- 26 long-range ground-based interceptors located in silos in Alaska and California;
- 32 standard missile (SM-3) sea-based interceptors;
- 18 Aegis cruisers (3) and destroyers (15) capable of engaging short- and medium-range missiles and performing long-range surveillance and tracking;
- 635 Patriot advanced capability (PAC)-3 missiles;
- A sea-based X-band radar capable of discrimination;
- Upgraded early warning radars in California and the United Kingdom, and an upgraded COBRA DANE radar in Alaska;
- Two forward-based X-band radars (AN/TPY-2 [FBM]) deployed in Japan and Israel, and;
- C2BMC (command, control, battle management, and communications) systems.[40]

This system of systems was declared operational for limited defense purposes in 2006, and has been undergoing a so-called spiral development process, which permits simultaneous deployment and development. Along the way, a number of tests of increasing complexity have registered success for the Aegis, THAAD, and ground-based interceptor components.[41] The inherent flexibility and functional integration of geographically dispersed sensors and mobile interceptor platforms was demonstrated with the successful intercept of a failing U.S. satellite in February 2008. Using radars located in the contiguous United States and Alaska, the United Kingdom, and at sea, along with a specially modified SM-3, the failed satellite's potentially hazardous load of unexpended hydrazine fuel was destroyed just outside of the atmosphere, with little to no persistent orbiting debris generated as a result.[42]

In addition to the U.S. component, there is a significant international piece to the BMD system. To date, the United States has developed international agreements and partnerships with six other nations, including Japan, the United Kingdom, Australia, Denmark, Italy, and the Czech Republic. The extent of the agreements varies depending on the partner country's needs and perceptions. For example, when the Japanese embarked on a defense development program after the 1998 DPRK launch of the TD-1, they leveraged off U.S. assets and technology to develop and deploy land- and sea-based capabilities, including SM-3 interceptors and the Aegis system on Japanese Maritime Self-Defense Force ships.[43] Another example was the proposed European component negotiated by the George W. Bush administration (2001–09), which consisted of a mid-course X-band radar sited in the Czech Republic and a field of ten ground-based interceptors in Poland for the purpose of intercepting ICBMs from Iran bound for Europe or the United States. A mid-2009 assessment by the U.S. intelligence community of the slowly developing long-range ballistic missile threat posed by Iran prompted a decision by the Obama administration to concentrate instead on a phased, adaptive approach dealing with the more immediate medium-range threat using current and proven, cost-effective technology (i.e., the Aegis BMD/SM-3 system).[44]

The key to success—and the challenge—is integration. The nature of BMD is such that a single platform cannot execute the mission by itself. Once sensors are cued, their data pass along a series of "kill chains" that tie in with multiple command and control nodes as well as weapon platforms, knitting together the whole into an effective web of redundant paths and capabilities. The wide range of missile threats generates requirements from BMD systems-of-systems that lend themselves to cooperative or collective defense measures between threatened states at both the bilateral and multilateral levels.

Missile Defense Contributions

The 2006 National Security Strategy of the United States mandated, among many changes, a new way to establish deterrence based on the changed threat environment of the new century.[45] Similarly, the U.S. Navy's "A Cooperative Strategy for 21st Century Seapower," released in 2007, states in its opening lines that: "[W]e believe that *preventing wars is as important as winning wars*."[46] BMD's contribution to securing freedom in and access to the global commons lies chiefly in the role it plays in deterrence calculations, and implicitly in the cooperation its development requires between nations and their respective armed forces.

New Deterrence Calculus

The twenty-first century is clearly emerging as a multi-polar environment whose emerging nodes exhibit varying strengths and weaknesses. While the final form, if indeed one can be defined, is still unclear, what is clear is that the symmetrical offsets that evolved during the Cold War and underpinned deterrence between the United States and Soviet Union will not be present in the foreseeable future. Nowadays, we face a significantly more complex environment with a multiplicity of state and non-state actors, numerous media channels for transmitting intent, and multiple vectors for inflicting varying degrees of harm to individual states or alliances.[47] Operationally deployed, credible missile defenses provide a necessary part of this new deterrence, primarily by (a) helping to deny the desired benefits of, and (b) imposing unacceptable costs on, an aggressor's deterrence calculations.[48]

Regional Stability Enabler

An additional benefit of BMD is the regional stability engendered when the United States and its regional partners and allies undertake joint and combined activities. During the Cold War, the extension of the U.S. nuclear deterrent "umbrella" over the European members of NATO, combined with the presence of U.S. forces on European soil, served as a guarantor of continued U.S. engagement in the region, even when tensions were high. This in turn removed any perceived need on the part of the allied non-nuclear states to obtain nuclear forces of their own.

The credibility of the guarantee, however, was directly tied to the credibility of the U.S. strategic nuclear forces, and a perception on the part of the Soviet Union that the United States would indeed be willing to "trade New York for Moscow" in the event of a nuclear exchange. The slightest variation in either side's forces—whether it was the re-deployment of U.S. missiles back to the United States or the emergence of a new capability like the Soviet SS-20 intermediate-range ballistic missile in the late 1970s—was bound to increase tensions and controversy within the transatlantic alliance.[49] Similar guarantees today may carry less credibility in certain regional conflicts and conditions.

Credible missile defenses, especially those that can be brought to a theater of conflict on sea-based platforms, may serve to supplement, if not supplant, nuclear weapons as a new guarantor of U.S. engagement and support because of the perceived greater willingness to use non-nuclear defenses against a nuclear threat. Indeed, the 2007 Maritime Strategy implies this is a viable course of action:

> Effective Theater Security Cooperation activities are a form of extended deterrence, creating security and removing conditions for conflict. Maritime ballistic missile defense will enhance deterrence by providing an umbrella of protection to forward-deployed forces and friends and allies, while contributing to the larger architecture planned for defense of the United States. . . . We will use forward based and forward deployed forces, space-based assets, sea-based strategic deterrence and other initiatives to deter those who wish us harm.[50]

Still, the demands in terms of training, sensor and network resources, and weapons can be daunting and exceptionally challenging to resource-constrained nations and regions. Nevertheless, adding regional partners to a defense network leverages capabilities, enhancing forward presence and domain security while bringing about improvements via integration and interoperability. Cooperating with partner nations and their forces early in the development process, especially those with common assets, will ensure a common baseline from which to work and build.

Summary and Transition

> "When all else fails—when all the negotiations have broken down, when there is a missile in the air—you have to have the ability to destroy it, because the only other ability that you would have would be to apologize to those that have died."
> Lieutenant General Henry 'Trey' Obering, USAF (retired)[51]

The qualitative and quantitative proliferation of ballistic missiles, and the widespread transition to nuclear or other WMD capability, is one of the most significant dangers to the global commons and to national decision makers in the new century. The advent of credible, conventional ballistic missile defenses, however, provides a means to address this threat. No one nation can go it alone, because of the multitude of threat sectors and delivery vehicles. Thus, cooperation among allies and partners on the development and deployment of missile defense assets is necessary to achieve the full benefits of missile defense.

Nations and their leaders need no longer face a Hobson's choice of escalating conflict or surrender in the face of aggressive action. Effective, credible ballistic missile defenses will provide the means to terminate conflict while protecting and securing homelands, deployed forces, and by extension, access to and use of the global commons.

9 Air Superiority

Mort Rolleston

Emerging Competition in the Air Domain

The first chapter of this book describes how the global commons are rapidly becoming more interwoven and interdependent through new developments in networking, connectivity, and speed. While these developments considerably strengthen the military combat power of the United States and its allies, they also have lowered the bar for state and non-state actors to compete effectively in the commons. This has been especially true in the air domain, the military sphere related to the global common of international airspace.

By connecting and integrating its sensors and shooters in air, space, and cyberspace, the American military, with some of its allies, has revolutionized its ability to achieve and maintain air superiority. At the same time, as the permeability of the outer space and cyberspace commons has grown, potential adversaries are learning to exploit this interdependence to pose new and serious threats to traditional allied superiority in the air domain. In tandem, state competitors are swiftly developing new capabilities that pose direct threats to air superiority. Together, these concerns will likely force the United States and its global partners to dramatically alter how they achieve and maintain air superiority, which is essential to ground and maritime operations.

This chapter briefly summarizes these issues to establish a framework for further discussion and analysis. It first defines and delineates air superiority and the operations necessary to achieve it. It then describes how air superiority greatly depends on space and cyberspace, and why air superiority is, in turn, often essential to the conduct of ground and maritime operations. Following this, the chapter turns to the emerging threats the United States and its allies face over the next decade or two as they work to achieve and maintain air superiority not only within the air domain, but also through preserving key enablers in space and cyberspace. It concludes with a discussion of possible ways to counter or mitigate these threats.

Defining Air Superiority and the Role of Counterair Operations

Freedom of access to, transit through, and the use of the air domain, which consists of the atmosphere up to the point where "air-breathing" vehicles can no longer sustain flight (roughly twenty-eight miles above the earth), requires air superiority. The U.S. Department of Defense (DoD) defines air superiority as "that degree of dominance in the air battle of one force over another that permits the conduct of operations by the former and its related land, sea, and air forces at a given time and place without prohibitive interference by the opposing force."[1]

Per U.S. joint doctrine, offensive and defensive counterair operations "attain the desired degree of air superiority required by the [Joint Force Commander] to accomplish the assigned mission . . . normally . . . as quick as possible."[2] The goal of offensive counterair operations is to "prevent the launch of enemy aircraft and missiles by destroying them and their overall supporting infrastructure prior to employment."[3] This is achieved by: (1) attack operations that target enemy air and missile forces on the surface and their infrastructure; (2) suppressive actions to neutralize, destroy, or degrade surface-based enemy air defense systems;[4] (3) fighter escort in support of air operations; and (4) fighter sweeps to seek out and destroy enemy aircraft or targets of opportunity in a designated area.[5] The goal of defensive counterair operations, in concert with offensive counterair operations, is "to provide an area from which forces can operate, secure from air and missile threats."[6] Defensive counterair operations consist of: (1) active air and missile defense that directly "destroy, nullify, or reduce the effectiveness of air and missile threats against friendly forces and assets";[7] and (2) passive air and missile defenses, which minimize the effectiveness of hostile air and missile threats by such means as detection, warning, camouflage, concealment, deception, dispersion, and protective construction.[8] Since Will Dossel examines missile defense in Chapter 8, this chapter will instead focus on the remaining aspects of joint counterair operations.

While counterair operations are a primary function of the Air Force in the

U.S. military, it is essential to emphasize that, given the importance of air superiority, all services play key roles. The U.S. Army Air and Missile Defense Command focuses on countering adversaries' offensive air and missile capabilities. The U.S. Navy provides fleet air and missile defense as well as theater-wide offensive counterair capabilities. The U.S. Marine Corps conducts counterair operations for its ground forces, as well as for the joint force commander.[9]

In addition to its basic doctrine, the U.S. Air Force articulates how it achieves and maintains air superiority in both its Global Strike (GS) and Global Persistent Attack (GPA) CONOPS (Concept of Operations). As described by the GS CONOPS, "previous strategies have depended on U.S. forces having sufficient time to build up in theater. . . . Potential adversaries may recognize and attempt to exploit this strategy. . . . They are acquiring advanced anti-access systems that threaten to discourage U.S. intervention, fracture coalitions, or prevent coalition forces from operating at desired locations."[10] To counter this, the GS CONOPS states that "in the initial hours of a developing conflict, joint forces will employ low-observable and standoff systems, to execute rapid strike against anti-access targets and/or other HVTs [high value targets] and to 'kick down the door' and gain access to denied battlespace. The advanced capabilities built into the GS CONOPS are designed to allow joint/coalition forces to survive against advanced and/or numerically overwhelming IADS [Integrated Air Defense Systems] at the onset of operations. It will be necessary to attack certain critical targets without waiting for degradation of the air defenses."[11] In turn, the GPA CONOPS discusses how the Air Force will sustain overall air superiority with both advanced air-to-air capabilities and the effective suppression of enemy air defenses in a theater after joint forces achieve initial access through the GS CONOPS.[12]

The key idea to take away from these concepts is that achieving and maintaining air superiority entails much more than just destroying enemy aircraft. It also means taking down enough of the adversary's air defense and ballistic missile systems so that the bulk of joint and allied forces can operate with an acceptable level of risk of attack from the air domain.

Reliance on other Military Domains

Especially since the first Persian Gulf War (August 1990 to February 1991), achieving and maintaining air superiority has increasingly required a combination of capabilities inherent to other military domains, especially space and cyberspace.[13] In part, this is because more counterair operations are conducted through cyberspace, using both computer network attack and electronic warfare to affect enemy command and control systems, air defenses, missile sites, and airfield facilities.[14] Counterair operations are also being more frequently conducted on land, especially though direct special operations and conventional ground force occupation of territory to deny the adversary the ability to hide air defenses or ballistic missiles.[15]

More importantly, allied forces are increasingly able to exploit space and cyberspace to achieve and maintain air superiority through network-centric warfare. For example, current counterair operations and their associated training assume ready access to precision intelligence, surveillance and reconnaissance, (ISR), and virtually unlimited bandwidth—which mostly preside in the space and cyberspace domains. Network-centric warfare is defined as "an information superiority-enabled concept of operations that generates increased combat power by networking sensors, decision makers, and shooters to achieve shared awareness, increased speed of command, higher tempo of operations, greater lethality, increased survivability, and a degree of self synchronization."[16] After experiencing considerable command-and-control difficulties and delays during Operation Desert Storm (1991), the U.S. military aggressively exploited new technology to greatly expand its command-and-control networks, largely through satellites that permit forces to go almost anywhere in theater with the same connectivity they would have within the United States. In addition, the U.S. military has generated new wide-area, but limited access, airborne networks dedicated to particular tasks (such as the NATO standard Link 16). Sensor and communications packages on current platforms are also being used in innovative ways to further improve network-centric warfare. For example, the stealthy F-22A Raptor has significant ISR capabilities in its existing configuration, with much more to come as the APG-77 (V) 2 Active Electronically Scanned Array radar and ALR-94 internal Electronic Support Measures system mature. Fighters are rapidly evolving beyond force application assets to also become very effective C2ISR (command, control, and ISR) platforms that feed a knowledge-based architecture.[17]

This unprecedented networking of sensors, decision makers, and shooters in the air, space, and cyberspace domains has revolutionized allied ability to achieve air superiority and allowed significant reductions in force structure. More specifically, network-centric warfare provides or allows:

- A "first view, first shot, first kill" capability for fighter aircraft;
- Precision navigation and positioning through the Global Positioning

System, plus targeting data to enable accurate strikes by aircraft-delivered precision-guided weapons;[18]

- Secure command and control that is essential for the planning, direction, warning, and deployment of forces (including key support functions such as refueling);

- Joint commanders to strike not only preplanned targets, but also unplanned targets of opportunity that unexpectedly emerge during a mission;[19]

- Unprecedented persistent global awareness, using satellites unconstrained by earthbound geopolitical limitations. In turn, this enhances real-time knowledge of enemy locations and the ability to map terrain, assess battle damage, and collect weather and environmental data;

- Improved survivability of air assets by rapidly detecting, locating, and tracking mobile air defense systems and immediately passing the data to threatened platforms;[20]

- Force Projection (particularly mobility) assets to much more effectively establish and maintain forward air bases and associated agile combat support; and

- Special operations to provide key intelligence on ground targets for air strikes and/or conduct direct action that destroys or disrupts adversary assets.

Indeed, the air, space, and cyberspace military domains have grown so interdependent that for many years the U.S. Air Force advocated the concept that air and space represented "a single and seamless 'aerospace' continuum."[21] In addition, after the stunning success of the integration of space-enabled capabilities with air operations during the first Gulf War, the Air Force took a number of actions to integrate space assets with the larger warfighting community.[22] Recently, the Air Force also amended its mission statement to reflect the importance and interdependency of these three military domains: "The mission of the United States Air Force is to fly, fight and win . . . in air, space and cyberspace."[23]

Air superiority, in turn, is a key enabler of joint and coalition operations on land and at sea, especially in so-called "high-intensity" conflicts. To quote U.S. joint doctrine: "Historically, air superiority has proven to be a prerequisite to success for an operation/campaign because it prevents enemy air and missile threats from interfering with operations of friendly air, land, maritime, space, and special operations forces (SOF), assuring freedom of action and movement."[24] The GS CONOPS adds that air superiority "is essential to sustained warfare and offers protection of friendly forces, enables access to the battlespace, provides freedom to maneuver, restricts adversary intelligence gathering, decision cycles and movement, and empowers the ability to project friendly engaging forces."[25] Many historical examples demonstrate how critical air superiority is to the success of operations.[26] Indeed, since World War Two, most enemy casualties in conventional conflicts have been inflicted from the air.[27]

Rising Threats through the Air Domain

The United States and its allies have enjoyed virtually unchallenged air superiority for many years, in part because they have been involved in operations against adversaries with limited means to challenge that superiority. The threats to air superiority are growing rapidly, however, and are amplified by the reality that, in many cases, adversaries only have to deny air superiority rather than establish it themselves to succeed.

In the air domain, the primary threat comes from so-called integrated air defense systems, which are a combination of fighter aircraft, ground-based tactical and strategic surface-to-air missiles (SAMs), anti-aircraft artillery systems, short-range air defenses, and man-portable air-defense systems that may be guided by infrared or radio frequency methods.[28] Today, there are over fifty nations (double that of ten years ago) that fly so-called fourth-generation fighter jets that are equivalent in performance to America's fourth generation fighters (the F-15, F-16, and F/A-18). These legacy fighters still comprise the bulk of the U.S. force structure and will for at least two more decades, until they are eventually replaced or retired. Non-U.S.-made fourth generation fighters include the Russian-made Su-27 Flanker and MiG-35 Fulcrum F, the Chinese-made Jian-F-10B and Shenyang J-11B, and the European-built Saab JAS 39 Gripen, Eurofighter Typhoon, and Dassault Rafale. Many possess the latest active electronically scanned array radars and beyond-visual-range air-to-air missiles.[29]

Since the 1973 Middle East "Yom Kippur" War, however, the primary battle for air superiority has been between fighters and surface-to-air missile (SAM) systems.[30] Potential adversaries are developing and deploying much-improved, longer range, more mobile, and more electronic-warfare-resistant air defense systems, often referred to as "double-digit SAMs." This new generation of mostly Russian-built SAMs includes the SA-10 (with a range of 49 nautical miles), SA-20 (108 nm), HQ-9 (81 nm), and SA-21 (over 200 nm), as well as the SA-N-20 and HHQ-9 naval SAMs. Currently, eleven nations possess these advanced SAMs, with a twelfth awaiting delivery; at least seven more countries are believed to be seriously interested in obtaining them.[31] SAMs have also become "more mobile and lethal, with some systems demonstrating a 'shoot and move' time in minutes rather than hours or days."[32] Making matters worse, they are easily hidden among non-combatants and in crowded urban environments, or protected in hardened and deeply buried bunkers that are difficult to affect with conventional weapons. As a result, many SAMs "may remain hidden until they actually engage";[33] allies thus require the ability to strike them within a mere five to ten minutes of detection before they are able to hide again.[34] In sum, many analysts believe that most, if not all, fourth-generation fighters are very vulnerable to this new generation of SAMs.[35]

The challenge of achieving air superiority is further complicated if a foe should choose to minimize the use of, and therefore expose to attack, its mobile air defense systems, and/or keep them defensively dispersed. This could potentially deny air superiority, regardless of adversaries' future capabilities. Indeed, during the 1999 conflict in Kosovo, the Serbs did just that. Serbia ended up firing only 800 SAMs at NATO aircraft over the seventy-eight day war, mostly without any radar guidance, and downed only two aircraft. However, "the persistence of a credible SAM threat throughout the Kosovo air war meant that NATO had to dedicate a larger-than-usual number of strike sorties to the SEAD mission to ensure reasonable freedom to operate in enemy airspace. Thus, fewer sorties were available . . . to allocate against enemy military and infrastructure targets. . . ." In addition, NATO had to place high-value ISR platforms in less-than-ideal orbits, and often had to adopt defensive tactics and flight patterns that limited the effectiveness of many sorties. Despite these extensive SEAD efforts, NATO could only confirm destruction of three out of the Serb's estimated twenty-five mobile SA-6 batteries and ten out of forty-one SAM radars.[36]

Beyond the fighter jets and mobile air-defense systems that potential adversaries are procuring, other considerations must be factored into achieving air superiority against a capable enemy, especially in the future. As articulated in a recent RAND Corporation analysis, air superiority requires that, in addition to uninterrupted access to the space and cyberspace domains, allied forces must possess: (1) secure bases within about 500 nautical miles to generate sufficient air sorties; (2) low-observable (often called "stealth") capabilities to penetrate the adversary's air-defense systems; and (3) beyond-visual-range missiles.[37] The

RAND analysts consider it an open question whether the U.S. military and its allies can depend on any of these key enablers of air superiority in the future.

First, most of the areas in which the United States and its allies expect to operate in the future will likely have: (1) limited access to forward bases (for political and/or geographical reasons, especially given the considerable distances inherent to much of Asia and the Pacific region); or (2) forward bases (including aircraft carriers) located in an anti-access environment threatened by evolving ballistic missiles (short-range, intermediate-range, and anti-ship) or cruise missiles (land and air-launched), air-to-ground or air-to-surface strike fighters or bombers, or diesel electric submarines equipped with torpedoes and anti-ship cruise missiles.[38] The lack of an adequate number of bases could hamper generation of the large number of air sorties needed to accomplish many operational objectives during a major conflict.

Second, the value of stealth capability in future conflict is being called into question by emerging sensor technologies, such as those currently being integrated into SA-20 and SA-21 air defense systems, as well as Russian- and Chinese-made fighters.[39] Stealth-type aircraft also have significant maintenance problems that may prevent them from being available in sufficient numbers to prevail against numerically superior foes.[40] Furthermore, most current and planned low-observable aircraft, even if their stealthy characteristics are not countered in the long run, are restricted to a limited combat radius because refueling tankers cannot penetrate heavily defended airspace.

Third, regarding the effectiveness of beyond-visual-range missiles, history shows that during the Vietnam War (1959–1975), the versatile AIM-7 Sparrow air-to-air missile was expected to achieve a 0.70 Pk (probability of kill) but in actual combat demonstrated a dismal 0.08 Pk. As of early 2009, the new-generation AIM-120 advanced medium-range air-to-air missile has demonstrated a 0.59 Pk (seventeen missiles fired for ten kills) only in permissive conditions, against aircraft without operative radars or electronic countermeasures. This raises concerns over the AIM-120's performance against technologically advanced fighters fitted with countermeasures.[41]

Mounting Threats in Other Domains

As described earlier, air superiority has become very dependent on a broad network of sensors, decision makers, and shooters that often reside in or use the space and cyberspace military domains. It is a double-edged sword, however, as those enablers that have revolutionized the ability of allied forces to achieve and maintain air superiority are also vulnerable to attack:

- Computer network attack capabilities in the cyberspace domain threaten the networks and information systems on which air superiority depends.[42]
- Electronic attack capabilities threaten to jam or otherwise disrupt data transmissions to assets in the air and space domain. Obvious key targets include the Global Positioning System, which supports almost every precision weapon and unmanned vehicle for navigation and near-precision targeting, and various satellite communications platforms. This category also includes use of ground-based lasers.
- High-altitude electromagnetic pulses (caused by nuclear detonations in the upper atmosphere) and high-power microwave devices (non-nuclear devices using a special coil component or reactive chemicals) threaten satellites, electrical systems, and microcircuits over thousands of miles (in the case of the former) or electronic equipment in a more limited area (in the case of the latter).[43]
- Anti-satellite weapons using kinetic-kill vehicles, electro-magnetic pulses, directed-energy, radiofrequency, high-power microwave, or micro-satellites will threaten satellite assets.[44]

Unfortunately, defenses against these threats, which are discussed in more detail by Glenn Zimmerman and Steven McPherson in Chapter 6 and Mike Manor and Kurt Neuman in Chapter 7, are quite limited. Establishing effective countermeasures will certainly require significant international agreement and cooperation, given the global scale of these domains and the scope of existing treaty regimes as outlined by James Kraska in Chapter 4.

How to Mitigate Imminent Threats

These growing challenges to air superiority beg the question of how to counter, or at least mitigate, those threats. While various studies and war games suggest some possible answers, most have their own constraints, tradeoffs, and limitations to consider.

Perhaps the most widely discussed alternative solution is to develop a force that can conduct counterair operations from beyond the range of enemy air-defense systems and ballistic missiles, instead of sending mostly short-range fighters from vulnerable forward bases to penetrate air defenses that will more than likely defeat them anyway. Indeed, this proposed solution was the focus of the first U.S. Air Force Future Capabilities Games in the late 1990s, after a 1995 study on future anti-access capabilities delivered alarming findings. Not surprisingly, during the first game in 1998, the alternative force, which possessed a long-range standoff strike capability, performed much better than the planned future force, which was capable only of mostly forward-based short-range strikes. The game also highlighted, however, that such a long-range strike force would require significantly enhanced C4ISR (command, control, communications, computers, ISR) capabilities.[45] Therefore, the second Future Capabilities Game in 1999 compared how an alternative force with target-quality ISR capabilities capable of looking deep into defended airspace would do compared to the baseline force that lacked this ability. Not surprisingly, the game strongly suggested that such "deep look" ISR is indispensable to a long-range, standoff strike force that intends to limit or neutralize an adversary's anti-access capabilities.[46] Many additional independent studies and analyses have reached a similar conclusion about the need to alter the balance between short- and long-range strike assets away from short-range and more towards long-range.[47]

The two Future Capabilities Games succeeded in bringing the issue of standoff warfare to the attention of the senior Air Force leadership and identifying the necessary capabilities (a long-range, standoff strike force with "deep look" ISR) to achieve it. The response, however, has been mixed. The senior leadership did add the term "Global Vigilance" to the Air Force Vision as a critical capability and committed to add more resources to ISR.[48] While the Air Force has spent significantly more on ISR over the past decade, especially for unmanned vehicles, a key ISR enabler, the Space Radar, still faces very significant technological and budget hurdles.[49] In addition, the U.S. Air Force has been hesitant to adjust its force-structure mix between short- and long-range strike assets, although recent budget constraints have forced it to reduce its short-range strike force structure.[50] Until the 2006 Quadrennial Defense Review directed the Air Force to develop a new long-range strike platform (known as the Next Generation Bomber) by 2018, it had not been actively pursuing such capabilities, waiting instead for expected revolutionary technologies to develop by the 2030s that would support a new generation of bombers. The Office of the Secretary of Defense, however, recently proposed to both buy more overall short-range tactical fighters (mostly additional F-35s), and "not pursue a development program for a follow-on Air Force bomber until we have a better understanding of the need, the requirement, and the technology."[51]

Another key component of an effective standoff strike force are extremely fast long-range missiles fired from outside the range of enemy air defenses that can strike designated critical targets before they can hide. The only apparent options in the foreseeable future are either hypersonic missiles (which are expected to travel at least Mach 5) or supersonic (Mach 3) cruise missiles. Hypersonic technology, however, is not expected to become available for at least twenty more years.[52] Supersonic missiles, while technologically feasible, may not be adequate from a time-sensitive targeting perspective. They would take twenty minutes to strike critical targets 500 nautical miles inside an air defense network, while the requirement is to strike mobile targets within ten minutes of detection before they can hide again. Even the twenty-minute timeframe would be under ideal circumstances, in which an adequate number of aircraft were already deployed in the air just outside of the adversary air defense range and had access to enough bases within 1,500 nautical miles.[53]

In addition to its dependence on some combination of the capabilities described above, another key question facing the standoff warfare concept is whether it can strike enough targets from long distance to adequately support joint operations against a major adversary. During Operation Iraqi Freedom (2003), for example, the United States expended nearly 20,000 guided munitions and almost 200,000 non-guided munitions over forty-three days, much of it by short-range fighters that could fly numerous sorties where they had complete control of the air domain.[54] Could so many targets be struck in a cost-effective manner from outside the range of advanced air defenses in the same time frame? One standoff warfare concept would be to have new "arsenal planes" and/or "arsenal ships" loaded with missiles just outside of enemy defenses. Even if such platforms could fire enough missiles to replace short-range fighter sorties, however, the cost might still be prohibitive. Even today's relatively slow standoff munitions are forty to one hundred times more expensive than direct-attack munitions delivered by short-range fighters, and future hypersonic or supersonic missiles would almost certainly be even more expensive by several orders of magnitude.[55] One way to mitigate this issue would be to use only enough standoff munitions to destroy adversary air defenses and ballistic missile threats to forward bases, to then enable short-range fighters to move forward to conduct the bulk of persistent strike operations.

Possible alternatives to long-range, standoff strike missiles would be to deploy expendable unmanned vehicles[56] or autonomous munitions that can penetrate heavily defended airspace from a distance and loiter close to a time-sensitive critical target, striking quickly when the target appears. Some very preliminary forays into this field have been made in recent years. The United States has already armed its first generation of unmanned vehicles, such as the Predator and Reaper, with air-to-ground munitions and used them frequently in operations over the past decade. Their cost, however, has yet to drop to a point at which they will be actually expendable, nor can they survive modern air defenses. The DoD has also begun to develop munitions that can autonomously strike targets if delivered to the general vicinity. The Wide Area Search Autonomous Attack Miniature Munition, formerly known as the Low Cost Autonomous Attack System, is an advanced-technology prototype started in 1998 by the U.S. Air Force and the Defense Advanced Research Projects Agency. To date, its biggest technological hurdle, autonomous target recognition algorithms, appears to have been overcome. The understandable cultural reluctance to remove a human from the decision loop, however, which is necessary for an effective standoff weapon in defended airspace, appears to be threatening its survival. The deployment of enough expendable unmanned aircraft or autonomous munitions to take down advanced air defenses at an affordable price will require further technological advances, not to mention changes to applicable law, doctrine, and international agreements—something that will likely take many years to achieve.

Another possibility might be to take down air defenses through more advanced information operations, especially using computer network attacks. It is far from clear, however, whether advances in these methods will: (1) be adequately capable in the foreseeable future to replace the need for air or missile strikes (the effectiveness of cyber attacks on such targets is arguably maximized when combined with kinetic strikes); and (2) be adequately measurable in terms of battle damage assessment to know whether the attack was successful.

Defeating or mitigating threats to key enablers of air superiority in space and cyberspace are addressed in more detail in other chapters. In very broad terms, maintaining superiority in space will first require effective capabilities that provide situational awareness to determine, for instance, whether damage to a space asset is actually caused by an adversary and, if so, trace the source of the attack. Then, it will likely require a way to either disrupt or destroy the adversary's counterspace capability, or successfully defend against it. Other possible options to mitigate the loss of critical space-based assets include: (1) creating redundancy by moving space-based C4ISR to air-breathing platforms such as aircraft or high-altitude airships, and/or creating backup capabilities on them; (2) developing a significant space response capability, so that damaged space assets could be replaced relatively quickly with new, small satellites; and (3) developing new technology to reduce or eliminate the dependence of counterair operations on space-based assets. Maintaining superiority in cyberspace will require corresponding attribution and attack capabilities within that domain. Given that such capabilities to maintain superiority in space and cyberspace are years from fruition, analysts and planners are exploring ways to adequately conduct joint operations should access to space or cyberspace be denied by a competitor.

Summary

"Since the air, space and cyber domains are increasingly interdependent, loss of dominance in any one could lead to loss of control in all. Thus, superiority and freedom of action—the historically proven predicates of all joint operations, in all warfighting domains—cannot be taken for granted. No modern war has been won without air superiority. No future war will be won without air, space and cyberspace superiority."
General Michael Moseley, Chief of Staff of the Air Force[57]

Superiority in the air domain, a key prerequisite of joint and allied military operations on land and at sea for the foreseeable future, especially in so-called "high intensity" conflicts, is at risk. While the United States and its allies have enjoyed virtually uncontested air superiority in recent decades, that luxury is quickly diminishing due to the development and proliferation of new threats—not only within the air domain, but also toward key enabling assets in space and cyberspace. Countering or at least mitigating these threats will be very difficult, but essential, if the United States and its allies wish to continue using the air domain to support and conduct joint and coalition operations. Future solutions will likely require significant changes in platform design, force structure, and concepts of operations that could, if all else fails, include the conduct of operations without air superiority, and all the resulting challenges that would create.

10 Sea Control

Thomas Bowditch

CONTROL OF THE SEAS—the term itself has almost a magical aura, having been blessed by the figurative father of American naval strategy, Alfred Thayer Mahan.[1] Sea control suggests at once distant access to the riches of foreign trade and near protection from foreign enemies. It has been especially meaningful for great maritime powers, particularly Britain for more than three centuries before the Second World War, and the United States across the decades since. Given the great changes the world has seen over the last quarter century, however, it is reasonable to ask whether our understanding of sea control has changed as well. This chapter will explore sea control within the context of its traditional meaning, and examine how today's security situation has potentially altered our calculus.

The singular characteristic of today's world is globalization, and nothing proves the connectedness of the planet more than the contagious financial meltdown that began in 2007. By the same token, no medium illustrates as aptly as the sea the altered significance of the world's commons in light of intensifying globalization and the ever-changing security situation. What happens in one place on the planet can have immediate repercussions in distant, once inaccessible, corners of a world now washed by the same universal commons. There is an unprecedented global movement of financial instruments such as money, currency value interactions, and the like, but also of goods, information, ideas and, naturally, people. An absolutely essential element of the interconnected global system is free trade among nations, and most of that trade moves by sea.[2]

What has changed today? As the international financial system and the network of interconnected economies, including commerce, become more and more sophisticated, they also provide more targets and become more susceptible to disruptions by hostile actors such as adversarial states, terrorist groups, or non-state actors. The global commons, especially the sea, facilitate the actions of these groups and individuals by giving them a space with limited controls or oversight in which to move around and in which to move things around. In this sense, the sea is the ideal medium, fluid and anonymous. What does control of the sea mean in this new interconnected world, where seafaring is both more useful and more dangerous?

The Meaning of Sea Control

Sea control is a conflict term: it connotes nations at war and the contest over freedom to use the interconnecting medium of the sea as part of a nation's grand strategy for victory. To quote Julian Corbett,

> The object of naval warfare must always be directly or indirectly either to secure command of the sea or to prevent the enemy from securing it. . . . [T]hat the object of naval warfare is to get command of the sea actually connotes the proposition that the command is normally in dispute. It is this state of dispute with which naval strategy is most nearly concerned.[3]

The essence of the matter is the ability to operate at will at sea, or within some specific area of the oceans. In defining sea control there is, as Corbett alludes, an element of conflict; when the sea is uncontested, we do not control it, we simply use it. While fighting in Iraq, for instance, the United States supplied its forces ashore in the Middle East largely from the sea. U.S. Navy Military Sealift Command shipping transited the Atlantic and the Mediterranean, through the Suez Canal and the Red Sea, out into the Indian Ocean, up to the Strait of Hormuz, and finally through the Persian Gulf to Kuwait's ports. Free use of the seas was nowhere contested along this route: no enemy submarines or aircraft threatened the ocean supply lines. Only in the Persian Gulf was there ever any suggestion of war-like hostility, and that came from the sometimes threatening posture of Iran's various naval forces. The re-supply of the war effort in Iraq represents the traditional use of the global commons as a non-sovereign highway, because opponents in Iraq did not have the wherewithal to challenge freedom of maritime transit.

Two important aspects of sea control have remained valid across the changing face of warfare, from the Peloponnesian Wars (431–404 BCE) to the Cold War. First, battle between ships at sea is seldom, if ever, a strategic end in itself. Navies fight at sea, and seek to control this or that patch of the great ocean, for the effect those engagements have on the situation on land.[4] Second, no sea power, however great, ever controls all of the oceans all of the time. Sea control is a transient phenomenon; it is never complete, either geographically or temporally. In war we do not hold the sea as we do the land; we use it and move on. As Mahan observed, "The first and most obvious light in which the sea presents itself from the political and social point of view is that of a great highway."[5] Not all parts of this highway are equally important, nor can any one country hope to control the entirety.

The government of the United States, as much or more than any other state, thinks globally about sea control. With a permanent battle fleet in Northeast Asia and another in the Persian Gulf, and the command structure for a third in the Mediterranean, the U.S. Navy has a right to claim near-global coverage. In addition, American warships routinely transit other important regions such as the Indian Ocean, the Southeast Asian archipelagos with their all-important choke points, and the great expanses of Oceania. More recently, the United States has even kept a naval presence in the Gulf of Guinea and off the coast of South America, areas where the need for sea supremacy is questionable. Still, no one would argue that it holds sway over all the oceans all of the time, nor does it need to. What the United States will not abide is a condition where it must seek any other country's leave to operate as it sees fit on the high seas, to ply its commerce freely in peacetime, and to deploy its warships as needed in wartime.

This is the reason the U.S. Navy will conduct freedom-of-navigation operations when the freedom of the high seas is contested by another power. It was upholding this principle when the Sixth Fleet's carriers clashed with the Libyan air force in the Gulf of Sidra in 1981. Without freedom of the seas, the United States and its Western allies could not have defeated either Germany or Japan in the Second World War.

Sea denial is the flip side of control: one side seeks to deny the use of the sea, or some part of the sea, to be accurate, to its enemy, while sea control is overcoming the enemy's efforts at denial. Denial is never as effective as control, nor is it a war-winning strategy; it buys time and might prevent some attacks, but it does not further strategy or push big objectives forward. In reality, there are only a small number of wartime uses that rely on control of the sea. The sea is used to move things across it, like goods, supplies, people, and equipment, and a part of the sea is also used to move things across the beach, like supplies for friendly forces, as well as some variety of power projection. To put something across a beach requires a port in a benign environment, or a sea base of some description in a hostile environment.[6] This is all the more important as the United States and its allies continue to see their access to forward bases in critical theaters diminish. Sea control is the essential facilitator of maritime power projection. In theory this is fairly simple, yet as will be described in more detail below, what complicates the equation in today's global commons is the evolution of weapons technology.

Another important concept is sufficiency. Total sea control, even in a geographic area of importance, is not always necessary to accomplish the strategic objective for which use of the sea is critical.[7] The corollary for air control is captured in the difference between "air superiority" and "air supremacy." When one side in a conflict enjoys air supremacy, the other side does not fly. When superiority is enough, there will be challenges, but not sufficient to deny the use of the air domain. The same is true at sea. Early in World War Two, the United States helped mount a sea-borne lifeline to Great Britain, without which the lone, embattled island would not have survived. Known as the Battle of the Atlantic, convoy escorts continued throughout the war despite staggering losses.[8] Enough got through to keep Britain alive, and later to carry the war to Berlin. It is interesting to note that while the early phase of the Battle of the Atlantic was clearly a defensive operation whose purpose was to keep enough sea control to supply Britain, once the United States was well engaged in the war, protection of the Atlantic convoys became a strategic engagement that reduced the German U-boat threat enough to allow the Normandy landings.[9] The role of sea control is aptly illustrated here: war in Europe was a land war, but the sea was its crucial enabler. Meanwhile, on the other side of the world, the Pacific was an oceanic theater, and the war there consisted mostly of battles at sea or on island outposts. Still, the final victory required a cruelly chastened Japan to accept its existential helplessness ashore.

Changes in the International System

Myriad changes in the international security system are changing all of the global commons, and the sea in particular. Piracy, terrorism, transnational crime, and the clandestine movements of WMD and other weapons all make the policing of international waters much more than a task for law enforcement. The vastness of the sea lends anonymity to its users, and awareness of the ocean's transient habitation is necessarily limited. Improving that awareness in peacetime is understood to be a function of maritime security; in war it becomes the essential role of intelligence, surveillance, and reconnaissance in sea control.

More recently, the distinction between sea control and maritime security has begun to blur. In the fight against international terrorists and increasingly bold and well-armed pirates, the weapons systems and the tactics, techniques, and practices of war are useful, but it does not require the kind of sea control described above; both kinds of operation fall within the realm of maritime security. For the forces of disorder, smuggling goods or contraband, even the elicit movement of people, by sea does not require controlling the sea, only the temporary use of it—sharing, as it were, Mahan's highway. Interdicting such illicit activities is a function of maritime security as well. Moreover, just as the commons belong to everyone, so the task of maintaining security in ordinary times falls alike to all users of the sea. Maritime powers like China and Japan recognize this when they send warships to the Gulf of Aden to help in the fight against piracy.[10] It is also obvious that these and most other countries have a direct interest in free passage of the sea lanes that carry their oil.

Another distinction that is blurring is the margin between the global commons themselves. Control of the sea, for example, can no longer be assured through ocean-going assets alone. Free use of the air commons, and space and cyberspace as well, is essential to operate effectively at sea, which is more than simply promoting joint operations. It means the sea can no longer be thought of as a discreet medium insofar as security is concerned.

The Evolution of Maritime Strategy

What, therefore, of the future of sea control? There is no question the security environment, and with it allied naval strategy, has changed dramatically since the end of the Cold War. The guiding principles for the operational use of the U.S. Navy at the height of the Cold War were contained in the unpretentiously named *Maritime Strategy*, which was developed through the early 1980s and first published as a classified document in 1984. By the time its third formal iteration was signed in 1985, this document was essentially the strategic blueprint for how the U.S. Navy intended to defeat the Soviet navy.[11] The strategy depended on global maritime superiority over the Soviet navy, integrating offensive operations in the seaward approaches to the Soviet Eurasian homeland with ground operations on the NATO flanks in Europe. It also depended on tying down Soviet naval forces into a defensive posture, to minimize threats to the reinforcement and resupply of Europe, and American allies and forces in Asia, by sea. This was, in short, a sea control strategy.

Everything changed with the collapse of the Soviet Union at the end of the 1980s. This was captured in the 1992 joint U.S. Navy and Marine Corps white paper, ". . . From the Sea," which signaled a shift by the naval services from an emphasis on Cold War-era power *at sea* to the projection of power *from the sea*.[12] The American Navy had come out of the Cold War the undisputed sovereign of the seas, without peer or even serious challenger. The focus in those early post-Soviet years was on the projection of power ashore as part of joint operations, and sea control was assumed, as was the ability to operate unfettered in proximity to potentially hostile coastlines.[13] This offensive power-projection ethic is nicely summed up in the following assertion by a Chief of Naval Operations at the time: "Sea Strike is what we are all about. It is first and most importantly about being on the offensive. It is the ultimate reason we remain forward deployed: To impose the will of our nation on our enemies when all else has failed."[14]

The notion of sea control shifted again with the events of the morning of 11 September 2001, and the Navy, like the rest of the American defense establishment, began thinking in terms of counterterrorism and asymmetric warfare. As the decade progressed, with the United States increasingly distracted in the Middle East, alterations in the international security situation became increasingly evident. The proliferation of better anti-ship missile technology, the rise of a near-peer competitor in China, a resurgent Russia, and the persistence of the global pestilence of terrorism, all combined to bring the U.S. Navy to another crossroads in strategic thinking.[15] The effort to produce the Navy's new strategy began under then-Chief of Naval Operations Admiral Michael Mullen, in 2006. The key concept—that deterrence by promise of punishment had to be understood in broader terms, including how to influence the maritime dimensions of societal conditions that lead to terrorism and insurgencies— found expression initially in the "Naval Operations Concept" and the "Navy Strategic Plan," produced respectively in 2006 and 2007.[16]

This transformed perspective was codified in "A Cooperative Strategy for 21st Century Seapower" (often referred to as the "New Maritime Strategy"), published in October 2007 and signed by the heads of all three U.S. maritime services: the Navy, the Marine Corps, and the Coast Guard.[17] This new strategic approach completes the shift from a narrow focus on power projection to an integrated effort to fold the Navy into the nation's "soft power" capabilities as a counter to the causes of terrorism and revolution, by providing humanitarian assistance and preventing conflict as opposed to waiting until combat becomes the only option.[18]

At the high end of conflict, the "New Maritime Strategy" also returns the Navy to a sea control emphasis:

> Critical to this notion is the maintenance of a powerful fleet—ships, aircraft, Marine forces, and shore-based fleet activities—capable of selectively controlling the seas, projecting power ashore, and protecting friendly forces and civilian populations from attack.[19]

In fact, the strategy calls for regionally concentrated, forward-deployed task forces with the combat power to do three things: limit regional conflict, deter major war, and win an undeterred war as part of a joint or combined force. The strategy is specific enough to identify the Western Pacific and the Persian Gulf as areas in which U.S. naval combat power will have a permanent presence.

Sea Control Remains Key

Sea control is once again central to the U.S. Navy's strategy for major war fighting. The United States, with its allies, will always fight its wars as far forward as possible, and control of the sea lines of communication is an essential prerequisite for serious fighting abroad. The in-place network of overseas bases the United States once relied on, however, has been largely dismantled since the end of the Cold War as the U.S. military has withdrawn from its forward posture of containment.[20] What this means, among other things, is that when allied countries seek to project serious power ashore in some future hostile land, they will more than likely do it from the sea. Control of the sea will be essential if a protracted conventional war is fought with a major state, and a dominant blue-water navy—to protect the critical sea lines of communications, escort trade, and contest challenges to freedom of navigation—remains vital to free and orderly use of the sea in an increasingly dangerous and crowded world.

In the traditional sense of sea control as described earlier, the United States is without peer. In a recent speech, the U.S. Secretary of Defense described the

U.S. Navy's battle fleet, in terms of tonnage, as being larger than the next thir-teen navies of the world combined.[21] In a future war, the increased lethality of ship-borne anti-aircraft defenses will likely make the modern nuclear attack submarine at least as important to offensive control of the high seas as the air-craft carrier was in the Pacific in 1943. Again, to quote "A Cooperative Strategy for 21st Century Seapower": "There are many challenges to our ability to exer-cise sea control, perhaps none as significant as the growing number of nations operating submarines, both advanced diesel-electric and nuclear propelled."[22] This is the reason the U.S. Navy has recently increased its emphasis on antisub-marine warfare.[23] It is also why the U.S. Navy's battle fleet continues to empha-size both aircraft carriers for power projection, of which there are eleven, and nuclear-powered attack submarines for offensive sea control, at a total of fifty-two.[24] For comparison, Russia and China operate a combined total of twenty-three nuclear subs. As Secretary Gates' assessment of tonnage indicates, the U.S. Navy outweighs any combination of possible competitors in terms of large cruisers, guided missile destroyers, and smaller frigates. The big fleet paradigm has a distinguished pedigree. For centuries, navies ranked themselves by sheer power, ship-to-ship match-up, weight of capital warships, number and caliber of guns, and overall destructive capacity, on the assumption that one day in some future conflict, the navies of the world's principal powers would meet at sea for a winner-take-all slugfest. Although such decisive naval confrontations have occurred throughout history, from Athens' defeat of Persia at Salamis in 480 BCE to the Battle of Midway in 1942, fleet-to-fleet engagements on the high seas are not likely to characterize warfare in the future.

The Extremities Fray: The High End

We are entering an era in which fleets will find themselves matched against asymmetric threats, both at the "high end," where adversaries launch anti-ship missiles from sea or shore while their targets are still hundreds of miles over the horizon, or at the "lower end," nearer the shore, where mines and swarms of deadly little boats and in-shore rocket launchers can overwhelm larger, more capable ships. At these two ends of the spectrum, allied superiority may no longer be certain. More likely than a war with a peer competitor nation that has a sophisticated blue water navy is a limited engagement over a specific flash point, in which allies seek to project power over an adversary's beach, or into the littoral waters close aboard an adversary's coast. This is most likely to happen in either of the two regions singled out for continuous naval presence in the "New Maritime Strategy," the Persian Gulf and the Western Pacific.

What does the spread of sophisticated anti-access weaponry, designed to keep power projection forces well back from the coast, mean for claims of allied sea control? In the 1990s and into the early years of the following decade, naval planners appeared confident that planned capabilities for countering the maritime anti-access threat would be sufficient to overwhelm emerging enemy systems, and allow the future operation of sea bases in relative proximity to an enemy's coast. This was at a time when the sea base was envisioned to lie fairly close, no more than twenty-five to one hundred fifty nautical miles off the enemy coast. The primary threat at the time was understood to be anti-ship cruise missiles, which the Navy anticipated destroying at the launch site with its own missiles, or defeating after launch, either with surface-to-air missiles or terminal defenses of one kind or another.[25]

In the early years of the twenty-first century, U.S. maritime strategy continued to assume the Navy had the technology to assure it access to the world's oceans, and to those littoral regions in which it might need to project power across a hostile shore.[26] A main pillar of "Naval Power 21," the sea services' strategy in 2002, sums up the prevailing wisdom about getting close enough to an adversary to make a difference: "*We assure access.* Assuring sea-based access world-wide for military operations, diplomatic interaction, and humanitarian relief operations. Our nation counts on us to do this."[27] Note the similarity of intent, if not in tone, in the following statement from the "New Maritime Strategy" of 2007:

> In times of war, our ability to impose local sea control, overcome challenges to access, force entry, and project and sustain power ashore, makes our maritime forces an indispensable element of the joint or combined force. . . . Reinforced by a robust sealift capability that can concentrate and sustain forces, sea control and power projection enable extended campaigns ashore.[28]

That level of confidence does not appear evident anymore among most fleet planners. Among emerging anti-access threats, the anti-ship missile seems most immediate. The Chinese, as the most serious example, are developing a medium-range ballistic missile equipped with maneuverable reentry vehicles (MaRVs) capable of steering the warhead after reentry, and with the ability to "recognize" the outlines of an aircraft carrier. This technology, in development since at least 2006, apparently makes use of the CSS-5 ballistic missile airframe (range in excess of 1,500 km), includes a mid-course target update, and has terminal geo-locating guidance for the warhead.[29] The missiles would be incorporated into a broad-area maritime surveillance and targeting system that includes very powerful over-the-horizon radars, and takes advantage of the electro-magnetic emissions of the carrier.[30] This medium-range networked anti-ship ballistic missile system represents a remarkable asymmetric attempt to control the sea from the shore.[31]

Such technology is by no means easy to achieve, but if the Chinese can get there so can others and it will change the sea control calculus dramatically.[32] China's interest in developing such weapons is essentially defensive. The Chinese seek to keep third parties, such as the United States and its allies, out of their coastal and near-island areas, so they are free to address territorial issues like Taiwan on their own terms, if need be. The U.S. military's assessment is that improvements in Chinese weaponry, such as anti-ship missiles, as well as investments in foreign-made systems, are actually changing the military balance in East Asia.[33] During the Vietnam War (1961–1975), the U.S. Navy enjoyed complete freedom on Yankee Station, the uncontested waters of the South China Sea from which American carriers bombed North Vietnam. More recently, U.S. carriers have operated unopposed in the Persian Gulf and North Arabian Sea off the coast of Pakistan, flying sorties into Iraq and Afghanistan in support of coalition operations. It has been a long time since a blue water navy has had to fight its way to an enemy's shores.

There would seem to be two choices for an offensive navy when confronted by long-range, land-based anti-ship weapons: avoid or defeat the shore-launched missiles while operating from the sea base, or stay out of harm's way altogether. On the one hand, a greater standoff range allows better maneuver, an open ocean where decoys can be used and surveillance avoided, and more time for disrupting the missile's targeting solution. On the other hand, however, standing well out from shore puts vulnerable attack airplanes a long way from the relative safety of the ship, of necessity reduces their weapons payload, and can require extensive refueling by the carrier strike group. When the mission is power projection, the launch platforms have to come to within some reasonable distance of the enemy shore.

Admiral Horatio Nelson famously warned, "A ship's a fool that fights a fort." What he meant was that a ship was foolish to stand off from the shore, in range of the long guns of a fortress, and slug it out. The fort could always take much more damage than the wooden ship of Nelson's era. Naval strategist Wayne Hughes suggests that the missile threat in this century can be addressed by maneuver: the fleet "must exploit the longstanding advantage of operational maneuver from the sea in such a way that the forces ashore will be a day late and a salvo short."[34] While maneuver, speed, deception, and more will all be used by any prudent commander, it seems clear that the source of the missile itself will need to be addressed. Given the range of, for example, a Chinese CSS-5, however, it is unlikely to be the current generation of carrier aircraft that does the addressing.[35] Allied forces will need the synergism of multi-service contributions to control this corner of the global commons. Air Force bombers could go after the missile launch sites before launch, provided targeting and intelligence about intent were sufficiently nuanced. Timing would be everything in this, especially since at least some of these missile launch systems are mobile. Also important will be networked battle geometry, meaning the ability of widely separated but interconnected elements of a battle force to be mutually supportive and reinforcing in their effects.[36]

In short, foolish though allied forces may be to fight a fort, maintaining freedom of the seas in the future will require joint forces, spearheaded by naval forces, to reach out and touch the land. This is another example of the blurring of the commons and the loss of the luxury of one-service offense and defense within a chosen corner of the global commons.

The Extremities Fray: The Low End

At the other, "lower" end of the anti-access spectrum, there is the matter of fighting a smaller, coastal navy that deploys asymmetric capabilities such as small, fast missile boats and small, quiet submarines designed to overwhelm larger capital ships. Just as at the higher end of this sea control spectrum, it is the possible need to project power over a hostile shore that could bring allies into conflict with a smaller coastal navy. There are a growing number of nations that operate more and more sophisticated submarines. Given the importance of the Arabian Gulf to many nations' energy security and other interests, and the open hostility of the government of Iran toward many Western nations, Iran's naval and other forces can serve as a good illustration of a low-end, asymmetric coastal threat. In addition to three Russian-built Kilo-class diesel-electric subs and a number of midget submarines, the Iranian Navy operates one destroyer, a small number of frigates and corvettes, and some twenty to twenty-five missile craft, mostly the French-designed Combattante II. Also of significance to sea control in the Gulf, Iran operates more than a hundred light patrol and coastal combatants. Iran's missile craft mount a number of sophisticated anti-ship sea-skimming missiles (mostly Chinese-built or based on Chinese designs) equipped with inertial navigation systems and ranges that are considerable for combat in the littorals.[37]

The threat from Iranian anti-ship cruise missiles, launched either from fast patrol boats or from shore installations, is significant in itself, but that threat is compounded by asymmetric tactics such as so-called "swarming." In this scenario, numerous small, rocket- and missile-armed patrol boats, referred to as fast inshore attack craft, would attack much larger, slower warships, overwhelming their close-in defense systems. In addition to the Aegis radar system, current plans for combating such threats include using the Hellfire missile coupled to a radar detection and laser illumination system.[38] Naval helicopters armed with Hellfire can extend the range of defenses. The U.S. Navy is busy now experimenting with new tactics, techniques, and procedures for countering swarm threats. A key element in responding to the challenge will be an increased dependence on air and sea coordination demanding the close integration of multiple service platforms. Iran also possesses a significant number of mines, many of which are much more powerful than those used effectively inside the Gulf during the so-called "tanker wars" in the 1980s.[39] Sophisticated counter-mine tactics are being developed based on combinations of high resolution sonar, video systems, and remote control mine detonating devises. The U.S. Navy will also rely on new classes of ships, including the recently fielded Littoral Combat Ship, to defeat the range of low-end, asymmetric coastal threats.

In an all-out contest in the Gulf, there can be little question how the fight would come out. During the above mentioned "tanker wars," the U.S. Navy swept the Iranian Navy from the Gulf with little difficulty.[40] Here, as at the high end, the option of standing off has appeal, given that small coastal navies suffer from restricted range and endurance. The problem is when some essential requirement, such as escorting friendly merchants or clearing mines, drives navies into range of the asymmetric enemy. Iran has continued to improve its arsenal of in-shore weapon systems, missiles, mines, submarines, and fast boats, and although the conventional superiority of allied naval forces would no doubt prevail, the contest would be costly. Reducing that cost will require both innovations in tactics and new technologies, and an increased reliance on coordinated operations and training with allied partners, who can contribute platforms such as minesweepers and smaller, but fast and well-armed vessels in the corvette class.

Conclusion

To reiterate, there are only two uses of the sea in war—moving things over the water and sending things over the shore. It is the evolution of anti-access weapons and techniques, medium-range networked anti-ship missile systems at the high end and asymmetric small platforms and swarm tactics at the low end, that threaten to prevent the essential functions of sea control.

The U.S. Navy, with its allies, can no longer assume it controls the oceans of the global commons, especially at the ends of the sea control spectrum. Allied naval forces are probably more vulnerable at the high end due to the emerging medium-range anti-access and area-denial threat from ballistic missiles. At either extremity, the difficulty will be getting close enough to an unfriendly coast to make a difference. Solutions will depend on a combination of technology and tactics as well as an understanding of the interdependence of the global commons. Joint training and operations that integrate disparate but contributory capabilities will also be essential, if allies really mean to both control the sea-lanes where they need them and project power when they have to.

PART III
THINKING ACROSS COMMONS

11 Leadership for Complexity and Adaptability

Sandra M. Martínez

Introduction

The interconnectivity of global actors, realized by continual interactions between and among individuals, teams, networked groups, organizations, and nations, has qualitatively changed the world and, by extension, the strategic environment in which we operate. The 2008 Joint Operating Environment report acknowledges this quality of the environment in its language: "There is one new watchword that will continue to define the global environment for the immediate future—interconnectedness."[1] Information and communication technologies have accelerated globalization, whereby goods, labor, capital, information, and knowledge flow through the media of the global commons, with relatively little interference.

In contrast to predictions that globalization would bring about a global convergence of culture, however, it has instead driven cultural and national groups to become increasingly reflexive about their own culture and identity in relationship to those of others.[2] The dynamics of the global environment are complex. From the interaction of agents (whether individuals, teams, networks, organizations, or nations), novel higher-level systemic patterns and structures emerge whose properties and capacities cannot be predicted by knowledge of the individual components of a system.[3]

Different institutions have coined various terms to refer to these types of natural and social systems that operate beyond equilibrium, with the capacity to learn, adapt, and evolve. The Santa Fe Institute, which has been a nexus of inquiry into complexity science and emergent principles, calls them "complex adaptive systems."[4] John Holland, a pioneer in nonlinear systems, described such a system as a dynamic network of many agents functioning in parallel, constantly acting and reacting to what the other agents are doing: "[T]he control of a complex adaptive system tends to be highly dispersed" and decentralized. "If there is to be any coherent behavior in the system, it has to arise from competition and cooperation among the agents themselves."[5] The overall behavior of the system is the result of a huge number of decisions made every moment by many individual agents based on their internal models of the world.

The interconnected global environment, characterized by interactions among many players with access to information at every moment, offers great opportunities for learning, innovation, collaboration, and the creation of wealth; yet at the same time, by its very nature it is unpredictable, uncertain, volatile, and rich with possibility for actors to leverage the same assets to destructive ends. How, then, can a society leverage the constructive elements of newer technology and the environment to gain a competitive advantage for itself and its allies, as well as advance the common good? Part of the solution might lie in leadership that influences the behavior of individuals, groups, and larger social entities to interact in configurations and patterns that encourage learning, collaboration, adaptation, and innovation. But what patterns of collaboration and competition characterize an effective team, a collaborative project or mission, an organization, or a society? And, significantly, how do we educate and support civil and military leaders to develop and exercise capabilities to engage constructively in this environment?

This chapter argues that sustaining competitive advantage and working toward the common good in this dynamic global environment that depends on the global commons require a new paradigm of leadership. It will not attempt to answer all of the foregoing questions, but rather to build a framework from which to approach them. A major tenet of this paradigm, which draws from constructive development theory, is that human development is more than simply acquiring new information, knowledge, or skills, but rather represents qualitative changes in how we interpret our experience, structure knowledge, and make sense of the world.[6] Foundational to this new paradigm of leadership is an understanding of social processes that enable the emergence of higher-level capabilities in order to respond effectively to the complexity of twenty-first-century challenges.

This new paradigm, however, encompasses more than simply identifying a different set of leadership capabilities. This approach understands these capabilities to be applicable in social entities of various scales, from individuals to work teams, business units, networked groups, and organizations, from cities to nation-states and world economies. These higher-level capabilities and this understanding of social reality are not unrelated to each other, in that many of the capabilities involve acknowledging the complexity and interrelatedness of agents and systems. This is a challenging notion because social science theories that influence our everyday understanding of reality, and thus our behavior, have generally advocated perspectives that favor one level of analysis or social entity over another, e.g., assuming the individual and individual action at the "micro" level satisfactorily explain behavior, as opposed to structural or more macro explanations, or vice-versa.[7]

An example of a reductionist explanation that favors the individual is the leader as "hero or scapegoat." From this perspective, the success or failure of a project or venture is explained primarily or solely by the mental framework and/or behavior of the leader, to whom the powers of prediction and control are attributed, whether consciously or not. These assumptions are embedded in most conventional theories of leadership. If the project succeeds, the leader is a hero; if the project does not meet the objectives, the leader becomes a scapegoat.[8] This perspective does not consider other explanations for success or failure at the intermediate and more macro levels of social reality, e.g., teams, interpersonal networks, organizations, and societies. Furthermore, not examining how social entities at multiple levels contribute to outcomes can lead to an illusory grasp of reality, miscalculation of actual levels of control, missed opportunities for shaping the environment, and accepting an unrealistically high or low level of risk. The perspective put forward in this chapter does not deny the influence and contributions that individual leaders make to successful outcomes for projects, missions, and organizations. It simply places individuals as a social entity in a larger perspective that more closely approximates reality, considers explanations from multiple levels of reality, and accounts for the emergent properties of systems whereby the interaction of parts of a whole create the properties of the whole.

Properties of a whole "are the result not of an aggregation of the components' own properties but of the actual exercise of their capacities. These capacities depend on component properties but cannot be reduced to them since they involve reference to the properties of other interacting entities."[9] With regard to an example in the global commons, non-state rogue actors on the high seas frequently act in informal networks whose structures may adapt to perceived threats and whose allegiances may migrate depending on changing circumstances. Our generally accepted understanding of social reality may not be sufficiently complex to capture the actual behavior of these types of social entities; we should therefore support the development of a strategic understanding of the interrelatedness of multiple entities and systems, especially among emergent and formal leaders. Furthermore, as much of the work of maintaining the security of the global commons could be identified as "systemic intervention," that is, purposeful action to create change, it is in our best interests to bring to bear all our collective physical, intellectual, social, and spiritual assets to further the common good.[10] In fact, the global commons, because they represent a context in which collaboration is required and sovereignty is shared, is the space that may offer the greatest opportunities for developing leadership models that are responsive and productive in an interdependent world.

This chapter discusses the need for co-existing models of leadership—formal, emergent, and shared[11]—as well as the complex leadership capabilities required to effectively meet the competing challenges of the global commons. Three short cases follow that illustrate leadership at different levels: 1) the individual leader with a formal role collaborating with groups representing multiple and diverse organizations, 2) the interactions among representatives of several nations developing collaborative structures and processes to address a common challenge, and 3) institutional change at the national level. Comments following each case highlight what can be learned both in terms of the existence and effectiveness of the co-existing models (explained below), as well as to what degree the case supports or disconfirms the veracity of the complex leadership capabilities associated with the new leadership paradigm. The first case discusses the experience of Rear Admiral Michael LeFever, when he served as director of all U.S. military elements participating in disaster relief after the massive 2005 earthquake in Pakistan. Next, the case of the cooperative mechanism developed for the Malacca and Singapore Straits demonstrates an international collaborative agreement that codifies governance and shared responsibilities among nations. Finally, the chapter considers the case of China, whose response to the availability and use of a broad spectrum of the electromagnetic field for defense transformed the country's military strategy. The author closes the chapter with recommendations for leadership education and some remarks on the role of leadership in the future.

Co-existing Models of Leadership

From the perspective of complexity science, the global environment consists of overlapping and intersecting complex physical, biological, and social systems that respond and adapt to internal and external conditions. These systems are not symmetrically nested within one another to build a seamless whole, but rather can interact as discreet structures or systems within systems, with permeable and changeable boundaries. Organizations adapt by seeking a constructive balance between exploitation and exploration to guide their decisions, a process that may or may not be deliberate. This method applies to social entities both larger and smaller than the organization, from the team to more macro collectives including the state and society, as well as international consortia consisting of multiple organizations or nations.

Within complex adaptive systems, an agent is an individual person or a group of individuals possessing a dominant purpose.[12] Emergent leadership arises from agents exercising their capabilities, and from interactions from which emerge novel structures, patterns of influence, and information flows that will allow the organization to adapt to the environment and respond to challenges as they develop. Within this churn of change, power relationships shift among agents over time. Ashby's law of requisite variety states that all living things must respond with sufficient heterogeneity to the variety of the environment in order to survive, while simultaneously making selective decisions about which capabilities to develop and which responses to choose, so that they do not waste resources.[13] This law applies equally to social systems.

Because of the paradoxical requirements for both efficient exploitation of existing capabilities and the need to invest in new capabilities, several leadership models must exist simultaneously within a social entity. First is the hierarchical type, the traditional model of formal leadership that efficiently orchestrates a centralized effort to exploit resources. Second is emergent leadership that arises from the interaction between agents, and which can exercise new and otherwise dormant capabilities to meet present and future challenges. A third leadership response, that of shared leadership, co-exists with formal and emergent leadership. It describes the patterns of exchange and relationships characterized by sharing power that often arise among team members.[14]

There is an inherent tension among these different models of leadership. Although this dilemma cannot be resolved with edicts from the top down, a formal leader can choose to build and/or support a culture or environment that encourages patterns of interaction that lead to emergent leadership and can engage in shared leadership. Viewing leadership in this way can help dispel the notion that leadership is necessarily embodied in one individual, in favor of an understanding of "leadership as a dynamic process where several forms of leadership (formal, emergent, shared) co-exist and co-evolve."[15]

Operation Lifeline:
Disaster Relief after the 2005 Earthquake in Pakistan

Although leadership is exercised at many levels within the hierarchy of a social system, and the process of social interaction results in several possibilities for leadership, the quality of leadership demonstrated by individuals continues to contribute to successful outcomes. Rear Admiral Michael LeFever, in his role as the chief of U.S. military activities during Operation Lifeline in Pakistan, is an example of a formal leader who is mindful of the legitimacy and the contributions of many individuals, teams, and other organizations to the success of the mission. The length of this chapter does not allow a comprehensive analysis of how LeFever's perspective and actions meshed with the contributions of these other entities, but such an analysis would be useful for an integral understanding of the interrelationship of all the systems and entities that contributed to the success of this operation.

On 9 October 2005, the day after the 7.6 magnitude earthquake struck Pakistan, most of the world was unaware of the scope and scale of the devastation to the remote North West Frontier and Kashmir regions of Pakistan, in the high, extremely rugged and mostly inaccessible foothills of the Himalayas. Initial estimates of 18,000 dead appeared exaggerated, but as the Pakistani government began to realize that the damage far exceeded its original estimates, President Pervez Musharraf asked for assistance from the United States. Within forty-eight hours, Admiral LeFever of the Pentagon's Combined Disaster Assistance Center and William S. Berger, a regional advisor with the United States Agency for International Development's (USAID) Office of Foreign Disaster Assistance, were in Pakistan. LeFever was asked to undertake the initial assessments and assume leadership of all U.S. military forces, many of which were disengaged from combat and stability operations in Afghanistan and others from units in Germany, the United States, and Japan as well. This event would turn out to be the worst natural disaster the Pakistani people had ever faced; final estimates were that 73,000 to 75,000 people died as a result of the earthquake.

U.S. military personnel worked collaboratively as a team with USAID to assist the Pakistani government in many ways. Engineers were sent to oversee the clearing of the rubble, including the debris blocking roadways into the two major valleys of the region. Heavy equipment such as backhoes, dump trucks, and bulldozers arrived by sea. Because most of the hospitals and medical units in the affected region had been destroyed, a MASH (Mobile Army Surgical Hospital) unit was sent into the worst-affected area, and was completely set up within a month of the earthquake, while a second hospital was erected in the adjacent province. Meanwhile, multiple sorties flew in daily to the affected areas to deliver relief supplies and take out injured Pakistanis. Before the end of the mission, which at six months had lasted longer than any previous U.S. relief effort, U.S. civilian and military personnel would attend to 34,914 injured Pakistanis, fly 5,204 relief missions, evacuate 3,782 injured Pakistanis, deliver 14,831 tons of humanitarian aid, and build 56 "seahuts" (temporary shelters from salvaged materials) and several schools. Yet, as attested to by LeFever and in testimonials by U.S. and Pakistani officials, one of the most powerful legacies of the mission was the friendships that were built.[16]

In e-mail correspondence with Admiral LeFever after this experience, he emphasized the important role of collaboration and trust-building among all the players. In his own words:

[F]or the U.S. team, it was unity of command with a common mission and a highly collaborative campaign plan. In real terms, the U.S. military and USAID aligned under the U.S. Ambassador to Pakistan, as the President's representative, and we agreed on a common mission: to provide humanitarian relief and improve US-Pakistani relations. Playing to the organizational strengths we each brought to the table—aligning diplomacy and policy with U.S. military where-withal and capacity with USAID's relief experience—we collectively forged the campaign plan that made it explicit who would handle what and how we would interact and work together. Collaboration among the agencies was a key to the success of this project. . . . There was a huge team-building role to my work to ensure that we capitalized on all contributors. . . . I learned a lot about the critical importance of relationship-building as a central tenet of leadership and to building productive working partnerships. . . . My leadership philosophy is based, in large part, on effective communication and feedback—of goals, expectations of performance, mission alignment, clear standards of accountability and responsibility, and two-way communication in well-defined channels.[17]

LeFever's leadership in this mission demonstrates several capacities that appear to be vital for the effective leadership of complex operations in a dynamic, uncertain, and volatile environment of the global commons. To effectively lead, cooperate with and, in general, work productively with a broad range of players, LeFever had to be able to accept and appreciate the multiple perspectives, mind-sets, and value systems with which others approached their work, and also have the capacity to bring these disparate groups together to achieve constructive outcomes. The level of adaptability he demonstrated points to a high level of cognitive complexity; that is, he has a sufficiently complex cognitive framework and related set of behavior patterns (a later stage action-logic[18]) to respond effectively to very diverse types of situations and challenges.

The capacity to collaborate, share power, accept new ideas, and work inclusively and effectively with agents representing different positions and points of view, is critical for success in complex environments. An ability to be profoundly aware of and frequently reassess one's own assumptions is a prerequisite for these sorts of capacities and level of leadership. Additionally, an understanding of the interrelationship of social systems and the learning process also contributes to successful leadership. The following list of capabilities[19] reflects the qualities leaders need if they are going to respond successfully to challenges in the global commons.[20] The case of Admiral LeFever's strategic leadership supports this model.

1. *Sufficient cognitive agility* to reconcile multiple and diverse mental frameworks.[21] Especially in the arena of national security, it is necessary to tolerate and strive to understand individuals and groups of people who have very different values and assumptions about reality.

2. *Sufficient cognitive complexity* to respond and adapt to diverse and changing environmental and internal stimuli. From the perspective of complexity, individuals, teams, organizations, and societies must have enough variety in their cognitive frameworks to be able to adapt to a range of circumstances. A subset of the capability is a high degree of self-awareness, which will enable the entity (whether an individual, organization, or society) to identify the assumptions being brought to a particular setting, and to understand the limits of their application.[22]

3. *A worldview consistent with complexity.* This ability is demonstrated by a willingness to embrace uncertainty and change as opportunity, to learn from diverse points of view, and to tolerate differences.[23]

4. *Willingness to accept mutual feedback and power sharing.* In a world where many have access to information and knowledge, it behooves even the most powerful agent (whether among systems of individuals, teams, organizations, or nations) to share power in order to draw from the resources of many, to learn more readily, and to successfully influence others to join in a larger collaboration for the common good.[24]

5. *An ability to recognize emergent patterns* in both social and physical systems.[25] In an increasingly complex and uncertain world where it is hard to predict and control events, and where the ability to influence and shape future conditions is our lever for constructive action, it is important to recognize patterns of behavior as they emerge.

6. *The flexibility to harness collective intelligence* by working in an inclusive, collaborative way. Effective leaders grow communities of trust by encouraging conversation, building the means to share information, and supporting mutual understanding.[26]

7. *An understanding of the social and cognitive processes that underlie learning.* A leader who understands how learning takes place will better be able to make decisions that support knowledge management—both the exploration and exploitation of ideas—to reach the organization's stated shorter-term goals and longer-term strategic objectives.[27]

8. *The presence of mind to maintain perspective from multiple temporal realities concurrently.* This is the capacity to be aware of and responsive to the present, while simultaneously maintaining an active awareness of how the past is influencing the present, as well as the possible consequences of current actions in the future.[28]

In terms of the three co-existing models of leadership—formal, emergent, and shared—Admiral LeFever's experience in coordinating Operation Lifeline illustrates patterns of interaction that run across social levels from the individual to the collective, as many diverse participants in the relief effort formed networks of influence that worked not only to respond to immediate needs, but also built relationships and capacity for the future. LeFever, as the formal leader of U.S. military operations, provided longer-term coherence and focus to the mission, yet at the same time, he and his team were able to share leadership with other teams representing many different groups. These teams exchanged information, made sense of the dynamic situation collectively, and to some degree made collaborative decisions. Success at this level of complexity also requires emergent leadership, whereby different leaders arise to take charge of different tasks dependent upon their competencies and qualities. Formal leaders working in these types of operations need to understand the dynamic complexity of social processes and the importance of collaboration, as well as support the emergent properties of the leadership process, as did LeFever.

The Co-operative Mechanism
for the Straits of Malacca and Singapore

The development of what is known as the Co-operative Mechanism as a framework for governance of the Straits of Malacca and Singapore represents a milestone in international maritime collaboration among the littoral states, users of the Straits, and other stakeholders with interests in this region. The framework emerged from years of collaborative dialogue among the three littoral states that border the Straits (Indonesia, Malaysia, and Singapore), working with the International Maritime Organization and its Secretary-General, Efthimios Mitropolous. Participants at the inaugural meeting in Singapore included representatives from major shipping and trading nations such as China, Japan, the United States, Germany, and Greece, as well as major trade organizations such as the International Chamber of Shipping and the International Association of Independent Tanker Owners. Launched in September of 2007, the Co-operative Mechanism offers collaborative arrangements within which participants can "exchange views, jointly undertake projects or make direct monetary contributions, via a regular platform for dialogue, a committee to co-ordinate and manage specific projects, and a Fund to receive and manage direct financial contribution for sustainability."[29]

This agreement was seen by many to reflect the commitment of the Straits' stakeholders to work cooperatively to address mutual concerns about navigational security, access, and environmental protection. As emphasized earlier, the highly interrelated quality of the global environment presents new challenges, especially to maritime safety and security. The problems of drug and human traffickers, terrorism, the proliferation of weapons of mass destruction, piracy, and hijacking tend to flourish in the progressively more congested global waterways. Some analysts identify the creation of social mechanisms and technological and political platforms to maintain global maritime domain awareness as the next critical step for improving maritime security and safety for all stakeholders.[30] Such an initiative involves gathering data on patterns of traffic and the characteristics of those using the seas and waterways, collectively "making sense" of the findings—that is, giving meaning to the patterns of behavior and changes in these patterns—and then acting on them.

The technological capacity exists to gather, pool, and process the data; to achieve a functional system, however, long-standing tendencies to mistrust and resist sharing information and knowledge, among both state and commercial users, must be overcome. Stakeholders also must be willing to develop and share their expertise in the area of data analysis, for example, create algorithms to separate real threats from false alarms, and develop threat evaluation matrices and anomaly detection processes. The high seas are vast in scale and scope, and such a system would require a high level of collaboration to achieve a real-time picture of the global flows of traffic along the world's oceans. This system will also require higher-level leadership capabilities.

The high levels of collaboration required to support the maritime security initiative call for leaders with broad capacities for sharing information, knowledge, and power, and the disposition to give and receive feedback. With regard to the analytical elements of the technology, leaders will need to maintain an explicit awareness of the assumptions embedded in the algorithms to make sense of the information, and to frequently re-evaluate these assumptions if the process is to render valid knowledge and insights. Further, overcoming the social and political hurdles of sharing information among many entities will require a tolerance and acceptance of differences, the ability to generate and maintain relationships of trust, and the capacity to harness collective intelligence to develop and maintain comprehensive maritime domain awareness. Whether their leadership is formal or emergent, those who exert influence to accomplish this broad initiative will need to create a process that is responsive to innovation, sense-making, learning, adaptation, and the larger strategic objectives of affected communities.

Transformation in China's Information Operations and Military Strategy

The transformation of Chinese military strategy in recent years offers a provocative case study of how flexible, adaptable leadership can meet the challenges of a rapidly changing strategic environment. The willingness to respond to new conditions by re-evaluating existing concepts and their relationship to one another is an important capability of leadership at all levels, from the individual or team

to the organizational and national levels. In this case, the Chinese have been in-
fluenced by and are acting on the possibilities offered to them by the electromagnetic spectrum and computer networks. This is not to say that China is foremost
in the areas of information, cyberspace, or network warfare; rather, the case describes what we can discern from open source documents about the learning
process at an institutional and national level in China, and how the abilities to
learn and adapt contribute to institutional and national change and innovation.

Since the late 1990s, the Chinese military has been rethinking, and then
reformulating, its military theories, planning, management, and strategies, in
a process that emphasizes the significance of information warfare (IW). Chinese leaders characterize this transformation as a response to the emergence of
technologies that support electronic warfare and computer network warfare,
which have brought about changes in the structure of combat power, the methods of combat operations, and the principles for directing combat operations.[31]
Chinese definitions of information operations emphasize control of information and countermeasures, rather than solely information superiority.[32] Major
General Dai Qingmin of the People's Liberation Army wrote in 2002 that the
Chinese concept of integrated network-electronic warfare is an offensive strategy with the objective to effectively destroy the enemy's electronic information
system.[33] Further, the theorists explicitly describe a cognitive focus for information operations, the objective of which in electronic, computer network, and
psychological warfare is to gain control of the opponent's cognition and belief
systems, and ultimately, decision-making processes.[34]

The Chinese science of military strategy uses formally defined comprehensive assessments to analyze the potential impact of several factors on strategy
and power. This approach is highlighted by Dai and his co-workers in the scope
they define for operations, targets, and outcomes, in the 2005 Study Guide for
Information Operations Theory:

> The broad sense of information warfare, also known as strategic information
> warfare, refers to countermeasures and combat using information and infor-
> mation technology by two sides in a conflict as a means of gaining information
> superiority in the areas of politics, the economy, science, technology, diplomacy,
> culture, and the military, both in the civilian and military realms, during peace-
> time or in times of war, either on the battlefield or off of it.[35]

Although Chinese theorists such as General Shen, whom many consider
to be the father of Chinese IW, began writing on the subject of IW in 1985,

little was done to advance the concept until the latter part of the 1990s. Since the late 1990s, many publications, especially books and conference proceedings from the Chinese Academy of Military Science, have appeared on the subject. Also, the Chinese learned from their observations of the use of IW during the conflict in Kosovo (1998–99), the Persian Gulf War (1991), and the second Iraq War (May through August 2003). Chinese forces have used organization, mobilization, exercises, and other types of action to implement integrated IW strategies and theories. The attempted penetration of U.S. government or corporate computers to gain competitive information, such as the April 2009 intrusion into the F-35 Joint Strike Fighter project data network,[36] and the acknowledgment, in April 2009, by Solutionary (a top-ranked managed security services provider) that it had identified 128 acts of cyber aggression *per minute* against clients by internet protocol addresses in China,[37] offer evidence that the Chinese have begun to put their theories to practice.

At the core of competitive advantage is the ability to process and share data and information, and thus to create and manage knowledge. One comparative analysis of the ways in which China and the United States deal with complexity found that the Chinese tend to absorb complexity by "creating options and risk-hedging strategies," for example, by means of collaborative relationships that allow them to consider "simultaneously multiple and sometimes conflicting, representations of the environment."[38] In contrast, the tendency of Westerners, and particularly Americans, is to reduce complexity by arriving at a specific understanding of the situation and acting directly on that understanding. The trade-off between these two approaches to complexity is that in the approach favored by the Chinese, complexity absorption, the "goodness of fit" between any one particular state of the environment and the response, may be less, but the range of states with which the response can deal more or less effectively is greater. The U.S. approach, complexity reduction, is specialized: while the strategy and responses match well with a particular state of the environment, they are unable to address effectively a broader range of environmental contingencies.

Taking a global view of the Chinese case, two observations can be made. First, the Chinese have used the emergence of electromagnetic and computer technology to explore and implement ideas to reformulate their military strategies. They have innovated by re-thinking the relationships among the agents and elements of war, while remaining cognizant of the social, cultural, economic, physical, and security implications. Second, as described above, the

Chinese have a different manner of responding to complexity from that of Americans and Europeans. This kind of cognitive complexity—a high level of self-awareness and awareness of others, and the ability to respond to diversity in the environment—is an important leadership quality.

As nations respond to threats in the global commons, a clear awareness of our own behavioral tendencies and those of our allies, partners, and opponents is necessary to forge adaptive tactics, operations, and strategies. Moreover, the assumptions and values we embed in our scanning systems, the technology and patterns we use to process and make sense of data, and the learning patterns characteristic of our approach to knowledge creation and management are critical to competitive advantage and long-term survivability.

Summary

The three cases described above illustrate different aspects of leadership that might apply to complex situations in the global commons. Admiral LeFever's leadership during Operation Lifeline in Pakistan embodies a highly collaborative leadership model and demonstrates the importance of developing trust among disparate agents working toward a common goal. The case of the Cooperative Mechanism for governance of the Straits of Malacca and Singapore illustrates the difficulty of reaching a shared understanding of what the problems are and how to address them. It highlights the importance of collaboration for information gathering, sharing, sense-making, and collective analysis. Finally, the case of the reformulation of Chinese military strategy represents an example of transformation at an institutional level, whereby leaders were willing to restructure their understanding of the nature of warfare and the relationships between elements of war.

This chapter describes a set of capabilities needed for effective leadership. These include an awareness of one's own behavior choices, and the assumptions behind them; high levels of cognitive complexity, including the capacity to act from a diverse repertoire of orientations and strategies; the capacity for sharing power, and giving and receiving feedback; a broad temporal orientation; and the ability to recognize emerging social and physical patterns. These capabilities can be exercised by individuals, teams, networks, organizations, institutions, and nation-states. The degree to which a social entity successfully adapts to the complexity of this environment will reflect, to a great extent, the level of cognitive development of the individual or collective.

Based on the models of leadership described in this chapter, and the abilities required for leaders to effectively succeed in complex operations in the global commons, leadership capabilities should be developed in a multi-modal manner through degree and certificate programs. This can be achieved in the following ways: 1) use leadership assessment tools that are designed to measure an individual's cognitive complexity and effectiveness in complex environments; 2) offer useful, reliable feedback to individuals that will help them meet the challenges of their current and future positions; and 3) design opportunities for participants to reflect on what they are learning, how they perceive and structure reality, and how this affects their behavior and overall effectiveness, both within their organization and in the larger network of individuals with whom they interact. The academic content of these programs should include carefully selected material about emergent principles and complex adaptive systems, so that students develop an understanding of the systems in which they operate, and have the tools to reflect on their own assumptions and behavioral tendencies when they find themselves in a leadership position. Participants will need to look for opportunities to experiment and develop these new capabilities, for example, by choosing low-risk situations at work or using computer-simulated environments, where they can try moving out of their comfort zone as a way to increase their levels of effectiveness.

This chapter proposes a new paradigm that sees effective leadership as an outcome of a process that fosters interaction among individuals, groups, organizations, and societies to stimulate adaptive, innovative, and constructive configurations of influence and abilities. Although individuals continue to play a critical role in emergent leadership, leadership is not accurately or productively conceived solely as the patterns of influence and abilities of one formal leader. The complexity of national and international security in the global commons calls for the simultaneous exercise of several models of leadership. In the first, formal leaders generally coordinate resources using a more centralized, hierarchical model. For the second, emergent leaders exert influence to harness collective intelligence, innovate, and/or develop trust, and mobilize other new and alternative resources to accomplish a project goal or mission. In the third model, power-sharing occurs among leaders, teams, and organizations. All these solutions acknowledge that leaders emerge according to the situation and the need, and organizations must find ways to nurture innovative, adaptable, and constructive leaders.

12 Advanced Technology Enablers

Marco Fiorello and Donald McSwain

A Decision Support Framework

The preceding companion chapters in this book present what the global commons are, why their security is important to the global community, and the ways in which occurrences in the commons affect national security and the global system of communications and trade. Decision makers concerned with national and international security need to know what the state of the global commons is, when they should be concerned about events or trends in the commons, and what effects if any can be correlated with the responsive actions they may take. They need a decision support framework that enables them to make programmatic decisions and institutional changes that will help ensure stability and prosperity in the global commons.

Such a framework can provide a means to both gain situational awareness and then measure the state of the commons and trends of concern. This chapter describes an advanced technology system that aggregates a "big picture" understanding of the commons through both high-level integration and sophisticated displays of measures of effectiveness and measures of performance. It uses a logic engine to combine both types of measures and normalize subjective and objective data, which can then be used at several levels of decision making (called decision-making perspectives), for example, from the national leadership down to operations and training. The chapter presents two scenarios to illustrate the application and utility of the decision support framework to monitor, assess, and affect the connectivity and stability of the global commons. It goes on to describe future steps for addressing several capability gaps, and to develop the concept from an "as is" situation awareness tool to a "what if" assessment tool.

From a military, civil, or commercial point of view, making programmatic and institutional changes that can help ensure security and prosperity in the commons requires decision support capabilities that:

- Provide situational awareness that encapsulates the current state of the commons (the global commons are similar to but less wide-ranging than the elucidation of the term military domains, which encompass the entire operating space of joint forces working with interagency partners and commercial entities);
- Facilitate the making and implementing of decisions that will help maintain the stability of the commons; and
- Ultimately, aid in the conduct of "what-if" assessments to revise policies, plans, and regimes that will improve the health of the commons.

The design and implementation of a decision support system (DSS) with the above capabilities faces significant challenges. This chapter will, in three subsections, lay out a preliminary logic structure that can be used as a building block toward the eventual creation of a functional system. Specifically, it will describe:

- The design considerations and essential characteristics of a system for global domain awareness. This discussion will pay particular attention to the design of a common operational picture for domain awareness, and offer a representative set of decision perspectives.
- Two illustrations of DSS, using notional conceptual displays for physically presenting information related to domain awareness, one dealing with a cyber attack and the second dealing with piracy incidents.
- Capability gaps and future improvements that will need to be addressed, to ensure the future security and freedom of the commons.

DSS Design Considerations

A principal focus of DSS design for the global commons is on the information needs of decision makers who lead or conduct missions associated with

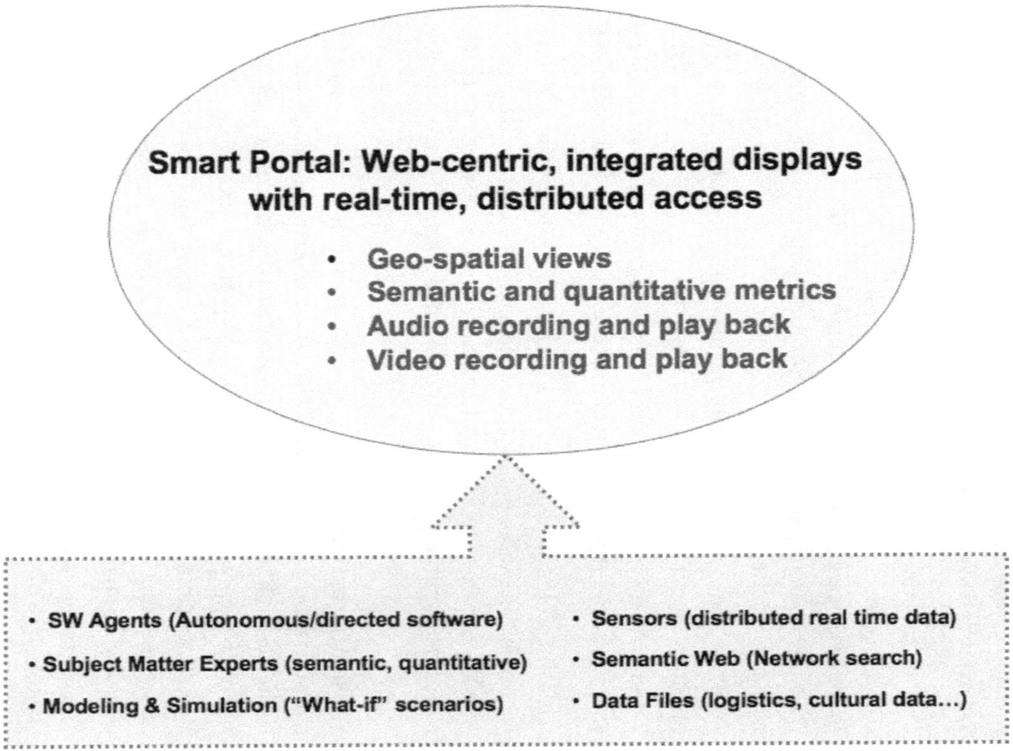

Smart Portal: Web-centric, integrated displays
with real-time, distributed access

- Geo-spatial views
- Semantic and quantitative metrics
- Audio recording and play back
- Video recording and play back

- SW Agents (Autonomous/directed software)
- Subject Matter Experts (semantic, quantitative)
- Modeling & Simulation ("What-if" scenarios)

- Sensors (distributed real time data)
- Semantic Web (Network search)
- Data Files (logistics, cultural data…)

FIGURE 12.1 DSS Design Concept

securing the global commons. This includes the development of an underlying logical framework for deriving timely, relevant information from collected data, and the choice of an appropriate display technology for presenting the information. The goal is to build a DSS that provides effective global domain awareness, that is, a comprehensive picture of events in the commons that could affect national security and the global system of commercial and community interests.[1]

The design of the decision support framework presented here takes a deliberate top-down approach that emphasizes, at this preliminary stage, the top two tiers (strategic and operational) of a decision hierarchy. Additional views, such as the tactical level or doctrine development, for example, are noted but are not addressed with any detail in this discussion.

Figure 12.1 depicts a conceptual net-centric architecture, with four critical system components—geo-spatial, metrics, audio, and video—integrated into a common operating picture for military and government decision makers. To support sustained and effective shared situational domain awareness and understanding, the DSS synthesizes information from four dimensions:

- dynamic *geo-spatial graphics and mapping*
- organized and unambiguous *descriptive semantic and quantitative metrics* as graphic representations;
- *audio statements* with question-answer exchanges; and
- *video presentations and reports.*

As shown in Figure 12.1, the DSS will synthesize information that has been collected at regular and irregular intervals and time-stamped, from a broad spectrum of semantic (descriptive, verbal) and quantitative data sources (traditional databases, dynamic sensors, domain modeling, subject matter experts, and web searches). Before they are presented, all the data for the four system components will be both temporally and logically correlated, to ensure they create accurate representations of "reality" across all the pre-defined relevant decision perspectives. Authorized system users will have access to the "smart portal," a network interface for the DSS database, from whatever point on the network they are working. They will also be able to search or "drill" down to more specific metrics and displays.

The U.S. Department of Defense Capstone Concept for Joint Operations envisions a future wherein U.S. joint forces, as a component of regional and theater international partnerships, will conduct a combination of combat, security,

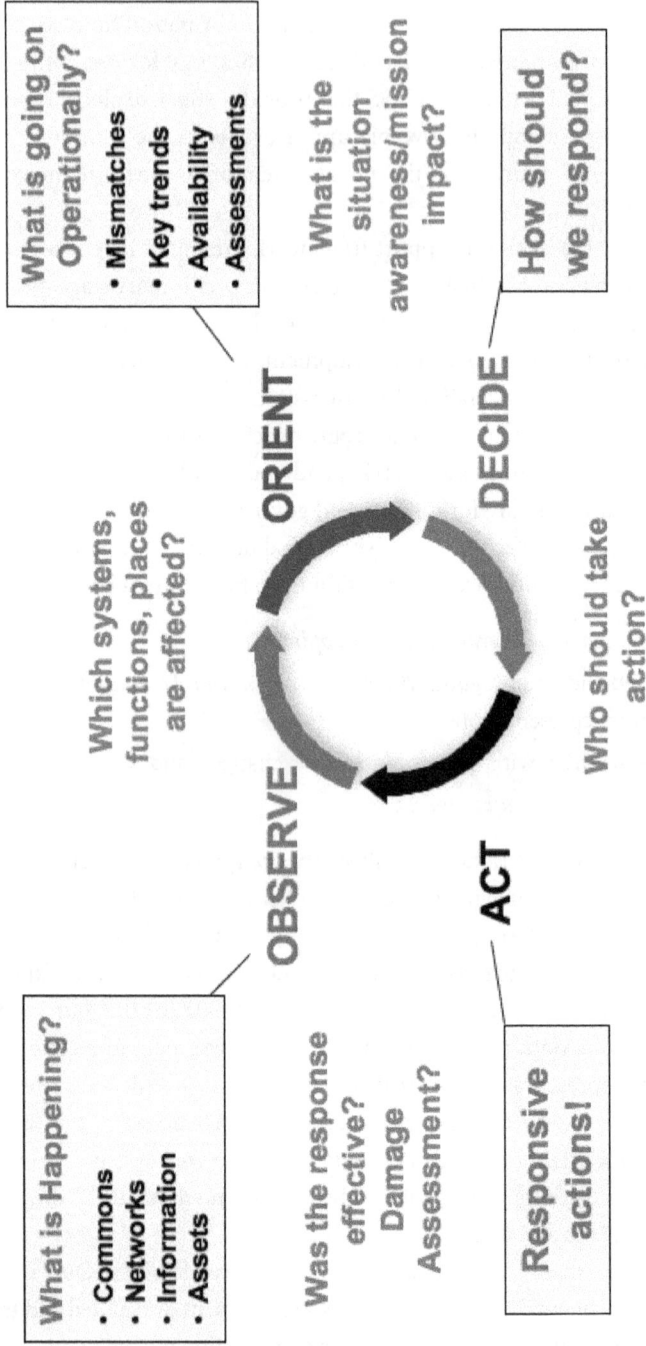

FIGURE 12.2 Basic Management Decision OODA Loop

SOURCE: Based on John Boyd's Observe, Orient, Decision, Act (OODA) Loop.

engagement, and relief and reconstruction activities in support of U.S. and part-ner interests. The concept recognizes that it will continue to fall to the United States and its partner nations to protect and sustain the peaceful global system of interdependent networks of trade, finance, information, law, and governance. Freedom of action and access around the globe is at least as much a requirement for the functioning of this global system as it is for the conduct of military oper-ations. Maintaining sufficient control of the global commons, which encompass the respective and interdependent military domains of sea, air, space, and cyber-space, thus will remain a vital piece of future joint force design.[2] A key enabler for the effective implementation of this overarching joint concept is a "generic process of operational adaptation designed expressly to cope with the complex-ity, uncertainty, and change that will define the future operating environment."[3] The DSS described in this chapter is intended to be a fundamental component for that process of operational adaptation.

An underlying conceptual building block for the proposed commons DSS design is an adapted version of what is known as the Observe, Orient, Decide, Act (OODA) Loop, developed by John Boyd and illustrated in Figure 12.2.[4] The DSS display and logic engine are applicable in any network-centric environ-ment, and provide the necessary "feed forward" and "feedback" loops between the four OODA nodes that are essential to effective decision making.[5]

The global commons DSS performs the analysis and synthesis functions in the Orient node of the OODA Loop. The DSS receives or subscribes to a broad spectrum of automated and human-generated data, and then synthesizes and transforms the data into displays of information that promote domain aware-ness for decision makers.

The logical foundation of this DSS design is a set of organized and unam-biguously defined terms, an ontology of domain awareness in the commons,[6] that derive explicitly from the principal decision-making organization's goals and objectives for the global commons. This specification of terms establishes the vocabulary for shared domain awareness. The terms are used in the defini-tion of measures of effectiveness and performance that are essential to achiev-ing the organization's goals. At the lowest metric level, meaningful intervals of achievement are defined for correlating subjective and objective source data into a logical construct that transforms data into information to build a common operating picture, and thus a shared understanding of the situation at hand.[7] Figure 12.3 presents the logic engine architecture for this data-to-information transformation process.

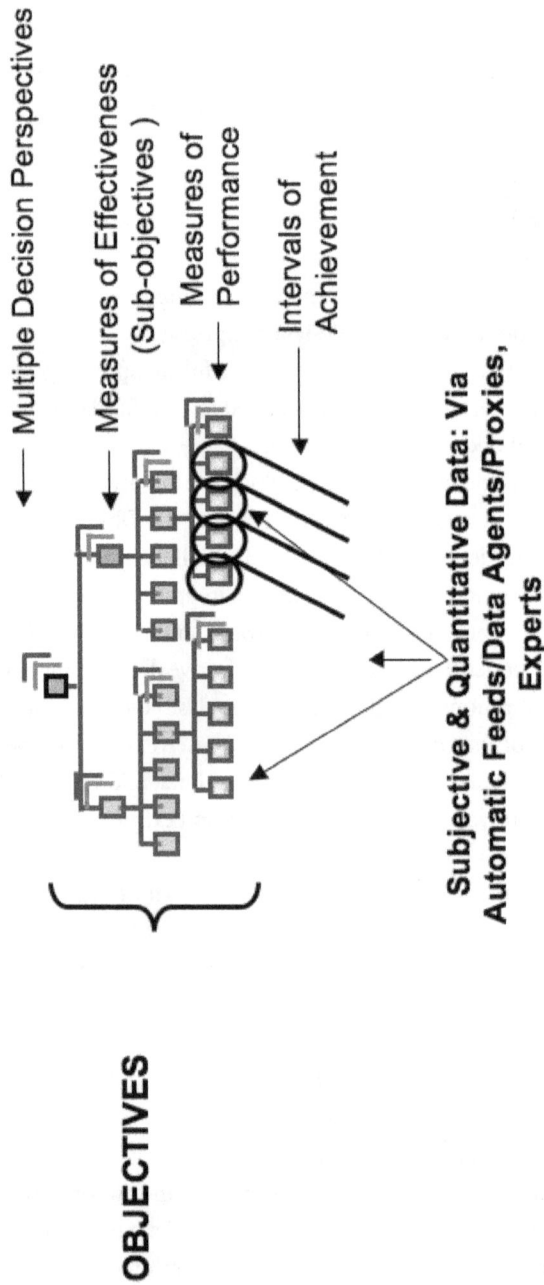

FIGURE 12.3 Logic Engine Architecture

Figure 12.4 presents a preliminary, high-level ontology for the global commons. In this version there are four principal categories for the information required for effective domain awareness:

1. *Military Goals*: The five freedoms listed in Figure 12.4 constitute high-level security goals that facilitate operating in the global commons. In the final version of the DSS, these freedoms will be further defined in lower-level measures of performance that are monitored by the DSS, and incorporated into the domain awareness presentations.

2. *Capability-Based Enablers*: These are the key processes that must be implemented to achieve organizational goals. These capability enablers include theater coalition arrangements, as well as agreements or tasks conducted with international governmental partners and non-governmental and commercial organizations.[8]

3. *Undesired Events* (natural and agent-based): These are occurrences and trends over which the military and its partners have no direct control. They include both agent-caused and natural phenomena that have negative impacts on the commons. Examples of the former are the hypothetical cyber attack and maritime piracy scenarios described below.

4. *Effects* on the global commons: The commons constitute the underlying structure of the global system, and they are where the effects of adversaries and allies will be felt.

Once source data are entered into the DSS and synthesized to create usable information, the information needs to be displayed to the decision makers in a way that facilitates domain awareness. Given the need to visualize simultaneously multiple aspects of the problem to "get the big picture," and uncover correlations and trends that can be related to the thresholds of acceptable performance values, a dynamic Kiviat chart works best for strategic and operations views.[9] This type of display allows multiple metrics to be incorporated on one radial diagram, the metric assessments and the desired-undesired threshold values noted for each metric for normalized or "individual" scales. "Connecting-the-dots" creates a profile for contemporaneous evaluations allowing decision makers to get the big picture. The solid lines on the diagram create profiles for the system of metrics which, when viewed in groups, can create very useful trend information.

The top-level set of metrics in Figure 12.4 is depicted in a Kiviat display in Figure 12.5. All the top-level goals are defined as separate vectors using

Securing Freedom in the Global Commons

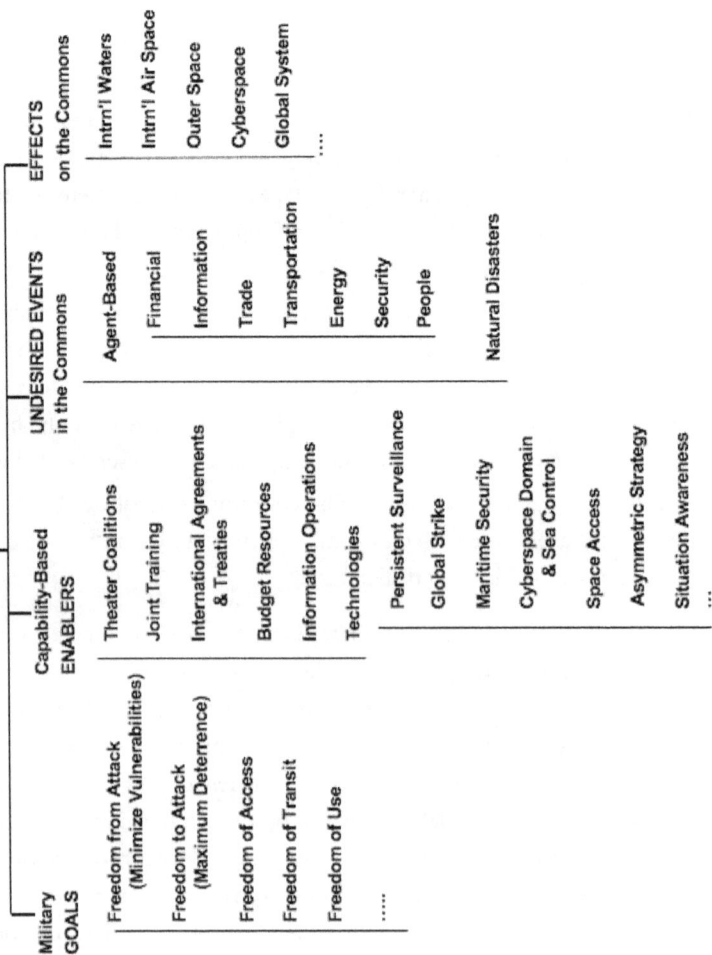

Military GOALS	Capability-Based ENABLERS	UNDESIRED EVENTS in the Commons	EFFECTS on the Commons
Freedom from Attack (Minimize Vulnerabilities)	Theater Coalitions	Agent-Based	Intrn'l Waters
	Joint Training	Financial	Intrn'l Air Space
Freedom to Attack (Maximum Deterrence)	International Agreements & Treaties	Information	Outer Space
	Budget Resources	Trade	Cyberspace
Freedom of Access	Information Operations	Transportation	Global System
Freedom of Transit	Technologies	Energy	....
Freedom of Use		Security	
....	Persistent Surveillance	People	
	Global Strike		
	Maritime Security	Natural Disasters	
	Cyberspace Domain & Sea Control		
	Space Access		
	Asymmetric Strategy		
	Situation Awareness		
	....		

FIGURE 12.4 Performance Metrics Framework Illustration

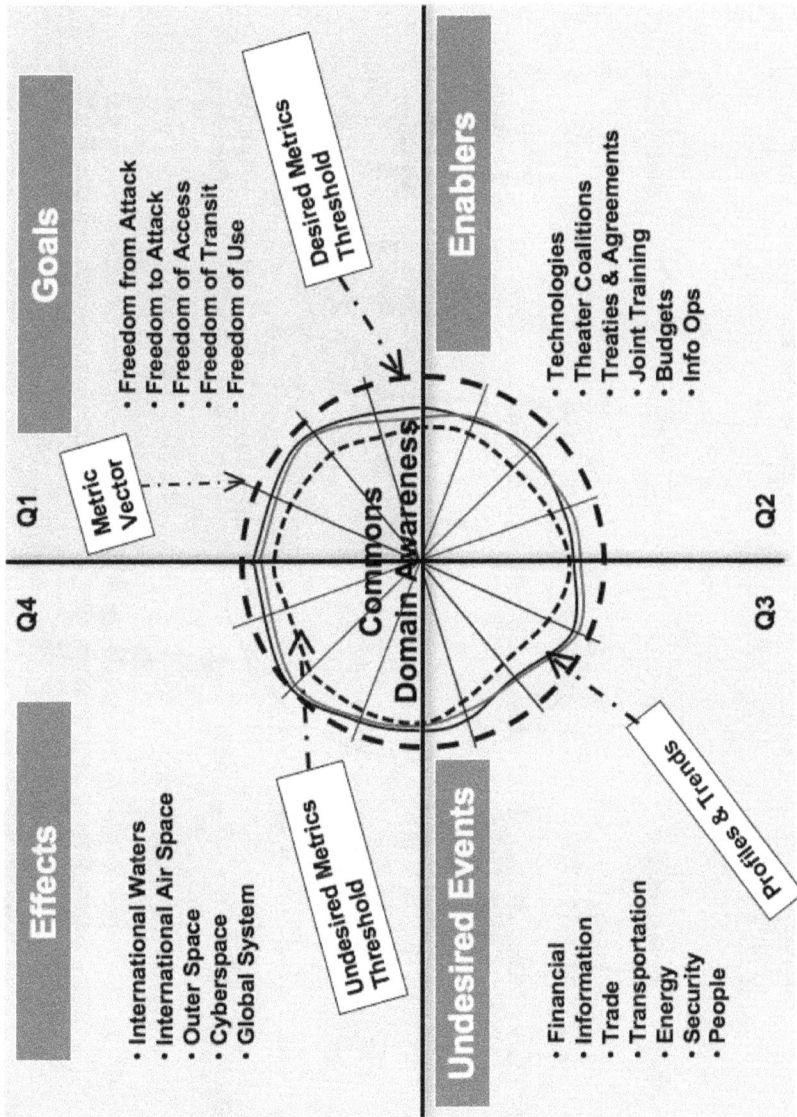

FIGURE 12.5 Highest-level Display for Domain Awareness

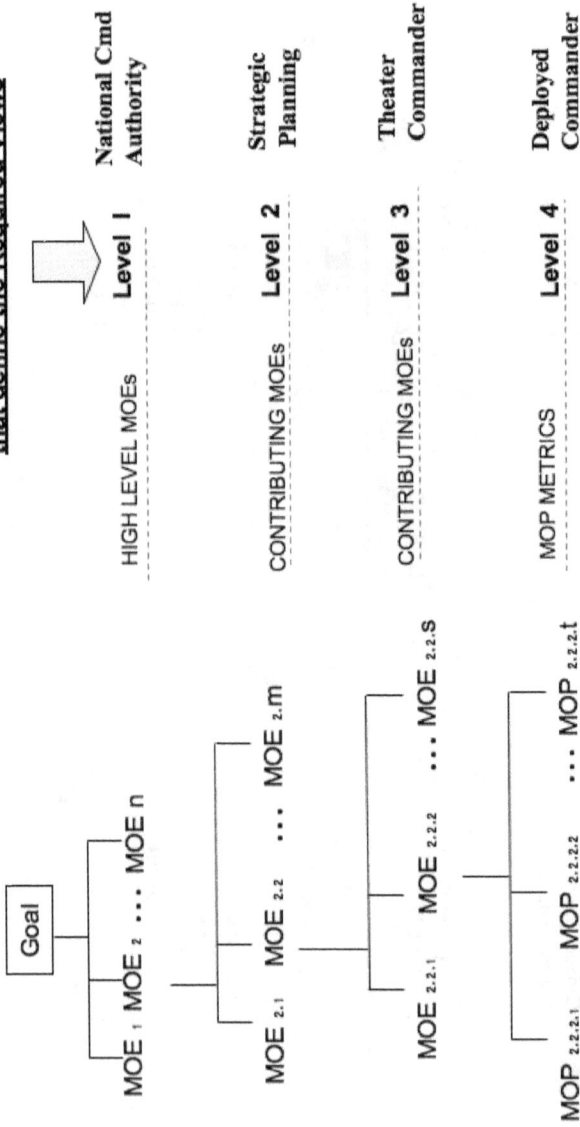

ECHELON OF DECISION MAKERS
that define the Required Views

	Level 1	National Cmd Authority
HIGH LEVEL MOEs	Level 1	
CONTRIBUTING MOEs	Level 2	Strategic Planning
CONTRIBUTING MOEs	Level 3	Theater Commander
MOP METRICS	Level 4	Deployed Commander

Each display vector category decomposes into sets and subsets of MOEs layer by layer until the underlying MOPs (preferentially distinguishable metrics) are shown.

FIGURE 12.6 DDS Tools Drill-down

normalized scales with "0 percent" at the origin and "100 percent" at the diagram perimeter. Each of the vectors has computed or imputed (assigned) threshold values for an undesired value and a desired value. Data are input at the lowest metric level and normalized using an appropriate algorithm to compute a value for each vector. Figure 12.5 shows two solid profile and trend lines generated by connecting the dots (computed points) across the vectors, plus a dotted line for the undesired threshold values and a dashed line for desired metric values. This illustration uses a four-quadrant graphic to highlight the relationship between goals, enablers, undesired events, and effects; fewer or more than four sectors can be used depending on the particular set of metrics and their preferred organization. It is important that all the vectors and their lower-level metrics be preferentially distinguishable,[10] so as to ensure consistency throughout the data-synthesizing process.

The top-level global commons vectors (goals, enablers, undesired events, and effects) are too macro and ambiguous to produce meaningful measures directly, and must be disaggregated into more specific component measures of performance, as shown in Figure 12.4, where for example the technologies vector under Capability-Based Enablers breaks down into seven constituents. The disaggregation process continues to the level at which an unambiguous metric can be identified. An example is a traffic flow-rate statistic for key maritime regions (tonnage per day), or an international data network (latency per message). This requirement is important, because it allows the source data to both be communicated easily and used for multiple decision perspectives. It also allows the collected data to be mapped unambiguously onto the measures-of-performance intervals of achievement. The decision perspectives (levels of decision making) define the combinations of data and computed values across the vectors, to create decision-specific information display-shots. For the global commons application, combinations of lower levels of metric computations are candidate decision perspectives, as depicted in Figure 12.6.

Two abbreviated, hypothetical scenarios, one for a cyber attack and one for a maritime piracy event, illustrate how the DSS framework can be used to generate domain awareness.

Cyber Attack Scenario
In Figure 12.7, a hypothetical cyber attack has occurred (in the global common of cyberspace) and appears to be focused primarily on disrupting leadership, public confidence, and financial stability by exploiting the common of cyberspace; it is not apparent whether the intent was to cause physical harm

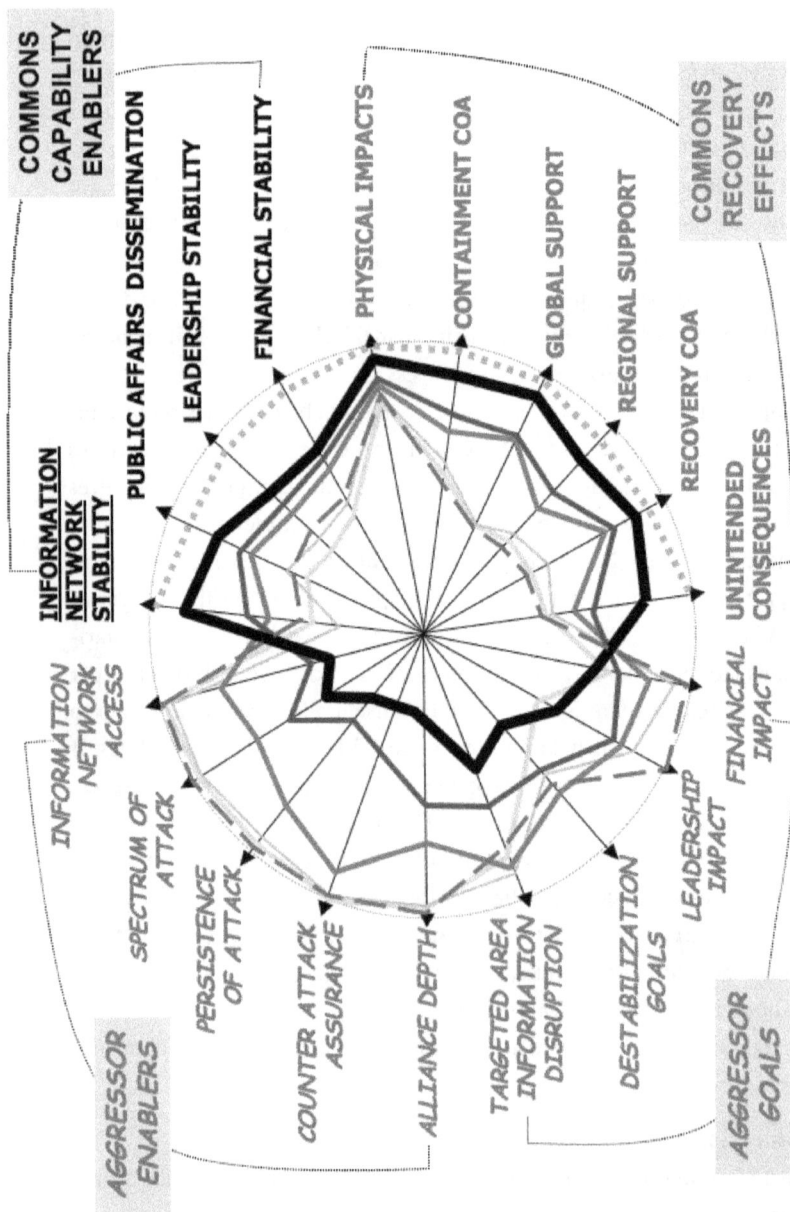

FIGURE 12.7 Cyber Attack Domain Awareness Theater-level View

KEY: Bold line is most current, lightest shade is oldest report. Dashed line is initial attack. Dotted line is desired Commons end state.

COMMONS CAPABILITY ENABLERS

COMMONS RECOVERY EFFECTS

AGGRESSOR ENABLERS

AGGRESSOR GOALS

PUBLIC AFFAIRS DISSEMINATION

LEADERSHIP STABILITY

FINANCIAL STABILITY

PHYSICAL IMPACTS

CONTAINMENT COA

GLOBAL SUPPORT

REGIONAL SUPPORT

RECOVERY COA

UNINTENDED CONSEQUENCES

FINANCIAL IMPACT

LEADERSHIP IMPACT

DESTABILIZATION GOALS

TARGETED AREA INFORMATION DISRUPTION

ALLIANCE DEPTH

COUNTER ATTACK ASSURANCE

PERSISTENCE OF ATTACK

SPECTRUM OF ATTACK

INFORMATION NETWORK ACCESS

INFORMATION NETWORK STABILITY

or permanently disable cyberspace network functions. By assembling a cross-section of the relevant high-level vectors from Figure 12.5 (Goal: Freedom from Attack; Capability-Based Enabler: Theater Coalitions; Undesired Events: Information; and Effects: Cyberspace), a set of metrics can be defined for the theater-level Cyber Attack Domain Awareness display shown in Figure 12.7.

In this view of the cyber attack scenario, the coalition's capability enablers and recovery effects to secure the common are shown on the right-hand side, while the aggressor's goals and enablers are shown on the left half. In this normalized view, the origin (central point) represents 0 percent (most undesired state) and the perimeter represents 100 percent (most desired state). The initial condition of both sides immediately following the attack, from the perspective of the common, is shown with the dashed line, and the desired end-state for the common, stability and full function, is the closely spaced dotted line. The darkest bold line is the most recent assessment, and the profiles, the bold lines shading from dark to light, are relevant reports going back in time (intervals can be months, weeks, days, or even hours if the situation warrants). In this view, the decision maker can see the initial cyber attack, and then over time, the recovery of the common to regain cyberspace superiority while the aggressor shows increasing failure.

If there was recovery in the common but little or no change for the aggressor, such a result would tell the decision maker that: 1) the recovery plan is incorrect; 2) the data sources are not sufficient to support his decision needs; or 3) that the aggressor is able to adapt to the defenses and over time is successfully defeating the recovery efforts. If the plan is effective enough to neutralize the breadth of the cyber attack across the aggressor's set of enablers, the displayed trends should show a relative collapse in the attack on the left side, and on the commons right side a recovery toward the dotted line that represents the desired end state.

As illustrated in Figure 12.7, the left hemisphere shows that all the attributes of the aggressor, represented by the dashed line, are initially high; the coalition's goal is to see all of them reduced. In the right hemisphere, the desired end-state for the commons is the dotted line toward the hemisphere's edge; the goal of the counter-attack plan in this illustration is to see the reported trend lines progress toward that desired end-state from the initial condition (dashed line). All the commons categories should show improvement as the plan progresses. If some do not improve, or actually decline, then the coalition's plan and ability to counter the aggressor's activities and goals are insufficient. If the aggressor's activities and goals are failing, and the enabling capabilities and recovery effects or

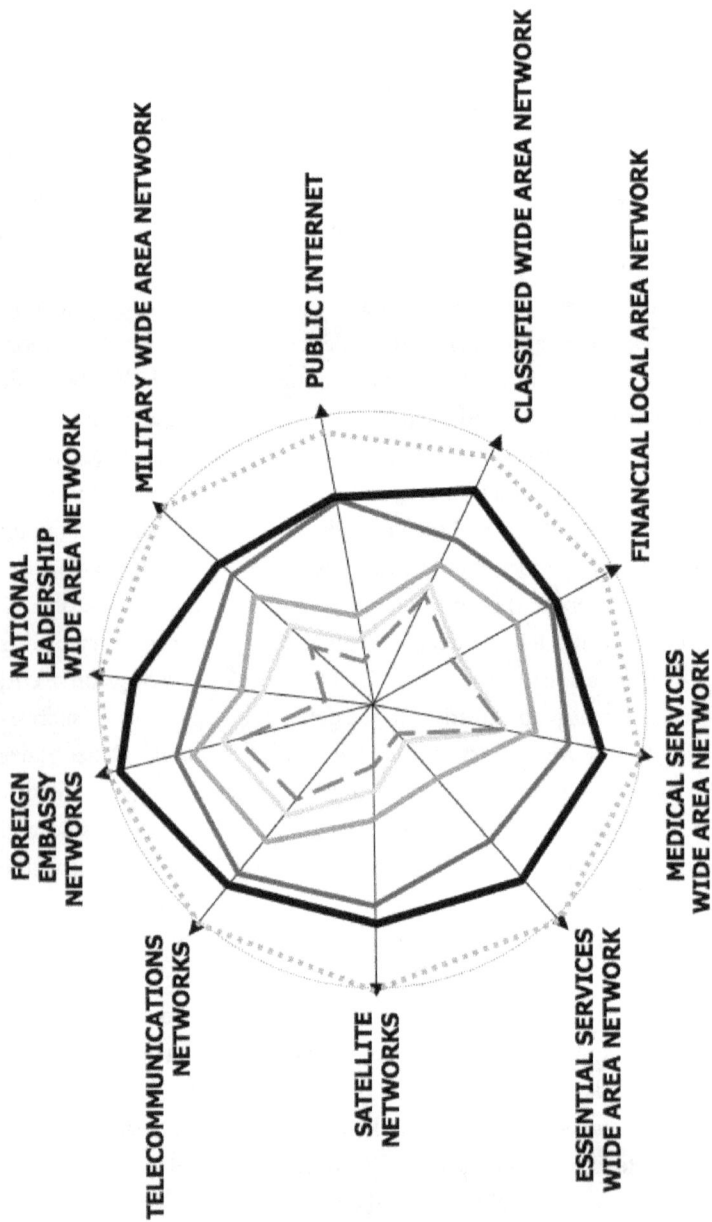

FIGURE 12.8 Information Network Domain Awareness Theater-level View

NOTE: This view is a "DSS drill-down," or disaggregation, of the *Information Network Stability* metric category from Figure 12.7.

Labels around the figure:

MILITARY WIDE AREA NETWORK

PUBLIC INTERNET

CLASSIFIED WIDE AREA NETWORK

FINANCIAL LOCAL AREA NETWORK

NATIONAL LEADERSHIP WIDE AREA NETWORK

MEDICAL SERVICES WIDE AREA NETWORK

FOREIGN EMBASSY NETWORKS

ESSENTIAL SERVICES WIDE AREA NETWORK

TELECOMMUNICATIONS NETWORKS

SATELLITE NETWORKS

goals for the commons are improving, then the actions of the coalition are successful. Metrics that do not move (are stagnant) or that move in an undesired direction need to be analyzed closely, to ensure both that the right metrics are being evaluated and that the plan is the optimum or desired course of action.

One way to better understand the attacker's intent is to examine specific aspects of, or "drill-down" on, several of the vectors for more detailed views. In this case, the Information Network Stability vector (underlined near the top of Figure 12.7), is expanded in Figure 12.8, so the decision maker can view the lower-level nodes and assessments that comprise the Information Network Stability vector. For consistency, the DSS displays data from the same intervals of time at all display levels, so that the decision maker can readily understand the trend line of the information, and thus more effectively formulate a plan of action or more accurately pose a question of interest.

Figure 12.8 displays ten Information Network Stability metrics that would be typical for a modern nation dependent on the global common of cyberspace. The instance of an attack is shown by the dashed-line profile that lies across the vectors, close to the 0 percent (undesired) value at the origin of the graphic. This indicates that the attack has had an adverse impact on network stability. Values close to the origin are undesired because they imply that the networks represented by the vectors have little to no capability. From this domain awareness view, the decision maker may be able to determine the intent of the cyber attack, or perhaps see what networks proved invulnerable to attack. The trend profiles in the figure show a very broad spectrum of cyberspace attack that has left medical services, foreign embassy communications, common commercial networks, and classified networks degraded but still functional, while the networks for national leadership, the public, and essential services are more seriously degraded. A review of the display could lead one to determine that the classified networks were difficult to disrupt or fully disable. One might also presume that since the other services are only partially disrupted, the cyber attack did not specifically target the general populace and their well-being, but was focused against the national leadership, military, and financial elements of the cyberspace common. Over time, we see that the latest (darkest bold line) assessment shows a significant neutralization of the attack. Each of the vectors in Figure 12.8 can in turn be investigated further by drilling down into their lower-level metrics. This would be warranted if, for example, in retrospect it was important to determine whether remediation worked as rapidly as the plan called for, or if there was some delay in implementing the remedial actions.

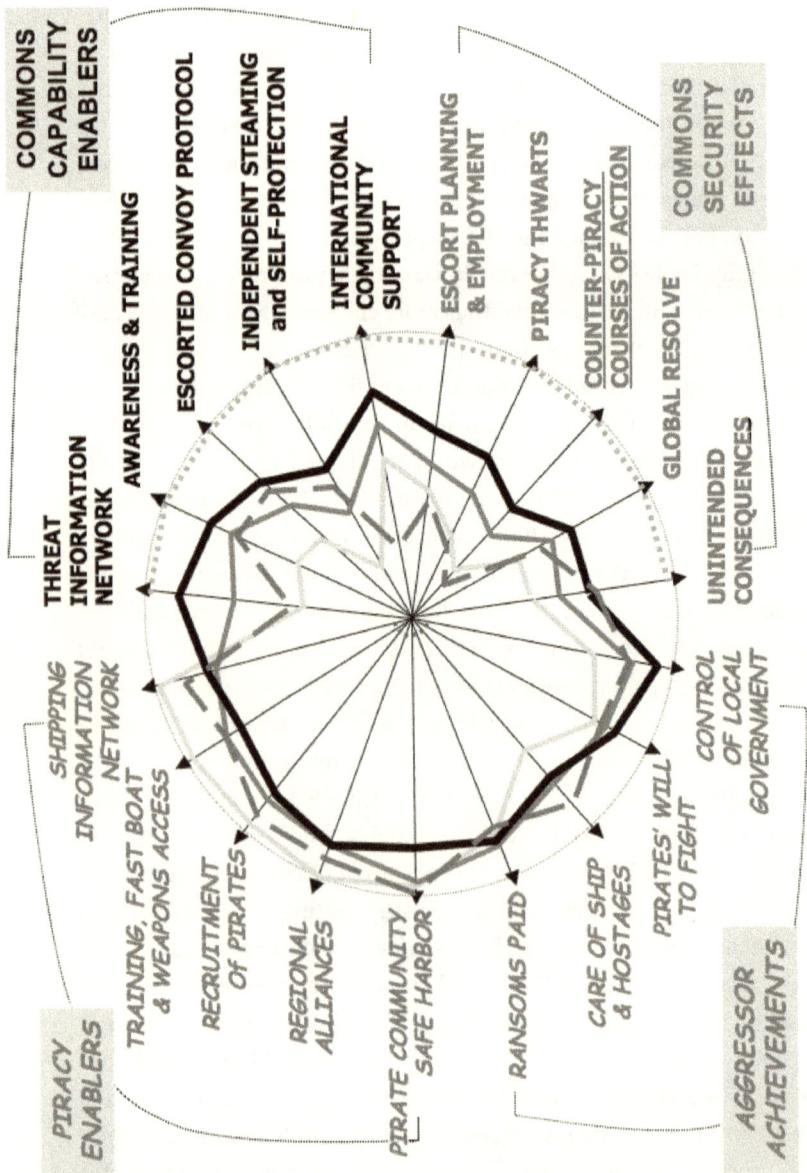

FIGURE 12.9 Maritime Piracy Domain Awareness Regional-level View

KEY: Bold line is most current, lightest shade is oldest report. Dotted line is the desired Commons end state. Dashed line is initial attack.

Maritime Piracy Scenario

The second hypothetical scenario concerns the seizure of commercial shipping at sea by third-world pirates seeking ransom. These modern day brigands are sometimes based in failing or failed nation states that directly or indirectly equip and train young men with weapons and fast watercraft to seek and seize commercial freighters and oil tankers and their crews for ransom. Some pirates foster the illusion that they are modern day "Robin Hoods" who take from the rich and give to the poor, and thus enjoy safe harbor and general public support from their countrymen. The nexus of the high-level vectors from Figure 12.5— in this case, Goal: Freedom from Attack; Capability-Based Enabler: Theater Coalitions; Undesired Events: Trade; and Effects: International Waters—bound a set of metrics for the nineteen vectors in Figure 12.9 that define piracy domain awareness at the regional level.

This maritime piracy DSS display portrays the adequacy of the freedom-from-attack plans (with associated enabling activities and resultant desired effects), while also revealing the intent and achievements of the pirates. In this perspective, the dotted line on the commons (right) side is the desired end state, and the dashed line represents the level of activity for the initial reporting timeframe, which serves as a baseline reference to measure progress. Here again, the origin represents 0 percent (undesired) and the perimeter 100 percent (desired) on the normalized scales. The left hemisphere of the figure shows the conditions that enable the pirates and their desired achievements, while the right hemisphere illustrates the coalition's capacity to defeat piracy through relative enablers and desired security effects. In this view from the perspective of the maritime common, the initial condition is the long dashed line and the desired end state is the small dotted line. The situation over time (lightest solid line to darkest) shows some progress against the maritime piracy problem, but counter-measures have not yet been fully successful. Likewise, the capabilities and achievements of the pirates are somewhat degraded, but not sufficiently to guarantee freedom of action in the maritime common or security from piracy.

The trends displayed in Figure 12.9, including the latest (darkest solid line), show that the overall capability of the pirates to operate at will is unrestrained by coalition defense measures. These measures have made progress, but have yet to show significant degradation or disruption of the pirates' activities or intent. The message coming from the Domain Awareness view is that there is consistent trend-line progress, albeit slow, from the coalition's anti-piracy efforts, and that they are having a negative effect on the brigands. Decision

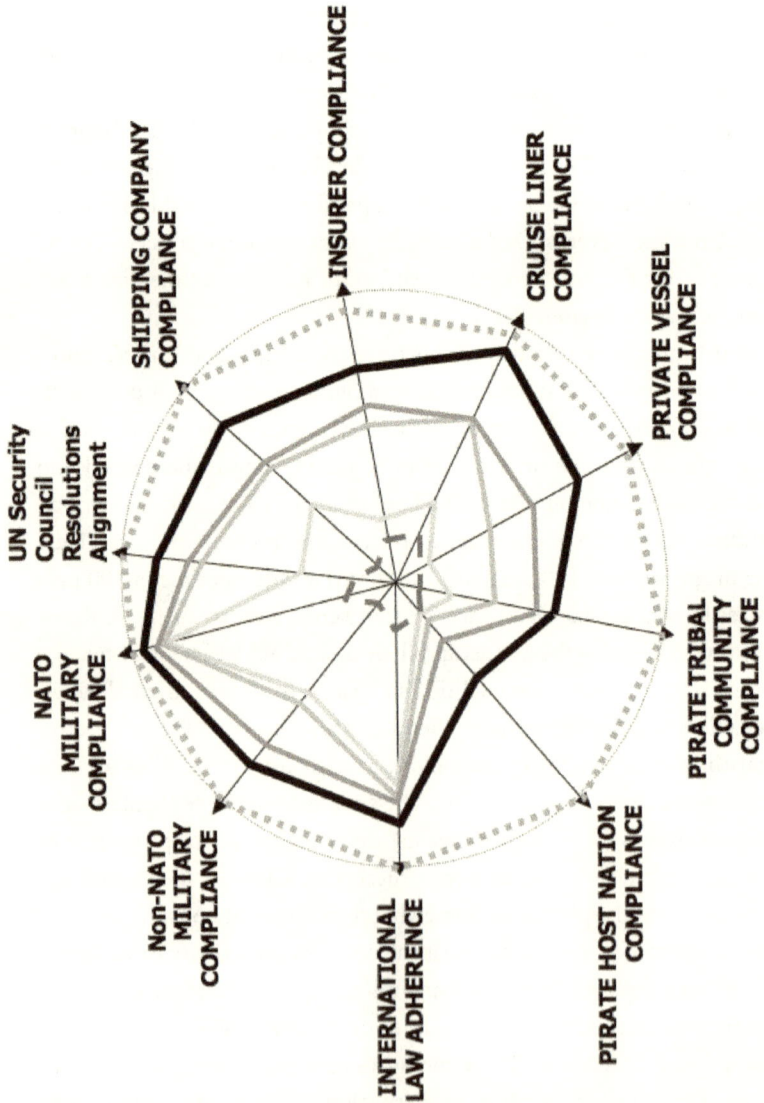

FIGURE 12.10 Counter-piracy COA Domain Awareness

NOTE: This view is a "DSS drill-down" or disaggregation of the *Counter Piracy COA* metric category from Figure 12.9.

Chart axis labels (clockwise):

- INSURER COMPLIANCE
- CRUISE LINER COMPLIANCE
- PRIVATE VESSEL COMPLIANCE
- PIRATE TRIBAL COMMUNITY COMPLIANCE
- PIRATE HOST NATION COMPLIANCE
- INTERNATIONAL LAW ADHERENCE
- Non-NATO MILITARY COMPLIANCE
- NATO MILITARY COMPLIANCE
- UN Security Council Resolutions Alignment
- SHIPPING COMPANY COMPLIANCE

makers should be encouraged, but not satisfied, by this information that they are on the right path. One reasonable strategy would be to ensure that all anti-piracy activities continue without falter, and continue to look for indications of failure on the pirates' side of the display. If such a trend emerged, decision makers must be ready to adapt their plans to exploit that emerging weakness. Additional insight can be gained by drilling down on several of the vectors for more detailed information. To illustrate this point, Figure 12.10 displays the ten counter-piracy COA (Course of Action) metrics that depict the alignment or compliance of various security partners in this environment.

This view shows the degree to which military and non-military partners and communities of interest are in compliance with the counter-piracy plan, rather than the impact of the plan on the actions of the pirates shown in the higher-level view in Figure 12.9. Figure 12.10 shows that there is little compli-ance with the plan in the host nation; that tribal players are also not aggressively supporting the plan; and that privately owned non-commercial vessels are not aware of or are not fully adhering to the plan. By contrast, since implementa-tion of the COA, NATO members, non-NATO military members, independent commercial shipping companies, passenger cruise lines, and maritime insur-ance companies have shown considerable progress toward full compliance with counter-piracy measures. The most rapid alignment has been with the NATO community and with the passenger cruise line companies. Overall, this chart does show progress in almost all of these defining areas, so the lack of stagna-tion is promising, but it is not an indication of victory. The decision maker should see a need to increase efforts to change attitudes and behaviors in the host nation and specifically amongst the tribal players as well.

Capability Gaps and Future Steps

The DSS described above can provide an effective "as is" domain awareness capability, and its specifications lie well within current available technology. There are, however, a number of improvements that should be addressed to make the design more effective for decision making, as well as to improve the design from an "as is" monitoring capability to a "what if" assessment tool. The objective is to create a DSS that can be used to both develop more effective strategies and evaluate doctrines. These suggested improvements are organized below into three categories.

Improving the "As-is" Design

A holy grail of any DSS is to collect and synthesize data about "ground truth" and generate relevant and timely information for specified decision perspectives (official levels of decision making). The fundamental obstacle to perfect information is that all data, regardless of the source (e.g., authorized databases, autonomous sensors, software agents, humans, models) are surrogates for reality and have inherent problems with incompleteness, inconsistency, and uncertainty. The challenge is magnified in dynamic settings with adaptive adversaries and cross-cultural semantic noise. Approaching, let alone achieving, consistent and timely individual and shared situational awareness and understanding in such settings is very difficult. The following three strategies can be used to understand and mitigate the inherent data and information uncertainty in the "as is" design.

1) Mission Vocabulary Creation and Management   There are two high payoff activities in this area that should be considered for implementation. The first addresses the mission vocabulary creation and documentation process. Typically, mission vocabularies are created in workshops, according to input from subject matter experts. The process is often ad hoc in nature, and would benefit from a formal, interactive wizard-like software application. The intent is to speed up the process, make it less burdensome, ensure self-documentation, and incorporate basic unity-of-purpose evaluation criteria. The second action introduces a formal validation step to test the degree of individual and shared understanding of vocabulary among the mission stakeholders.

2) The Definition and Representation of Data Uncertainty   The development of both "as is" and "what if" systems require a logical framework to deal with the inevitable uncertainty that arises from the semantic ambiguity of using surrogate data and statistical sampling errors at the data collection levels, and the propagation of that uncertainty into the different higher-level decision perspectives. Figure 12.1, the uppermost domain awareness smart portal, shows a user-definable, collaborative system that supports a decision maker's needs for relevant information delivered in a timely manner. It must necessarily help the decision maker with risk mitigation, and should provide a measurable degree of confidence or certainty in the information it provides. This DSS is supported by an intelligent software interface, or portal, that retrieves requested data along with complementary geo-spatial views and historically relevant information. Given the inherent semantic nature of most source data and the assessment process, we recommend a Fuzzy Logic approach to connote a level of data uncertainty, and to propagate that uncertainty upwards through the decision perspective levels.[11] The objective is to create an appropriate means to normalize uncertainty, and to portray the aggregate uncertainty in a meaningful way to decision makers.

3) Monitoring and Managing the OODA Tempo and Quality   In a narrow sense, the OODA paradigm is all about how team members can work together harmoniously in dynamic competitive or adversarial settings to accomplish a mission objective; in the broader context, it is about organization adaptation for survival and prosperity. An inevitable question is, how does one know if the OODA process is being implemented effectively by the DSS for the mission of securing the commons?

Two measures of effectiveness are noted here as a basis for assessing the commons DSS-OODA model: tempo and quality. The tempo metric (cycle time) is relevant to determine whether the decision process is maintaining the required tempo and has not become too slow or, worse yet, fallen into a "stuttering" mode. It is important to note that the tempo metric "desired" and "undesired" thresholds depend on context and decision perspective.

The second metric is about the quality of OODA performance; namely, whether it is producing effective decisions and winning actions. A suggested surrogate, and a subject for future research, is a "requisite variety" metric of the COAs being used or considered based on Ross Ashby's "Principle of Requisite Variety."[12] Though not explicitly addressed by Boyd in the OODA formulation, it is clearly implicit. Requisite variety is a fundamental principle of all control processes, wherein a system experiencing perturbations from its environment seeks to neutralize or control the adverse impacts through actions it can initiate. Simply put, a successful system will have the requisite variety of actions at its disposal relative to the actions taken by its adversary or environment. The key metric is the ratio of "our-to-their" requisite variety. COA strategies inherently address either or both the creation of greater variety for "us" and the reduction of the adversary's ability to take certain actions—"their" requisite variety. Research is needed to define the appropriate aspects (space, time, complexity, and so on) of variety for a given context, and a process to measure action relevancy.

A requisite variety index would provide a useful metric to assess the robustness and likelihood of success for an ongoing or planned action, and should be included in all COA plans and candidate option assessments. In addition, monitoring and measuring the effectiveness of the feedback loops (particularly the implicit ones) in the OODA Loop would be very useful to determine whether stakeholders' implicit knowledge is being shared effectively, and whether needed adjustments in the data collection-observe node are being communicated and implemented.

Developing a "What-if" Capability

Real-world decision processes inherently entail developing and evaluating alternative COA plans and options. In the "as-is" DSS, alternative actions can be assessed for their contribution to the mission goals, because in both the "as-is" and "what-if" systems the decision spaces are the same. The difference in the "what-if"-capable DSS is that the system helps to generate candidate options and rank them in terms of their assessment scores. In effect, we are recommending a formal net-centric process as part of the DSS design that will permit authorized users to participate in the generation of multiple options, their assessment, and, importantly, the interpretation of the options' effects. An additional dimension to the "what-if" formulation is to tie the DSS to exercises, and evaluate training with the purpose of speeding up the OODA Loop.[13]

Recognizing the "Larger" Affects

In addition to the above "technical" improvements, there is, in a systems sense, the larger view that encompasses the four commons addressed in this book. That view includes shared resources, the physical environment, migration patterns, and the troubling behavior of resource users in the commons characterized by Garrett Hardin in his "Tragedy of the Commons."[14] Hardin's thesis is that degradation or ruin of common resources is inevitable where competing parties can freely access and use the resource. Though Hardin focused on consumable, limited resources (such as grazing land, fisheries, forests, fresh water) the argument is relevant and applicable to the commons addressed in this book. Where competitive interests for material gain, power, prestige, or malfeasance exist and the medium is the commons, the commons will suffer. The question is, given those inherent human and organizational non-altruistic proclivities, what are the appropriate and effective strategies for securing the commons by neutralizing unrestrained competitive behavior? Any successful strategy must be based on shared interests at a minimum, or ideally on shared values. Strategies based on shared economic interests can take the form of privatization, or outside enforcement with formal international agreements. The proposed maritime partnerships strategy discussed earlier is one example of outside enforcement. A third alternative is to create joint and collective welfare frameworks with voluntary constraints, and a common Pareto goal embraced by all the participants.[15]

The DSS described in this chapter is intended to monitor events that affect the security of the commons but are not, in general, the underlying causes. The DSS design should, however, use a framework with metrics to monitor relevant events in those states with commons infringement issues. The analytical framework introduced by Susan Buck offers additional DSS metrics that can monitor effects on failed states with commons infringement issues.[16] Some examples from that framework include: commons boundary definitions, extant operational rules, monitoring processes, sanctions, active enterprises, and representation forums. The intent would be to enrich the information representing the situation and, importantly, delineate what can be done to achieve the desired effects. The value added would come from addressing and portraying cultural characteristics and traditions that are relevant to the mission of securing the global commons. Incorporating some of these metrics, for example, in the Undesired Events set in Figure 12.4, can provide additional discriminators between candidate COAs under consideration.

Conclusion

The modern decision maker charged with managing the security of the global commons requires a structured framework that organizes key decision parameters and facilitates the formulation of correct perspectives, problem descriptions, and solutions that can handle the variety of events, actions, and choices he is confronted with. The DSS described in this chapter provides that basic capability and, as well, a logical building block for additional useful enhancements such as moving from an "as-is" monitoring tool to a "what-if" assessment capability. John Boyd's OODA loop is used as the underlying decision process paradigm because it is an excellent framework for organizational adaptation and decision-centric applications.[17] The DSS design explicitly incorporates Ross Ashby's principle of requisite variety, a logic engine for normalizing semantic and quantitative data, controlled vocabularies with metric intervals of achievement, a multi-attribute utility construct for aggregating assessment valuations by decision perspectives, and advanced displays of measures of effectiveness and measures of performance.

This DSS provides a means to gain situational awareness and measure the state of the commons and trends of concern. It will:

- Identify and monitor factors that facilitate or obstruct security;
- Assess the wide range of threats to security;
- Support the development of tailored regional partnerships; and
- Provide on-time shared situational awareness for stakeholders.

The value added for this proposed commons DSS is as an enabling capability for making programmatic decisions and assessing institutional changes that ensure stability and prosperity in the global commons.

13 Integrated Training Systems

Scott Jasper and Scott Moreland

Building Security Partnerships

> "Today, our nations and the world are facing new, increasingly global threats, such as terrorism, the proliferation of weapons of mass destruction, their means of delivery and cyber attacks."
>
> *NATO Declaration on Alliance Security*[1]

The North Atlantic Treaty Organization recognizes that its members' national interests are inextricably tied to a stable and secure international environment. While there is a significant role for the military to play in global security assurance, recent experience in the Balkans and Afghanistan demonstrates that today's security challenges require a comprehensive approach by the international community that combines civil and military measures and coordination. Direct military intervention will still be required to overcome acute threats, but such actions should aim to create or sustain opportunities for strong and positive civil engagement, to defuse and eventually eliminate the causes of conflict. Such a comprehensive approach to security requires all international actors to contribute to a concerted effort with a shared sense of openness and determination, based on their respective strengths and mandates.[2]

In the United States, there has been an explicit shift in national security policy toward cooperative relationships between the Defense Department and interagency partners, nongovernmental organizations, and private or commercial interests that share common goals. Internationally, the United States has made building partner nations' security capabilities a priority,[3] but the successful integration of partners with their U.S. military counterparts in some operations, like stabilization and reconstruction, has proven a difficult task. The much-maligned "nation-building under fire"[4] strategy that was pursued by U.S. military personnel in Iraq and Afghanistan evolved as a strategy of necessity, not design: there was simply no civil authority or international organization able to take a lead role in these hostile environments. Nation-building, with its range of security dilemmas that transcend national borders and authority, is just one of many operations that raise the question of civil versus military leadership and responsibility.

The military's traditional responsibility to maintain security may make it the obvious lead in some activities in the global commons, such as ballistic missile defense or sea control. Other activities may demand extensive multilateral and interagency cooperation to address the political, economic, and social issues that are crucial for long-term security assurance.[5] This is especially true of emerging situations in the commons that lack the guidance of mature and tested national and international policies. For instance, do we pursue a policy of arms control or military supremacy in space?[6] Should national navies control piracy in international waters, or should commercial interests invest in private security escorts? Is the military a capable and appropriate lead for information security in the cyberspace commons? Although the answers to these individual questions may be elusive, in all cases the theme of integration and cooperation is clear. One effective way to determine and practice appropriate roles and responsibilities, overcome capability gaps or shortfalls, and promote integration in operations with multinational defense and interagency partners, is through joint training forums and activities.

The Imperative for Security Cooperation

> "We will act in concert with those who value cooperation and collaboration to foster security and stability."
> *Admiral Timothy J. Keating, U.S. Navy, Commander, U.S. Pacific Command*[7]

The United States' maritime security training program for partners in the Gulf of Guinea demonstrates the necessity of cooperation in the global commons. The U.S. Navy, with assistance from Italian and Spanish military experts, began training personnel from partner countries around Africa's Gulf of Guinea to help improve maritime security in a region beset by piracy, drug smuggling, and raids on off-shore oil facilities. Many African navies lack the capabilities necessary to stop increasingly bold attacks in sovereign coastal waters. The United States, NATO members, and other stakeholder nations augmented these regional navies with warships to fight piracy, but their agile adversaries rapidly shifted tactics. Sidestepping the coalescing foreign naval power in the open waters of the Gulf, renegade gunmen in fast launches started to target oil and fishing boats, and even coastal towns in areas where foreign intervention is limited or legally constrained by sovereign interests.

To counter this development, the U.S. Navy began training African volunteers, as part of the Africa Partnership Station under U.S. Africa Command, to improve situational awareness and response capability at the regional and local level.[8] As mentioned by Jeff Kline in Chapter 5, the Africa Partnership Station represents a shift toward a more cooperative strategy for maritime security. U.S. naval amphibious ships serve as a sea-based staging area to support scientists, personnel from aid organizations, and military trainers from the United States and allied militaries, who are working to build regional maritime security and humanitarian assistance capacity. The goal is to identify and overcome root causes of instability in the region under U.S. Secretary of Defense Robert Gates' people-centric philosophy that "ultimate success or failure will increasingly depend more on shaping the behavior of others—friends and adversaries, and most importantly, the people in between."[9]

Security cooperation encompasses not only exchanges between multinational defense institutions, but also interaction with interagency partners, foreign ministries, regional and international organizations, and private sector interests. This inclusive interpretation of the joint security community acknowledges the vital role that non-defense sector actors play in national, regional, and international stability and defense. Unfortunately, military support for civil agencies is a concept that has not matured apace with demand. For the United States, the 2008 National Defense Strategy emphasizes that the military "must improve its ability to deploy civilian expertise rapidly, and continue to increase effectiveness by joining with organizations and people outside of government—untapped resources with enormous potential."[10]

The integration of defense and interagency partners into a balanced security strategy requires planning approaches, training scenarios, and implementation methods that are universally applicable and relevant. The roles and relationships are often unfamiliar and difficult, even contentious. Joint training can provide a forum for the development of unified goals, cooperative and mutually supportive tasks, and the resolution of integration problems. Joint training can include a host of activities, which may be as simple as collaborative scenario-based workshops or notional table-top war games, or as complex and resource-intensive as a full field-training exercise replete with realistic threats in a challenging simulated or real-world venue.[11]

Joint training events further provide a means to orchestrate complex activities involving multiple players and to harmonize command and cooperative relationships. The service components and regional combatant commands of the United States possess a unique capability and responsibility not only to facilitate training for the joint uniformed services, but also to integrate interagency and multinational partners through training. The services boast excellent joint training venues, such as the U.S. Army's National Training Center and the U.S. Air Force's Red Flag program at Nellis Air Force Base, while combatant and functional commands can offer the planning, funding, and expertise required to sponsor high quality, integrated training and exercises.[12] But perhaps the most important U.S. training capability, one that is applicable for international and interagency community consideration as an integration framework, is a deliberate and coherent training process known as the *Joint Training System.*

Joint Training System Applicability

The Joint Training System (JTS) is the official United States Armed Forces joint training instrument. The JTS has two fundamental and mutually supporting purposes: *capabilities development* and *requirements-based (mission-to task) training.*[13] In general terms, the purpose of joint training is to prepare in advance to accomplish key tasks and succeed in anticipated missions. The JTS provides a process to determine what capabilities are critical for mission accomplishment, then focuses its training program on the development of those capabilities. The JTS can assist commanders first to identify tasks essential to mission accomplishment, then to determine the required scope of training and participation necessary to achieve proficiency in task performance. The JTS also provides evaluation tools to determine training effectiveness, capture lessons learned, and guide future training efforts.[14]

Under the JTS, training events are planned, resourced, and executed to mirror the real-world activities they represent. Training ideally should be a deliberate and organized activity that ties training objectives to mission-essential tasks. Training events will be most useful when they are conducted under realistic and rigorous conditions, and their tasks are evaluated against measurable and meaningful standards. The training "end-state" is the successful development of a *capability*, defined as "the ability to achieve a desired effect under specified standards and conditions through combinations of means and ways to perform a set of tasks."[15] Mission readiness is achieved through a combination of capabilities development and the proficient execution of mission-essential tasks.[16]

The JTS is specifically designed to support "the synchronization, coordination, and/or integration of the activities of governmental and nongovernmental entities with military operations to achieve unity of effort."[17] As previously mentioned, the global commons are complex settings where the military may alternately lead or be called to provide support to other lead agencies. To achieve mission readiness, military commanders must pursue joint training objectives that develop the right military capabilities to support a comprehensive approach, combining the contributions of allied and coalition forces with governmental and nongovernmental agencies. To accomplish this, the JTS must fully integrate foreign military and civilian participants into a universally applicable and achievable training program that accurately reflects the complex challenges of the twenty-first century security environment.

The Joint Training System utilizes a four-phase methodology driven by commanders' assessments and needs, as illustrated below in Figure 13.1. In Phase I (Requirements), the joint force commander determines the capabilities the force requires to accomplish assigned or anticipated missions. These capabilities are defined in terms of tasks, conditions, and standards, and are delegated to specific organizations. During Phase II (Plans), participating commands and agencies develop their Joint/Agency Training Plans, which specify comprehensive training requirements and objectives. Because joint training requires extensive preparation, synchronization, and resource allocation, it is also imperative during this phase that planners start to develop the training activity's scope and design, resource requirements, and training event milestones and timelines. In Phase III (Execution), planners finalize details and allocate the resources needed to support the capstone training activity; once their forces have completed the training events, commanders evaluate the exercise and report the outcomes. Finally, in Phase IV (Assessment), the lead agency's commander or director evaluates joint training performance relative to the mission-essential task requirements specified in Phase I, the results of which help gauge progress toward capability development and guide future training efforts.[18]

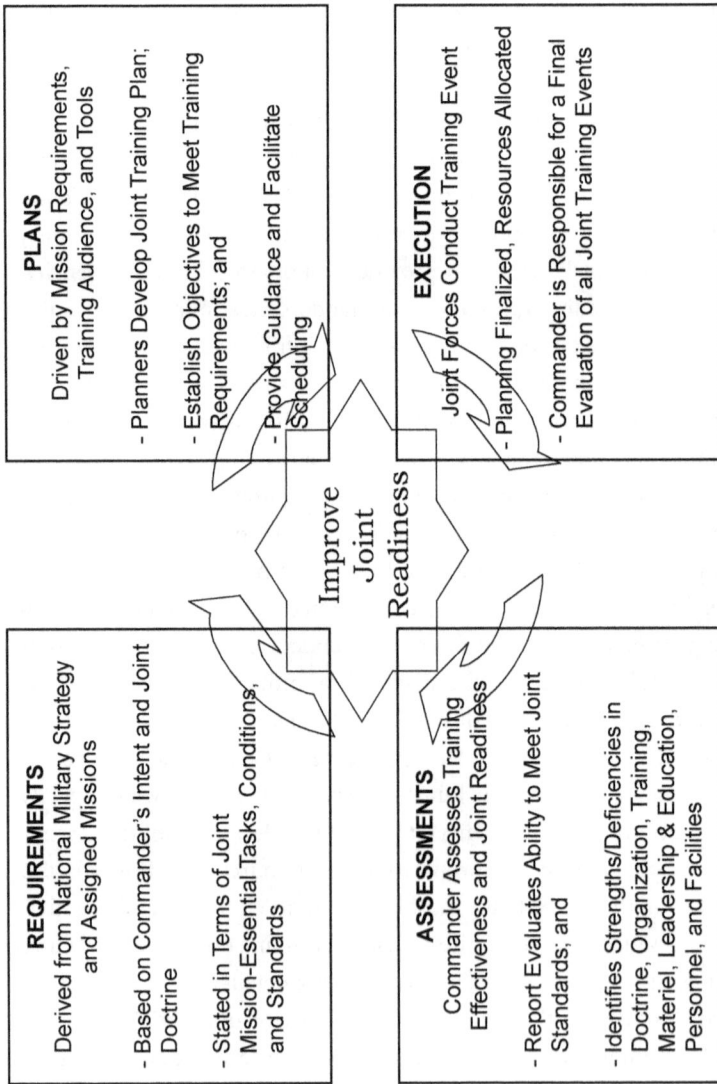

REQUIREMENTS

Derived from National Military Strategy and Assigned Missions

- Based on Commander's Intent and Joint Doctrine

- Stated in Terms of Joint Mission-Essential Tasks, Conditions, and Standards

PLANS

Driven by Mission Requirements, Training Audience, and Tools

- Planners Develop Joint Training Plan;

- Establish Objectives to Meet Training Requirements; and

- Provide Guidance and Facilitate Scheduling

ASSESSMENTS

Commander Assesses Training Effectiveness and Joint Readiness

- Report Evaluates Ability to Meet Joint Standards; and

- Identifies Strengths/Deficiencies in Doctrine, Organization, Training, Materiel, Leadership & Education, Personnel, and Facilities

EXECUTION

Joint Forces Conduct Training Event

- Planning Finalized, Resources Allocated

- Commander is Responsible for a Final Evaluation of all Joint Training Events

Improve Joint Readiness

FIGURE 13.1 The Joint Training System

source: Modified from "Joint Training Manual for the Armed Forces of the United States," Chairman of the Joint Chiefs of Staff Manual (CJCSM) 3500.03B, Washington, D.C., 31 August 2007: B–1, 2.

Phase 1: Requirements

"Do essential things first. There is not enough time for the commander to do everything. Each commander will have to determine wisely what is essential, and assign responsibilities for accomplishment. . . . This is especially true of training. Nonessentials should not take up time required for essentials."

General Bruce C. Clarke, former Commander-in-Chief, U.S. Army—Europe[19]

The first, or "Requirements," phase guides commanders as they identify the critical tasks that underpin success in their assigned missions. Requirements-based, or "mission-to-task" training hinges on an ability to first identify and codify in concrete terms *what* must be done to achieve success. The Universal Joint Task List (UJTL) is a JTS tool that assists commanders in this endeavor by providing a common lexicon that defines the *what*, according to a comprehensive and multi-echelon series of *tasks*.[20] The tasks are jointly applicable by design, and are generally sufficient to "address what the U.S. military needs to be able to undertake when working with [interagency], multinational, and coalition partners" in integrated operations.[21] Unit commanders determine which tasks they *must* be able to perform to support designed operational requirements. These "must-do" tasks comprise the command's *mission-essential task list*, or METL.

Requirements-based training definitively ties the command training program to the commander's METL. The METL reflects wartime requirements, and will ultimately determine a unit's capability to perform its mission. In the past, mission assignments were intended to counter named threats that operated according to well-defined and understood doctrine under specific geographical and environmental conditions. Because of this, under the events-based training model that corresponded to previous threat-based planning strategies, METL tasks were traditionally "stabilized," and only modified when there was a change in wartime missions.[22]

In the last decade, however, the term "wartime mission" has largely lost its reference point. Units are routinely mobilized and deployed to conduct non-traditional operations in unfamiliar locations across the spectrum of conflict, working in concert with multinational and civilian partners. The operational need for more flexible and adaptive units has led to a conceptual shift in training, from being events-based to a more generic requirements basis, which necessitates a more fluid approach to METL development. The shift away from threat-based planning has had a further de-stabilizing effect on training. Each significant revision of a unit's mission set has forced major changes to its METL and, as a consequence, required major modifications or wholesale changes to events-based training methodologies.[23]

Army and Marine ground forces have been especially stressed by the man-power-intensive and ever-changing strategies used in expeditionary operations in Central Asia and the Middle East over the past decade. This high operational tempo, coupled with the transformation to brigade-centric and modular-component force packaging has forced commanders to discover new ways to identify METLs and internalize them into effective training programs that will prepare forces for both current deployments and future battles against conventional and irregular threats.

The Army Task List, which is the service equivalent of the Universal Joint Task List, reflects a new emphasis on U.S. Army operations in the emerging battle spaces of the global commons. Ground-force tasks that may be mission-essential to joint operations in the commons might include such Army tasks as *5.6-Integrate Space Operations, 6.1-Employ Air and Missile Defense,* or *6.3-Conduct Information Protection.*[24] The U.S. Army's 6th Air Defense Artillery Brigade, for example, is conducting pre-fielding experimentation and training with the Terminal High Altitude Area Defense, or THAAD, missile defense system. Designed to have tactical to strategic national utility, the THAAD system is intended to provide "broad area coverage against threats to military forces and critical assets, such as population centers and industrial resources."[25] As a major emerging component in the ballistic missile defense system, when it is operational THAAD is expected to intercept short- to medium-range missiles from mobile and flexible ground-based launchers, as mentioned by Will Dossel in Chapter 8.

One of the most radical shifts in U.S. Army mission readiness and training is the bold-faced concession that Army training simply cannot aspire to fully prepare individual units to meet all of the assigned or anticipated METL tasks. Army full-spectrum operations are categorized into broad sets: offensive, defensive, stability, or civil support operations. Tactical tasks are then associated with operational themes: military engagements, limited interventions, peace operations, irregular warfare, and major combat.[26] For a single unit to be proficient in the essential tasks that would support this diverse range of operations across such an expansive set of themes is simply not a realistic goal. Full METL proficiency, once a sacrosanct training requirement, has been replaced by a new Army training concept: *aim point* training prioritization.

The Army Field Manual points out that the aim point concept represents "a major cultural change for Army leaders, Soldiers, and units."[27] In essence, it is the

Army's acknowledgement that it must balance the more traditional focus of its training on major combat operations with the persistent requirement for its hard-won "proficiency in irregular warfare and limited intervention."[28] Figure 13.2 depicts where the Army's training aim point currently lies (the bold oval) relative to present and *most likely* future requirements, which are shown by the dotted oval. It clearly illustrates the Army's need to shift its training focus inexorably leftward toward tasks that support a broader range of operational themes.

The U.S. Army is just one of many security contributors that are re-focusing their training programs to better reflect task requirements in the commons. The UN Department of Peacekeeping Operations has also embraced requirements-based training for military peacekeepers to "optimize military training and education efforts preparing for the evolving, demanding environment in which future peace support operations will be conducted."[29] The UN's framework documents for requirements-based training, titled "33 Common

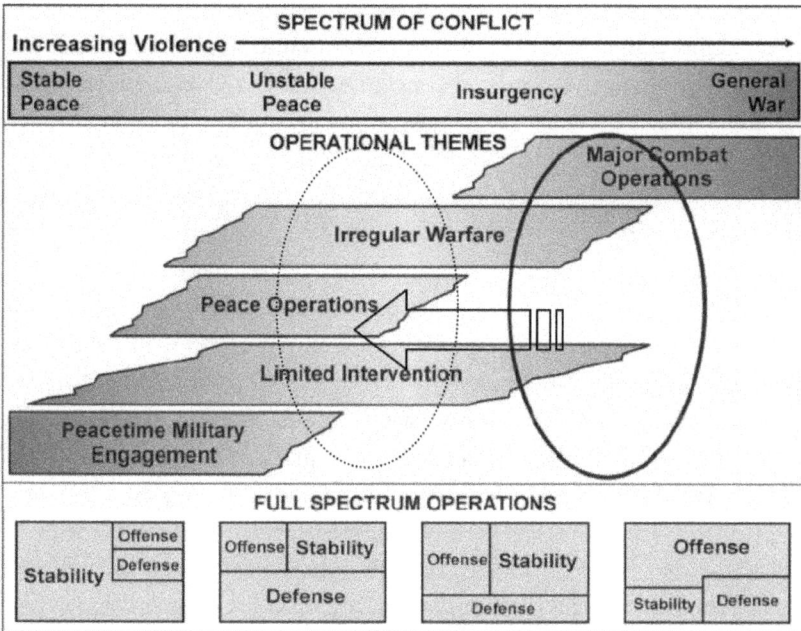

FIGURE 13.2 Aim Point for Army Training and Leader Development

SOURCE: Modified from "Training for Full-spectrum Operations," United States Army Field Manual (FM) 7–0, Headquarters, Department of the Army, Washington, D.C., December 2008: 1–7.

Peacekeeping Tasks," make significant reference to the Joint Mission-Essential Task List Handbook and the Universal Joint Task List, a tribute to international confidence in the Joint Training System.[30]

Phase 2: Plans

> "You can always amend a big plan, but you can never expand a little one. I don't believe in little plans. I believe in plans big enough to meet a situation which we can't possibly foresee now."
>
> *Harry S. Truman, 33d U.S. president*[31]

The second JTS phase, Plans, is perhaps the most demanding and vital to training success. Military commanders set the foundation for the Plans phase by comparing their current capabilities to the mission-essential tasks and identifying capabilities shortfalls. The training objectives that derive from this initial step clearly describe the level of capability development that forces will require to attain proficiency in an essential task. Related objectives can then be grouped together to form the basis for a training activity.

The U.S. Pacific Command-sponsored exercises provide excellent examples of combining complementary training objectives into a cogent training event. The majority of Pacific Command's operational space resides in the maritime commons, which encompasses layered dimensions of international airspace, outer space, and cyberspace. Preceding chapters in this volume highlight the complex operational, legal, and environmental considerations for operating in the global commons that must be reflected in the commander's Joint/Agency Training Plan. Out of necessity, Pacific Command exercises combine military training objectives with those of coalition and interagency participants, supported by industry partners. To provide realistic training for the Pacific Command area of responsibility, exercises are set in multi-dimensional live and virtual training venues. According to Pacific Command staff, exercise planning should involve "almost every imaginable type of war fighting capability . . . underwater, on water, over water, airspace, land, cyber."[32]

Effective warfare training scenarios should challenge participants with simultaneous conflicts that span the breadth of the global commons: maritime engagements at strategic chokepoints, ballistic missile exchanges, and cyberwarfare are just a few potential concurrently occurring scenarios. Exercise planning requires careful venue development and exhaustive synchronization of events with training objectives—in fact, the majority of time allocated to a training event can easily be consumed by planning activities. The Joint Training System emphasizes deliberate planning of training events, but it saves time and improves planning synchronization with an automated planning support tool: the Joint Training Information Management System (JTIMS).

A responsibility of the Joint Chiefs of Staff, JTIMS "is used by the joint staff and major commands to manage all large-scale military training and operational events."[33] JTIMS supports the task-based, multi-phased structure of the JTS by integrating all four JTS phases and linking them to assigned missions and mission-essential tasks through a web-based network available to the collaborative training community. The collaborative capability and standardized processes of the JTIMS provide training stakeholders with on-demand access to both the tools and the critical operational, administrative, and logistical data that support each command's training plan.[34]

Although JTIMS is a powerful joint training management tool, one of its primary shortfalls is a lack of interoperability for integrated training events with non-military participants. Interagency and multinational partners have limited JTIMS access and system familiarity, so training planners will often supplement the JTIMS planning tools with an inclusive *synchronization matrix*. The planning phase of Lightning Rescue 2008 offers a good example of the utility of the synchronization matrix for integrated training. Set in the Hawaiian Islands, Lightning Rescue is "a Joint Task Force—Homeland Defense exercise designed to test federal, state, and local agencies' coordinated efforts in responding to pandemic influenza or other . . . disasters throughout the Pacific."[35]

During the exercise's final planning conference, participating military and interagency representatives used the synchronization matrix to thoroughly review the training scenario events to ensure realism, applicability to training objectives, and the feasibility of implementation. Working together, stakeholders applied their unique areas of expertise to each of the scenario events as they created the master scenario events list; they then were able to identify and resolve conflicting plans, shortfalls, and omissions as they coordinated their assigned tasks and response actions for each scenario event. The exercise director, Lieutenant Colonel Ed Toy, emphasized the utility of the synchronization matrix beyond the training event, asserting that "once it has been vetted and refined through the exercise, the synchronization matrix becomes the basis for your integrated response plan. Lead agency authority, level of response, and who is providing the resources: all of that is hashed out as you build the synch[ronization] matrix."[36]

Phase 3: Execution

> "We must replicate the fast-paced, chaotic conditions of future battle-fields in our training environments."
>
> *General James N. Mattis, Commander, U.S. Joint Forces Command and*
> *NATO's Supreme Allied Commander Transformation* [37]

The success of the third joint training phase, Execution, is largely dependent on the methodical implementation of the preceding phases. In fact, although the Execution phase is certainly the climactic point of the process, it can also be the most simple to conduct. Training events that are guided by a commander's clear intent, coordinated through a participant synchronization matrix, and thoroughly scripted with a realistic master scenario events list will generally accomplish stakeholder training objectives. If requirements have been properly identified and the event has been purposefully planned and supported, then the training execution phase can focus concisely on building mission-critical capabilities based on a pre-designated set of conditions and standards.

Venue preparation is critical for training success in the Execution phase. The twenty-first century battlefield demands a complex and diverse training arena with interconnected activities across the global commons. The training venue, for instance, may need to virtually connect training participants from around the world. The U.S. military's Joint National Training Capability (JNTC) accomplishes the daunting task of realistic venue development in a joint, multinational, and interagency context, by providing an integrated network of live training sites, virtual manned simulators, and computer-simulated training nodes and events.[38] Its global community of over forty interoperable training sites can provide a broad spectrum of joint training needs without geographic or other physical limitations. Further, JNTC provides consistent, standards-based training regardless of the training participants' physical location or training venue, by ensuring that each training node undergoes the same accreditation and certification process.

The JNTC continues to improve security and cross-domain information sharing; network-enabled interaction between live, virtual (platform simulators), and constructive (computer-simulated) training capabilities; and joint systems compatibility through the development of the Joint Training and Experimentation Network (JTEN). The JTEN "globally and persistently connects sites, allowing seamless training in a common operational environment."[39] Service training networks, such as the Air Force Distributed Mission Operations Network and the Navy Continuous Training Environment, as well as service training sites and models and simulations, can be linked to the JTEN in order to bring joint context to service-specific training programs. Significantly, JTEN is expanding beyond the U.S. joint military community to connect allied and coalition partners through compatible training interfaces such as the NATO Joint Warfare Center in Norway, and Australia's Defence Training and Experimentation Network.[40]

Since 2007, combatant command-level exercises have validated the JTEN by conducting networked training between the United States and partners such as Australia, Japan, and South Korea across live and simulated air, maritime, ground, space, and cyberspace domains.[41] To ensure defensive preeminence against adversaries' asymmetric strategies, JTEN training venues must cover the spectrum of the global commons. JTEN has made great strides in the cyber-training domain in particular, with the establishment of an Information Operations range. This range provides a venue to develop capabilities and validate cyber-engagement options against threats ranging from direct attacks by sophisticated national-level adversaries to irregular and transnational cyber engagements. The range also provides a cyber-environment where information operations can provide options other than direct military force to shape behavior or respond to events such as military deception, electronic warfare, psychological operations, computer network operations, and operations security.[42]

The JTS Execution phase ends with a command evaluation of whether the exercise achieved the joint training objectives. Stakeholder commands and directorates conduct an After Action Review to report outcomes of responses and activities from the master scenario event list, lessons learned and best practices, observations on exercise management and logistical support, and recommendations for further training. The evaluation products that are generated during the Execution phase (written reports and observer notes) are recorded in JTIMS to facilitate the transition to a more thorough examination of the training.

Phase 4: Assessment

A training assessment is "the analytical process used by commanders to determine an organization's proficiency to accomplish the capability requirements."[43] The assessment phase of the Joint Training System provides participating commanders and their staffs with valuable training information that describes their current level of mission capability, based on the observations and evaluations of their ability to accomplish assigned mission-essential tasks.

The goal of the assessment phase is to determine whether the organization is sufficiently trained to be considered "mission-capable," or if personnel require additional training to achieve adequate proficiency in an essential task.

The JTS provides a standards-based assessment methodology that utilizes quantitative *measures* and *criteria* to evaluate successful task execution. *Measures* describe levels of task performance. Their supporting *criteria* define the acceptable level of performance to determine task proficiency. Together, measures and criteria comprise the task *standard*.[44] Commanders determine the appropriate task standards and associated measures and criteria, using the Universal Joint Task List as their guide. For example, if a commander wishes to evaluate unit proficiency in the operational task *OP 6.1—Provide Operational Air, Space, and Missile Defense,* he or she could select a combination of kinetic engagement measures (e.g., *M9—Percent of hostile aircraft and missiles engaged and destroyed*), and non-kinetic performance measures (e.g., *M1—Errors in performance of air surveillance, identification, and track monitor procedures*), and then determine the criteria for each measure that would best reflect successful accomplishment of that task.[45]

The Assessment phase also assists commanders to determine the effectiveness of their training program in developing critical capabilities. The assessment provides clear measurements of force strengths and weaknesses, identifies training issues and lessons learned, and offers recommendations for refinement of the joint training program to meet command training objectives.[46] Service component commanders, multinational participants, interagency directors, and other supporting organization leaders can all utilize this training assessment method to evaluate their organization's training effectiveness and determine its readiness to perform unified missions. The assessment phase of the JTS describes how the collective training results are:

(1) Translated into requirements for subsequent training cycles;

(2) Developed into lessons learned;

(3) Used to identify and resolve issues; and

(4) Made available to other users of training information.[47]

Lessons learned and best practices noted in the Assessment phase of joint training should be reflected in doctrinal updates, policy revisions, and concept documents. The development of the U.S. Department of Defense's Maritime Domain Awareness Joint Integrating Concept (MDA JIC) provides an example of how using assessment to validate concepts and generate capability requirements can in turn help shape training objectives. Maritime Domain Awareness is a critical component of maritime security, as explained in detail in Chapter 5. In November 2008, the draft MDA JIC was reviewed by a Joint Staff Red Team of experts on future scenarios and adversary strategies. The Red Team agreed with the concepts presented in the draft, but felt that the document "lacked specific details of the solution and a common theme." The Red Team comments were then used to perform a substantial rewrite of the MDA JIC, which led to a subsequent adjustment of capability requirements; these were validated at a Limited Objective Experiment held in March 2009.[48]

The MDA JIC capabilities generally center on the ability to: exercise command and control of MDA assets; collect essential information on entities of interest; aggregate, display, and analyze maritime information; predict activity within the maritime domain; and exchange information with U.S., international, nongovernmental, and commercial partners. These requirements highlight the need for a network approach to Maritime Domain Awareness that mandates joint military, interagency, and international partner cooperation, as well as ubiquitous network communications, web-based information-sharing, and space satellite effect technologies. The MDA JIC also goes further, however, to offer tasks with standards that can help determine capability requirements for both military commands and non-military stakeholders.[49]

These types of concepts can assist commanders to effectively identify the tasks, resources, and players that must be incorporated into training events to achieve refined training objectives. For example, Combined Joint Task Force—Horn of Africa (CJTF-HOA) hosted regional cooperation working groups in June 2008 to demonstrate how the MDA JIC could help identify training tasks for developing critical capabilities. The Horn of Africa encompasses a strategically vital maritime common wherein international and regional partners must deal with de-stabilizing issues ranging from violent extremist movements to piracy. The success of the CJTF-HOA workshop confirms that maritime domain awareness is an essential regional capability requirement, as expressed by Ugandan Lieutenant Colonel Michael Nyayrwa: "We looked at how maritime security and safety strategies could be developed in the workshop and we came to understand these strategies are not about navies, but about maritime domain awareness. It is about partnership, it is about cooperation, it is about countries pooling their resources [and] sharing information."[50] The MDA JIC offers a conceptual framework that commanders can use to determine the best way to train to achieve maritime domain awareness as a core capability for maritime security.

Externally-Imposed Training Challenges

Military training has long been a target of media interest and public protest, and for good reason. Regional command-level training exercises, in particular, reflect both preparedness and the will to protect sovereign borders, honor alliance commitments, or even preemptively engage an immediate threat. The REdeployment of FORces to GERmany (REFORGER) exercises in Europe during the Cold War era not only prepared U.S. troops for deployment to a potential ground war in Western Europe, but also sent a powerful message that the United States was unwaveringly committed to its NATO allies and was fully prepared to deploy, engage, and destroy a named aggressor: the Soviet Union.[51]

Despite its longevity, however, the REFORGER exercises were beset with fierce opposition from German protestors. The culmination came in 1988, a year during which eighteen NATO planes crashed on West German soil while training, and seven people, including five German civilians, were killed during REFORGER exercises.[52] These training disasters, coupled with a waning Soviet threat, led to the cancellation of REFORGER in 1989. When it re-surfaced from 1990–1993, REFORGER had been reduced largely to a computer-simulated command post exercise, and the once awe-inspiring division-level tank maneuvers were banned outright to avoid infrastructure and environmental damage, and demonstrate respect for German citizens weary of living in a simulated war zone.[53]

Commanders face similar challenges in contemporary operational-level training. The biennial, bilateral U.S.-Australian Talisman Saber exercise is a clear case in point. Talisman Saber, according to its press release, is "designed to provide both countries' military forces enhanced combined and joint war fighting skills while furthering the U.S.-Australia defense relationship."[54] In 2007, the field training was conducted at the "Shoalwater Bay Training Area, Defence Practice Area (marine) adjacent to Cowley Beach Training Area, and within the Coral Sea within the Australian Maritime limits of the Territorial Sea zone and the Exclusive Economic Zone."[55] Since its inception in 2005, the conduct of the exercise has met with staunch opposition from protestors "against U.S. nuclear policy and environmentalists fearful of Shoalwater Bay being turned into a wasteland."[56]

Talisman Saber's exercise planners realized the importance of addressing legitimate protests in a forthright fashion. During the second iteration of the exercise in 2007, the Australian Department of Defence commissioned an exhaustive and openly available Public Environment Report. This detailed document, far more than a cursory response to inconvenient grievances, carefully considered the political, environmental, and social impacts of this large-scale military exercise. The Australian Defence Department seized the opportunity to dispel rumors and assuage concerns by openly inviting even the most vocal exercise opponents to review and comment on the report. Meanwhile, commanders from both countries explicitly "committed to promoting a strong culture of sustainable environmental management in all combined military activities."[57]

The candid approach to public concerns regarding Talisman Saber's 2007 exercise facilitated balanced and integrated training, while moderating public perceptions and safeguarding military legitimacy through public affairs outreach. Although the training took place largely within Australian sovereign territory, international concerns over impacts in the global commons were also addressed. For example, exercise participants vowed to heed the International Whaling Commission's warnings about the "potential effects of naval mid-frequency sonar devices on whales and dolphins" by avoiding areas known to be frequented by cetaceans and maintaining active whale lookouts.[58]

Joint and integrated training activities in the commons will certainly face similar opposition from regional and international environmental groups, peace activists, and geo-political opponents. Solutions such as networked simulated training venues, careful effects planning, voluntary restraint (e.g., reduced sonar transmissions), and public outreach are all means to mitigate potential training disruptions, maintain military legitimacy, and foster public goodwill. Training that includes interagency and multinational partners not only supports a balanced approach to security in the commons, but demonstrates the military's willingness to cooperate with the broader civilian and international community.

Conclusion

> "I believe that the operational environment will feature at least three core challenges: rising tensions in the global commons; increasingly hybrid forms of warfare; and frequent threats . . . associated with state weakness or failure."
>
> *Michèle Flournoy, U.S. Under Secretary of Defense for Policy*[59]

In the twenty-first century, training programs must be responsive to converging modes of warfare arising from a broad range of adversaries. Hybrid threats incorporate combinations of conventional capabilities, irregular tactics, terrorist acts, and criminal disorder to overcome Western conventional military primacy.[60] Training for operations in the global commons is an integral component of a comprehensive approach that recognizes that military dominance is insufficient to address global security challenges. Military, civilian, and commercial stakeholders each have an important role to play. Joint, multinational, and integrated training is the key to developing the required collective capabilities for security assurance.

The Joint Training System provides a framework to determine what critical capabilities are needed and how to focus training tasks, functions, and people to help generate those capabilities.[61] The system can assist commanders to decide what types of training events to conduct and what partner stakeholders should be incorporated. The JTS offers a standards-based assessment mechanism that measures how effective the joint training was in generating required capabilities, which in turn guides future training efforts and resource commitments.

The United States and its partner nations will continue to play a decisive role in international security, especially in the global commons. Allies must be able to fulfill their responsibilities through a comprehensive approach to international security assurance. Joint training must prepare military commands not only to serve as the guardians of national sovereignty, but also to work with civil actors to protect the essential networks of information, commerce, and governance that comprise the global system.

REFERENCE MATTER

Notes

Foreword

1. Andrew J. Bacevich, "The Petraeus Doctrine," *The Atlantic*, October 2008: http://www.theatlantic.com/doc/200810/petraeus-doctrine.

2. Robert M. Gates, "A Balanced Strategy: Reprogramming the Pentagon for a New Age," *Foreign Affairs*, vol. 88: 1 (January/February 2009): 28–40; http://www.foreignaffairs.com/articles/63717/robert-m-gates/a-balanced-strategy.

3. Robert M. Gates, U.S. Secretary of Defense, remarks delivered at the U.S. Naval War College, Newport, Rhode Island, 17 April 2009: http://www.defenselink.mil/speeches/speech.aspx?speechid=1346.

4. Frank Hoffman, "Towards a Balanced and Sustainable Defense," E-Notes, the Foreign Policy Research Institute, 6 March 2009: http://www.fpri.org/enotes/200903.hoffman.balancedsustainabledefense.html.

5. Patrick M. Cronin, "Introduction," in *Global Strategic Assessment 2009: America's Security Role in a Changing World*, Patrick M. Cronin, ed. (Washington, D.C.: National Defense University Press, 2009), iii.

6. Frank Hoffman, "Conflict in the 21st Century: The Rise of Hybrid Wars," The Potomac Institute for Policy Studies, Arlington, Virginia, December 2007: http://www.potomacinstitute.org/media/pressreleases/2008/013108HyrbidWars.htm.

7. Michèle Flournoy and Shawn Brimley, "The Contested Commons," *Proceedings*, U.S. Naval Institute, Annapolis, Maryland, Vol. 135/7/1,277 (July 2009): 16–21. Also see Jason Sherman, "Flournoy: QDR Must Prepare For End of U.S. Hegemony in 'Global Commons'," *Inside Defense*, 2 July 2009: http://defensenewsstand.com.

8. Paul S. Giarra and Michael J. Green, "Asia's Military Balance at a Tipping Point: America's Deterrent is Shrinking in the Region," *Asian Wall Street Journal*, 17 July 2009: http://online.wsj.com/article/SB124776820445852755.html.

9. Andrew F. Krepinevich Jr., "The Pentagon's Wasting Assets," *Foreign Affairs* (July/August 2009): 18–33; http://www.foreignaffairs.com/articles/65150/andrew-f-krepinevich-jr/the-pentagons-wasting-assets.

10. See "The Global Redistribution of Economic Power," in *Global Strategic Assessment 2009: America's Security Role in a Changing World*, Patrick M. Cronin, ed. (Washington, D.C.: National Defense University Press, 2009): http://www.ndu.edu/inss/index.cfm?secID=8&pageID=126&type=section.

11. Robert M. Gates, "Defense Budget Recommendation Statement," as prepared for delivery, U.S. Department of Defense, Arlington, Virginia, 6 April 2009: http://www.defenselink.mil/speeches/speech.aspx?speechid=1341.

Chapter 1

1. General John Craddock, U.S. Army, Supreme Allied Commander, Europe, "SACEUR Address to the NATO Parliamentary Assembly," 19 November 2008: 2; http://www.nato.int/shape/opinions/2008/s081219a.htm.

2. Donald H. Rumsfeld, U.S. Secretary of Defense, "The National Defense Strategy of the United States of America," Office of the U.S. Secretary of Defense, March 2005: 13.

3. Lynn White Jr., *Medieval Technology & Social Change* (London: Oxford University Press, 1962), 44, 51–55.

4. "Global Commons," Glossary of Statistical Terms, Organization for Economic Co-operation and Development (OECD) Statistics Portal: http://stats.oecd.org/glossary/detail.asp?ID=1120.

5. General James T. Conway, U.S. Marine Corps, Admiral Gary Roughhead, U.S. Navy, and Admiral Thad W. Allen, U.S. Coast Guard, "A Cooperative Strategy for 21st Century Seapower," Washington, D.C., October 2007: 1.

6. Susan J. Buck, *The Global Commons: An Introduction* (Washington, D.C.: Island Press, 1998), 1, 45–68. Antarctica, the only terrestrial landmass that does not fall under any national jurisdiction, has been maintained as a commons by international treaty since 1961. Its security is not at issue, not least because of its climate, and so Antarctica is not a subject of this book.

7. Christopher J. Castelli, "Defense Department Adopts New Definition for Cyberspace," *Inside the Pentagon*, 22 May 2008: http://www.insidedefense.com.

8. Barry R. Posen, "The Military Foundation of U.S. Hegemony," *International Security*, Vol. 28: 1 (Summer 2003): 8.

9. Jaap de Hoop Scheffer, NATO Secretary General, "Transatlantic Leadership For a New Era," speech at the Security and Defense Agenda, Brussels, Belgium, 29 January 2009: 2.

10. Eleanor Keymar, "Space-saving Devices: Militaries Look to Make the Most of Commercial Satellites," Jane's Defense Systems News, 8 October 2008.

11. "Air Combat Platforms and ISR," Feature Report, *Defense Today* (March 2009): 5.

12. Tom Espiner, "U.S. Reveals Plans to Hit Back at Cyberthreats," *CNET News*, remarks by Lt. Gen. Robert J. Elder, USAF, at the Cyber Warfare Conference 2008 in London, 4 April 2008: http://news.cnet.com.

13. Dana A. Shea, "Critical Infrastructure: Control Systems and the Terrorist Threat," CRS Report for Congress RL31534, Congressional Research Service, Washington, D.C., 20 January 2004: 1–11.

14. General J. N. Mattis, U.S. Marine Corps, "The Joint Operating Environment: Challenges and Implications for the Future Joint Force," United States Joint Forces Command, Norfolk, Virginia, 25 November 2008: 10–19.

15. Stephen D. Krasner, *International Regimes* (Ithaca, New York: Cornell University Press, 1983), 1–2.

16. Susan J. Buck, *The Global Commons*, 6–10, 27–31.

17. George W. Bush, president of the United States, "U.S. National Space Policy," Office of the President, 31 August 2006: 2.

18. "Space Security 2008," Space Security Index, September 2008: 46–55; http://www.spacesecurity.org/publications.htm.

19. Peter Schrank, "International: Newly Nasty: Cyberwarfare," *The Economist*, 26 May 2007: 76.

20. General James L. Jones, U.S. Marine Corps (Retired), "A Transition Plan for Securing America's Energy Future," Institute for 21st Century Energy, U.S. Chamber of Commerce, November 2008: 34; http://energyxxi.org/pages/reports.aspx.

21. Clay Wilson, "Botnets, Cybercrime, and Cyberterrorism: Vulnerabilities and Policy Issues for Congress," CRS Report for Congress RL32114, Congressional Research Service, Washington, D.C., 29 January 2008: 5–6.

22. "Emerging Cyber Threats Report for 2009," Georgia Tech Information Security Center, 15 October 2008: 1–2.

23. "Intelligence Note: Storm Worm Virus," Internet Crime Complaint Center, 31 July 2008: http://www.ic3.gov/media/2008/080730.aspx.

24. Iain Thomson, "Russia Hired Botnets for Estonia Cyber-War," *Computing*, 31 May 2007.

25. "Internet Security Threat Report: Trends for July-December 07," Symantec Corporation, Volume XIII, April 2008: 2–9.

26. "Dark Market TakeDown: Exclusive Cyber Club for Crooks Exposed," Headline Archives, Federal Bureau of Investigation, 20 October 2008: http://www.fbi.gov/page2/oct08/darkmarket_102008.html.

27. John D. Sutter, "Twitter hit by denial-of-service attack," Technology section, CNN.com, 6 August 2009.

28. William Matthews, "U.S. Security Experts Differ on Impact of Cyberattacks," *Defense News*, 13 July 2009: 14.

29. Tony Skinner, "War and PC," *Jane's Defense Weekly*, 24 September 2008: 38.

30. Caitlin Talmadge, "Closing Time: Assessing the Iranian Threat to the Strait of Hormuz," *International Security*, Vol. 33: 1 (Summer 2008): 82–117.

31. James A. Lewis, "Securing Cyberspace for the 44th Presidency," Center for Strategic and International Studies, December 2008: 13.

32. Azadeh Ansari, "Smugglers sink 'drug subs,' but not feds' case," Crime section, CNN.com, 14 January 2009.

33. Tom Walters, "Drug cartels using submarines to smuggle cocaine," CTV.ca, 19 July 2008: http://www.ctv.ca/servlet/ArticleNews/story/CTVNews/20080719/sub_drugs_080719/20080719?hub=SciTech.

34. "Piracy and Armed Robbery against Ships," International Chamber of Commerce (ICC) International Maritime Bureau, Annual Report: 1 January—31 December 2008: 1–22.

35. Barbara Surk, "Somali pirates hijack Saudi tanker loaded with oil," *International Herald Tribune,* 17 November 2008; and "Pirates Hijack Two Tankers Within 24 Hours Off Somali Shore," Fox News, 27 March 2009: http://www.foxnews.com/story/0,2933,510766,00.html

36. Mike Pflanz, "Cruise ship opens fire to beat back Somali pirates," Telegraph .co.uk, 26 April 2009.

37. Andrew Scutro, "Pirates Still Defiant Aboard Tank-Carrying Cargo Ship," *Navy Times,* 13 October 2008: 18–19.

38. Julian Hale, "EU Extends Anti-Piracy Effort to Seychelles" *Defense News,* 1 June 2009: 22.

39. Andrew Scutro, "Sailors, Coasties Nab 17 Pirates off Yemen," *Navy Times,* 25 May 2009: 26.

40. "Pirates' luxury lifestyles on lawless coast," International section, CNN.com, 19 November 2008.

41. Peter Chalk, "The Maritime Dimension of International Security," RAND Corporation, Santa Monica, California, 2008: 20–21.

42. Ibid.: 22–24.

43. Eric Sayers, "An Outer Space Defense Bargain," *Armed Forces Journal* (October 2008): 28.

44. Robert M. Gates, U.S. Secretary of Defense, "A Balanced Strategy," *Foreign Affairs* (January/February 2009): 3.

45. Steven J. Lambakis, "Reconsidering Asymmetric Warfare," *Joint Forces Quarterly,* 36 (December 2004): 102–8.

46. Michael W. Wynne, U.S. Secretary of the Air Force, "Cyberspace as a Domain in which the Air Force Flies and Fights," remarks to the C4ISR Integration Conference, Crystal City, Virginia, 2 November 2006: 2.

47. Thomas Harding, "Terrorists 'Use Google Maps to Hit UK Troops,'" *The Sunday Telegraph,* 13 January 2007.

48. "Digital Globe Announces General Availability of Worldview-1 Imagery," DigitalGlobe.com, 3 January 2008: http://media.digitalglobe.com/index.php?s=43&item=135.

49. "Global Positioning System: Serving the World," Timing Applications Fact

Sheet, National Space-Based Positioning, Navigation, and Timing Coordination Office, 10 October 2008: http://www.gps.gov/.

50. "Military Power of the People's Republic of China," Annual Report to Congress, Office of the Secretary of Defense, 2009: 14.

51. Roger Cliff, Mark Burles, Michael S. Chase, Derek Eaton, and Kevin L. Pollpeter, "Entering the Dragon's Lair: Chinese Antiaccess Strategies and Their Implications for the United States," RAND Corporation, Santa Monica, California, 2007: 55.

52. Lieutenant General Stanley A. McChrystal, U.S. Air Force, "Space Operations," Joint Publication 3–14, 6 January 2009: II-1—II-3.

53. "Space Security 2008": 137–173.

54. Craig Covault, "Chinese Test Anti-Satellite Weapon," *Aviation Week*, 17 January 2007.

55. Peppino A. DeBiasco, Director of the Office of Missile Defense Policy, U.S. Department of Defense, "Missile Defense and NATO Security," *Joint Forces Quarterly*, 51 (4th quarter 2008): 46–48; http://www.ndu.edu/inss/Press/jfq_pages/editions/i51/13.pdf

56. Lauren Gelfand, "Iran Tests Sajil-2 Missile," *Jane's Defense Weekly*, 27 May 2009: 16.

57. Choe Sang-Hun, "North Korea Claims to Conduct 2nd Nuclear Test," *New York Times*, 25 May 2009: A1; and Borzou Daragahi, "Iran, Russia Test Joint Nuclear Reactor in Bushehr," *Los Angeles Times*, 26 February 2009: http://www.latimes.com/news/nationworld/world/la-fg-iran-nuclear26-2009feb26,0,7858717.story.

58. Pam Benson, "Gates: Iran's test shows missile defense need in Europe," CNN Politics.com, 9 July 2008; http://www.cnn.com/2008/POLITICS/07/09/us.iran/index.html.

59. James Phillips and Baker Spring, "Iran's Satellite Launch Underscores Growing Military Threat," WebMemo No. 2270, Heritage Foundation, 4 February 2009: 1.

60. Jie-Ae Sohn, Charley Keyes, and Elise Labott, "'Satisfaction' from Kim over N. Korea launch," CNN.com, 5 April 2009; http://us.cnn.com/2009/WORLD/asiapcf/04/05/north.korea.rocket/index.html

61. Wendell Minnick, "China's Sub-Building Surprises Experts: Possible Third Ballistic-Missile Submarine Seen in Satellite Photo," *Navy Times*, 10 December 2007: 22.

62. Reuben Johnson, "Sukhoi's T-50 PAK-FA Fighter Enters First Stages of Assembly," *Jane's Defense Weekly*, 14 January 2009: 7.

63. Lauren Gelfand, "Moscow Plays Political Chess with Iran S-300 sale," *Jane's Defense Weekly*, 25 March 2009: 16.

64. John Pike, "S-300PMU2 Favorit SA-20 Gargoyle, S-300PMU3/S-400 Triumf/SA-21 Growler, SA-18 Grouse Igla 9K38," GlobalSecurity.org, 11 September 2008: http://www.globalsecurity.org/military/world/russia/.

65. Ronald O'Rourke, "China Naval Modernization: Implications for U.S. Navy Capabilities—Background and Issues for Congress," CRS Report for Congress RL33153, Congressional Research Service, Washington, D.C., 29 May 2009: 11.

66. Lauren Gelfand, "Iran Launches New Submarine Production Line," *Jane's Defense Weekly*, 3 September 2008: 19.

67. "Iran tests super-fast torpedo," BBC News, 3 April 2006.

68. Andrew Scutro, "Strait Showdown Analysts: Hormuz incident Could Have Been Iranian Practice Run for 'Swarm Tactics'," *Navy Times*, 21 January 2008: 8, 10.

69. Hossein Aryan, "A New Line of Defense: Iran's Naval Power Projection Continues to Gain Momentum . . . ," *Jane's Defense Weekly*, 28 January 2009: 26.

70. Robin Hughes, "Iran and Syria Equip Tir-Class Fast Attack Craft with ASCMs," *Jane's Defense Weekly*, 25 July 2007: 18.

71. Ted Parsons, "China Shores Up Coastal Units with Long-Range YJ-62C Missile," *Jane's Defense Weekly*, 11 June 2008: 17.

72. Andrew S. Erickson and David D.Yang, "On the Verge of a Game-Changer," *Proceedings* (May 2009): 27–32.

73. O'Rourke, "China Naval Modernization," 4.

74. Robert Hewson, "China Rolls Out Z-9 Helo Naval Variant with Anti-Ship Missile," *Jane's Defense Weekly*, 6 August 2008: 8.

75. Reuben F. Johnson, "Talks Twist and Turn as Chinese Navy Eyes Su-33," *Jane's Defense Weekly*, 18 March 2009: 4.

76. Admiral Timothy J. Keating, U.S. Navy, Commander U.S. Pacific Command, "Statement before the House Armed Services Committee on U.S. Pacific Command Posture," 110th Congress, 2nd Session, 12 March 2008: 11.

77. Lieutenant General Gary L. North, USAF and Colonel John Riordan, USAF, "The Role of Space in Military Operations: Integrating and Synchronizing Space in Today's Fight," *High Frontier*, Volume 4: 2 (February 2008): 3–7.

78. Major General William T. Lord, U.S. Air Force, "Air Force Cyber Command Strategic Vision," U.S. Air Force Cyber Command, 2008: 11–12.

79. Admiral M. G. Mullen, U.S. Navy, "CJCS Guidance for 2008–2009," Office of the Chairman, Joint Chiefs of Staff, 1 October 2008: 4.

80. John Markoff, "Before the Gunfire, Cyberattacks," *New York Times*, 13 August 2008: A1.

81. Colonel Stephen W. Korns, U.S. Air Force, "Botnets Outmaneuvered," *Armed Forces Journal* (January 2009): 26–28.

82. Bobby Junker, "Office of Naval Research Maritime Domain Awareness Vision," presentation to Maritime Security and Domain Awareness Conference, San Diego, 19 September 2008: 9.

83. Samuel Black, "Components of a Space Assurance Strategy," *High Frontier*, Volume 5: 1 (November 2008): 16–20.

84. General T. Michael Moseley, U.S. Air Force, Chief of Staff, "Global Strike Concept of Operations," 27 December 2006: 8–12.

85. Robert O. Work, "The US Navy: Charting a Course for Tomorrow's Fleet," Center for Strategic and Budgetary Assessments, Washington, D.C., 17 February 2009: 64.

86. Milan Vego, "Trade Protection," *Armed Forces Journal* (November 2008): 43.

87. Admiral M. G. Mullen, U.S. Navy, "Capstone Concept for Joint Operations," version 3.0, Joint Chiefs of Staff, Washington, D.C., 15 January 2009: 3.

88. Robert O. Work, "The Future Security Environment: Multidimensional Challenges in a Multi-Player World," Center for Strategic and Budgetary Assessments, Washington, D.C., 21 August 2008: 9; http://www.csbaonline.org/4Publications/PubLibrary/S.20080820.Future_Security_En/S.20080820.Future_Security_En.pdf.

89. Robert M. Gates, U.S. Secretary of Defense, *National Defense Strategy*, Office of the U.S. Secretary of Defense, Washington, D.C., June 2008: 2–13.

90. General Richard B. Myers, U.S. Air Force, Chairman of the Joint Chiefs of Staff, *National Military Strategy of the United States of America*, 2004: 10.

91. General James E. Cartwright, U.S. Marine Corps, Commander, U.S. Strategic Command, "Deterrence Operations Joint Operating Concept," version 2.0, U.S. Strategic Command, Offutt AFB, Nebraska, December 2006: 7–25.

Chapter 2

1. George Friedman, *The Next 100 Years, A Forecast for the 21st Century* (New York: Doubleday Press 2009), 3.

2. William James, *The Principles of Psychology*, Volume I (New York: Alice James Publishing, 1890), 496.

3. Mika Mannermaa, "Traps in Futures Thinking and How to Overcome Them," in Howard Didsbury Jr., ed., *Thinking Creatively in Turbulent Times* (Bethesda: World Futurist Society, 2004), 41–53.

4. Thucydides, *History of the Peloponnesian War* (trans. Richard Crawley), Chapter III, Verse 68.

5. U.S Census Bureau, World Population Clock: http://www.census.gov/main/www/popclock.html.

6. World Population Prospects 2008 Revision, United Nations, New York: http://esa.un.org/unpp/p2k0data.asp

7. Mark Steyn, "It's the Demography, Stupid," *Wall Street Journal*, 4 January 2006: http://www.opinionjournal.com/extra/?id=110007760.

8. Anthony Faiola, "A Baby Bust Empties Japan's Schools: Shrinking Population Called Greatest National Problem," *Washington Post*, 3 March 2005: A01.

9. Robert Clifford Ostergren and John G. Rice, *The Europeans* (London: Guildford Press, 2004), 95.

10. Richard Jackson and Neil Howe, "The Graying of the Great Powers: Major Findings Report," Center for Strategic and International Studies, Washington, D.C., 2008: 2.

11. U.S. Department of Energy, *International Energy Outlook 2009*, 27 May 2009: http://www.eia.doe.gov/oiaf/ieo/world.html.

12. Jeff Rubin, *Why Your World is About to Get A Whole Lot Smaller: What the Price of Oil Means for the Way We Live* (London: Virgin Books, 2009).

13. "World Energy Outlook 2008," International Energy Agency, 2008: 103.

14. "United Nations Human Development Report 2006," United Nations, New York, 2006: 5.

15. Erik Peterson, "Below the Surface: U.S. International Water Policy," Washington, D.C., Center for Strategic and International Studies, 2007: 2.

16. A. T. Wolf, S. B. Yoffe, and M. Giordano, "International Waters: Identifying Basins at Risk," *Water Policy*, Issue 5: 1 (2003): 29–60.

17. Ibid.: 7. The vast majority of disputes over waters that cross international boundaries are governed under bi- or multi-lateral conflict resolution mechanisms.

18. John Robb, "Global Guerillas and Temporary Autonomous Zones," 20 August, 2004, at Globalguerillas.com: http://globalguerrillas.typepad.com/globalguerrillas/2004/08/global_guerrill_1.html.

19. George Backus and James Strickland, "Climate-Derived Tensions in Arctic Security," Sandia National Laboratories, Albuquerque, New Mexico, 2008: 3.

20. "With a high degree of likelihood, Russia will be able to increase its continental shelf by 1.2 million square kilometers [460,000 square miles] with potential hydrocarbon reserves of not less than 9,000 to 10,000 billion tonnes of conventional fuel beyond the 200-mile [322-kilometer] economic zone in the Arctic Ocean." Viktor Posyolov, official in the Agency for Management of Mineral Resources, Russian Federation, quoted in Richard A. Lovett, "Russia's Arctic Claim Backed by Rocks, Officials Say," National Geographic News, 21 September 2007. http://news.nationalgeographic.com/news/2007/09/070921–arctic-russia.html

21. James Clay Moltz, "Space Jam," *New York Times,* Op-ed, 18 February 2009.

22. Edward Cody, "China Confirms Firing Missile to Destroy Satellite," *Washington Post,* 24 January 2007: A08; and William J. Broad, "Debris Spews into Space after Satellites Collide," *New York Times,* 12 February 2009: A28.

23. Colin Gray, *Another Bloody Century: Future Warfare* (London: Orion Books, 2005), 301.

24. Mark Williams, "Mining the Moon," *Technology Review* (23 August 2007): http://www.technologyreview.com/energy/19296; and, Robert S. Walker, Former Chairman of the House Science Committee, "The Race into Space," *Washington Times,* 28 May 2003: http://www.washingtontimes.com/news/2003/may/28/20030528 –092308–4284r/.

25. John Robb, *Brave New War: The Next Stage of Terrorism and the End of Globalization* (New Jersey: John Wiley and Sons, 2007), 32.

26. David S. Alberts and Richard E. Hayes, "Power to the Edge: Command and Control in the Information Age," Command and Control Research Program, Washington, D.C.: 113.

27. A meme is a unit or element of cultural ideas or symbols. It was coined by Richard Dawkins in *The Selfish Gene* (London: Oxford University Press, 1976), 189. The idea of memes and "memetics" describes the evolution of ideas and concepts in genetic and biological terms.

28. "The JOE (Joint Operating Environment) 2008: Challenges and Implications

for the Future Joint Force," United States Joint Forces Command, Norfolk, Virginia, 25 November 2008: 3.

29. Richard Rosecrance, *The Rise of the Virtual State* (New York: Basic Books, 1999).

30. David Theis, "Crisis Reveals Growing Finance Gaps for Developing Countries," World Bank News Release, 8 March 2009: http://go.worldbank.org/U05NMJJNZ0.

31. Economist Intelligence Unit, "Special Report: Manning the Barricades, Who's at Risk as Deepening Economic Distress Foments Social Unrest," March 2009: 5.

32. Jamil Anderlini, "China Calls for New Reserve Currency," *Financial Times*, 23 March 2009 http://www.ft.com/cms/s/0/7851925a-17a2-11de-8c9d-0000779fd2ac .html?nclick_check=1; and Breitbart.com, "Russia, China Cooperate on New Currency Proposals," 30 March 2009.

33. Lori Montgomery, "Deficit Projected to Swell Beyond Earlier Estimates," *Washington Post*, 21 March 2009: A01; Wayne M. Morrison and Marc Lebonte, "China's Holdings of U.S. Securities: Implications for the U.S. Economy," CRS report RL34314 for Congress, 5 March 2009: 2; and Brad Setser and Nouriel Roubini "How Scary Is the Deficit?" *Foreign Affairs* (July/August 2005): http://www.foreignaffairs .com/articles/60840/brad-setser-et-al/how-scary-is-the-deficit

34. John Robb, "Bigger than a President 2," at *Global Guerrillas* (22 January 2009), http://globalguerrillas.typepad.com/globalguerrillas/2009/01/bigger-than-a -presiden.html

35. Economist Intelligence Unit: 2.

36. Robert Kaplan, "The Shrinking Superpower: Why the Recession Could Spell the End of American Dominance," *The Atlantic* (9 March 2009): http://www.the atlantic.com/doc/200903u/military-budget

37. Shrinking economic and military capabilities may force the US into a difficult set of tradeoffs between domestic versus foreign policy priorities. National Intelligence Council, *Global Trends 2025: A Transformed World* (Washington: Government Printing Office, 2008): iv.

38. Defense Science Board Summer Study, *21st Century Strategic Technology Vectors*, February 2007.

39. Airland Battle (also Air Land, or AirLand) originated in the 1980s as the U.S. Army's warfighting doctrine for a Soviet invasion of Europe. It was premised on highly maneuverable land forces operating in close coordination with air attacks against the enemy's rear echelon to prevent reinforcement and re-supply. For more detail, see Douglas W. Skinner, "Airland Battle Doctrine," Center for Naval Analysis, Alexandria, Virginia, September 1988.

40. Paul Boutin, "Biowar for Dummies" at KurzweilAI.net, 11 July 2006: http:// www.kurzweilai.net/meme/frame.html?main=/articles/art0682.html. For more on the dramatic implications of artificial life, see Alan H. Goldstein "I, Nanobot," 9 March 2006: http://www.salon.com/tech/feature/2006/03/09/nanobiobot/index .html.

41. Kim Zetter, "Botnets Took Control of 12 Million New IPs this Year," *Wired*

(5 May 2009): http://www.wired.com/threatlevel/2009/05/botnets-took-control-of -12-million-new-ips-this-year/.

42. Photosynth is a software application that analyzes digital photographs and generates a three-dimensional model of the photos and a "point cloud" of a photographed object. Pattern recognition components compare portions of images to create points, which are then compared to convert the image into a model. Users are able to view and generate their own models based on dozens, hundreds, or even thousands of uploaded photographs. See the Microsoft website: http://photosynth.net/.

43. *Global Trends 2025: A Transformed World*, National Intelligence Council, Washington, D.C., 2008: 29.

44. Ann Scott Tyson, "Navy Sends Destroyer to Protect Ship Near China," *Washington Post*, 13 March 2009: A12.

45. On 18 November 2008, INS Tabar, a frigate of the Indian Navy patrolling the Somali coast, engaged and sank a suspected pirate vessel in a five-hour engagement. Hari Kumar and Alan Cowell, "Indian Navy Says it Sank Pirate Ship," *New York Times*, 19 November 2008: http://www.nytimes.com/2008/11/20/world/africa/20 pirate.html

46. Frank Hoffman, "Hybrid Warfare and Challenges," *Joint Forces Quarterly*, Issue 52: 1 (2009): 35.

47. Robert Gilpin, *War and Change in World Politics* (New York: Cambridge University Press, 1981), 36.

48. Jim Lacey, ed., *A Terrorist's Call to Global Jihad, Deciphering Abu Musab Al-Suri's Islamic Jihad Manifesto* (Annapolis, Maryland: Naval Institute Press, 2008), 1.

49. Hedley Bull notes the tension between order and justice in the international system. See Hedley Bull, *The Anarchical Society: A Study of Order in World Politics*, 3rd edition (New York: Columbia University Press, 2002).

50. Quoted NPR (National Public Radio) interview, 30 November 1999: Time code 11: 55.

Chapter 3

1. The author wishes to thank Lieutenant General James Soligan, U.S. Air Force (ret.), for his patience and the numerous insights he provided in reviewing this paper. While his recommendations and counsel were important, any subsequent errors in fact are mine alone.

2. General J. N. Mattis, U.S. Marine Corps, Supreme Allied Commander Transformation, "Multiple Futures Project: Navigating towards 2030," Final Report, NATO Allied Command Transformation, Norfolk, Virginia, April 2009.

3. Peter Schwartz, *Inevitable Surprises: Thinking Ahead in a Time of Turbulence* (New York: Gotham Books, 2003), 13.

4. In this context, the term "globalized" refers to those post-industrial, industrial, and developing nations that are linked into global commerce and communications networks.

5. Lt. Col. Richard H. Estes, U.S. Air Force, "Giulio Douhet: More on Target Than He Knew," *Airpower Journal* (Winter 1990); http://www.airpower.maxwell.af.mil/airchronicles/apj/apj90/win90/6win90.htm.

6. Russia's population is in an even steeper decline, from a peak of 148.5 million in 1995 to about 140.5 million today; it is projected to drop another 20% to about 111 million by 2050. "World Population Prospects: The 2008 Revision," UN Report ST/ESA/SER.A/261/ES: 9.

7. Thomas J. Pyle, "2008 Year in Review," Institute for Energy Research, Houston: 3.

8. Robert D. Kaplan, "The Revenge of Geography," *Foreign Policy Magazine* (May/June 2009): 102.

9. Ibid.

10. Frank G. Hoffman, "Hybrid Warfare and Challenges," *Joint Forces Quarterly*, issue 52: 1 (2009): 34–37.

11. "Strasbourg/Kehl Summit Declaration," NATO Press Release: (2009) 044, issued by the Heads of State and Government at the meeting of the North Atlantic Council, 4 April 2009: 4.

12. China has developed and in some cases fielded cyber warfare units to hack into space control systems; co-orbital ASAT systems to covertly disable enemy satellites; radiofrequency weapons to jam satellite signals; and high-powered microwave weapons to destroy satellites from Earth. Ian Easton, "The Great Game in Space: China's Evolving ASAT Weapons Programs and Their Implications for the Future U.S. Strategy," Project 2049 Institute, Arlington, Virginia, June 2009: 5.

13. Ralph Peters, "Wishful Thinking and Indecisive Wars," *The Journal of International Security Affairs*, no. 16 (Spring 2009): 6; http://www.securityaffairs.org/issues/2009/16/peters.php.

14. John C. Rood, U.S. Acting Under Secretary of State for Arms Control and International Security, Remarks at the Twenty-fifth International Workshop on Global Security, Rome, 21 June 2008: http://www.state.gov/t/us/rm/107502.htm.

15. "The JOE (Joint Operating Environment) 2008: Challenges and Implications for the Future Joint Force," U.S. Joint Forces Command, Norfolk, Virginia, 25 November 2008: 39.

16. Philip H. Gordon, Assistant Secretary of State, Bureau of European and Eurasian Affairs, statement before the Subcommittee on Europe, House Foreign Affairs Committee, U.S. House of Representatives, 111th Congress, 1st session, Washington, D.C., 16 June 2009: http://www.state.gov/p/eur/rls/rm/2009/124870.htm.

17. Rebecca Santana, Associated Press, "Activists Take to the Streets—and the Tweets." *New York Post*, 16 June 2009; http://www.nypost.com/seven/06162009/news/worldnews/activists_take_to_the_streets___and_the__174524.htm.

18. Martin Van Creveld, *The Transformation of War: The Most Radical Reinterpretation of Armed Conflict since Clausewitz* (New York: The Free Press, 1991), 194.

19. Ibid.: 197.

20. Captain Daniel Helmer, Australian Army, "Not Quite Insurgency: A Cautionary Tale for U.S. Forces Based on Israel's Operation Change of Direction," Australian

Army Journal (Counterinsurgency, Land Warfare Studies Centre, Duntroon), special edition, vol. V: 2 (Winter 2008): 120.

21. John M. Richardson, "The Joint Narrative," *Joint Forces Quarterly*, vol. 54: 3 (2009): 83.

22. Nik Gowing, "Skyful of Lies and Black Swans: The New Tyranny of Shifting Information Power in Crises," RISJ Challenges series, Reuters Institute for the Study of Journalism, Oxford, U.K., July 2009: 2.

23. Tim Blanning, *The Pursuit of Glory: The Five Revolutions that Made Modern Europe: 1648–1815* (New York: Penguin Group, May 2008), 296.

24. Colin S. Gray, "The 21st Century Security Environment and the Future of War," *Parameters*, vol. 38: 4 (Winter 2008–09): 16–17.

25. Winston Churchill, "Air Parity Lost," speech to British House of Commons, London, U.K., 2 May 1935. Transcript available at: http://www.winstonchurchill.org/learn/speeches/speeches-of-winston-churchill.

26. Preamble to the North Atlantic Treaty, Washington, D.C., 4 April 1949: http://www.nato.int/docu/basictxt/treaty.htm.

27. David H. Gurney, "An Interview with Admiral James G. Stavridis," *Joint Forces Quarterly*, Issue 50: 3 (2008): 128.

28. Major Thomas Single, U.S. Air Force, "JAPCC NATO Space Operations Assessment," Joint Air Power Competence Centre, Kalkar, Germany, (revised January 2009): 33.

29. Jeffrey Simon, "NATOs Uncertain Future: Is Demography Destiny?" *Strategic Forum*, No. 236, Institute for National Strategic Studies, National Defense University, Washington, D.C., October 2008: 6.

30. Mattis, "Multiple Futures Project": 67.

31. Peters, "Wishful Thinking and Indecisive Wars": 8.

Chapter 4

1. The concept of natural law or the law of nature is derived from the concept of nature or God, and thus is considered inalienable and applicable everywhere. The concept grew out of the Renaissance, and has become a feature of Anglo-American common law, informing the creation of human rights and international humanitarian law.

2. Lori Fisler Damrosch, with Louis Henkin, Richard Pugh, Oscar Schachter, and Hans Smit, *International Law: Cases and Materials and Basic Documents Supplemental*, 4th ed. (St. Paul, Minnesota: West Publishing Company, 2001), xxviii.

3. United Nations Convention on the Law of the Sea, 30 April 1982, UN Doc. A/CONF.62/122 (1982), 10 December 1982, 1833 U.N.T.S. 3, 397, 21 I.L.M. 1261 (1982) (entered into force on 16 November 1994), United Nations, New York (hereafter, the LOS Convention). A nautical mile is equivalent to one minute of latitude at the equator and is 1,852 meters or 6,076 feet in length. A statute mile on land is 5,280 feet in length.

4. Juridical Regime of Historic Waters, Including Historic Bays, UN Doc. A/CN.4/143 United Nations, New York, (1962): 56.

5. "World Oil Transit Chokepoints—Strait of Hormuz," Energy Information Administration, U.S. Department of Energy, Washington, D.C., January 2008; http://www.eia.doe.gov/cabs/World_Oil_Transit_Chokepoints/Hormuz.html.

6. LOS Convention, Art. 57: Art. 5–16.

7. Ibid., Art. 56: Para. 1.

8. Ken Booth, *Law, Force & Diplomacy at Sea* (London, Boston: Allen & Unwin, 1985), 38.

9. On 9 March 2009, for example, five vessels from the PLA Navy and other Chinese government agencies interfered with military survey activities being conducted by USNS Impeccable 120 km from China. Similarly, in April 2001, a Chinese fighter aircraft collided with a U.S. Navy EP-3 surveillance and reconnaissance flight over China's EEZ, causing the loss of the Chinese fighter jet and pilot, and forcing an emergency landing of the EP-3 on Hainan Island, where the U.S. crew was subsequently detained. Michael Swaine, "The U.S.–China Spat at Sea," *Foreign Policy*, 11 March 2009: 1; http://experts.foreignpolicy.com/posts/2009/03/11/the_us_china_spat_at_sea.

10. 1972 Convention on the International Regulations for Preventing Collisions at Sea (COLREG), 1977 UKTS 77, 12 ILM 1973 734.

11. According to Shen Dingli, director of the Center of American Studies at Shanghai's Fudan University, "China considers that international law only allows innocent passage for military vessels [in the EEZ], not activities that could be considered to have a military purpose." James Kraska and Brian Wilson, "China Wages Maritime 'Lawfare'," *Foreign Policy*, 11 March 2009: 1; http://experts.foreignpolicy.com/posts/2009/03/11/china_wages_maritime_lawfare.

12. U.N. Doc. A/RES/1472 (XIV), United Nations, New York (12 December 1959). See, "Memorandum from Secretary of State Rusk to President Kennedy," 2 February 1961, reprinted in *Foreign Relations of the United States*, Vol. XXV (1961–1963), Document # 414 (Washington: Office of the Historian, United States Department of State, 2001): http://www.state.gov/r/pa/ho/frus/kennedyjf/xxv/6025.htm.

13. International Cooperation in the Peaceful Uses of Outer Space, U.N. Doc. A/RES/1721 (XVI), United Nations, New York (20 December 1961).

14. Declaration of Legal Principles Governing the Activities of States in the Exploration and Use of Outer Space, U.N. Doc. A/RES/1962 (XVIII), United Nations, New York (13 December 1963).

15. Treaty on Principles Governing the Activities of States in the Exploration and Use of Outer Space, Including the Moon and Other Celestial Bodies, 18 U.S.T. 2410, 610 U.N.T.S. 205, United Nations, New York (27 January 1967).

16. "Declaration of the First Meeting of Equatorial Countries" (known as the Bogotá Declaration) (3 Dec. 1976), reprinted in 6 J. Space L. 193 (1978).

17. "Canada, Claim against the USSR for Damage Caused by Soviet *Cosmos* 954," Notes of 23 Jan. 1979 and 15 Mar. 1979, 18 I.L.M. 899, 902 (1979). In the section of its claim titled "General Principles of International Law," Canada asserted:

The intrusion of the Cosmos 954 satellite into Canada's air space and the deposit on Canadian territory of hazardous radioactive debris from the satellite constitutes a violation of Canada's sovereignty. This violation is established by the mere fact of the trespass of the satellite, the harmful consequences of this intrusion, being the damage caused to Canada by the presence of hazardous radioactive debris and the interference with the sovereign right of Canada to determine the acts that will be performed on its territory.

18. See, for example, McGeorge Bundy, "National Security Action Memorandum No. 183, Subject: Space Program of the United States," 27 August 1962, reprinted in *Foreign Relations of the United States*, Vol. XXV, 1961–1963, Document #425 (2001). Bundy asserts that before the U.N. Committee on the Peaceful Uses of Outer Space, the United States must develop and advocate objectives that show, inter alia, "that the distinction between peaceful and aggressive uses of outer space is not the same as the distinction between military and civilian uses."

19. William Gibson, *Neuromancer* (San Francisco: New Ace, 1984), 5.

20. John Markoff, "Vast Spy System Loots Computers in 103 Countries," *New York Times*, 29 March 2009: A1.

21. Constitution and Convention of the International Telecommunication Union, with annexes (concluded 22 December 1992, entered into force 1 July 1994), 1825 UNTS 1.

22. Similarly, chemical and biological weapons constitute use of force because they "are employed for the destruction of life and property." Ian Brownlie, *International Law and the Use of Force by States* (Oxford: Clarendon Press, 1963), 362.

23. See Kathryn Westcott, "Pirate in the Dock," BBC News Online, 21 May 2009; http://news.bbc.co.uk/2/hi/africa/8059345.stm.

24. Michael D. Carsten, "International Law and Military Operations," in Carsten, ed., *International Law Studies*, vol. 84 (Newport: Naval War College, 2008), preface: xii.

Chapter 5

1. R. P. Anand, "The Influence of History on the Literature of International Law," in *The Structure and Process of International Law: Essays in Legal Philosophy Doctrine and Theory*, R. St. J. Macdonald, ed. (The Hague: Martinus Nijhoff Publishers 1983), 345–47.

2. "International Trade Facts and Figures November 2008," International Maritime Organization (IMO) Maritime Knowledge Center, November 2008, taken from the IMO web site: http://www.imo.org/includes/blastDataOnly.asp/data_id%3D23754/InternationalShippingandWorldTrade-factsandfigures.pdf.

3. "Yearbooks of Fisheries Statistic Tables 2006," Food and Agriculture Organization (FAO) of the United Nations, taken from the FAO website: http://www.fao.org/fishery/statistics/en.

4. These threat categories correlate with those discussed in the United States Na-

tional Strategy for Maritime Security, Homeland Security Presidential Directive 13 and National Security Presidential Directive 41, 5 September 2005.

5. "International Trade Facts and Figures November 2008."

6. Virginia Lunsford, "What makes Piracy Work," *Proceedings*, vol. 134/12/270 (December 2008): 28–33.

7. Captain Pottengal Mukundan, Director, International Maritime Bureau, "IMB reports unprecedented raise in maritime hijackings," International Maritime Bureau, International Chamber of Commerce, 19 January 2009: http://www.icc-css.org/.

8. Peter Chalk, "The Maritime Dimension of International Security: Terrorism, Piracy, and Challenges for the United States," RAND Corporation, Santa Monica, California, 2008: 16; http://www.rand.org/pubs/monographs/MG697/.

9. Louis Hansen, "Anti-Piracy Task Force Hits Choppy Waters in African Seas," *Norfolk Virginian-Pilot*, 30 January 2009: http://hamptonroads.com/2009/01/anti piracy-task-force-hits-choppy-waters

10. Rawle O. King, "Ocean Piracy and Its Impact on Insurance," Congressional Research Service (CRS) Report for Congress, R40081, Congressional Research Service, Washington, D.C., 6 February 2009: 1.

11. Chalk, "The Maritime Dimension of International Security."

12. Stephanie Elam, Mohammed Jamjoom, and Barbara Starr, "Pirates repel sailors attempting to reach captain," CNN.com, 11 April 2009: http://www.cnn.com /2009/WORLD/africa/04/11/somalia.u.s.ship/index.html.

13. James Kraska, *The Report on the U.S. Naval War College Workshop on Somali Piracy: Fresh Thinking for an Old Threat*, Countering Maritime Piracy, International Law Department, U.S. Naval War, 28 April 2009: 3; http://www.nwc.navy.mil/cnws/ ild/documents/Countering%20Maritime%20Piracy.pdf

14. Martin N. Murphy, *Small Boats, Weak States, and Dirty Money: Piracy and Maritime Terrorism in the Modern World* (New York: Columbia University Press, 2009), 17.

15. Michael McNicholas, *Maritime Security: An Introduction* (Boston: Butterworth-Heinemann Publishers, 2008), 248–53.

16. Ibid.

17. Margashirsha Shuddha Dwitiya, "Mumbai Attack: Clear and Present Danger from Sea," *Hindu Janajargruti Samiti*, 29 November 2008: http://www.hindujagruti .org/news/5865.html.

18. "What's the Problem?" Convention on Biological Diversity, Marine and Coastal Biological Diversity, 02 July 2008: http://www.cbd.int/marine/problem .shtml.

19. Richard Black, "Pirate Fishing Boats Target Africa," *BBC News*, 02 July 2008: http://news.bbc.co.uk/2/hi/science/nature/7485839.stm.

20. The triad of requirements for effective maritime security comes from Admiral Thad W. Allen, Commandant, U.S. Coast Guard, "The U.S. Coast Guard Strategy for Maritime Safety, Security, and Stewardship," Washington, D.C., January 2007; www .uscg.mil/COMDT/speeches/docs/CGS-Final.pdf.

21. "National Plan to Achieve Maritime Domain Awareness for the National Strategy for Maritime Security," Department of Homeland Security, Washington, D.C., October 2005; http://www.dhs.gov/xprevprot/programs/editorial_0753.shtm.

22. Gabrielle Pickard, "Sea-Horse Satellite System to Seek Out Illegal Immigrants," *Russian Times*, 13 January 2009: http://www.russiatoday.com/Top_News/2009–01 –13/'Sea-Horse'_satellite_system_to_seek_out_illegal_immigrants.html.

23. "Citizen Action Network," U.S. Coast Guard, 13th District, 11 March 2009, taken from the U.S. Coast Guard website: http://www.uscg.mil/d13/can.

24. "IMB Piracy Reporting Center," International Chamber of Commerce website: http://www.icc-ccs.org/index.php?option=com_content&view=article&id=30 &Itemid=12.

25. Josh Martin, "Project Seahawk in the Port of Charleston," *Government Security News Magazine*, 29 May 2007, found on the Charleston Regional Development Alliance website: http://www.crda.org/news/local_news/project_seahawk_in_port _of_charleston-782.

26. "Maritime Component Commands," Commanders, Allied Maritime Component Commands Northwood and Naples, 2008: 8; for information contact the NATO Public Information Office: www.afsouth.nato.int.

27. For more information on ReCAAP, see: http://www.recaap.org/index_home .html.

28. "Maritime Security Partnerships," Naval Studies Board, National Research Council of the National Academies, Washington, D.C., 2008: 52.

29. Ibid.: 60.

30. Mukundan, "IMB reports unprecedented raise."

31. Leo Shane III, "Pirate Attacks Down, but Concerns Linger," *Stars and Stripes*, 6 March 2009: http://www.stripes.com/article.asp?section=104&article=61148.

32. Denise Hammick, "Turning the Tide: Indonesia, Malaysia and Singapore Have Joined Forces in the Battle for Maritime Security in Southeast Asia, Particularly in the Strait of Malacca," *Jane's Defense Weekly*, 21 November 2007: 19–22.

33. U.N. Resolution S/res/1851 (2008), United Nations Security Council, 16 December 2008.

34. Paulo Prada and Alex Roth, "On the Lawless Seas, It's Not Easy Putting Somali Pirates in the Dock," *Wall Street Journal*, 12 December 2008: http://online.wsj .com/article/SB122903542171799663.html.

35. Sandra Jontz, "9 Suspected Pirates Freed in Somalia," *Stars and Stripes*, 4 March 2009: http://www.stripes.com/article.asp?section=104&article=61100.

36. Admiral G. Roughead, U.S. Navy, "Executing our Maritime Strategy," CNO Guidance for 2009, November 2008: 8.

37. National Strategy for Maritime Security: 2.

38. "International Outreach and Coordination Strategy for Maritime Security," NSPD-41/HSPD-13, Department of Homeland Security, Washington, D.C., November 2005: 4.

39. For a discussion on a holistic yet regional approach toward combating piracy

in Somalia, see James Kraska, "Coalition Strategy and the Pirates of the Gulf of Aden and the Red Sea," *Comparative Strategy*, 28: 3 (1 July 2009): 197–216, found at: http://dx.doi.org/10.1080/01495930903025250.

40. "Intelligence-Gathering Centers Planned for Somalia's Neighbors to Battle Piracy," *Mainichi Daily News*, 6 February 2009: 2a.

41. ReCAAP Information Sharing Centre Half Year Report, 1 January 2009–30 June 2009: 2.

42. James T. Conway, Gary Roughead, and Thad Allen, "A Cooperative Strategy for 21st Century Seapower," Department of the Navy, Washington, D.C. October 2007: p 11; http://www.navy.mil/maritime/MaritimeStrategy.pdf.

43. "Active Endeavour Briefing," NATO Public Diplomacy Division, 14 February 2008: 1–5; for more information see: http://www.jfcnaples.nato.int/JFCN_Operations /ActiveEndeavour/Endeavour.htm.

44. David Sagunski, "Improving our Maritime Vision," Atlantic Council of the United States, Washington, D.C., 2 December 2008: http://www.acus.org/new_atlan ticist/improving-our-maritime-vision.

45. "Building Maritime Partnerships," *Rhumb Lines*, Navy Office of Information, 20 March 2009: 1.

46. For information on the Container Security Initiative, see the U.S. Customs and Border Patrols web site: http://www.cbp.gov/xp/cgov/trade/cargo_security/csi/.

47. Report of the Second Joint FAO/IMO ad hoc Working Group on IUU Fishing and Related Matters, Maritime Safety Committee, 83rd Session, 31 July 2007, International Maritime Organization Document: 8; http://www.illegal-fishing.info/uploads/ IMO-FAO-working-group-report2.pdf.

Chapter 6

1. Norbert Wiener, *The Human Use of Human Beings* (Boston: Houghton Mifflin Co., 1950), 2–3.

2. Michael Howard, *Clausewitz* (Oxford: Oxford University Press, 1983), 39.

3. Alfred Thayer Mahan, *The Influence of Sea Power Upon History* (Charleston: Bibliolife, 2007), 51.

4. Ibid.

5. Ibid.

6. Alfred Thayer Mahan, *Mahan on Naval Warfare: Selections from the Writings of Rear Admiral Alfred T. Mahan* (Mineola, New York: Dover Publications, 1999).

7. James R. Blaker, *Transforming Military Force* (Santa Barbara: Praeger Publishers, 2007), 166.

8. Arthur K. Cebrowski, Director of Force Transformation, Office of the Secretary of Defense, Statement before the Subcommittee on Strategic Forces, Armed Services Committee, United States Senate, 108th Congress, 2nd session, 25 March 2004: http://ftp.fas.org/irp/congress/2004_hr/032504cebrowski.pdf.

9. Doyle E. Larson, "Exploiting Electronic Warfare," *Air Force Magazine*, vol. 64: 7, July 1981.

10. Jim Hu, "Outrage a deliberate attack, Yahoo says," CNET news, 7 February 2000; http://news.cnet.com/2100–1023–236594.html.

11. John Borland, "E-commerce site breached by credit card thieves," CNET news, 1 March 2000; http://news.cnet.com/E-commerce-site-breached-by-credit-card-thieves/2100–1017_3–237512.html?tag=mncol.

12. "E-Stats: Measuring the Electronic Economy," U.S. Census Bureau, Washington, D.C., March 2001: http://www.census.gov/estats.

13. "E-Stats: Measuring the Electronic Economy," U.S. Census Bureau, Washington, D.C., May 2009: http://www.census.gov/estats.

14. Ibid.

15. "Business-to-Consumer E-commerce Statistics," Directorate for Science, Technology, and Industry, Organization for Economic Development, Berlin, Germany, 13–14 March 2001: www.oecd.org/dataoecd/34/36/1864439.pdf.

16. Hamanaka Elji, "Over Secure Networks," *Japan Journal* (in English), vol. 6: 3, March 2006.

17. "Business-to-Consumer E-commerce Statistics."

18. Rod Beckstrom, "A New Model for Network Valuation," research paper, National Cybersecurity Center, Department of Homeland Security, Washington, D.C., 13 March 2009: 3–4.

19. Robert Vamosi, "Ransom-based malware attacks specific companies," CNET news, 17 July 2007; http://news.cnet.com/8301–10784_3–9746130–7.html ?tag=mncol.

20. "Russia/Georgia Cyber War—Findings and Analysis," Project Grey Goose: Phase I Report, 17 October 2008: 4–5; http://www.scribd.com/doc/6967393/Project-Grey-Goose-Phase-I-Report.

21. "Emerging Cyber Threats Report for 2009," Georgia Tech Information Security Center, Georgia Institute of Technology, Atlanta, Georgia,15 October 2008: 1–2.

22. "Cyber-attacks batter web heavyweights," CNN.com, 9 February 2000: http://archives.cnn.com/2000/TECH/computing/02/09/cyber.attacks.01/index .html.

23. Larry Greenemeier, "Estonian 'Cyber Riot' was Planned, but Mastermind Still a Mystery," *Information Week* online, 3 August 2007: http://www.informationweek .com/news/internet/showArticle.jhtml?articleID=201202784; Noah Shachtmann, "Georgia Under Online Assault," *Wired* online, 10 August 2008: http://www.wired .com/dangerroom/2008/08/georgia-under-o/.

24. Carlo Kopp, "The Electromagnetic Bomb: A Weapon of Electrical Mass Destruction," report, GlobalSecurity.org (1996): http://www.globalsecurity.org/military /library/report/1996/apjemp.htm.

25. Kevin Poulsen, "'Cyberwar' and Estonia's Panic Attack," *Wired* online, 22 August 2007: http://www.wired.com/threatlevel/2007/08/cyber-war-and-e/.

26. Rebecca Grant, "Victory in Cyberspace," Air Force Association, Arlington, Virginia, October 2007: 8.

27. John Markoff, "Before the Gunfire, Cyberattacks," *New York Times*, 13 August 2008: A1.

28. "Improvised Explosive Devices (EIDs)—Iraq," GlobalSecurity.org [no date]: http://www.globalsecurity.org/military/intro/ied-iraq.htm.

29. Kelley Beaucar Vlahos, "Radical Islamic Groups Exploit Internet for Jihad," FoxNews.com, 21 December 2006: http://www.foxnews.com/story/0,2933,237879,00 .html.

30. Tony Skinner, "War and PC," *Jane's Defense Weekly*, 24 September 2008: 38–39.

31. Ben Worthen, "Wide Cyber Attack is Linked to China," *Wall Street Journal*, 30 March 2009: A18.

32. Mike Harvey, "Chinese Hackers 'Using Ghost Network to Control Embassy Computers'," *Times* online, 30 March 2009: http://www.timesonline.co.uk/tol/news/uk/crime/article5996253.ece.

33. Tom Standage, *The Victorian Internet* (New York: Walker Publishing Co., 1998), VII.

Chapter 7

1. Ben Sakrisson, "Space as a contested environment debuts," Air University Public Affairs, 31 March 2009: 1; http://www.afspc.af.mil/news/story.asp?id=123142103.

2. In collating this work, the authors are grateful for the assistance of Ms. Shawna Pugmire for research, formatting, and editing.

3. "National Space Policy," National Security Presidential Directive-49 (NSPD-49), 31 August 2006.

4. David Usborne, "Satellite's Failure Leaves Millions Speechless in US," *London Independent*, 21 May 1998.

5. LTG Joseph M. Cosumano, Jr., "A Day Without Space: Ensuring It Doesn't Happen," *Army Space Journal* (Summer 2002): 3.

6. Treaty on Principles Governing the Activities of States in the Exploration and Use of Outer Space, Including the Moon and Other Celestial Bodies, 18 U.S.T. 2410, 610 U.N.T.S. 205, United Nations General Assembly, New York, 27 Jan. 1967.

7. Warren Ferster and Colin Clark, "NRO Confirms Chinese Laser Test Illuminates U.S. Spacecraft," *Defense News*, 2 October 2006.

8. Craig Covault, "Chinese Test Anti-Satellite Weapon," *Aviation Week*, 17 January 2007.

9. John J. Klein, *Space Warfare Strategy, Principles and Policy* (New York: Routledge, 2006), 62.

10. Ibid.

11. Mancur Olson, *The Logic of Collective Action: Public Goods and the Theory of Groups* (Cambridge: Harvard University Press, 1971), 2.

12. The National Security Space Office was created in 2004 by merging several existing agencies. See the website: http://www.acq.osd.mil/nsso/index.htm.

13. Michael Krepon, "Space Security," testimony before the House Committee on Armed Services Subcommittee on Strategic Forces," 18 March 2009: 2; http://armed services.house.gov/pdfs/SF031809/Krepon_Testimony031809.pdf

14. James Clay Moltz, "Space Jam," *New York Times*, 19 February 2009; http://www.nytimes.com/2009/02/19/opinion/19moltz.html.

15. Ibid.

16. "Final Report," Commission to Assess United States National Security Space Management and Organization, Washington, D.C., 2001.

17. "Final Report": 18–20.

18. "TV Stations," *Post-Soviet Media Law and Policy Newsletter*, Issue 55 (1 May 1999); http://www.vii.org/monroe/issue55/reports.htm.

19. "Final Report to the Prosecutor by the Committee Established to Review the NATO Bombing Campaign Against the Federal Republic of Yugoslavia," United Nations International Criminal Tribunal for the former Yugoslavia, New York, 2000; http://www.un.org/icty/pressreal/nato061300.htm.

20. Jim Mathews, "U.S. Navy Shoots Down Satellite" *Aviation Week*, 20 February 2008: http://www.aviationweek.com/aw/generic/story_channel.jsp?channel=defense&id=news/ERIE02208.xml; Laura Grego, "A History of Anti-satellite (ASAT) Programs," Union of Concerned Scientists, 27 August 2008; http://www.ucsusa.org/nuclear_weapons_and_global_security/space_weapons/technical_issues/; and Ian Easton, "The Great Game in Space: China's Evolving ASAT Weapons Programs and Their Implications for Future U.S. Strategy," Project 2049 Institute, 2009: 2–5.

21. Dave Ahern, "Senator Urges Funding Space-Based Satellite Defense," *Defense News*, 31 January 2007: 1; Vago Muradian, "China Attempted to Blind U.S. Satellites with Laser," *Defense News*, October 2006: 1; http://www.DefenseNews.com.

22. Toby Harden and Alex Massie, "Chinese Missile Destroys Satellite in Space," *Telegraph*, 19 January 2007: 1.

23. "China Jamming Test Sparks U.S. Satellite Concerns," *USA Today*, 5 October 2006: http://www.usatoday.com/tech/news/2006-10-05-satellite-laser_x.htm.

24. Gary Anthes, "Ray Kurzweil: IT Will Be Everything," *Computerworld*, 6 January 2006; http://www.computerworld.com/action/article.do?command=viewArticleBasic&articleId=107494.

25. "Orbital Express Space Operations Architecture," Tactical Technology Office, Defense Advanced Research Projects Agency, Arlington, Virginia [no date]: http://www.darpa.mil/tto/programs/oe.htm.

26. Kelly Young, "Autonomous Military Satellite to Inspect Others in Orbit," *New Scientist*, 12 April 2005; http://www.newscientist.com/article/dn7255.

27. Kristen Chick, "Piracy 'Surge' Off Somali Coast," *Christian Scientist Monitor*, 7 April 2009; http://www.csmonitor.com/2009/0407/p99s01–duts.html.

28. Bob Brewin, "Homemade GPS jammers raise concerns," article, Computerworld.com, 17 January 2003.

29. J. Michael Waller, "Iran and Cuba Zap U.S. Satellites," *INSIGHT*, 19 August 2003; http://findarticles.com/p/articles/mi_m1571/is_2003_August_19/ai_106701632/.

30. Tom Carter, "Castro Regime Jamming US Broadcasts into Iran," *Washington Times*, 16 July 2003; http://www.washtimes.com/world/20030715–114937–2635r.htm.

31. Immanuel Kant, "Perpetual Peace," in Kant, *On History*, Lewis White Beck, ed. and trans. (Indianapolis: Bobbs-Merrill, 1963), originally published in 1795.

32. Bruce Russett and John R. Oneal, *Triangulating Peace: Democracy, Interdependence, and International Organizations* (New York: W. W. Norton & Company, 2001).

33. The National Security Space Office is a single office within DoD, distinct from the National Security Space enterprise mentioned earlier, which is a much broader collection of offices and agencies that includes members from the commercial and private sectors.

34. For more regarding U.S. assurance of the space commons, see Everett Dolman, *Astropolitik: Classic Geopolitics in the Space Age* (London: Frank Cass Publishers, 2002).

35. Olson, *The Logic of Collective Action*, 49, 57.

36. "Australia to Fund Sixth WGS Satellite," *Satellite Today*, 4 October 2007; http://www.satellitetoday.com/st/topnews/19168.html.

37. "EU And US To Make GPS And Galileo Compatible," *GPS Daily*, 26 July 2007; http://www.gpsdaily.com/reports/EU_And_US_To_Make_GPS_And_Galileo_Compatible_999.html.

38. Lani Kass, "Rethinking Deterrence," *High Frontier*, vol. 5: 2 (2009): 19.

39. Ibid.: 20.

40. Ibid.: 21.

41. Discusses effects of nuclear detonation and possible alternatives to space systems. Dennis Papdopoulos, "Satellite Threat Due To High Altitude Nuclear Detonations," University of Maryland Physics Department, College Park, Maryland, October 2002: http://www.lightwatcher.com/chemtrails/Papadopoulos-chemtrails.pdf.

42. Rep. Geoff Davis (R-KY) and General Lance W. Lord, Hearing on Fiscal Year 2006 National Defense Authorization Act—Budget Request for Military Space Activities, House Armed Services Committee, 109th Congress, 1st session, 9 March 2005: http://commdocs.house.gov/committees/security/has068290.000/has068290_0f.htm.

43. Eleanor Keymer, "Space-Saving Devices: Militaries Look to Make the Most of Commercial Satellites," Jane's Defense Systems, 8 October 2008: http://www.janes.com/news/defence/systems/idr/idr081008_1_n.shtml.

44. Robert K. Ackerman, "Military Users Boost Commercial Imagery," *Signal Magazine*, December 2003.

Chapter 8

1. The text and protocols of the Treaty Between the United States of America and the Union of Soviet Socialist Republics on the Elimination of their Intermediate-Range and Shorter-Range Missiles, 8 December 1987, commonly known as IMF, can be found at: http://www.state.gov/www/global/arms/treaties/inf1.html.

2. For more on the Missile Technology Control Regime see: http://www.mtcr .info/english/index.html.

3. The A-4/V–2 (German: *Vergeltungswaffe* or Reprisal weapon) had its first successful flight on 3 October 1942. Production began shortly thereafter and eventually would total over 5200 missiles. "German Missiles," Weapons of Mass Destruction section, Globalsecurity.org, 19 March 2009: http://www.globalsecurity.org/wmd/world/ germany/missile.htm.

4. "Iran-Iraq War (1980–1988)," GlobalSecurity.org: http://www.globalsecurity .org/military/world/war/iran-iraq.htm.

5. "Gaza's rocket threat to Israel," *BBC News* online, 21 Jan 2008: http://news.bbc .co.uk/1/hi/world/middle_east/3702088.stm.

6. There is an extensive body of literature that covers the origin of nuclear deterrence theory and theories of nuclear war fighting. Examples of the former include *The Absolute Weapon*, Bernard Brodie, ed. (New York: Harcourt, 1946); Henry A. Kissinger, *Nuclear Weapons and Foreign Policy* (Washington, D.C.: Council on Foreign Relations, 1958); Bernard Brodie, *Strategy in the Missile Age* (Princeton, New Jersey: Princeton University Press, 1959); Herman Kahn, *On Thermonuclear War* (Princeton, New Jersey: Princeton University Press, 1962); and Scott D. Sagan and Kenneth N. Waltz, *The Spread of Nuclear Weapons: A Debate* (New York: W.W. Norton & Co., 1995). For a reexamination of the role of nuclear weapons and how, in the hands of the so-called "great powers," they ensure peace in the post-Cold War world, see John J. Mearsheimer, *The Tragedy of Great Power Politics* (New York: W. W. Norton, 2001); and Robert J. Art, *A Grand Strategy for America* (Ithaca, New York: Cornell University Press, 2003). An extensive dialogue on the shift in the nuclear balance toward U.S. primacy may be found in Keir A. Liebler and Daryl G. Press, "The End of MAD? The Nuclear Dimension of U.S. Primacy," *International Security*, vol. 30: 4 (Spring 2006): 7–44.

7. Robert Powell has an extensive discussion of nuclear deterrence based on brinkmanship and game theory in Powell, "Nuclear Deterrence Theory, Nuclear Proliferation, and National Missile Defense," *International Security*, vol. 27: 4 (Spring 2003): 86–118.

8. Wang Wei, "The Effect of Tactical Ballistic Missiles on the Maritime Strategy of China," translated by Danling Cacioppo, *The Naval War College Review*, 61: 3 (Summer 2008): 133–140.

9. The basis of this discussion may be found in Marshal V. D. Sokolovskiy, *Soviet Military Strategy*, 3rd edition, Harriet Fast Scott, ed. (New York: Crane, Russak, 1975).

10. "China's Preliminary Assessment of Operation Iraqi Freedom," *Chinese Mili-*

tary Update, RUSI, vol. 1: 2 (July 2003): 1–3; http://www.rusi.org/downloads/assets/AN00039.pdf.

11. *Annual Report to Congress: Military Power of the People's Republic of China*, Office of the Secretary of Defense, Washington, D.C., 2009: 17, 21.

12. Elaine Scoliono, "Documents Detail Israeli Missile Deal With the Shah," *New York Times*, 1 April 1986: A17.

13. *The Whirlwind War: The United States Army in Operations DESERT SHIELD and DESERT STORM*, Frank N. Schubert and Theresa L. Kraus, eds. (Washington, D.C.: Center of Military History Publication, 1995); available online: http://www.history.army.mil/books/www/284a.htm.

14. These totaled 20 SCUD-B missiles and 2 MAZ-543P mobile transporter/erector vehicles; see "Country Profiles: Iran," Nuclear Threat Initiative (NTI): http://www.nti.org/e_research/profiles/Iran/Missile/.

15. "Hwasong 5/SCUD B," Federation of American Scientists, 30 May 2008: http://www.fas.org/nuke/guide/dprk/missile/hwasong-5.htm.

16. "Iran's Weapons of Mass Destruction," Jane's Intelligence Review, Special Report No. 6, 1 June 1995: 20; see NTI: http://www.nti.org/e_research/profiles/Iran/Missile/chronology_1987.html. That same year, the Chinese helped construct a plant to produce 600 to 1,000 *Oghab* rockets per year, provided Iran was able to import ammonium perchlorate for the solid-fueled motors. Derivatives of these same rockets would later factor in the 2006 Hezbollah and 2008 Hamas campaigns against Israel.

17. NTI, "Country Profiles: Iran."

18. Joseph S. Bermudez, Jr., "Iran's Missile Development," *The International Missile Bazaar: The New Supplier's Network*, William C. Potter and Harlan W. Jencks, eds. (San Francisco: Westview Press, 1994), 48; see NTI.org: http://www.nti.org/e_research/profiles/Iran/Missile/3876.html.

19. In an interview with Jane's Defense Weekly, the former director of Israel's Ballistic Missile Defense Organization, Uzi Rubin, declared, "The Safir is the basis for a future Iranian intercontinental ballistic missile." Alon Ben-David, "Iranian Satellite Launch Evokes Nuclear Concerns," *Jane's Defense Weekly*, 11 February 2009: 5.

20. Executive Summary Of The Report Of The Commission To Assess The Ballistic Missile Threat To The United States, 104th Congress (Washington, D.C. 1998); http://www.fas.org/irp/threat/bm-threat.htm; and http://www.fas.org/irp/threat/missile/rumsfeld/index.html.

21. Charles P. Vick, "Taep'o-dong 2 (TD-2), NKSL-X-2," GlobalSecurity.org., 20 March 2007: http://www.globalsecurity.org/wmd/world/dprk/td-2.htm.

22. "Non-proliferation/Democratic People's Republic of Korea," UN Security Council Resolution (UNSCR) 1718; .pdf file at: http://www.un.org/Docs/sc/unsc_resolutions06.htm; and "Letter dated 4 July 2006 from the Permanent Representative of Japan to the United Nations addressed to the President of the Security Council (S/2006/481)," UNSCR 1695: .pdf file at: http://www.un.org/Docs/sc/unsc_resolutions06.htm.

23. Jie-Ae Sohn, Charley Keyes, and Elise Labott, "'Satisfaction' from Kim over

N. Korea launch," CNN.com/asia, 5 April 2009: http://edition.cnn.hu/2009/WORLD/asiapcf/04/05/north.korea.rocket/index.html.

24. Jeffrey Park, "The North Korean Nuclear Test: What the Seismic Data Says," *Bulletin of the Atomic Scientists*, 26 May 2009: http://www.thebulletin.org/web-edition/features/the-north-korean-nuclear-test-what-the-seismic-data-says/.

25. Choe Sang-Hun, "In Defiance, North Korea Is Said to Test More Missiles," *New York Times*, 26 May 2009: http://www.nytimes.com/2009/05/27/world/asia/27korea.html?_r=1&hp.

26. The Code calls upon all countries to show greater restraint in their own development of ballistic missiles capable of delivering weapons of mass destruction, and to reduce their existing missile arsenals if possible. Aidan Harris, "Basic Notes: The International Code of Conduct Against Ballistic Missile Proliferation," British American Security Information Council, 18 July 2002: http://www.basicint.org/pubs/Notes/2002international_code.htm.

27. "Countering Air and Missile Threats," Joint Publication 3–01, Chairman Joint Chiefs of Staff, Washington, D.C., 1 Feb 2007: GL-13.

28. This phase of CROSSBOW saw significant losses in allied aircraft and airmen, including over 770 airmen killed and 154 aircraft lost by the RAF and USAAF. Adam L. Gruen, *Preemptive Defense: Allied Airpower Versus Hitler's V-Weapons, 1943–1945*, Air Force History Studies Office, Washington, D.C., 1998: 26.

29. Christopher Andrew, *For the President's Eyes Only* (New York: Harper Collins, 1996), 524.

30. "Rocket threat from the Gaza Strip, 2000–2007," Intelligence and Terrorism Information Center, Israel Ministry of Foreign Affairs, 16 Dec 2007: http://www.mfa.gov.il/MFA/Terrorism-+Obstacle+to+Peace/Terror+Groups/Rocket+threat+from+the+Gaza+Strip+2000–2007.htm.

31. Tony Karon, "The Homemade Rocket That Could Change the Mideast," *Time*, 11 February 2002: http://www.time.com/time/world/article/0,8599,202159,00.html; and Martin Sieff, "Israel's defense against Qassam rockets still a BMD shambles," UPI.com, 11 March 2009: http://www.upi.com/Security_Industry/2009/03/11/Israels_defense_against_Qassam_rockets_still_a_BMD_shambles/UPI-48921236781900/.

32. "Joint Publication 1–02, Department of Defense Dictionary of Military and Associated Terms," U.S. Department of Defense, Washington, D.C., 12 April 2001 (as amended through 17 October 2008): 411; and "Countering Air and Missile Threats": GL-14.

33. Existing Defense Support Program satellites, now orbiting the earth in a geosynchronous orbit, provide global coverage for early warning, tracking, and identification. "BMD Basics: Sensors," Missile Defense Agency (MDA), Washington, D.C., 1 March 2009: http://www.mda.mil/mdalink/html/sensors.html.

34. "Defense Support Program Satellites," Air Force Link Factsheets, Air Force Space Command, Peterson AFB, Colorado, January 2008: http://www.af.mil/factsheets/factsheet.asp?id=96.

35. Philip E. Coyle III and Victoria Samson, "The Proliferation Security Initia-

tive: Background, history and prospects for the future," Center for Defense Information, January 2009: 1–3; http://www.icnnd.org/latest/research/Proliferation_Security _Initiative.pdf.

36. A succinct summary may be found in "Missile Defense: The First Sixty Years," Missile Defense Agency (MDA), Washington, D.C., 15 August 2008: http://www.mda .mil/mdalink/pdf/first60.pdf.

37. Ballistic, exo-atmospheric flight consists of three distinct phases: boost, midcourse and terminal. The boost phase is the part of a missile flight path from launch until it stops accelerating under its own power. Typically the boost phase ends within the first three to five minutes of flight. The midcourse phase, lasting up to twenty minutes for ICBMs, is the point where the missile has stopped thrusting and follows a more predictable glide path. The terminal phase occurs when a missile (or its warhead) falls back into the atmosphere. This phase is typically the shortest and most difficult for intercepts, generally lasting from thirty seconds to one minute.

38. Typically land-based PATRIOT PAC-3 and sea-based Standard SM-2 Blk 4 surface-to-air missiles.

39. "Testing: Building Confidence," Missile Defense Agency, Washington, D.C., 25 March 2009: 1; http://www.mda.mil/mdalink/pdf/2009MDAbook.pdf.

40. Ibid.: 5.

41. According to MDA, the overall intercept success rate for individual programs is: 19 of 23 Aegis interceptors that included Japanese shots; 6 of 6 THAAD; and 8 of 13 ground-based interceptors. "BMD Test Record," Missile Defense Agency Fact Sheet, MDA, Washington, D.C., 31 July 2009: http://www.mda.mil/mdalink/html/factsheet .html.

42. "(U) OASD Satellite Engagement Communications Plan," Office of the Assistant Secretary of Defense, Washington, D.C., 14 Feb 2008: http://www.governmentattic.org/docs/(U)_OASD_Satellite_Engagement_Communications_Plan_(1400_ hrs_14_Feb_08).pdf.

43. "RIM-161 SM-3 Japan Maritime Self Defense Force Deployment," GlobalSecurity.org, 28 March 2009: http://www.globalsecurity.org/space/systems/sm3– japan.htm.

44. "Fact Sheet on U.S. Missile Defense Policy: A 'Phased, Adaptive Approach' for Missile Defense in Europe," Office of the Press Secretary, The White House, Washington, D.C. 17 September 2009: http://www.whitehouse.gov/the_press_office/ FACT-SHEET-US-Missile-Defense-Policy-A-Phased-Adaptive-Approach-for-Missile -Defense-in-Europe/.

45. "2006 National Security Strategy of the United States," National Security Council, Washington, D.C., 16 March 2006, 22; www.marforres.usmc.mil/docs/ nss2006.pdf.

46. "A Cooperative Strategy for 21st Century Seapower," Chief of Naval Operations (CNO), United States Navy, Washington, D.C., October 2007 [emphasis in original]: 5; http://www.navy.mil/maritime/MaritimeStrategy.pdf.

47. General Kevin Chilton, USAF, and Greg Weaver, "Waging Deterrence in the

Twenty-First Century," *Strategic Studies Quarterly* (Spring 2009): 32–33; http://www
.au.af.mil/au/ssq/.

48. "Deterrence Operations Joint Operating Concept Version 2.0, December
2006," Department of Defense, Washington, D.C., 2006: 38–39.

49. "SALT and European Security," in *NATO's Strategic Options*, David S. Yost,
ed. (Oxford: Pergammon, 1981), 114.

50. CNO, "A Cooperative Strategy": 13.

51. "33 Minutes: Protecting America in the New Missile Age," documentary film
by the Heritage Foundation, 21 Nov 2008: http://www.heritage.org/33–minutes/.

Chapter 9

1. U.S. Department of Defense Dictionary, taken from the Defense Department
website: http://www.dtic.mil/doctrine/jel/doddict/data/a/00283.html.

2. "Joint Publication 3–01: Countering Air and Missile Threats," U.S. Department of Defense, Washington, D.C., 5 February 2007: I–2.

3. Ibid.: I–3.

4. Targets for the suppression of enemy air defenses include radars for early
warning/ground-controlled intercept, acquisition, surface-to-air missiles, and anti-
aircraft artillery and their associated command and control systems. General T. Michael Moseley, US Air Force, "Global Strike CONOPS," Washington, D.C., 27 December 2006: 10.

5. "Joint Publication 3–01": I–4, 1–5.

6. Ibid.: I–5.

7. Ibid.

8. Ibid.: I–6.

9. Ibid.: II–4, II–5.

10. "Global Strike CONOPS": 4. A comprehensive list of anti-access capabilities
can be found on page 7.

11. Ibid.: 20.

12. General T. Michael Moseley, USAF, "Global Persistent Attack CONOPS,"
Washington, D.C., 28 July 2006: 17–19.

13. These are derived from *Joint Publication 3–01*: III–23—III–27; "Global Strike
CONOPS": 8, 21; and Lambeth, *The Transformation of American Air Power*, 248–249.

14. For example, see Benjamin S. Lambeth, "Kosovo and the Continuing SEAD
Challenge," Aerospace Power Journal, Summer 2002: http://www.airpower.maxwell
.af.mil/airchonicles/apj/apj02/sum02/lambeth.html.

15. Compiled from *Joint Publication 3–01*: III–25; "Global Strike CONOPS": 11;
and Lambeth, *The Transformation of American Air Power*, 235.

16. David Albert, John Garstka, and Frederick Stein, "Network Centric Warfare,"
DoD Command and Control Research Program, Washington, D.C., 1999: 2.

17. Lieutenant General David A. Deptula, U.S. Air Force, Deputy Chief of Staff
for Intelligence, Surveillance, and Reconnaissance, "Air combat platforms and ISR,"

Defense Today Feature Report, March 2009: 2–3; http://www.defencenews.com.au/defence-today-feature-report.cfm.

18. During the first Gulf War, the Global Positioning System revolutionized coalition operations by, among other things, "facilitating the unerring 100-hour ground sweep across the flat and featureless Iraqi desert into the blind side of Iraqi troops hunkered down [in Kuwait]." Lambeth, *The Transformation of American Air Power*, 236.

19. Rebecca Grant, "Victory in Cyberspace," Air Force Association, Arlington, Virginia, 2007: 14.

20. "Global Strike CONOPS": 21.

21. This was officially ended only by the Commission to Assess United States National Security Space Management and Organization, which expressed concerns that training all U.S. Air Force officers to be both air and space conversant was threatening to produce the proverbial "jack of all trades and master of none." Benjamin Lambeth, *Mastering the Ultimate High Ground: Next Steps in the Military Uses of Space*, Monograph Series No. MR-1649–AF, RAND Corporation, Santa Monica, California, 2003: 64, 90–91.

22. Lambeth, *The Transformation of American Air Power*, 238–241.

23. The U.S. Air Force mission statement, taken from the USAF website: http://www.af.mil/main/welcome.asp.

24. "Joint Publication 3–01": I–1.

25. "Global Strike CONOPS": 11.

26. For example, see *Case Studies in the Achievement of Air Superiority*, Benjamin Franklin Cooling, ed. (Washington, D.C., U.S. Government Printing Office, 1994); and Clayton K. S. Chun, "Aerospace Power in the Twenty-First Century: A Basic Primer," Air University Press, Maxwell Air Force Base, 2001.

27. Richard Hallion and Michael Irish, "Air and Space Superiority," in Daniel Goure and Christopher Szara, eds. *Air and Space Power in the New Millennium* (Washington, D.C.: Center for Strategic and International Studies, 1997), 88.

28. "Joint Publication 3–01": IV–9.

29. Craig Caffrey, "Fewer, but Fitter," *Jane's Defense Weekly*, 1 April 2009: 25–31.

30. Daniel Goure and Stephen A. Cambone, "The Coming of Age of Air and Space Power," in Daniel Goure and Christopher Szara, eds., *Air and Space Power in the New Millennium* (Washington, D.C.: Center for Strategic and International Studies, 1997), 18.

31. John Tirpak, "The Double Digit SAMs," *Air Force Magazine*, June 2001: 48–49; and Barry Watts, "Long-Range Strike: Imperatives, Urgency and Options," report, Center For Strategic and Budgetary Assessments, April 2005: 39–47; www.csbaonline.org/4Publications/PubLibrary/R.20050406.LRPS/R.20050406.LRPS.pdf.

32. "Joint Publication 3–01": IV–9.

33. "Global Strike CONOPS": 21; Watts, "Long-Range Strike": 49–57.

34. "Alternatives for Long-Range Ground-Attack Systems," Congressional Budget Office study, Washington, D.C., March 2006: 21.

35. For example, see Christopher Bolkhom, "Military Suppression of Enemy Air Defenses (SEAD): Assessing Future Needs," CRS Report for Congress No. RS21141, Congressional Research Service (CRS), Washington, D.C., 11 May 2005: 2–4; "Why Raptor? The Logic of Buying the World's Best Fighter," Lexington Institute, Arlington, Virginia, 2004; Tirpak, "Double Digit SAMs"; and Lambeth, "Kosovo and the Continuing SEAD Challenge."

36. Lambeth, "Kosovo and the Continuing SEAD Challenge"; and Bolkhom, "Military SEAD."

37. John Stillion and Scott Perdue, "Air Combat Past, Present and Future," Project Air Force briefing, RAND Corporation, August 2008: 1–5; http://www.scribd.com /doc/7774389/Rand-StudyFuture-of-Air-Combat.

38. Also see Watts, "Long-Range Strike": 45–49; Christopher Bowie, "The Anti-Access Threat and Theater Air Bases" report, Center for Strategic and Budgetary Assessments, Washington, D.C., 23 August 2002; and John Stillion and David Or-letsky, "Airbase Vulnerability to Conventional Cruise-Missile and Ballistic-Missile Attacks," Monograph Series No. MR-1028–AF, RAND Corporation, Santa Monica, California, 1999.

39. Also see Bill Sweetman, "Radical and Cheap Anti-Stealth Radar," 6 December 2007, *Aviation Week Defense Technology International*: http://www.military.com/ features/0,15240,157743,00.html; Watts "Long-Range Strike"; Martin Libicki "Technology in Warfare" in *2015: Power and Progress*, Patrick Cronin, ed. (Washington, D.C.: National Defense University, 1996), 134; Mort Rolleston, "A Peek into the Future: Results of the 2007 USAF Future Capabilities Game," *The Wright Stuff*, Vol. 3: 22 (26 November 2008); and Bolkhom, "Military SEAD."

40. The Project on Government Oversight, "High Maintenance F-22 Stealth Features Keeping It in the Shop," 20 February 2009; http://www.pogo.org/pogo-files/ alerts/national-security/ns-f22–20090220.html.

41. Stillion and Perdue, "Air Combat Past, Present and Future": 19–28.

42. For more details, see, for example, "Emerging Cyber Threats Report for 2009: Data, Mobility and Questions of Responsibility will Drive Cyber Threats in 2009 and Beyond," Georgia Tech Information Security Center, Atlanta, Georgia, 15 October 2008; Clay Wilson, "Information Operations, Electronic Warfare, and Cyberwar: Capabilities and Related Policy Issues," CRS Report for Congress RL31787, CRS, Washington, D.C., 5 June 2007: 1–16.

43. For more details, see Clay Wilson, "High Altitude Electromagnetic Pulse (HEMP) and High Power Microwave (HPM) Devices: Threat Assessments," CRS Report for Congress RL32544, CRS, Washington, D.C., 26 March 2008: 1–16.

44. Ian Easton, "The Great Game in Space: China's Evolving ASAT Weapons Programs and Their Implications for Future U.S. Strategy," Project 2049 Institute, Arlington, Virginia, 2009: 2–5.

45. Also see Watts, "Long-Range Strike": 55–57.

46. Michael Barzelay and Colin Campbell, *Preparing for the Future: Strategic*

Planning in the U.S. Air Force (Washington, D.C.: Brookings Institution Press, 2003), 201–205.

47. For example, see "Alternatives for Long-Range Ground-Attack Systems"; and Watts, "Long-Range Strike."

48. Barzelay and Campbell, *Preparing for the Future,* 206–207.

49. One analysis strongly suggests that the planned program (with an estimated total cost of $35–52 billion over twenty years in 2007 dollars), while adequate for other uses, will lack the radar aperture necessary to detect ground targets moving slower than about twenty miles per hour. "Alternatives for Military Space Radar," Congressional Budget Office study, Washington, D.C., January 2007): xv–xx.

50. For a fairly detailed analysis of U.S. military investment in short-range vs. long-range strike, see Watts, "Long-Range Strike": 20–22.

51. Secretary of Defense Robert M. Gates, press briefing on the Pentagon budget, Office of the Secretary of Defense, Arlington, Virginia, 6 April 2009.

52. Congressional Budget Office, "Alternatives for Long-Range Ground-Attack Systems": 13.

53. Ibid.: 11–12. For perspective, 1,500 nautical miles is nearly the distance between Guam and Fuijian Province in China.

54. Watts, "Long-Range Strike": 35.

55. Bowie, "The Anti-Access Threat and Theater Air Bases": 59.

56. Players in the 2007 Future Capabilities Game did just that. See Mort Rolleston, "A Peek into the Future: Results of the 2007 USAF Future Capabilities Game," *The Wright Stuff,* vol. 3: 22 (26 November 2008); http://www.au.af.mil/au/aunews/archive/2008/0322/Articles/Q2008–09–03%20Rolleston%20revised%20(6%20Nov%2008).htm.

57. General T. Michael Moseley, U.S. Air Force, 18th Chief of Staff, "The Nation's Guardians: America's 21st Century Air Force," Chief of Staff, Air Force (CSAF) White Paper, Washington, D.C., 29 December 2007: 2.

Chapter 10

1. For an analysis of Mahanian thought, see Jon Tetsuro Sumida, *Inventing Grand Strategy and Teaching Command: The Classic Works of Alfred Thayer Mahan Reconsidered* (Baltimore: Johns Hopkins University Press, 1997).

2. On globalization and naval power, see *Globalization and Maritime Power,* Captain Sam Tangredi, U.S. Navy, ed. (Washington, D.C.: National Defense University, 2002).

3. Julian Stafford Corbett, *Some Principles of Maritime Strategy* (Annapolis: Naval Institute Press, 1988), 87.

4. This key observation was made by Colin S. Gray in *The Leverage of Sea Power: The Strategic Advantage of Navies in War* (New York: The Free Press, 1992), 1.

5. Alfred Thayer Mahan, *The Influence of Sea Power upon History, 1660–1783* (Boston: Little, Brown and Company, 1918), 25.

6. The meaning here of "sea base" is simply some platform on or under the ocean, from which power can be projected, such as an aircraft carrier, a submarine, or a squadron of amphibious ships.

7. The concept of sufficiency applies most particularly to conflict between nations. The worldwide efforts to control terrorism, narcotics smuggling, and WMD proliferation require a much wider blanket of security across the global maritime common.

8. Samuel Eliot Morison, *The Battle of the Atlantic: September 1939–May 1943* (New York: Little, Brown and Company, 1947). 1,315 allied ships were lost to the U-boat, compared to a total 2,177 ships lost to all causes in the Battle of the Atlantic. Total crew lost to U-boats were 22,898, and to all causes, 30,132. From Terry Hughes and John Costello, *The Battle of the Atlantic* (New York: Dial Press, 1977). See also, Stephen W. Roskill, *The War at Sea, 1939–1945* (London: H. M. Stationary Office, 1954–56); and, John Barratt, "The Bitter End, The U-Boat War, 1939–1945," *MilitaryHistoryOnline.com* (15 December 2002); http://www.militaryhistoryonline.com/wwii/atlantic/bitterend.aspx.

9. Gray, *The Leverage of Sea* Power, 240. In spite of their own devastating losses while interdicting Allied shipping on the Atlantic, the U-boats were a threat until the very end of the war. By 1944, however, their efforts at sea denial having ultimately failed, the Germans did not have enough submarines left to prevent the Allied landings in France.

10. "U.S. Praises China Anti-Piracy Role off Somalia," *USA Today*, 28 February 2009; http://www.usatoday.com/news/world/2009–02–28–somalia-pirates_N.htm. and, "Japan Navy Ships Depart for Anti-Piracy Mission," *USA Today*, 14 March 2009; http://www.usatoday.com/news/world/2009–03–14–japan-piracy_N.htm.

11. For an in-depth discussion of the strategic thinking that went into the *Maritime Strategy*, see John B. Hattendorf, "The Evolution of the U.S. Navy's Maritime Strategy, 1977–1986," Newport Paper 19, Center for Naval Warfare Studies, U.S. Naval War College, Newport, Rhode Island, 2004. For the actual successive texts of the *Maritime Strategy*, see "U.S. Naval Strategies in the 1980s," John B. Hattendorf and Peter M. Swartz, eds., Newport Paper 33, Center for Naval Warfare Studies, U.S. Naval War College, Newport, Rhode Island, 2008; and, "U.S. Naval Strategies in the 1990s," John B. Hattendorf, ed., Newport Paper 27, Center for Naval Warfare Studies, U.S. Naval War College, Newport, Rhode Island, 2006.

12. Sean O'Keefe, Secretary of the Navy ". . . From the Sea: Preparing the Naval Service for the 21st Century," Office of the Secretary of the Navy, Washington, D.C., September 1992. For a good discussion of the shifting strategic underpinnings of the Navy's doctrine, see Geoffrey Till, "A Cooperative Strategy for 21st Century Seapower: A View from Outside," *Naval War College Review*, vol. 61: 2 (Spring 2008): 25–38.

13. Robert Rubel, "The Navy's Changing Force Paradigm," *Naval War College Review*, Vol. 62:2 (Spring 2009): 13–24.

14. Admiral Vern Clark, U.S. Navy, quoted in Andrew Krepinevich, Barry Watts,

and Robert Work, "Meeting the Anti-Access and Area-Denial Challenge," *Center for Strategic and Budgetary Assessments*, Washington, D.C., 2003: 41.

15. Robert Rubel, "Changing Force Paradigm": 16.

16. Admiral Michael Mullen, U.S. Navy, and General Michael Hagee, U.S. Marine Corps, "Naval Operations Concept," Department of the Navy, Washington, D.C., 2006; Admiral Michael Mullen, U.S. Navy, Navy Strategic Plan in Support of POM 10 (Washington, D.C.: Office of the Chief of Naval Operations, 2007). Mullen became Chairman of the Joint Chiefs of Staff in 2007.

17. General James T. Conway, U.S. Marine Corps, Admiral Gary Roughead, U.S. Navy, and Admiral Thad Allen, U.S. Coast Guard, "A Cooperative Strategy for 21st Century Seapower," Department of the Navy, Washington, D.C., October 2007: p 11; http://www.navy.mil/maritime/MaritimeStrategy.pdf.

18. See Joshua Ho, "US: A Cooperative Plan for 21st Century Sea Power," S. Rajaratnam School of International Studies, Singapore, 30 July 2008.

19. "A Cooperative Strategy": 9.

20. Krepinevich et al., "Meeting the Anti-Access Challenge."

21. Secretary of Defense Robert M. Gates, speech at the National Defense University, Washington, D.C., 29 September 2008.

22. "A Cooperative Strategy": 13.

23. In a recent statement before Congress, the commander, U.S. Pacific Command, stated that antisubmarine warfare "remains a challenge, and is the number one priority for the Pacific Fleet." See "Statement of Admiral Timothy J. Keating, U.S. Navy, Commander U.S. Pacific Command, Before the Senate Armed Services Committee on U.S. Pacific Command Posture," Senate Armed Services Committee, Washington, D.C., 24 March 2009.

24. Robert O. Work, "The US Navy: Charting a Course for Tomorrow's Fleet," Center for Strategic and Budgetary Assessments, Washington, D.C., 2008: 6.

25. Krepinevich et al., "Meeting the Anti-Access Challenge": 53.

26. Ibid.: 1.

27. Gordon England, Secretary of the Navy, Admiral Vern Clark, U.S. Navy, General James Jones, U.S. Marine Corps, "Naval Power 21 . . . A Naval Vision," Department of the Navy, Washington, D.C., October 2002: 1.

28. "A Cooperative Strategy": 10.

29. Ronald O'Rourke, "China Naval Modernization; Implications for U.S. Navy Capabilities—Background and Issues for Congress," Congressional Research Service (CRS) Report for Congress RL33153, Congressional Research Service, Washington, D.C., 29 May 2009: 4.

30. During the Cold War, the U.S. Navy went to considerable lengths to operate in relative quiet. When its control of sea was assured, the Navy worried less about minimizing its electronic signals, something that will have to be re-thought in light of a missile threat that relies on detecting the carrier at extended ranges.

31. Paul S. Giarra, "Watching the Chinese," *U.S. Naval Institute Proceedings*, Vol. 135/5/1275 (May 2009): 12.

32. Naval analyst Rear Admiral Michael McDevitt U.S. Navy (Ret.) at the Center for Naval Analyses observes, "If the PLA can master and field this weapon system, it will be able to present as serious a challenge to the U.S. Navy as the one presented by the Soviet Backfire-launched cruise missiles before the introduction of the Aegis radar system." See Michael McDevitt, "The Strategic and Operational Context Driving PLA Navy Building," in *Right-Sizing the People's Liberation Army: Exploring the Contours of China's Military,* Roy Kamphausen and Andrew Scobell, eds. (Carlisle, Pennsylvania: Army War College, 2007), 502.

33. "Military Power of the People's Republic of China," Annual Report to Congress, Office of the Secretary of Defense, Washington, D.C., 2009.

34. Wayne P. Hughes, Jr., Captain, U.S. Navy (Ret.), *Fleet Tactics and Coastal Combat* (Naval Institute Press: Annapolis, Maryland, 2000).

35. See Wendell Minnick, "China Developing Anti-Ship Ballistic Missiles," *Defense News* (14 January 2008).

36. On the evolution of these networks, see Norman Friedman, *Network Centric Warfare* (Annapolis: Naval Institute Press, 2009).

37. For information on the Iranian "order of battle," see Anthony H. Cordesman and Martin Kleiber, *Iran's Military Forces and Warfighting Capabilities* (Washington, D.C.: Greenwood Publishing Group, 2007).

38. See "Protecting Naval Surface Ships from Fast Attack Boat Swarm Threat," Defense Update, *International Online Defense Magazine* (10 January 2007); http://defense-update.com/newscast/0107/news/110107_fiac.htm.

39. For an in-depth discussion of Iran's mining capability and the threat to shipping in the Strait of Hormuz, see Caitlin Talmadge, "Closing Time; Assessing the Iranian Threat to the Strait of Hormuz," *International Security,* Vol. 33: 1 (Summer 2008): 82–117.

40. For the definitive analysis of the tanker wars see, Martin S. Navias and E.R. Hooton, *Tanker Wars: The Assault on Merchant Shipping During the Iran-Iraq Crisis, 1980–1988* (London and New York: I.B. Tauris & Co. Ltd, 1996). See also Lee Allen Zatarin, *Tanker War: America's First Conflict with Iran, 1987–1988* (Drexel Hill: Casement Publishers and Book Distributors, 2008).

Chapter 11

1. "The JOE (Joint Operating Environment) 2008: Challenges and Implications for the Future Joint Force," United States Joint Forces Command, Norfolk, Virginia, 25 November 2008: 15.

2. Mauro F. Guillen, "Is Globalization Civilizing, Destructive, or Feeble? A Critique of Key Debates in the Social Science Literature," *Annual Review of Sociology,* 27 (2001): 235–260.

3. Ilya Prigogine, *The End of Certainty: Time, Chaos, and the New Laws of Nature* (New York: The Free Press, 1997), 39, 57, 71–72; John H. Holland, *Hidden Order:*

How Adaptation Builds Complexity (New York: Basic Books, 1995), 10–11, 14–15, 87, 141–42.

4. From "An Introduction," Santa Fe Institute: http://www.santafe.edu/about/.

5. Holland quote cited in M. Mitchell Waldrop, *Complexity: The Emerging Science at the Edge of Order and Chaos* (New York: Simon and Schuster, 1992), 145.

6. Nancy Popp and Kathryn Portnow, "Our Developmental Perspective on Adulthood," in R. Kegan, M. Broderick, E. Drago-Severson, D. Helsing, N. Popp, and K. Portnow, eds., *Toward a New Pluralism in ABE/SOL Classrooms: Teaching to Multiple "Cultures of Mind,"* research monograph no. 19, National Center for the Study of Adult Learning and Literacy, Harvard Graduate School of Education, Cambridge, Mass., August 2001.

7. Chris Argyris and Donald Schön, *Theory in Practice: Increasing Professional Effectiveness* (San Francisco: Jossey-Bass, 1974), 6–7, 30; Chris Argyris and Donald Schön, *Organizational Learning: A Theory of Action Perspective* (Reading, Mass: Addison Wesley, 1978), 2–3.

8. Donde Ashmos Plowman and Dennis Duchon, "Emergent Leadership: Getting Beyond Heroes and Scapegoats," in J. K. Hazy, J. A. Goldstein, & B. B. Lichtenstein, eds., *Complex Systems Leadership Theory* (Mansfield, N.J.: ISCE Publishing, 2007), 109–27.

9. Manuel DeLanda, *A New Philosophy of Society: Assemblage Theory and Social Complexity* (London: Continuum, 2006), 11.

10. Gerald Midgley, "Complexity and Philosophy: Systems Thinking, Complexity and the Philosophy of Science," *Emergence: Complexity and Organization (E:CO)* vol. 10: 4 (2008): 55–73.

11. Carmen Panzar, James K. Hazy, Bill McKelvey, and David R. Schwandt, "The Paradox of Complex Organizations: Leadership as Integrative Influence," in *Complex Systems Leadership Theory*, J. K. Hazy, J. A. Goldstein, and B. B. Lichtenstein, eds. (Mansfield, Mass.: ISCE Publishing, 2007), 305–25.

12. Midgley, "Complexity and Philosophy": 55–73.

13. R. W. Ashby, *An Introduction to Cybernetics* (London: Methuen, 1956).

14. Panzar et al., "The Paradox of Complex Organizations," 305–25.

15. Ibid., 324.

16. Lieutenant Commander Robert Loughran, U.S. Navy, "Who's in Charge Here? Civil-Military Coordination in Humanitarian Assistance," Report OMB No. 0704–0188, Naval War College, Newport, Rhode Island, 28 April 2008: 8–12, 15–18; "Operation Lifeline in Pakistan," video produced by Defense Information School, Great Americans series (2005): http://www.greatamericans.com/videos/6a6fccc854/operation-lifeline.

17. Author email correspondence with Adm. Michael LeFever, U.S. Navy, January through July 2009.

18. An action-logic is a cognitive map and corresponding set of strategies that drives how an individual or collective gives meaning to and structures experience to create a coherent world view that influences and justifies patterns of action. See Bill

Torbert and Associates, *Action Inquiry: The Secret of Timely and Transforming Leadership* (San Francisco: Berrett-Koehler Publishers, 2004).

19. These capabilities of emergent leadership are further described in the Leadership Development Framework presented in David Rooke and William Torbert, "Organizational Transformation as a Function of CEO's Developmental Stage," *Organization Development Journal* 16 (1998): 11–28; David Rooke and William Torbert, "Seven Transformations of Leadership," *Harvard Business Review* (April 2005): 67–76; as well as Torbert et al., *Action Inquiry.*

20. John J. Garstka, Jon Geis, Ted Hailes, Richard Hughes, Sandra M. Martinez, and Lin Wells, "Challenges for National Security Organizations and Leadership Development: Trends and Shocks in Complex Adaptive Systems," in *Trends and Shocks,* Neyla Arnas, ed. (Washington, D.C.: National Defense University, forthcoming).

21. Robert Kegan, *In Over Our Heads: The Demands of Modern Life* (Cambridge, Mass.: Harvard University Press, 1994); Rooke and Torbert, "Organizational Transformation"; Rooke and Torbert, "Seven Transformations of Leadership."

22. *Higher Stages of Human Development,* Charles N. Alexander and Ellen Langer, eds. (New York: Oxford University Press, 1990); Argyris et al., *Theory in Practice*; C. Otto Scharmer, *Theory U: Leading from the Future as it Emerges* (Cambridge, Mass.: Society for Organizational Learning Press, 2007); William Torbert, "Cultivating Post-formal Adult Development: Higher Stages and Contrasting Interventions," in *Transcendence and Mature Thought in Adulthood: The Further Reaches of Adult Development,* M. Miller and S. Cook-Greuter, eds. (Lanham, Maryland: Rowman & Littlefield), 181–203.

23. Peter M. Senge, C. Otto Scharmer, Joseph Jaworski, and Betty Sue Flowers, *Presence: An Exploration of Profound Change in People, Organizations, and Society* (New York: Doubleday, 2005).

24. Chris Argyris, *Knowledge for Action* (San Francisco: Jossey-Bass, 2004); Torbert et al., *Action Inquiry.*

25. Plowman et al., "Emergent Leadership," 109–26; Scharmer, *Theory U.*

26. Plowman et al., "Emergent Leadership," 109–26; Senge et al., *Presence.*

27. Max H. Boisot and Ian C. MacMillan, "Crossing Epistemological Boundaries: Managerial and Entrepreneurial Approaches to Knowledge Management," in *Explorations in Information Space: Knowledge, Agents, and Organization,* M. H. Boisot, I. C. MacMillan, and K. S. Han, eds. (New York: Oxford University Press, 2007), 48–76; Peter Senge, *The Fifth Discipline: The Art & Practice of the Learning Organization* (New York: Doubleday, 1990); Karl E. Weick, *Sense-making in Organizations* (Thousand Oaks, Calif.: Sage Publications, 1995)

28. Elliott Jaques, *The Form of Time* (New York: Crane Russak, 1984); Jacques E. Elliott, *Requisite Organization: The CEO's Guide to Creative Structure and Leadership* (Arlington: Cason Hall & Co., 1989); Senge et al., *Presence*; Torbert et al., *Action Inquiry.*

29. "New Historic Milestone in International Co-operation for Straits of Malacca and Singapore," *MPA News,* Maritime and Port Authority of Singapore, 2009: http://

www.mpa.gov.sg/sites/global_navigation/news_center/mpa_news/mpa_news_detail
.page?filename=nr070904.xml.

30. LTC Irvin Lim, Singapore Armed Forces, "Comprehensive Maritime Domain Awareness: An Idea Whose Time Has Come?" *Pointer*, vol. 33: 3 (2007): 1–6; http://www.mindef.gov.sg/pointer/imindef/publications/pointer/journals/2007/v33n3/feature2.html.

31. Timothy L. Thomas, *Dragon Bytes: Chinese Information-War Theory and Practice from 1995–2003* (Fort Leavenworth, Kansas: Foreign Military Studies Office, 2004), 14–15, 28–29, 35–37, 43–47, 51–54, 58–61, 135; Timothy L. Thomas, *Decoding the Virtual Dragon: Critical Evolutions in the Science and Philosophy of China's Information Operations and Military Strategy* (Fort Leavenworth, Kansas: Foreign Military Studies Office, 2007), 75–82, 84–90, 94–96.

32. Thomas, *Dragon Bytes*, 12, 14, 32–41, 49–50; Thomas, *Decoding the Virtual Dragon*, 181–244.

33. Timothy L. Thomas, "Chinese and American Network Warfare," *Joint Forces Quarterly* 38 (2005): 76–83.

34. Thomas, *Decoding the Virtual Dragon*, 296–97; Thomas, *Dragon Bytes*, 6, 17, 32–37, 44.

35. Thomas, *Decoding the Virtual Dragon*, 284–86.

36. Siobhan Gorman, August Cole, and Yochi Dreazen, "Computer Spies Breach Fighter-Jet Project," *Wall Street Journal*, 21 April 2009; http://online.wsj.com/article/SB124027491029837401.html

37. Kevin G. Coleman, senior fellow at Technolytics, "China's Cyber Espionage Directed against the United States," statement at the U.S.-China Economic and Security Review Commission, Washington, D.C., 30 April 2009: 5.

38. Max Boisot and John Child, "Organizations as Adaptive Systems in Complex Environments: The Case of China," *Organization Science*, vol. 10: 3 (May–June 1999): 238, 237–52.

Chapter 12

1. For examples of contemporary definitions for domain awareness, all of which concern the degree to which decision makers can achieve an understanding of the operating environment when they view information provided by an information system; see "National Plan to Achieve Maritime Domain Awareness," Maritime Security Policy Coordinating Committee, Washington, D.C., October 2005; and, "Maritime Domain Awareness Concept (U)," Chief of Naval Operations, Department of the Navy, Washington, D.C., 29 May 2009.

2. Admiral M. G. Mullen, U.S. Navy, "Capstone Concept for Joint Operations," version 3.0, Joint Chiefs of Staff, Washington, D.C., 15 January 2009: 3; www.dtic.mil/futurejointwarfare.

3. Ibid.: 12.

4. The OODA (Observe, Orient, Decide, Act) Loop paradigm was created by mili-

tary strategist Col. John Boyd, U.S. Air Force, and first presented in his unpublished 1976 briefing manuscript, "A Discourse on Winning and Losing." Various versions of the OODA loop as illustrated in Figure 12.2 have been reproduced in a number of publications; see, for example, the Defense and National Institute website: http://www.d-n-i.net; and Chet Richards, *Certain to Win: The Strategy of John Boyd Applied to Business* (Atlanta, Georgia: Xlibris Corporation, 2004), 173. A recent and excellent source for information about Boyd's OODA loop can be found in Frans P. B. Osinga, *Science, Strategy and War: The Strategic Theory of John Boyd* (New York: Routledge, Taylor & Francis Group, 2007).

5. The authors have applied the OODA framework and principles in our DSS designs for a number of years; independently of our DSS research and development, the Capstone document also identifies Boyd's OODA loop as a well-known model of operational adaptation. See "Capstone Concept for Joint Operations": 39.

6. As used here, an ontology is a controlled and subject-specific vocabulary of terms with generic-to-specific relationships noted and often represented in a hierarchical taxonomy. In the context of a DSS, taxonomies are used not only to convey the preferred and common vocabulary for the subject matter in question, but are embedded into a "purpose oriented" framework, effectively transforming them into a teleology. In this way, the high-level decision perspective (e.g., national leadership) establishes the purpose, and all the metrics used in the DSS are interpreted with that purpose in mind.

7. This frequently requires that both semantic (subjective) and quantitative data be normalized. A practical and pragmatic approach used by the authors entails a combination of Fuzzy Logic to accommodate semantic data, and Multi-attribute Utility Theory to accommodate distinguishable "child-parent" relationships and the assignment of relative weight to those relationships. That formulation also is an effective means to account for the semantic, temporal, and classical statistical characterizations for uncertainty in and about the source data.

8. A good example of an activity that would be monitored and assessed in the "capability enabler" category is the U.S. proposal for international maritime agreements to create regional or theater security partnerships. See, for example, Naval Studies Board, *Maritime Security Partnerships* (Washington, D.C.: National Academies Press, 2008); and General James T. Conway, U.S. Marine Corps, Admiral Gary Roughead, U.S. Navy, and Admiral Thad Allen, U.S. Coast Guard, "A Cooperative Strategy for 21st Century Seapower," Department of the Navy, Washington, D.C., October 2007.

9. Also referred to as radar or radial phase-space charts, Kiviat charts are named after Phil Kiviat, who pioneered their use in the 1970s at the RAND Corporation. See Kenneth W. Kolance and Phillip J. Kiviat, "Software Unit Profiles and Kiviat Figures," *ACM Sigmetrics Performance Evaluation Review*, Vol. 2: 3 (September 1973): 2–12. There is a host of display techniques that can be used in place of—or along with—Kiviat charts for this DSS, but none captures the essence of the domain awareness display as clearly as the Kiviat. Note that ours differs from the original and from the usual rendering of Kiviat charts by using profiles instead of areas, and by creating a

dynamic sequence of profiles for trending information. A useful discussion about information visualization is provided in David Tegarden, "Business Information Visualization," *Communications of the Association for Information Systems*, Volume 1, Paper 4 (January 1999). Also, Edward Tufte offers six attributes for graphical excellence that any graphic or display designer should apply. See Edward R. Tufte, *The Visual Display of Quantitative Information* (Cheshire, Connecticut: Graphics Press, 1997), 13.

10. There is a decision concept that utilizes the notion of subjective assessments in the form of "improper linear models" vice "proper linear models," the latter being derived using statistical regression techniques. The improper linear model method uses expert subjective determinations to establish preferential distinguish ability between variables, and is what we use to define the separate decision space metrics. See R. M. Dawes and B. Corrigan, "Linear Models in Decision Making," *Psychological Bulletin*, vol. 81: 2 (1974): 95–106; and R. M. Dawes, "The Robust Beauty of Improper Linear Models," *American Psychologist*, vol. 34: 7 (1974): 571–82.

11. A useful start at this problem can be found in Jerry Mendel, *Uncertain Rule-Based Fuzzy Logic Systems* (New Jersey: Prentice Hall, 2001); and Kurt J. Schmucker, *Fuzzy Sets, Natural Language Computations, and Risk Analysis* (Rockville, Maryland: Computer Sciences Press, 1986).

12. W. Ross Ashby, *An Introduction to Cybernetics* (London: Chapman & Hall, 1956). Also see W. Ross Ashby, *Design for a Brain: The Origin of Adaptive Behavior* 2nd edition (New York: John Wiley, 1960).

13. Concepts such as Gary Klein's recognition primed decisions could be helpful to reduce the time from observation to action. For more on this idea, see Gary Klein, *Sources of Power: How People Make Decisions* (Cambridge, Mass.: MIT Press, 1999).

14. Garrett Hardin, "The Tragedy of the Commons," *Science*, vol. 162 (13 December 1968): 1243–48.

15. Elinor Ostrom, *Governing the Commons* (New York: Cambridge University Press, 1990).

16. Susan J. Buck, *The Global Commons, An Introduction* (Washington, D.C.: Island Press, 1998).

17. Osinga, *Science, Strategy and War.*

Chapter 13

1. "Declaration on Alliance Security," NATO Press Release (2009) 043, issued by the Heads of State and Government at the meeting of the North Atlantic Council, 4 April 2009: 1.

2. "Strasbourg/Kehl Summit Declaration," NATO Press Release (2009) 044, issued by the Heads of State and Government at the meeting of the North Atlantic Council, 4 April 2009: 4.

3. Eric Edelmen, Undersecretary of Defense for Policy, "Train and Equip Authority," testimony before the House Armed Services Committee, 109th Congress, 2nd

session, 7 April 2006: 3; http://www.globalsecurity.org/military/library/congress /2006_hr/060407–edelman.pdf.

4. Robert M. Gates, U.S. Secretary of Defense, "A Balanced Strategy: Reprogramming the Pentagon for a New Age," *Foreign Affairs*, vol. 88: 1 (January/February 2009): 1.

5. Stewart Patrick, "U.S. Policy Toward Fragile States: An Integrated Approach to Security and Development," in *The White House and the World: A Global Development Agenda for the Next US President*, Nancy Birdsall, ed. (Washington, D.C.: Center for Global Development, October 2008), 332–345.

6. Donald Mahley, "State of Space Security," speech to George Washington University, Essential Documents Collection, Council on Foreign Relations, 24 January 2008: http://www.cfr.org/publication/15365/state_of_space_security.html.

7. Admiral Timothy J. Keating, U.S. Navy, "USPACOM Strategy," United States Pacific Command, Camp H.M. Smith, Hawaii, 14 November 2008: 7.

8. "The Africa Partnership Station," *Strategic Comments*, International Institute for Strategic Studies, vol. 14: 6 (August 2008): 1–2.

9. U.S. Secretary of Defense Robert M. Gates, remarks to Air War College, Maxwell, Alabama, 21 April 2008: http://www.defenselink.mil/speeches/speech .aspx?speechid=1231.

10. "National Defense Strategy," Department of Defense, Washington, D.C., June 2008: 17; http://www.defenselink.mil/news/2008%20national%20defense%20 strategy.pdf.

11. "The Joint Training System: A Primer for Senior Leaders," Chairman of the Joint Chiefs of Staff Guide (CJCSG) 3501, Washington, D.C., 31 July 2008: 7.

12. Michael Spirtas, Jennifer D. P. Moroney, Harry J. Thie, Joe Hogler, and Thomas-Durell Young, "Department of Defense Training for Operations with Interagency, Multinational, and Coalition Partners," RAND National Defense Research Institute report prepared for the Office of the Secretary of Defense, RAND Corp., Santa Monica, 2008: 2.

13. CJCSG 3501, "The Joint Training System": 16–17.

14. Spirtas et al., "Department of Defense Training": 7.

15. "Joint Training Policy and Guidance for the Armed Forces of the United States," Chairman of the Joint Chiefs of Staff Instruction (CJCSI) 3500.01E, Washington, D.C., 31 May 2008: D-2.

16. Ibid.: A-5, D-1.

17. General Peter Pace, U.S. Marine Corps, "Doctrine for the Armed Forces of the United States," Joint Publication (JP) 1, Washington, D.C., 14 May 2007: II–2.

18. "Joint Training Manual for the Armed Forces of the United States," Chairman of the Joint Chiefs of Staff Manual (CJCSM) 3500.03B, Washington, D.C., 31 August 2007: B-1, 2.

19. "Mission Essential Task List Development," Field Manual 25–101, Department of the Army, Washington, D.C., 30 September 1990: 2–1.

20. "Universal Joint Task List (UJTL) Policy and Guidance for the Armed Forces of the United States," CJCSI 3500.02, Washington, D.C., 1 February 2008: B-2.

21. Spirtas et al., "Department of Defense Training": 12.

22. "Training the Force," United States Army Field Manual (FM) 25–100, Department of the Army, Washington, D.C., 15 November 1988: 2–2.

23. "Training for Full-Spectrum Operations," United States Army Field Manual (FM) 7–0, Department of the Army, Washington D.C., December 2008: 1–2, 1–5 to 1–9.

24. "The Army Universal Task List," United States Army Field Manual (FM) 7–15, Department of the Army, Washington, D.C., February 2009: 5–73 to 5–76; 6–2 to 6–11; 6–19 to 6–24.

25. "Terminal High Altitude Area Defense," Missile Defense Agency Fact Sheet, Department of Defense, available at: http://www.mda.mil/mdalink/html/thaad1.html.

26. FM 7–15: section Full Spectrum Operations: 7–1; section Operational Themes: 7–30.

27. FM 7–0: 1–6.

28. Ibid.

29. Seminar: Requirements-Based Training, UN Center for Excellence in Disaster Management and Humanitarian Assistance, Phnom Penh, Cambodia, 2–6 July 2007: http://coe-dmha.org/PKO/Cambodia07/index.htm.

30. Ibid.

31. As quoted by former Secretary of the Navy John H. Dalton in his remarks at the Paul Hall Memorial Lecture, Washington, D.C., 7 May 1997: http://www.navy.mil/navydata/people/secnav/dalton/speeches/paulhall.txt.

32. Donna Miles, "Terminal Fury Prepares PACOM to Confront Crisis, Threats," quote attributed to Navy Captain Mark Donahue, American Forces Press Service, 6 April 2008: http://www.globalsecurity.org/military/library/news/2008/04/mil-080406–afps02.htm.

33. "JTIMS-Joint Training Information Management System," Joint Staff official JTIMS website: http://drc010076.drc.com/jtims/homepage.do.

34. JTIMS mission statement, from ibid.

35. Sergeant First Class Jason Shepherd, "Avian Influenza Epidemic played out during Exercise 'Lightning Rescue '08,'" Army Knowledge Online, 25 July 2008: http://www.army.mil/-news/2008/07/25/11252–avian-influenza-epidemic-played-out-during-exercise-lightning-rescue-08/.

36. Lieutenant Colonel Ed Toy, comments at the Lighting Rescue 2008 Final Planning conference in Shafter Flats, Hawaii, 2–3 June 2008.

37. General James N. Mattis, U.S. Marine Corps, Commander, U.S. Joint Forces Command, Statement to the House Armed Services Committee, 111th Congress, 2nd session, 18 March 2009: 9; http://armedservices.house.gov/pdfs/FC031809/Mattis_Testimony031809.pdf.

38. "Joint National Training Capability (JNTC)," Fact Sheets, U.S. Joint Forces Command, Norfolk, Virginia: http://www.jfcom.mil/about/fact_jntc.htm.

39. Frank DiGiovanni, "DoD Has Made Great Progress in Live Training Capabilities," *Military Training Technology*, vol. 13: 2 (13 April 2008): 3; http://www.military
-training-technology.com/mt2–archives/43–mt2–2008–volume-13–issue-2/291–
dod-has-made-great-progress-in-live-training-capabilities.html.

40. Mattis, Statement: 21–22. See also, Chris Hoffpauir, "USJFCOM gets approval
to connect U.S., Australian networks," U.S. Joint Forces Command public affairs
press release, 21 December 2006: http://www.jfcom.mil/newslink/storyarchive/2006/
pa122106.html.

41. DiGiovanni, "DoD Has Made Great Progress": 4.

42. Maryann Lawlor, "Range Accelerates Information Operations Planning,"
Signal, AFCEA International, December 2008: http://www.afcea.org/signal/articles/
templates/Signal_Article_Template.asp?articleid=1770&zoneid=245#.

43. Joint Chiefs of Staff, "Joint Training Manual": F-1.

44. "Universal Joint Task List (UJTL)," CJCSM 3500.04D, Joint Staff, Washington, D.C., 1 August 2005: section Change 1 (15 September 2006); section Appendix B
to Enclosure B, Measures and Criteria: B-B-1.

45. "Pdf. Version of Approved Universal Joint Task List (UJTL) Database with
conditions," Joint Staff Action Package (JSAP) J7–A 30017–09, Version 3, Joint Chiefs
of Staff, Washington, D.C., 12 March 2009: 962–64.

46. Captain Mark A. Stearns, U.S. Navy, "Joint Training's Role in Transformation: Capability Improvements for the Warfighter," Joint Forces Command presentation, dated 27 March 2009: www.dtic.mil/doctrine/training/9_jfcomtrans.ppt.

47. Joint Chiefs of Staff, "Joint Training Manual": F-1.

48. "Maritime Domain Awareness Joint Integrating Concept," Version 0.5
(Draft), Department of Defense, Washington, D.C., 3 February 2009: 42–43.

49. "Universal Joint Task List (UJTL)": Appendix C, Table of Capabilities: 1–8.

50. Scott Cohen, "African Nations Work Together for Maritime Security," CJTF-
HOA Public Affairs article, 24 Jun 2008: http://www.hoa.africom.mil/getArticle.asp
?art=1808&lang=.

51. The first REFORGER exercises took place in 1969. Amy Holmes, "Direct Action: Maneuver Obstructions and Base Blockades in the American Sector of Germany
during the Last Decade of the Cold War," doctoral dissertation, John Hopkins University, Baltimore, Maryland, 2007: http://www.lse.ac.uk/Depts/global/PDFs/Peace
conference/Holmes.doc 1–3.

52. Ibid.: 22–23.

53. K. M. Shimko, "REFORGER 1990: Centurion Shield," *Spearhead*, publication
of the U.S. Army 3d Armor Division (January 1990): http://www.3ad.com/history/
cold.war/feature.pages/reforger.1990.htm.

54. "Special Press Summary: Talisman Saber 2007," Asia-Pacific Area Network (APAN) Virtual Information Center, 9 July 2007: http://www1.apan-info.net/
Portals/45/VIC_Products/2007/07/070709–SPS-TalismanSabre2007.doc.

55. "TS 07 Public Environment Report," prepared for the Australian Department
of Defence by Maunsell Australia Party, Ltd., Melbourne, April 2007: ii.

56. APAN, "Special Press Summary": 2.

57. "TS 07 Public Environment Report": ii.

58. APAN, "Special Press Summary": 8.

59. Michèle Flournoy, as quoted at panel on "Stability Operations: A Comprehensive Approach to the 21st Century," Brookings Institution, Washington, D.C., 27 March 2009: 30; transcript available at: http://www.brookings.edu//media/Files/events/2009/0327_stability/20090327_stability.pdf.

60. Frank G. Hoffman, "Hybrid Warfare and Challenges," *Joint Forces Quarterly*, Issue 52 (1st Quarter 2009): 34–37; http://www.ndu.edu/inss/Press/jfq_pages/editions /i52/9.pdf.

61. "The Joint Training System": 29.

About the Authors

SCOTT JASPER teaches courses in International Defense Transformation in the National Security Affairs (NSA) Department and Center for Civil-Military Relations (CCMR) at the Naval Postgraduate School (NPS). As a United States Navy Captain, Jasper served as the deputy for Joint Experimentation at Headquarters, U.S. Pacific Command. He drove the creation and implementation of a revolutionary concept for joint warfare that produced standardized procedure sets, mission-focused training tasks, and routine technology integration exercises for Joint Task Force component commands. His most recent publications include defense transformation-related articles in the Partnership for Peace Consortium of Defense Academies' quarterly journal, *Connections*; *Joint Force Quarterly*, a professional military journal; and the Marine Corps *Gazette*. His first edited volume is entitled *Transforming Defense Capabilities: New Approaches for International Security* (Lynne Rienner Publishers, 2009). Captain Jasper received his MA in national security and strategic studies from the Naval War College and an MBA from San Jose State University.

JEFFREY BECKER is a Futures analyst for U.S. Joint Forces Command, and a senior analyst with Science Applications International Corporation. Mr. Becker has contributed to military futures studies, as well as concept development and experimentation efforts for a wide variety of Department of Defense and NATO organizations. At U.S. Joint Forces Command's Joint Futures Group, Mr. Becker was responsible for writing, research, and analysis for three editions of the "Joint Operating Environment" report, which addresses changes in the geopolitical and military landscape that will confront future joint force commanders. During his time at NATO's Allied Command Transformation, he developed a concept to transform the Alliance's crisis management information systems, and conducted the first set of military experiments within NATO Headquarters in Brussels. Mr. Becker has a Bachelor's degree in political science from the University of Iowa, including a year studying politics and international relations at the University of Lancaster, UK. Mr. Becker completed his doctoral coursework (ABD) in international studies at Old Dominion University in Norfolk, Virginia.

DICK BEDFORD is the branch head for Strategic Engagement and Vision at the Supreme Headquarters for Allied Command Transformation in Norfolk, Virginia. A former naval officer, Captain Bedford served in a variety of command, operational, and staff billets in both the United States and Europe. Captain Bedford holds an engineering degree from Tulane University, an MA in public administration from the John F. Kennedy School of Government at Harvard University, and an MA in national security studies from the Walsh School of Foreign Service at Georgetown University. He is also a seminar graduate of the National Defense University's School for Information and Resources Management, and a graduate of the Harvard University School for Senior Executive Fellows.

THOMAS BOWDITCH is the director of Strategic Initiatives at the Center for Naval Analysis (CNA) in Alexandria, Virginia. Dr. Bowditch's work at CNA has focused on broad issues of national security, in particular the maritime component of national security strategy, with an emphasis on assessing real-world military operations including transformational initiatives. During the summer of 2007, Dr. Bowditch was temporarily assigned to the Commander, U.S. Central Command in Tampa where he completed a special project for the commander on strategic options for the way ahead in Iraq. This assignment required several trips to Iraq, where he visited the major U.S. commands and had multi-level discussions with American and Iraqi commanders. Earlier in Operation Enduring Freedom, he was in the Persian Gulf and Afghanistan during the first half of 2002, providing analytical support to the Marine Corps Combat Assessment Team. Dr. Bowditch is a retired Marine Colonel and holds a Ph.D. in international relations from the University of Virginia.

The Honorable PATRICK M. CRONIN is the director of both the Institute for National Strategic Studies and the Center for the Study of Chinese Military Affairs. Prior to these positions, Dr. Cronin served for over two years at the London-based International Institute for Strategic Studies, where he was director of studies. Previous assignments include posts as the director of research and senior vice president at the Center for Strategic and International Studies, assistant administrator for Policy and Program Coordination at the United States Agency for International Development, and director of research at the United States Institute for Peace. Dr. Cronin was an adjunct professor at Georgetown University's Security Studies Program, the Johns Hopkins University's Paul H. Nitze School of Advanced International Studies, and the University of Virginia's Woodrow Wilson Department of Government. He is the editor and co-author of numerous publications, including: "Global Strategic Assessment 2009: America's Security Role in a Changing World," Institute for National Strategic Studies, 2009; "Civilian Surge: Key to Complex Operations," Center for Technology and National Security Policies, July 2009; *The Impenetrable Fog of War: Reflections on Modern Warfare and Strategic Surprise* (Praeger, 2008); *The Evolution of Strategic Thought* (Routledge, 2008); *Double Trouble: Iran and North Korea as Challenges to International Security* (Praeger, 2007); and *The United States and Coercive Diplomacy* (U.S. Institute of Peace, 2003). Dr. Cronin earned his Master's and doctorate degrees in international relations at St. Anthony's College, University of Oxford.

WILL DOSSEL is a senior subject matter expert for Ballistic Missile Defense operations with a top-five defense firm. He has participated extensively in the development of BMD policy and guidance, joint/service integration, and the daily and contingency operations of the global BMD system. During his naval career, Captain Dossel was a naval flight officer, commanding an E-2C Hawkeye squadron, and served on joint and service staffs as an air- and missile-defense expert, technical intelligence analyst, political-military specialist in Soviet issues, and a strategic planner. From 2001–2004 he served as the deputy director for Strategy and Policy (N51B) on the OPNAV Staff, and as special assistant to the Chief of Naval Operations for Joint Matters. Captain Dossel has a Bachelor's degree in political science from The Citadel; a Master's with Distinction in national security studies (Soviet/East European Studies) from NPS, and is a graduate of the U.S. Naval War College (Command and Staff) with Highest Distinction.

MARCO FIORELLO is the chief scientist in the Sullivan International Energy and Advanced Technology Group DoD Mentor Protégé Program. His principal activities include renewable energy systems evaluation, and the development of a software architecture and decision support system for Sullivan's RobonostiX(tm), an unmanned vehicle platform and payload services health management and condition-based maintenance system to support defense and security command and control decision making. Dr. Fiorello has 30 years' experience in operations research, information science, and cost analysis, with an emphasis in decision-support system design. He is a principal designer of The Assessment Profiling System (TAPS), a decision-support system for command and control and training and readiness decision making. Dr. Fiorello holds a Ph.D. in Operations Research and Information Science, an MBA, and Bachelor of Science degrees in Production Management and Mechanical Engineering, all from the University of California, Berkeley, and is an Institute of Cost Analysis Certified Cost Analyst.

PAUL GIARRA is the president of Global Strategies and Transformation, a defense consulting firm. Previously a senior program manager at Hicks and Associates, Inc., he has supported transformation and experimentation in the Office of the Secretary of Defense, at United States Joint Forces Command, at NATO Headquarters, and at NATO Allied Command Transformation. During his naval career, Commander Giarra was a naval aviator; a naval strategic planner; a political-military strategic planner for Far East, South Asia, and Pacific issues; and managed the United States-Japan alliance in the Office of the Secretary of Defense. He has a BA in history from Harvard College, an MA in international relations from Salve Regina University, is a graduate of the U.S. Naval War College (Command and Staff) with Highest Distinction, and attended the National Institute of Defense Studies in Tokyo, Japan. He is the author, most recently, of "Asia's Military Balance at a Tipping Point," an op-ed, with Michael Green, for the *Asian Wall Street Journal*, 17 July 2009; and "A Chinese Anti-Ship Ballistic Missile: Implications for the U.S. Navy," in *Chinese Aerospace Developments*, Andrew S. Erickson, ed. (U.S. Naval Institute Press, forthcoming early 2010).

JEFF KLINE is a senior lecturer in the Operations Research Department and Program Director for Maritime Defense and Security research programs at NPS. A retired United States Navy Captain, he has over 26 years of naval operational experience, including commanding two U.S. Navy ships and serving as deputy of operations for Commander, Sixth Fleet. In addition to his sea service, Captain Kline spent three years as a naval analyst in the Office of the Secretary of Defense. He is a 1992 graduate of NPS's Operations Research program, where he earned the Chief of Naval Operations Award for Excellence in Operations Research, and is a 1997 distinguished graduate of the National War College. Captain Kline's NPS faculty awards include the 2007 Hamming Award for interdisciplinary research, 2007 Wayne E. Meyers Award for Excellence in Systems Engineering Research, and the 2005 Northrup Grumman Award for Excellence in Systems Engineering.

JAMES KRASKA is a professor of international law at the U.S. Naval War College. Commander Kraska is author of numerous scholarly articles, which have appeared in journals such as *Ocean Development & International Law*, *World Policy Journal*, *International Journal of Marine & Coastal Law*, *Stanford Journal of International Law*, *Columbia Journal of International Affairs*, and *Yale Journal of International Law*. He has taught international law in the United States, Europe, and Japan, and is an elected member of the International Institute of Humanitarian Law in San Remo, Italy. Past military assignments include service as oceans policy adviser for Director, Strategic Plans & Policy, Joint Chiefs of Staff and Deputy Chief of Naval Operations for Plans, Policy and Operations. Commander Kraska is a graduate of the University of Virginia Law School, Indiana University Law School, and the School of Politics and Economics, Claremont Graduate School. Commander Kraska was awarded a post-doctoral fellowship in naval oceanography and national security from the Office of the Chief of Naval Research, which he served in residence at Woods Hole Oceanographic Institution, where he currently holds appointment as a guest investigator.

MIKE MANOR is the deputy chief of strategic studies at the United States Air Force Space Command, where he is actively engaged in shaping the strategic direction of space power through critical analysis of emerging space defense trends and challenges. A major in the United States Air Force, Manor is a career space operator and acquisitions officer, with experience ranging from satellite engineer on the Global Positioning System and classified programs in the National Reconnaissance Organization to crew commander in the 614th Air and Space Operations Center during Operation IRAQI FREEDOM. Major

Manor has a Bachelor's degree in management from the U.S. Air Force Academy, an MBA from Golden Gate University, and Master's degrees in military operational art and science at the Air Command and Staff College and in airpower art and science from the School of Advanced Air and Space Studies.

SANDRA M. MARTÍNEZ is a recognized expert in institutional and organizational change, organizational culture, and leadership development. As a National Security Education Program doctoral fellow, she studied institutional change in Mexico in the three years following the peso devaluation of December 1994. She was a co-investigator on the Global Leadership and Organizational Behavior Effectiveness project, and has published articles and book chapters on the influence of societal and national culture on management processes, and on leadership. Dr. Martinez is a former chair of Defense Transformation at the U.S. Army War College, where she focused her research and teaching on the impact of complexity on leadership, leadership development, and the social and cognitive domains of defense transformation. As a visiting professor with the Cebrowski Institute of NPS, she develops new curriculum for security professionals. Dr. Martinez holds a Ph.D. in business administration from New Mexico State University and an MA with distinction from the University of New Mexico in Latin American studies and international management. Her BA is in music, from Colorado Women's College.

STEVEN H. "MAC" MCPHERSON is an Air Force officer serving as the chief of staff for the Director, National Cyber Security Center, Department of Homeland Security. Prior to this assignment, he was the deputy director for both the USAF Chief of Staff's Strategic Studies Group, CHECKMATE, and the USAF Cyberspace Task Force. Colonel McPherson has held a variety of positions in both flying and non-flying operational areas, with multiple command assignments including the 23rd Information Operations Squadron and 11th Bomb Squadron. He is a B-52 weapons officer and master navigator with over 2,700 flying hours in multiple aircraft, including 163 combat hours during DESERT STORM. He holds a BA in biology from Southern Illinois University and an MA in Aeronautical Science Technology from Embry Riddle Aeronautical University. His articles have been published in the Stanford Jet Propulsion Laboratory *Proceedings*, *Defense News*, and the *Air Force Times*, and he has conducted presentations at numerous conferences and security fora on the cyber domain.

DONALD W. MCSWAIN served in the U.S. Navy for 24 years, accumulating over 4,800 flight hours as pilot in command in Navy tactical jets. Recognized for his planning expertise in joint and coalition warfare, he serves as an on-call presenter at the Air War College and the Naval War College. Commander Mc-Swain served as senior naval strike liaison officer to support the Commander, 9th AF CENTAF/ JFACC for planning and executing Operations Desert Shield, Eastern Exit, and Desert Storm. As commanding officer TACRON 22, he deployed with members of the USMC 26th MEU(SOC) and RAF elements to Polce, Federal Republic of Yugoslavia, during Operations Provide Promise, Deny Flight, and Sharp Guard. His awards include the Bronze Star, Meritorious Service Medal, and Air Medal (5). He co-developed the TAPS for net-centric situational awareness and decision support for disaster relief, information operations, fourth-generation warfare, and other effects-based strategies.

SCOTT MORELAND is a lecturer, program facilitator, and research associate at the Center for Civil-Military Relations at NPS. He has participated in CCMR Transformation and Civil-Military Crisis Response events and interagency exercises throughout Europe, Latin America, and the Pacific. Prior to his arrival at CCMR, Mr. Moreland served in the U.S. Army. During his military career, he participated in multinational combat and civil-military operations with NATO Civil Military Integration Centers, the Iraqi and Panamanian National Police, and the El Salvadoran Special Forces. His last assignment was service as a Civil-Military Operations team leader and military liaison to the Babel Province Developmental Assistance Coordination Council during Operation Iraqi Freedom II. His most recent publication was a chapter entitled "Pressing Contemporary Issues," with James Mattox, in *Transforming Defense Capabilities* (Lynne Rienner Press, 2009).

KURT NEUMAN is a senior policy analyst for Northrop-Grumman, and supports the Strategic Studies, Policy and Doctrine Branch for Headquarters Air Force Space Command (AFSPC). In this capacity he is responsible for developing military space strategy, doctrine, and policy in support of the Commander, AFSPC. Recent projects include an assessment of international space cooperation and an examination of space deterrence for the Eisenhower Center's *Space and Defense* journal. Mr. Neuman retired from the Air Force as a lieutenant colonel, having served assignments in operations research; satellite command and control; launch operations; war gaming; and strategic planning and policy development. Mr. Neuman holds a BA in aerospace engineering and mechanics from the University of Minnesota, along with an MA in business administration from the Anderson School of Management, University of New Mexico. In addition, he is a graduate of the Air Command and Staff College and Air War College.

MORT ROLLESTON is a Science Applications International Corp. defense analyst working onsite for the Headquarters Air Force Future Concepts Division (AF/A8XC). He authored all three annual editions of the U.S. Air Force Transformation Flight Plan at the direction of the Secretary of Defense, and has provided planning, analytical, and execution support to the Air Force's Title 10 "Future Capabilities Game," which explores alternative long-term force structures that may better address future operational challenges. Before arriving on the Air Staff, Mr. Rolleston was one of the primary analysts who conducted the Information Operations Joint Warfighting Capabilities Assessment (IO JWCA) for the Joint Staff, J-39. Prior to graduate school, he spent four years on the legislative staffs of two U.S. congressmen. Mr. Rolleston has a BA in Central and Eastern European affairs from the University of Colorado at Boulder and an MA in security policy studies from George Washington University's Elliott School of International Affairs.

GLENN ZIMMERMAN is an Air National Guard officer on active duty working in the USAF Chief of Staff's Strategic Studies Group—CHECKMATE. He is a recognized subject matter expert regarding cyber issues and developments, and is a featured presenter at venues around the globe. Prior to this assignment, Colonel Zimmerman was the Director of the Air National Guard Network Operations and Security Center, which provided operational oversight and administration of the ANG Enterprise, comprising 54 states and territories and over 106,000 users. While in this assignment, he was chosen to be part of the USAF Cyberspace Task Force, where he worked to establish the foundation for the Air Force's future in cyberspace operations, doctrine, and policy. He holds a dual BA in electrical engineering and computer science from the University of Colorado, and an MBA from Webster University. Additionally, he holds 14 current Information Technology certifications in specializations ranging from operating system and network design to security analysis.

Selected Bibliography

Abizaid, John P., Lieutenant General, U.S. Army. "Chairman of the Joint Chiefs of Staff Manual (CJCSM) 3500.03B: Joint Training Manual for the Armed Forces of the United States." Office of the Chairman, Joint Chiefs of Staff, Washington, D.C. (31 August 2007).

Albert, David, John Garstka, and Frederick Stein. *Network Centric Warfare*. Command and Control Research Program, Department of Defense, Washington, D.C. (1999).

Allen, Thad W., Admiral, U.S. Coast Guard. *The U.S. Coast Guard Strategy for Maritime Safety, Security, and Stewardship*. Department of the Navy, Washington, D.C. (January 2007).

Anand, R.P. "The Influence of History on the Literature of International Law," in *The Structure and Process of International Law: Essays in Legal Philosophy Doctrine and Theory*, R. St. J. Macdonald, ed. The Hague: Martinus Nijhoff Publishers, 1983.

Andrew, Christopher. *For the President's Eyes Only*. New York: Harper Collins, 1996.

Argyris, Chris. *Knowledge for Action*. San Francisco: Jossey-Bass, 2004.

———, and D. Schön. *Organizational Learning: A Theory of Action Perspective*. Reading, Mass.: Addison Wesley, 1978.

———, and D. Schön. *Theory in Practice: Increasing Professional Effectiveness*. San Francisco: Jossey-Bass, 1974.

Art, Robert J. *A Grand Strategy for America*. Ithaca, New York: Cornell University Press, 2003.

Ashby, W. Ross. *Design for a Brain: The Origin of Adaptive Behavior*, 2nd edition. New York: John Wiley, 1960.

———. *An Introduction to Cybernetics*. London: Methuen, 1956.

Bacevich, Andrew J. "The Petraeus Doctrine," *The Atlantic* (October 2008).

Backus, George, and James Strickland. "Climate-Derived Tensions in Arctic Security." Sandia National Laboratories, Albuquerque, New Mexico (2008).

Barratt, John. "The Bitter End, the U-Boat War, 1939–1945," *MilitaryHistoryOnline .com* (15 December 2002).

Barzelay, Michael, and Colin Campbell. *Preparing for the Future: Strategic Planning in the U.S. Air Force.* Washington, D.C.: Brookings Institution Press, 2003.

Bermudez, Joseph S. Jr. "Iran's Missile Development," in *The International Missile Bazaar: The New Supplier's Network*, William C. Potter and Harlan W. Jencks, eds. Boulder, Colo.: Westview Press, 1994.

Birdsall, Nancy, ed. *The White House and the World: A Global Development Agenda for the Next US President.* Washington, D.C.: Center for Global Development, 2008.

Blaker, James R. *Transforming Military Force: The Legacy of Arthur Cebrowski and Network Centric Warfare.* Westport, Conn.: Praeger Security International, 2007.

Blanning, Tim. *The Pursuit of Glory: The Five Revolutions that Made Modern Europe, 1648–1815.* New York: Penguin Group, 2008.

Boisot, Max, and John Child. "Organizations as Adaptive Systems in Complex Environments: The Case of China." *Organization Science* 10: 3 (May–June 1999).

Boisot, Max, and Ian C. MacMillan. "Crossing Epistemological Boundaries: Managerial and Entrepreneurial Approaches to Knowledge Management," in M. H. Boisot, I. C. MacMillan, and K. S. Han, eds. *Explorations in Information Space: Knowledge, Agents, and Organization.* New York: Oxford University Press, 2007.

Boltz, Donna G. "Information Technology and Peace Support Operations." United States Institute for Peace Virtual Diplomacy Report, 13 (22 July 2002).

Booth, Ken. *Law, Force & Diplomacy at Sea.* London, Boston: Allen & Unwin, 1985.

Bowie, Christopher. "The Anti-Access Threat and Theater Air Bases." Report, Center for Strategic and Budgetary Assessments, Washington, D.C. (23 August 2002).

Brodie, Bernard. *Strategy in the Missile Age.* Princeton, N.J.: Princeton University Press, 1959.

———. *The Absolute Weapon.* New York: Harcourt, 1946.

Brownlie, Ian. *International Law and the Use of Force by States.* Oxford: Clarendon Press, 1963.

Buck, Susan J. *The Global Commons: An Introduction.* Washington, D.C.: Island Press, 1998.

Bull, Headley. *The Anarchical Society: A Study of Order in World Politics*, 3rd edition. New York: Columbia University Press, 2002.

Bush, George W. President of the United States. "U.S. National Space Policy." Office of the President, Washington, D.C. (31 August 2006).

Carsten, Michael D. " International Law and Military Operations." *International Law Studies* (Newport: Naval War College), 84 (2008).

Cartwright, James E., General, U.S. Marine Corps. "Deterrence Operations Joint Operating Concept." Version 2.0. U.S. Strategic Command, Offutt AFB, Nebraska (December 2006).

Cebrowski, Arthur K., Director of Force Transformation, Office of the Secretary of

Defense. Statement before the Subcommittee on Strategic Forces, Armed Services Committee, United States Senate. 108th Congress, 2nd session (25 March 2004).

Chalk, Peter. "The Maritime Dimension of International Security: Terrorism, Piracy, and Challenges for the United States." RAND Corporation, Santa Monica, California (2008).

Chilton, Kevin, General, U.S. Air Force, and Greg Weaver. "Waging Deterrence in the Twenty-First Century." *Strategic Studies Quarterly* (Spring 2009).

Chun, Clayton K. S. *Aerospace Power in the Twenty-First Century: A Basic Primer.* Air University Press, Maxwell Air Force Base (2001).

Cliff, Roger, Mark Burles, Michael S. Chase, Derek Eaton, Kevin L. Pollpeter. "Entering the Dragon's Lair: Chinese Antiaccess Strategies and Their Implications for the United States." RAND Corporation, Santa Monica, California (2007).

Commission to Assess United States National Security Space Management and Organization. *Final Report.* Washington, D.C. (2001).

Conway, James T. General, U.S. Marine Corps, Admiral Guy Roughhead, U.S. Navy, and Admiral Thad W. Allen, U.S. Coast Guard. "A Cooperative Strategy for 21st Century Seapower." Department of the Navy, Washington, D.C. (October 2007).

Cooling, Benjamin Franklin, ed. *Case Studies in the Achievement of Air Superiority.* Seattle: University Press of the Pacific, 2005.

Corbett, Julian Stafford. *Some Principles of Maritime Strategy.* Annapolis, Md.: Naval Institute Press, 1988.

Cordesman, Anthony H., and Martin Kleiber. *Iran's Military Forces and Warfighting Capabilities.* Washington, D.C.: Greenwood Publishing Group, 2007.

Cosumano, Joseph M. Jr., Lieutenant General, U.S. Army. "A Day Without Space: Ensuring It Doesn't Happen." *Army Space Journal* (Summer 2002).

Cronin, Patrick, ed. *2015: Power and Progress.* Washington, D.C.: National Defense University Press, 1996.

———. (2009) ed. *Global Strategic Assessment 2009: America's Security Role in a Changing World.* Washington, D.C.: National Defense University Press.

Damrosch, Lori Fisler, with Louis Henkin, Richard Pugh, Oscar Schachter, and Hans Smit. *International Law: Cases and Materials and Basic Documents Supplemental.* 4th ed. St. Paul, Minn.: West Publishing Company, 2001.

Dawes, R. M. "The Robust Beauty of Improper Linear Models." *American Psychologist* 34 (1979).

———, and B. Corrigan. "Linear Models in Decision Making." *Psychological Bulletin* (University of Oregon and Oregon Research Institute) 81 (1974).

DeBiasco, Peppino A. Director of the Office of Missile Defense Policy, U.S. Department of Defense. "Missile Defense and NATO Security." *Joint Forces Quarterly* 51 (4th quarter 2008).

DeLanda, Manuel. *A New Philosophy of Society: Assemblage Theory and Social Complexity.* London: Continuum, 2006.

———. *War in the Age of Intelligent Machines.* New York: Swerve Editions, 1991.

Dolman, Everett. *Astropolitik: Classic Geopolitics in the Space Age.* London: Frank Cass Publishers, 2002.

Easton, Ian. "The Great Game in Space: China's Evolving ASAT Weapons Programs and Their Implications for Future U.S. Strategy." Project 2049 Institute, Arlington, Virginia (2009).

Edelmen, Eric, Office of the U.S. Under Secretary of Defense for Policy. "Train and Equip Authority." Testimony before the House Armed Services Committee, 109th Congress, 2nd session (7 April 2006).

Elji, Hamanaka. "Over Secure Networks," *Japan Journal* (in English) 6: 3 (March 2006).

Endsley, M. R., and D. J. Garland, eds. *Situation Awareness Analysis and Measurement.* Mahwahk, N.J.: CRC Press, 2000.

Endsley, M. R., B. Bolte, and D. G. Jones. *Designing for Situation Awareness.* London and New York: Taylor and Francis, 2003.

England, Gordon, Admiral Vern Clark, U.S. Navy, and General James Jones, U.S. Marine Corps. "Naval Power 21." Department of the Navy, Washington, D.C. (2002).

Erickson, Andrew S., and David D. Yang. "On the Verge of a Game-Changer," *Proceedings* (U.S. Naval Institute) 135/5/1,275 (May 2009).

Fingar, C. Thomas. "Global Trends 2025: A Transformed World." Office of the Chairman, National Intelligence Council, Washington, D.C. (2008).

Flournoy, Michèle, and Shawn Brimley. "The Contested Commons." *Proceedings* (U.S. Naval Institute) 135/7/1,277 (July 2009).

Friedman, George. *The Next 100 Years: A Forecast for the 21st Century.* New York: Doubleday Press, 2009.

Friedman, Norman. *Network Centric Warfare.* Annapolis, Md.: Naval Institute Press, 2009.

Gates, Robert M., U.S. Secretary of Defense. "A Balanced Strategy: Reprogramming the Pentagon for a New Age." *Foreign Affairs* 88: 1 (January/February 2009).

———. "National Defense Strategy." Office of the U.S. Secretary of Defense, Washington, D.C. (2008)

Giarra, Paul S. "Watching the Chinese." *Proceedings* (U.S. Naval Institute) 135/5/1,275 (May 2009).

———, and Michael J. Green. "Asia's Military Balance at a Tipping Point: America's Deterrent is Shrinking in the Region." *Asian Wall Street Journal* (17 July 2009).

Gilpin, Robert. *War and Change in World Politics.* New York: Cambridge University Press, 1981.

Goure, Daniel, and Christopher Szara, eds. *Air and Space Power in the New Millennium.* Washington, D.C.: Center for Strategic and International Studies, 1997.

Gowing, Nik. "Skyful of Lies and Black Swans: The New Tyranny of Shifting Information Power in Crises." RISJ Challenges series, Reuters Institute for the Study of Journalism, Oxford, U.K. (July 2009).

Grant, Rebecca. "Victory in Cyberspace." Air Force Association Special Report, Arlington, Virginia (October 2007).

Gray, Colin S. "The 21st Century Security Environment and the Future of War." *Parameters* 38: 4 (Winter 2008–2009).

———. *Another Bloody Century: Future Warfare.* London: Orion Books, 2005.

———. *The Leverage of Sea Power: The Strategic Advantage of Navies in War.* New York: The Free Press, 1992.

Grego, Laura. "A History of Anti-satellite (ASAT) Programs." Union of Concerned Scientists, Cambridge, Mass. (20 October 2003).

Guillen, Mauro F. "Is Globalization Civilizing, Destructive, or Feeble? A Critique of Key Debates in the Social Science Literature." *Annual Review of Sociology* 27 (2001).

Hardin, Garrett. "The Tragedy of the Commons." *Science* 162 (13 December 1968).

Harris, Aidan. "Basic Notes: The International Code of Conduct Against Ballistic Missile Proliferation." British American Security Information Council, London and Washington, D.C. (18 July 2002).

Hattendorf, John B., ed. "U.S. Naval Strategies in the 1990s." Newport Paper 27, Center for Naval Warfare Studies, U.S. Naval War College, Newport, Rhode Island (2006).

———. "The Evolution of the U.S. Navy's Maritime Strategy, 1977–1986." Newport Paper 19, Center for Naval Warfare Studies, U.S. Naval War College, Newport, Rhode Island (2004).

Hazy, J. K., J. A. Goldstein, and B. B. Lichtenstein, eds. *Complex Systems Leadership Theory.* Mansfield, N.J.: ISCE Publishing, 2007.

Helmer, Daniel, Captain, Australian Army. "Not Quite Insurgency: A Cautionary Tale for U.S. Forces Based on Israel's Operation Change of Direction." Special edition, "Counterinsurgency." *Australian Army Journal* (Land Warfare Studies Centre, Duntroon) 5: 2 (Winter 2008).

Hildreth, Steven A., and Carl Elk. "Long-Range Ballistic Missile Defense in Europe." Congressional Research Service (CRS) Report for Congress RL34051, Washington, D.C. (21 January 2009).

Ho, Joshua. "US: A Cooperative Plan for 21st Century Sea Power." S. Rajaratnam School of International Studies, Singapore (30 July 2008).

Hoffman, Frank G. "Hybrid Warfare and Challenges." *Joint Forces Quarterly* 52: 1 (2009).

Hughes, Terry, and John Costello. *The Battle of the Atlantic.* New York: Dial Press, 1977.

Hughes, Wayne P. Jr., Captain, U.S. Navy (Ret.). *Fleet Tactics and Coastal Combat.* Annapolis, Md.: Naval Institute Press, 2000.

International Chamber of Commerce. "Piracy and Armed Robbery against Ships." Annual Report, International Maritime Bureau, London (1 January–31 December 2008).

Jackson, Richard, and Neil Howe. "The Graying of the Great Powers: Major Findings Report." Center for Strategic and International Studies, Washington, D.C. (2008).

Jones, James L., General (Retired), U.S. Marine Corps. "A Transition Plan for Securing America's Energy Future." Institute for 21st Century Energy, U.S. Chamber of Commerce, Washington, D.C. (November 2008).

Kahn, Herman. *On Thermonuclear War*. Princeton, N.J.: Princeton University Press, 1962.

Kant, Immanuael. "Perpetual Peace," in Kant, *On History*, Lewis White Beck, ed. and trans. Indianapolis: Bobbs-Merrill, 1963, originally published in 1795.

Kaplan, Robert D. "The Revenge of Geography." *Foreign Policy Magazine* online (May/June 2009): www.foreignpolicy.com

Kass, Lani. "Rethinking Deterrence." *High Frontier* 5: 2 (2009).

Keating, Timothy J., Admiral, U.S. Navy, Commander U.S. Pacific Command. Statement before the House Armed Services Committee on U.S. Pacific Command Posture. 110th Congress, 2nd Session (12 March 2008).

———. "USPACOM Strategy." United States Pacific Command, Camp H.M. Smith, Hawaii (2008).

Kegan, Robert. *In Over Our Heads: The Demands of Modern Life*. Cambridge, Mass.: Harvard University Press, 1994.

Kissinger, Henry A. *Nuclear Weapons and Foreign Policy*. New York: Council on Foreign Relations, 1958.

Klein, John J. *Space Warfare Strategy, Principles and Policy*. New York: Routledge, 2006.

Kopp, Carlo. "The Electromagnetic Bomb: A Weapon of Electrical Mass Destruction." Report, GlobalSecurity.org (1996).

Krepinevich, Andrew F., Jr. "The Pentagon's Wasting Assets." *Foreign Affairs* (July/August 2009).

Krepon, Michael, and C. Clary. "Space Assurance or Space Dominance? The Case Against Weaponizing Space." Henry L. Stimson Center, Washington, D.C. (2003).

Krasner, Stephen D. International Regimes. Ithaca, New York: Cornell University Press, 1983.

Lacey, Jim, ed. *A Terrorist's Call to Global Jihad, Deciphering Abu Musab Al-Suri's Islamic Jihad Manifesto*. Annapolis, Md.: Naval Institute Press, 2008.

Lambakis, Steven J. "Reconsidering Asymmetric Warfare." *Joint Forces Quarterly* 36 (December 2004).

Lambeth, Benjamin. "Mastering the Ultimate High Ground: Next Steps in the Military Uses of Space." Monograph Series No. MR-1649-AF. RAND Corp., Santa Monica, California (2003).

———. *The Transformation of American Air Power*. Ithaca: Cornell University Press, 2000.

Larson, Doyle E. "Exploiting Electronic Warfare." *Air Force Magazine* 64: 7 (July 1981).

Lewis, James A. "Securing Cyberspace for the 44th Presidency." Center for Strategic and International Studies, Washington, D.C. (December 2008).

Liebler, Keir A., and Dryl G. Press. "The End of MAD? The Nuclear Dimension of U.S. Primacy." *International Security* 30: 4 (Spring 2006).

Lord, William T., Major General, U.S. Air Force. *Air Force Cyber Command Strategic Vision*. U.S. Air Force Cyber Command (Provisional), Barksdale Air Force Base, Louisiana (2008).

Lunsford, Virginia. "What Makes Piracy Work." *Proceedings* (U.S. Naval Institute) 134/12/270 (December 2008).

Mahan, Alfred Thayer. *The Influence of Sea Power upon History, 1660–1783*. Boston: Little, Brown and Company, 1918.

———. *Mahan on Naval Warfare: Selections from the Writings of Rear Admiral Alfred T. Mahan*. Mineola, N.Y.: Dover Publications, 1999.

Mannermaa, Mika. "Traps in Futures Thinking and How to Overcome Them," in Howard Didsbury Jr., ed. *Thinking Creatively in Turbulent Times*. Bethesda: World Futurist Society, 2004.

Marion, Russ. *The Edge of Organization: Chaos and Complexity Theories of Formal Social Systems*. Thousand Oaks, Calif.: Sage Publications, 1999.

Mattis, J. N., General, U.S. Marine Corps. "Multiple Futures Project: Navigating towards 2030, Final Report." NATO Allied Command Transformation, Norfolk, Virginia (April 2009).

———. "The Joint Operating Environment: Challenges and Implications for the Future Joint Force," U.S. Joint Forces Command, Norfolk, Virginia (2008).

McChrystal, Stanley A., Lieutenant General, U.S. Air Force. *Space Operations*. Joint Publication 3-14 (6 January 2009).

———. "Chairman of the Joint Chiefs of Staff Manual (CJCSM) 3500.04E: Universal Joint Task Manual." Office of the Chairman, Joint Chiefs of Staff, Washington, D.C. (2008).

McDevitt, Michael. "The Strategic and Operational Context Driving PLA Navy Building," in "Right Sizing the People's Liberation Army: Exploring the Contours of China's Military." Strategic Studies Institute, U.S. Army War College, Carlisle, Pennsylvania (28 January 2007).

McNicholas, Michael. *Maritime Security: An Introduction*. Boston: Butterworth-Heinemann Publishers, 2008.

Mearsheimer, John J. *The Tragedy of Great Power Politics*. New York: W. W. Norton, 2001.

Mendel, Jerry. *Uncertain Rule-Based Fuzzy Logic Systems*. Upper Saddle River, N.J.: Prentice Hall, 2001.

Morison, Samuel Eliot. *The Battle of the Atlantic: September 1939–May 1943*. New York: Little, Brown and Company, 1947.

Moseley, T. Michael, General, U.S. Air Force Chief of Staff. "Global Strike Concept of Operations." Department of the Air Force, Washington, D.C. (27 December 2006).

———. "Global Persistent Attack Concept of Operations." Department of the Air Force, Washington, D.C. (2006).

Mullen, Michael G., Admiral, U.S. Navy. "Capstone Concept for Joint Operations," version 3.0. Joint Chiefs of Staff, Washington, D.C. (15 January 2009).

———. "CJCS Guidance for 2008–2009." Office of the Chairman, Joint Chiefs of Staff, Washington, D.C. (2008).

———. "The Joint Training System: A Primer for Senior Leaders." Chairman of the Joint Chiefs of Staff Guide 3501. Office of the Chairman, Joint Chiefs of Staff, Washington, D.C. (2008).

———. "Joint Training Policy and Guidance for the Armed Forces of the United States." Chairman of the Joint Chiefs of Staff Instruction 3500.01E. Office of the Chairman, Joint Chiefs of Staff, Washington, D.C. (2008).

———. "Navy Maritime Domain Awareness Concept." Office of the Chief of Naval Operations, Department of the Navy, Washington, D.C. (2007).

———, and General Michael Hagee, U.S. Marine Corps. "Naval Operations Concept." Department of the Navy, Washington, D.C. (2006).

Murphy, Martin N. *Small Boats, Weak States, and Dirty Money: Piracy and Maritime Terrorism in the Modern World.* New York: Columbia University Press, 2009.

Myers, Richard B., General, U.S. Air Force, Chairman of the Joint Chiefs of Staff. "National Military Strategy of the United States of America." Office of the Chairman, Joint Chiefs of Staff, Washington, D.C. (2004).

Naval Studies Board. "Maritime Security Partnerships." National Research Council of the National Academies, Washington, D.C. (2008).

Navias, Martin, and S.E.R. Hooton. *Tanker Wars: The Assault on Merchant Shipping During the Iran-Iraq Crisis, 1980–1988.* London and New York: I.B. Tauri, 1996.

North, Gary L., Lieutenant General, U.S. Air Force, and Colonel John Riordan, U.S. Air Force. "The Role of Space in Military Operations: Integrating and Synchronizing Space in Today's Fight." *High Frontier* 4: 2 (February 2008).

Olson, Mancur. *The Logic of Collective Action: Public Goods and the Theory of Groups.* Cambridge: Harvard University Press, 1971.

O'Hanlon, Michael. *Technological Change and the Future of Warfare.* Washington, D.C.: Brookings Institution Press, 2000.

O'Keefe, Sean, U.S. Secretary of the Navy. " . . . From the Sea: Preparing the Naval Service for the 21st Century." Office of the Secretary of the Navy, Washington, D.C. (September 1992).

O'Neal, John R., and Bruce Russett. *Triangulating Peace: Democracy, Interdependence, and International Organizations.* New York: W. W. Norton, 2001.

O'Rourke, Ronald. "China Naval Modernization: Implications for U.S. Navy Capabilities—Background and Issues for Congress," CRS Report for Congress RL33153 (29 May 2008).

———. "Navy Ship Deployments: New Approaches—Background and Issues for Congress." CRS Report for Congress RS21338, Washington, D.C. (2006).

Ostergren, Robert Clifford, and John G. Rice. *The Europeans*. London: Guildford Press, 2004.

Ostrom, Elinor. *Governing the Commons*. New York: Cambridge University Press, 1990.

Peters, Ralph. "Wishful Thinking and Indecisive Wars." *The Journal of International Security Affairs* 16 (Spring 2009).

Peterson, Erik. "Below the Surface: U.S. International Water Policy." Center for Strategic and International Studies, Washington, D.C. (2007).

Posen, Barry R. "The Military Foundation of U.S. Hegemony." *International Security* 28: 1 (Summer 2003).

Powell, Robert. "Nuclear Deterrence Theory, Nuclear Proliferation, and National Missile Defense." *International Security* 27: 4 (Spring 2003).

Richards, Chet. *Certain to Win: The Strategy of John Boyd Applied to Business*. Atlanta: Xlibris Corporation, 2004.

Richardson, John M. "The Joint Narrative." *Joint Forces Quarterly* 54: 3 (2009).

Robb, John. *Brave New War: The Next Stage of Terrorism and the End of Globalization*. Hoboken, N.J.: John Wiley and Sons, 2007.

Rolleston, Mort. "A Peek into the Future: Results of the 2007 USAF Future Capabilities Game." *The Wright Stuff* 3: 22 (26 November 2008).

Rooke, David, and William Torbert. "Seven Transformations of Leadership." *Harvard Business Review* (April 2005).

———. "Organizational Transformation as a Function of CEO's Developmental Stage." *Organization Development Journal* 16 (1998).

Roskill, Stephen W. *The War at Sea, 1939–1945*. London: H. M. Stationary Office, 1954–56.

Roughhead, Gary, Admiral, Chief of Naval Operations, U.S. Navy. "Executing our Maritime Strategy." CNO Guidance for 2009, Department of the Navy, Washington, D.C. (November 2008).

Rubel, Robert. "The Navy's Changing Force Paradigm," *Naval War College Review* 62: 2 (Spring 2009).

Rubin, Jeff. *Why Your World Is About to Get a Whole Lot Smaller: What the Price of Oil Means for the Way We Live*. London: Virgin Books, 2009.

Rumsfeld, Donald H., U.S. Secretary of Defense. "The National Defense Strategy of the United States of America." Office of the Secretary of Defense, Washington, D.C. (March 2005).

Sagunski, David. "Improving our Maritime Vision." Atlantic Council of the United States, Washington, D.C. (2 December 2008).

Sagan, Scott D., and Kenneth N. Waltz. *The Spread of Nuclear Weapons: A Debate*. New York: W. W. Norton, 1995.

Scharmer, C. Otto. *Theory U: Leading from the Future as It Emerges*. Cambridge, Mass.: Society for Organizational Learning Press, 2007.

———, Peter Senge, Joseph Jaworski, and Betty Sue Flowers. *Presence: Human*

Purpose and the Field of the Future. Cambridge, Mass.: Society for Organizational Learning Press, 2004.

Schmucker, Kurt J. *Fuzzy Sets, Natural Language Computations, and Risk Analysis.* Rockville, Md.: Computer Sciences Press, 1986.

Schubert, Frank N., and Theresa L. Kraus, eds. *The Whirlwind War: The United States Army in Operations DESERT SHIELD and DESERT STORM.* Washington, D.C.: Center of Military History Publication, 1995.

Schwartz, Peter. *Inevitable Surprises: Thinking Ahead in a Time of Turbulence.* New York: Gotham Books, 2003.

Senge, Peter. *The Fifth Discipline: The Art & Practice of the Learning Organization.* New York: Doubleday, 1990.

Sharp, Walter L., Lieutenant General, U.S. Army. "Joint Publication 3-01: Countering Air and Missile Threats." Joint Chiefs of Staff, Washington, D.C. (5 February 2007).

Shea, Dana A. "Critical Infrastructure: Control Systems and the Terrorist Threat." CRS Report for Congress RL31534, Washington, D.C. (20 January 2004).

Sherman, Jason. "Flournoy: QDR Must Prepare for End of U.S. Hegemony in 'Global Commons'." *Inside Defense* (2 July, 2009).

Simon, Jeffrey. "NATO's Uncertain Future: Is Demography Destiny?" *Strategic Forum* (Institute for National Strategic Studies, National Defense University) 236 (October 2008).

Sokolovskiy, Marshal V. D. *Soviet Military Strategy*, 3rd edition. Harriet Fast Scott, ed. New York: Crane, Russak, 1975.

Spirtas, Michael, et al. "Department of Defense Training for Operations with Interagency, Multinational, and Coalition Partners." RAND Corp., Santa Monica, California (2008).

Standage, Tom. *The Victorian Internet.* New York: Walker Publishing Co., 1998.

Stillion, John, and David Orletsky. "Airbase Vulnerability to Conventional Cruise-Missile and Ballistic-Missile Attacks." RAND Corp., Santa Monica, California (1999).

Sumida, Jon Tetsuro. *Inventing Grand Strategy and Teaching Command: The Classic Works of Alfred Thayer Mahan Reconsidered.* Baltimore: Johns Hopkins University Press, 1997.

Tagredi, Sam, Captain, U.S. Navy, ed. *Globalization and Maritime Power.* Washington, D.C.: National Defense University, 2002.

Talmadge, Caitlin. "Closing Time: Assessing the Iranian Threat to the Strait of Hormuz." *International Security* 33: 1 (Summer 2008).

Tegarden, David. "Business Information Visualization." *Communications of the Association for Information Systems* 1: Paper 4 (January 1999).

Thomas, Timothy L. *Decoding the Virtual Dragon: Critical Evolutions in the Science and Philosophy of China's Information Operations and Military Strategy.* Fort Leavenworth, Kans.: Foreign Military Studies Office (2007).

———. "Chinese and American Network Warfare," *Joint Forces Quarterly* 38 (2005).

———. *Dragon Bytes: Chinese Information-War Theory and Practice from 1995–2003.* Fort Leavenworth, Kans.: Foreign Military Studies Office, 2004.

Till, Geoffrey. "A Cooperative Strategy for 21st Century Seapower." *Naval War College Review* (Spring 2008).

Torbert, Bill. *Action Inquiry: The Secret of Timely and Transforming Leadership.* San Francisco: Berrett-Koehler Publishers, 2004.

Tufte, Edward R. *The Visual Display of Quantitative Information.* Cheshire, Conn.: Graphics Press, 1997.

United Nations. "United Nations Human Development Report 2006," New York (2006).

———. "Final Report to the Prosecutor by the Committee Established to Review the NATO Bombing Campaign Against the Federal Republic of Yugoslavia." United Nations International Criminal Tribunal for the Former Yugoslavia, New York (2000).

———. "Constitution of the International Telecommunication Union, with annexes," 1825 U.N.T.S. 1., New York (1992, entered into force 1 July 1994).

———. "Convention on the Law of the Sea." UN Doc. A/CONF.62/122 (1982), 10 December 1982, 1833 U.N.T.S. 3, 397, 21 I.L.M. 1261, New York (1982, entered into force 16 November 1994).

———. "Treaty on Principles Governing the Activities of States in the Exploration and Use of Outer Space, Including the Moon and Other Celestial Bodies." 18 U.S.T. 2410, 610 U.N.T.S. 205 (1967), New York (1967, entered into force 10 October 1967).

———. "International Cooperation in the Peaceful Uses of Outer Space." U.N. Doc. A/RES/1721 (XVI), New York (1961).

U.S. Department of the Army. "Training the Force." Field Manual (FM) 7-0, Washington, D.C. (December 2008).

U.S. Department of Homeland Security. "National Plan to Achieve Maritime Domain Awareness for the National Strategy for Maritime Security." Washington, D.C. (October 2005).

———. "International Outreach and Coordination Strategy for Maritime Security." NSPD-41/HSPD-13, Washington, D.C. (November 2005).

Valencia, Mark J. "Co-operation in the Malacca and Singapore Straits: A Glass Half-Full." *Policy Forum Online*, Northeast Asia Peace and Security Project 06-103A, Nautilus Institute for Security and Sustainable Development, San Francisco, California (12 December 2006).

Van Creveld, Martin. *The Transformation of War: The Most Radical Reinterpretation of Armed Conflict since Clausewitz.* New York: The Free Press, 1991.

Waldrop, M. Mitchell. *Complexity: The Emerging Science at the Edge of Order and Chaos.* New York: Simon and Schuster, 1992.

Watts, Barry. "Long-Range Strike: Imperatives, Urgency and Options." Report, Center for Strategic and Budgetary Assessments, Washington, D.C. (April 2005).

Wei, Wang. "The Effect of Tactical Ballistic Missiles on the Maritime Strategy of China." Danling Cacioppo, trans. *The Naval War College Review* 61: 3 (Summer 2008).

Weick, Karl E. *Sense-making in Organizations.* Thousand Oaks, Calif.: Sage Publications, 1995.

White, Lynn, Jr. *Medieval Technology & Social Change.* London: Oxford University Press, 1962.

Wiener, Norbert. *The Human Use of Human Beings.* Boston: Houghton Mifflin, 1950.

Wilson, Clay. "Botnets, Cybercrime, and Cyberterrorism: Vulnerabilities and Policy Issues for Congress." CRS Report for Congress RL32114, Washington, D.C. (29 January 2008).

———. "Information Operations, Electronic Warfare, and Cyberwar: Capabilities and Related Policy Issues." CRS Report for Congress No. RL31787, Washington, D.C. (2007).

Wolf, A. T., S. B. Yoffe, and M. Giordano. "International Waters: Identifying Basins at Risk." *Water Policy* 5: 1 (2003).

Work, Robert O. "The U.S. Navy: Charting a Course For Tomorrow's Fleet." Center for Strategic and Budgetary Assessments, Washington, D.C. (2008).

Zatarin, Lee Allen. *Tanker War: America's First Conflict with Iran, 1987–1988.* Drexel Hill: Casement Publishers and Book Distributors, 2008.

Index

AIS. *See* Automatic Information System (AIS)

Al Qaeda, 7–8, 26, 71

ALR-94 Electronic Support Measures, 134

Antarctica, 2, 56, 220n6

Anti-access weaponry, 151–56

Anti-air warfare, 10

Anti-satellite (ASAT) weapons, 9–10, 25, 39, 102, 107

Anti-ship missiles, 10–11, 151–55

Antisubmarine warfare, 151, 249n23

APG-77 (V) 2 Active Electronically Scanned Array radar, 134

Arabian Gulf, 23, 154–55

Archipelagic nations, 55–56

Arctic region, 25, 56

Army, U.S.: Airland Battle, 29, 227n37; and Army Task List, 206; National Training Center, 202

Army Air and Missile Defense Command, U.S., 133

ASAT. *See* Anti-satellite (ASAT) weapons

Atlas V launch vehicle, 106

Automatic Information System (AIS), 71, 74, 76, 81

Backfire-launched cruise missiles, 250n32

Ballistic missiles: active defense against, 124–27; anti-ship ballistic missiles, 11; anti-ship missiles, 10–11, 151–55; asymmetric attack by, 119; capabilities required for ballistic missile defense, 13; for deterrence, 116, 118, 128; nations with, 116–17; pillars of missile defense, 122–27, 130; proliferation of, 115, 120–22, 129–30; and weapons of mass destruction (WMD), 10, 115, 118–19, 122, 129–30

Ballistic missile submarines, 10

Battle of the Narrative, 26, 39–41

Beckstrom's Law, 90–91

Biological weapons, 10, 39, 42, 232n22

Birthrate, 21. *See also* Demographics

BMD. *See* Ballistic missiles

Bogotá Declaration, 103, 110

"Botnets," 5, 6

Boyd, John, 179, 197, 254n4

C2BMC, 126

C2ISR, 134

C4I, 122

C4ISR, 119, 140, 143

Capability enabler, 254n8

Capstone Concept for Joint Operations, U.S., 14, 177, 179

Chemical weapons, 10, 118, 232n22

China: anti-satellite (ASAT) weapons of, 9–10, 25, 102, 107, 229n12; and anti-ship missiles, 152–54; and ballistic missiles, 10, 116, 119; and cyber attacks, 93, 97, 170–71; economy of, 27, 28; and exclusive economic zone (EEZ), 55; fight against piracy by, 148; and fighter aircraft of, 136, 138; government control over information access in, 40; information operations and military strategy of, 162, 169–72; and international law, 231n11; naval encounters in South China Sea (2009) between U.S. and, 30; nuclear submarines of, 151; and *Oghab* rockets, 241n16; oil resources for, 23; population of, 21; rise of, xi, xii–xiii, 149; space program of, 104,

CJTF-HOA. *See* Combined Joint Task Force-Horn of Africa (CJTF-HOA)

Cold War: ballistic missiles in, 119; deterrence doctrine of, 111, 118, 128; GIUK Gap and containment of Soviet Navy, 24; mutual assured

The authorized representative in the EU for product safety and compliance is:
Mare Nostrum Group
B.V Doelen 72
4831 GR Breda
The Netherlands